AFRICAN
FLY-FISHING
HANDBOOK

A guide to freshwater and saltwater fly-fishing in Africa

AFRICAN
FLY-FISHING
HANDBOOK

*A guide to freshwater and saltwater
fly-fishing in Africa*

Bill Hansford-Steele

SOUTHERN
BOOK PUBLISHERS

ISBN 1 86812 700 1

First edition, first impression 1997
First edition, second impression 1998

Published by
Southern Book Publishers (Pty) Ltd
PO Box 3103, Halfway House, 1685

Cover design by Abdul Amien, Cape Town
Cover photograph: ABPL Viesti
Illustrations by the author, Dale Hansford-Steele and Michael Thayer
Maps by CartoCom, Pretoria
Set in Palatino/Neue Helvetica 9 on 10.5 point
Design and typesetting by Wim Reinders
Scans by Scanshop, Cape Town
Printed and bound by Colorgraphic, Durban

Title page:
The author with a 6,86 kg (15lb 1oz), 75 cm long rainbow trout – the largest trout ever caught in Africa.
Taken at Trout Hideaway in South Africa on 21 July 1997.

This book is dedicated to my father
William James Joseph Hansford-Steele
Who set me on the road, opened the doors of my mind,
and led me to the river ... and the great joys of fishing!

CONTENTS

FOREWORD

This book could not have come at a better time, nor could there be a better author to write it. I have known and have fished with Bill for several years. Bill is one of those very special persons to whom the sport of angling, and especially fly-fishing, means far more than a pleasant way to spend a weekend. To Bill, angling is a way of life, a state of mind, and the ultimate challenge.

Fly-fishing with an artificial fly is the IN way of fishing at the moment. One has only to see the growth in fly-fishing clubs, and the increase in sales of things 'fly-fishing', to realise this. The angling press has become much more responsive to the needs of fly-fishing, and the information disseminated on the noble art has exploded in the last decade.

The subject covered by this volume is comprehensive indeed. From fly-fishing for trout to the mighty tigerfish and the great sport fishes of the salt. A coverage which spreads across the continent of Africa and its fabulous waters. Should you wish to hunt trout in South Africa or Kenya; tigerfish in the Zambezi River or the great lakes of the Rift Valley; kingfish off the archipelago of Bazaruto or in the surf of Kosi; bass in mountain lakes or slow rivers; and so on and so on. It's all here, and much more besides!

Perhaps the greatest step to success in fly-fishing is the path of properly imitating the fishes' food forms ... the insects, the small fishes, and the crustaceans. For the first time, the deep secrets of African fly-fishing are presented here.

Herein is the uniqueness of this book. As you step into the mysteries of this book and pursue your dream trophies, you will unravel even more unique aspects. For the fly-fisherman, this is a book full of real life facts, and full of the enthusiasm of a totally dedicated angler.

Bill Hansford-Steele is not just a very capable writer; he is indeed a very competent fly-fisherman. He has fished more waters, using more fly-fishing methods, than most anglers dream about. Because of this, you can be sure that the techniques and strategies described here do work. They have been used extensively by Bill and by many other extremely successful anglers. Bill has been described as a perfectionist when it comes to flies. He would say he is just an enthusiast, but those who have spent time fly-tying with him know his artistry, his dedication to correctness, and his uncanny ability to design deadly flies from a base of broad knowledge of insects and other creatures.

This book takes a quantum leap by bringing Africa's latest fly-fishing techniques into the next century. By doing so, it becomes a standard work on the subject, and will remain so for a very long time.

Cyril Ramaphosa
February 1997

ACKNOWLEDGEMENTS

Barry Kent, friend, skilled angler and master fly-tier; Mike Salomon, a superb sport angler; Malcolm Meintjes, the ultimate enthusiast, writer, and angler extraordinaire; Louis van der Westhuizen, to many the only master; Steve Stephens, who taught me so much, the best of the best; 'PJ' Jacobs, editor of *Complete Fly-fisherman* magazine, great fly-fisherman, and a source of unending fly-fishing knowledge; Anthony Shepherdson, life-long angling companion; Ron Clay, for ideas, photography, and all-round fishing know-how: Ken Jessop, master story-teller, splendid angler and great outdoors man; Charles Norman, for inspiration, photographs, and enviable mastery of angling; Angelo Komis, for more enthusiasm than anyone deserves; also Ken Bateman, for saltwater photographs and help; Mark Yelland, for help in tracking things down and his freely given expertise; Hilton Kinlock, for fishing with me; Nolan Owen-Johnstone, entomologist, fishing friend, fellow instructor and currently general manager of Zomba Flies; Rod Cross of 'Fly-fishing Adventures'; Irving Stevenson (currently operating out of Inhaca Island in Mozambique), for photographs and ideas for this book; John Costello (the doyen of African saltwater fly-fishing); Stuart Hemingway, for enthusiasm; Sean Pare, the master streamside angler; and my son-in-law Quinn Coetsee, who doesn't know what 'quit' means, loves fishing with a passion, and works at it with enviable persistence.

To Murray Peddar, my deepest appreciation for tying many of the flies used for illustration; and to Steve Collins of Kenya for introductions, manuscripts and ongoing support. Lt Col Unwin of Kenya, for information on flies; Rupert Watson of Kenya for fly-fishing with me, and for his broad knowledge of African trout; the late Don Lort for magnificent photography, field work, and his freely given vast knowledge of fly-fishing; and, finally, to Steve Barrow for checking the entire text, and for his contribution to field work.

Thanks to Adolf and Isobel Nicklaus who own Trout Hideaway in South Africa, the best trout fishery in Africa! Adolf's enthusiasm and encouragement are without match. Without his help, and access to his magnificent fishery, this book would have been much more difficult.

My wife Christina read the entire manuscript and freely gave of advice. To her a special thanks, for being my best fishing friend, and for her unending encouragement. My sons Ryan and Dale have accompanied me on countless fishing trips and have always supported my fishing, been good companions and put up with my single-mindedness with great patience.

Louise Grantham of Southern Book Publishers deserves special thanks for getting this project off the ground, and for her guidance and patience.

Lastly, the opinions given in this book are mine alone, and may be disagreed with in whole or in part by other authorities or persons.

INTRODUCTION

Africa conjures up pictures of steaming jungles, mighty wild beasts and mystery. But for some people it means fishing, and fishing so good it can match any other place in the world. Africa is a huge continent, with every conceivable biotype from snow-capped mountains to grass plains, deserts and equatorial forests. In this 'Garden of Eden' are rivers, lakes and water features unmatched by any other continent on the planet. Here then is a fisherman's paradise, a wonderland where angling dreams come true, and nothing is impossible.

Fly-fishing is an ancient art, traditionally steeped in mystique, bounded by misplaced snobbery, and replete with secrets guarded closely by its followers; it took a leash of centuries before the ordinary folk could participate! But, here we are ... fly-fishing is available to all in this enlightened age. New members swell our ranks daily! Today, fly-fishing, in all its forms, is the fastest growing participatory field sport. And the hunt for new species on the fly rod ... well, this is perhaps the fastest growth area of all. Saltwater fly-fishing, far from being the preserve of the slightly crazy, has an extraordinary number of super-keen followers. No one thinks twice about barbel on the fly, or tigerfish, or even the mighty Nile perch. Who would have conceived of bottlenose and moggel on the fly a scant ten years ago? There are many more species hungrily pursued by a growing band of generalist and even 'species specialist' fly-fishermen. No species is immune from the enquir-

ing modern fly-fisherman, and all species are great challenges to the angler with the long rod.

All the beginnings of fly-fishing are centred around the trout and the salmon. From the age of Tudors, and even before, the downfall of huge salmon and wily trout has been studied with a fervour almost frightening in its intensity. Fly-fishing began in antiquity, but the British turned it into an art form; from them it spread to the rest of Europe, and as the Europeans spread their wings around the world, fly-fishing went with them. They successfully introduced trout, and to a far lesser extent salmon, into remote corners of the world. Today, trout can be found in surprising places ... and where there are trout, there are fly-fishermen. The spread was inexorable in the nineteenth century, and continues even into the present.

It was inevitable that before the coming of trout, the fly-fisherman's attention would turn to local species in the out-of-the-way places. Great sport was enjoyed with them. In South Africa, yellowfish on the fly was well established in the late 1800s. But with the coming of the trout they were forgotten. Time went by and sometimes the indigenous fishes were caught by mistake; sometimes (almost secretly) they were caught deliberately. And, occasionally, these same 'non-trout' would amaze their captors by putting up a fight of such ferocity that it remained burned in the mind of the angler for ever. 'You know ... I took a yellowfish at Sterkfontein Dam on an Invicta the other day. It fought so hard my arms were aching. It was half the size of my last rainbow trout and twice as lively!'

The fighting merits of many local species ensured that a few dedicated anglers would eventually fish for indigenous species in preference to the traditional trout. In South Africa there was a strong tendency toward this shift, which was accelerated by the government's downgrading of some trout fisheries as a result of supposed destruction of local minnows and other fauna. However, once the word spread, the hunt for indigenous fishes on the fly grew rapidly. It arose out of the basic tenets of fly-fishing for trout. Saltwater, tigerfish, catfish, bass fly-fishing and the associated specialist techniques all evolved from trouting know-how. Thus, although we see the pursuit of most fish species with the fly rod, we should never forget that the roots, the basic strategies and knowledge, started with the trout and to a lesser extent the salmon. Some of this development has proceeded so far as to be almost unrecognisable, but make no mistake, the techniques of Isaac Walton, Cotton and others have survived the mists of time, they have been crystallised in the crucible of experience, and they have finally metamorphosed into the methods of today. This book is about modern-day methods and strategies. It is about fishing for trout, it is about fishing for other species in freshwater, and it is about fishing for the mighty gamefish of estuary and surf.

The book is designed for the fly-fisherman of today. Travel has become less difficult and a lot less expensive than it was 50 years ago. Places are easier to get to – even remote places! Anglers visit Africa from all over the world, and the African angler thinks nothing of journeying vast distances in his own country (most African countries are big); certainly he will visit neighbouring countries, and even remote ones, several times in his angling life. 'Have rod, will travel' ... how apt in this age of easy movement and communication. Techniques are well developed for most species. Fly rod anglers can be found on steaming tropical rivers, vast lakelands of the rift valley, mountain streams, golden beaches, and anywhere you care to think of. Madagascar, Kenya, South Africa, Malawi,

Zambia, Zimbabwe, Sierra Leone and plenty more ... the names roll off of the tongue. In all these places good fishing is available for the enthusiast. Thus, this is a book about African fly-fishing, a book about fly-fishing for many kinds of fishes, and mostly a book about methods which have worked for me, and for a great many successful anglers.

This book is immersed in African fly-fishing lore, not only that discovered by the author, but also the hard-won secrets of many fly-fishing experts who have helped in the compilation of the knowledge between these pages. Anyone who reads this book from cover to cover, should be on the way to mastering many fly-fishing situations. However, Africa and its fly-fishing are unpredictable entities; mysteries are there in profusion, and, thank goodness, fly-fishing is a challenge that can never be mastered in one lifetime. The jungle-edged Zambezi sums up the enchantment of African fly-fishing! As the blood courses through the veins and the adrenalin goes round in lumps to the flashing leap of a white-fanged tigerfish; as the reel screams and the rod bows to the great fish's majesty ... then is the fly-fisherman in tune with his world, then is he steeped in its mysteries, and then is he truly and vibrantly living his life!

In Africa, you can travel and travel, and never see it all. If you are from elsewhere in the world, a rod, an air ticket, and a few flies can open the doors to stunning fishing. If you live here, then count your blessings. In Africa you can fly-fish for superb gamefishes in estuary and surf, you can take on tigerfish, catfish, bass, yellowfish, and many others, and you can enjoy trout fishing as good as anywhere else in the world. Africa has it all!

In a world context, Africa suffers from pollution, deforestation, water abstraction and other evils, just like the rest of the world. And although Africa has survived better than others in places, there is no room for complacency. The attack of industry, government, and the uninformed poor, is insidious and deadly. Humanity in any guise no longer has the right to destroy a natural heritage that belongs to all the peoples of the world. The water, the plants and the whole delicate ecological balance give us life, and keep alive both us and all the creatures of the world. Anyone who destroys this heritage surely murders each of us a little. All anglers, as lovers of the world and its wild places, should think of themselves as protectors and watchers. It is the same for bird watchers, botanists, entomologists, rock climbers ... indeed anyone who loves life and this planet. We must all fight for the life-giving natural world. We can do it in part by contributing towards education and the institutions that look after these things. But our main weapons are our voices and our votes, and we must make these count.

This book has taken some thirteen years of research to put together. It has led me into dusty libraries, forgotten manuscripts, and the writings of anglers long gone. It has introduced me to the great fly-fishermen, and the great fly-tiers of Africa, it has taught me many things, and opened doors to new explorations in angling strategies; but mostly it has taught me to be a better angler. I have made life-long friends, and have visited corners of Africa which I shall never forget. There is wonderful fly-fishing, great fishes, and fantastic places in Africa. I trust that this book will equip you to enjoy it even more than I have!

When I was a small boy, a very wise angler took it upon himself to teach me a basic fishing philosophy. In essence it was this: 'To catch your fish you need to be able to put yourself in the fish's place ... think like him, understand his needs, and imagine his world. In the imagina-tion of this fish's world, the angler should strive to know it as well as the fish himself ... he should know about the teeming food forms that sustain the fish, and understand the vagaries of the fish's environment. If you know his address, you can knock on his door! Like us, the fish has comfort zones, he needs food and security, he likes the easy life. But, our fish is cold blooded, he lives in a world where expended energy and energy intake are in critical balance. Survival, let alone comfort, can be in the balance at a whimsical change in the state of the water. There, at the atom-thick layer of the water's surface, the world changes. All below is essentially mystery, the surface is merely a key which sometimes works, and often doesn't. Much of the joy of fly-fishing is in penetrating this mystery, strategising on the largely unknown, and tempting the quarry to partake of the inedible edible.'

That wise man was a dedicated fisherman naturalist ... he was my father, and after 50 or so years of my own angling life, I can only say he was absolutely correct. As a small boy it was always difficult to understand how Dad could catch a good dozen fishes to my one ... but he taught me well, and nowadays I could probably catch eleven to his twelve. I doubt I will ever match him. The older people, from an age when there were still horse-drawn carts and life was lived at a relaxing pace, had an indefinable closeness to nature. A natural feel for things wild; a feel which cannot be easily synthesised in this crazy high-speed concrete jungle we are immersed in today.

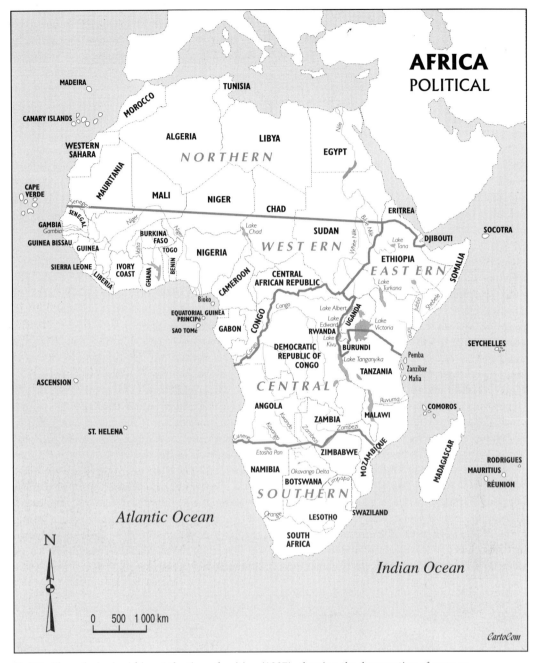

AFRICA
POLITICAL

MADEIRA

CANARY ISLANDS

CAPE VERDE

TUNISIA

MOROCCO

WESTERN SAHARA

ALGERIA

LIBYA

EGYPT

NORTHERN

MAURITANIA

MALI

NIGER

CHAD

ERITREA

SOCOTRA

GAMBIA
Gambia

SENEGAL

GUINEA BISSAU

GUINEA

Niger

BURKINA FASO

TOGO

NIGERIA

Volta

BENIN

SIERRA LEONE

IVORY COAST

LIBERIA

GHANA

Lake Chad

SUDAN

WESTERN

White Nile

Blue Nile

Lake Tana

DJIBOUTI

ETHIOPIA

EASTERN

Lake Turkana

SOMALIA

Shebele

Juba

Bioko

CAMEROON

CENTRAL AFRICAN REPUBLIC

EQUATORIAL GUINEA
PRINCIPÉ

SAO TOMÉ

GABON

CONGO

Congo

Lake Albert

Lake Edward

UGANDA

RWANDA

Lake Kivu

Lake Victoria

BURUNDI

DEMOCRATIC REPUBLIC OF CONGO

Congo

Lake Tanganyika

TANZANIA

Pemba

Zanzibar

Mafia

SEYCHELLES

ASCENSION

CENTRAL

ANGOLA

ZAMBIA

Kwando

Kavango

Zambezi

MALAWI

Ruvuma

COMOROS

ST. HELENA

Cunene

Etosha Pan

Zambezi

ZIMBABWE

MOZAMBIQUE

MADAGASCAR

RODRIGUES

MAURITIUS

RÉUNION

NAMIBIA

Okavango Delta

BOTSWANA

Limpopo

SOUTHERN

Orange

LESOTHO

SWAZILAND

SOUTH AFRICA

Atlantic Ocean

Indian Ocean

N

0 500 1 000 km

CartoCom

Political boundaries in Africa at the time of writing (1997), showing the demarcation of areas as used in this book.

CHAPTER 1

WHAT, WHEN AND WHERE?

I speak of Africa and golden joys.

William Shakespeare

Talk of fly-fishing tends to lead straight away to trout. In Africa, however, anglers should think in far wider terms. In southern African freshwater alone, you can cast a fly for several species of fighting yellowfish, catfish. kurper, bass tigerfish, and others. More and more fishes join the list as you progress northward, until finally you tangle with the mighty Nile perch.

Along an endless African coastline, pitted with innumerable estuaries, there are tremendous fighting fishes to be found everywhere. And if you venture out to sea, the limit of what you can catch with a fly rod has yet to be explored. The Americans may think they have the biggest bonefish in the world, but they don't! The biggest are here in Africa, and here too are tarpon, kingfish and an endless list of other fighting gamefishes. Books could be written on each of the species alone, sagas could be

The beautiful South African Swartwater Dam is typical of many high-country African waters. With trout in excess of 6 kg and with hotel facilities nearby, it is always worth a visit. (Photo: Don Lort)

1

A set-up specimen of a goliath tigerfish (Hydrocynus goliath). *These monsters are said to grow to massive weights (40 kg plus).* (Photo: Irving Stevenson)

told of fishing adventures to whet the appetites of the world's most successful anglers, and encyclopedias could be drafted on the insects and food forms that are the basis of African fly-fishing. Time is of the essence, however, and space is confined, so this book offers only a taste of the possibilities. But others will come,

and all the tales will one day be told ... perhaps this could be their starting point?

In southern Africa the potential of fly-fishing has at least been well sampled, and sufficient is known to form a basis for most species of game-fish. But, as you go northward through the continent, less and less has been discovered. West and Central Africa are the least known of all, and anglers may well find themselves in uncharted territory, explorers on the path to knowledge. However, the techniques developed for the lionhearted fighting machine we call the tigerfish will be good enough to handle anything you may find in freshwater. As for the salt – well, you can very nearly get away with the same tackle. So, in fact, all you need to handle anything Africa can throw at you, is a decent AFTM 9 or 10 outfit for the big stuff, a 7 or 8 for the big trout waters and for bassing, and a 5 or 6 for small stream work. Three rods, an assortment of lines, flies and tippet materials, and you can take on anything.

Most of what you will find in this book is based on experience of fishing the eastern African countries from Ethiopia all the way down to South Africa, and the coastline from Kenya to the Cape. If you find yourself some-

A quiet corner of a Kenyan trout lake, high in the Aberdares. Large populations of dragonflies demand patterns like the Mrs Simpson for good results.

where else in Africa, the flies and the techniques for using them will certainly still work. Tigerfish exist in several locations, and other fishes such as kurper, mudfish, yellowfish and catfish are to be found almost everywhere. The Atlantic coast is equally well served by the flies used in the Indian Ocean, except that blue-backed saltwater flies are probably more effective in the Atlantic than the green-backed versions which work so well on the Indian Ocean coastline.

In this chapter, I have provided introductory information on some of the countries, and this is augmented in Chapters 9 and 10 by information on the species you are most likely to come across. The information on locations is necessarily brief, and hopefully just enough to whet your appetite. You can obtain more detail from the tourist boards of each country, or from a specialist Africa travel bureau. Where information is supplied here on a specific country, you can be sure that the country is set up, at least in some areas, to cater for the visiting angler. In many African countries there is no such assurance, and one may perforce have to take pot luck in terms of transport and road systems, local knowledge, guides, and even supplies. One can of course make up a party under the auspices of a local safari company. Many of these are very professional, but even then the experience can be exceedingly rugged, to say the least! Stories of taking ten days to travel 50 km in the Congo basin during the rainy season are quite true. When you literally build your own bridges from forest trees and rocks, it tends to slow you up! The developed countries are much easier, and there it is quite possible to find every facility you might imagine, the only limitation being the depth of your purse.

SEASONAL CHANGES

Most of Africa has definite dry and wet seasons. The effect on small streams and rivers can be quite marked, especially in high-altitude trout and yellowfish streams. Such rivers become low and often crystal clear in the dry season, making fishing quite difficult. The onset of the rains is often sudden, commencing in October/November in the south and moving to-

An exquisite damselfly from the South African highveld. This one came from a rocky, fast-flowing stream with deep pools at Trout Hideaway.

wards March/April as you go north to Kenya. The weather is quite capable of going from several months of zero rainfall to torrential downpour within a period of a few days. Rivers suddenly run at full force, often cutting away banks and changing their entire character virtually overnight. Managed fisheries tend to build weirs and dams to control this, but in the wild anything may happen.

For a week or two after the commencement of the rains, the rivers are coloured and fast flowing. But, surprisingly, they often yield a fish or two to the persistent angler. Within a short time, the rivers usually adapt to the summer flow, and fishing becomes very good in the slightly tinted and fast-flowing water. Often the wet season relents a little in the middle of its period (e.g. January is often fairly rain-free in South Africa), followed by another intense two to three month rainy period that is often wetter than that at the beginning of the season.

The African trout and yellowfish stream fly-angler has to cater for these changes, which often bring about vast alterations in insect hatches, the location of fishes, and the tackle needed to fish successfully in varying flows and depths of water. The angler needs to be very adaptable as the season progresses. The winter can be very cold at high altitude in Africa. Many a European is stunned to learn that it can snow in South Africa and in Kenya,

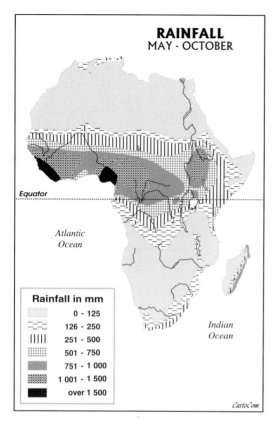

RAINFALL
MAY - OCTOBER

Equator

Atlantic
Ocean

Indian
Ocean

Rainfall in mm
0 - 125
126 - 250
251 - 500
501 - 750
751 - 1 000
1 001 - 1 500
over 1 500

CartoCom

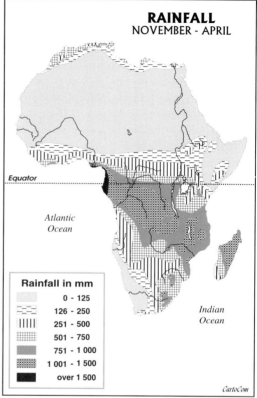

RAINFALL
NOVEMBER - APRIL

Equator

Atlantic
Ocean

Indian
Ocean

Rainfall in mm
0 - 125
126 - 250
251 - 500
501 - 750
751 - 1 000
1 001 - 1 500
over 1 500

CartoCom

but they forget that this is at altitudes of 1 500 to 3 000 metres or higher.

At low altitude the tropical and subtropical rivers are also affected by the weather, although to a much lesser extent than the high-altitude waters. The great rivers such as the Zambezi run crystal clear towards the end of the dry season, providing excellent conditions for fly-fishing. The last dry weather, the brief season before the rains, is excellent for tigerfish.

Winter dry season

Throughout much of Africa dry season and winter coincide, and trout, living at high altitude, often have to contend with severe conditions. The river flows are reduced, sometimes to mere trickles, the water becomes gin clear and subject to fierce temperature differences from daytime to night time. At high altitude, air temperatures can vary from zero at night to 24 °C during the day. Large otters and other mammalian predators are common, and there are herons and cormorants, ospreys and fish eagles to contend

with. The fishes become ultra-cautious. The slap of a line, the flash of gut or rod, the smallest awareness of movement or sound, and they are either gone, or off the feed for hours. Many of the wet season lies are now just boulders in almost still water, water weeds have died back, and waterside trees and bushes are bare leafed in the grip of winter. Where they can, the fishes will drop back into deep water, and this is the best place to catch them with fast-sink lines and a small Gold-ribbed Hare's Ear, Walker's Yellow Nymph, or Pheasant-tail Nymph.

Occasionally, insects such as small sedges and medium-sized dark brown mayflies will hatch, but little else. The odd trout can be seen flashing as he knocks nymphs off submerged rocks, but many will go for long periods without feeding, perhaps grabbing a luckless dragonfly nymph now and then. Only the finest tippets and small well-presented flies will score over the shallows, and then not too often. A warm spell or unseasonable rain may change all this, but the change will be short-lived. This is a time

4

for the skilful stream angler, and many African fly-fishermen turn their attention to still waters, where the pickings are easier.

Winter wet season

In the Cape, winter rain and sometimes snow visit the streams simultaneously with dropping temperatures from April to September. This climate comes close to that experienced in some parts of Europe, where swollen streams of coloured water are part and parcel of winter. Yellow (when it is very cold) and also black flies sometimes work, as do bushy and well-hackled flies which are sensed by the fish's lateral line. Seek out the quieter water where food would seem most likely to collect, where a fish can hold without expending much energy and where detritus and nymphs accumulate.

A lowering of flow rate as a result of a lull in rainfall can bring fishes onto the feed, even in cold water. The slightly coloured fast-flowing water hides the angler, and simultaneously tempts the trout to take up the lies where they can best feed.

Summer dry season

The South African Cape experiences a summer dry season from October to March. The rainfall dwindles as summer approaches and the streams lessen their flow, but they are not as badly affected as the African winter streams in their dry season. In most summers a reasonable flow remains in the Cape streams. Trout still hold in their lies, and the insect hatches are good. The prelude to summer, the months of September, October and November, is the best time for the insects, and the time of best feeding for the trout. The streams become very clear through the ensuing summer months. However, there is still plenty of rough water to hide the angler, and fishing through deep pools and runs can also be profitable. Dry fly, with flies immersed in the surface film, is a favoured method, but the wet fly-fishermen can still find fishes aplenty. Clear water demands skill in approach and presentation, and Cape fly-fishermen have brought it down to a fine art: 'in the surface dry flies' developed by them have become world famous.

Summer wet season

The warmth of summer brings back leaves to the waterside vegetation, and with the leaves of spring come insects. Grasshoppers and other terrestrial insects are important items on the menu of African fishes. As spring draws to an end, the rains come, and swell the rivers into raging torrents. After the initial downpours they settle somewhat, becoming slightly coloured and fast-flowing, and enormous hatches of insects appear in the summer warmth. Dragonflies and damselflies abound, sedges hatch everywhere, and mayflies drift the surface like tiny yachts in a regatta. This is the best of the seasons, and from now until autumn the fishing can be good. Feeding trout are in their lies, and the cautious angler can usually look forward to limit 'bags' in the days ahead. But the African climate is fickle, and in some years unseasonal drought can reduce the rivers to shallow, crystal clear, too warm, slow-flowing streams in which fishing is almost impossible.

In wild places, the thick African vegetation filters out the storm-fed ground water, and thus the running water and streamlets which fill the rivers remain clearer than one might expect. However, around developed farmland, such as often borders rivers in South Africa and in Kenya, the running water picks up plenty of colour and the streams run thick and brown with suspended matter.

OVERVIEW OF LOCATIONS
Southern Africa

Southern Africa is all that land which stretches south of the Zambezi and down to the Cape of Good Hope. In commercial terms, the most well-developed area is South Africa.

South Africa

This is a modern country, First World in most respects, and only Third World in terms of currency values. Here you may find every service you could expect in Europe; sometimes, even better. There are excellent fishing camps, many of which offer additional opportunities for viewing wildlife and other outdoor pursuits. South Africa offers first-class fishing for many species including trout and bass inland, and some of the best saltwater fly-fishing, Kosi Bay being the prime site. Move up the coast into Mozambique, and the coastal fishing becomes magnificent. Gulley fishing is a favourite pursuit, but most of the good saltwater fly-fishing is found in or near the estuaries. Some of the north-coast beaches from St Lucia to Kosi Bay offer superb saltwater fly-fishing in the surf. The northern west coast, extending right up into Namibia, is teeming with cold-water Atlantic fish. But much of the surf is unsuitable for fly-fishing, and one has to search carefully for suitable locations ... find them, and the fishing is first class!

All the South African provinces offer trout fishing in the high-altitude areas (over 1 700 metres). Perhaps the best is to be found in the Highveld, the areas adjacent to the Lesotho border, and at lower altitudes in the extreme south and south-east.

Great trout locations are Trout Hideaway near Pilgrim's Rest, Machadodorp, Dullstroom, Swartwater Dam some 60 km from Harrismith, the Himeville and Underberg area, Eastern Cape and most of the higher areas around Cape Town. Trout fishing is year-round in most waters; the best times are from September to November and from March to May.

Bass waters are everywhere: tops is Heys Hope Dam near Piet Retief. The summer months of October to April are best, although some anglers pursue bass all year round.

Tigerfish are found in the giant Jozini Dam. Several species of yellowfish are to be found in almost all the river systems; likewise catfish, with the best catches in the Vaal/Orange system where specimens over 100 kg are known to exist. The giant Sterkfontein Dam provides matchless yellow fishing as well as moggel and good trout. Blue kurper are found in all the northern provinces and large specimens may come from surprisingly small waters, but favourite locations are the big waters such as Loskop and Hartebeespoort.

Tackle and flies are easily purchased in South Africa, and information, and sometimes guiding services, are available at most major fly-fishing tackle dealers.

Lesotho

This is a magnificent land of lofty peaks and glassy clear rivers, aptly named the mountain kingdom (Tolkien used it as a location for part of his *Lord of the Rings*). The huge Highlands Water Scheme is approaching completion and promises to provide the best trout fishing in the world in the next decade. Lesotho is surrounded by South Africa, and is remarkable for an absence of pollution and often abundant wildlife. Conditions are primitive! In general, take your own tackle and a 4x4. An excellent location, with good road access, is the New Oxbow Lodge, 70 km in from Ficksburg on the South African border. Fishing is best from October to April. The mountains attract early snow and can become quite dangerous in the winter months.

Zimbabwe

Zimbabwe has everything from trout (at Nyanga) to tigerfish (in most of the northern rivers, with the best at Kariba). The Zambezi is one of the greatest fishing rivers of the world. Kurper and catfish (including the enormous vundu, only in the Zambezi) are found everywhere, together with all kinds of mudfish, bottlenose, Cornish jack, chessa, and others. The Zambezi offers superb fly-fishing ... some say the tigerfish are the attraction, others will eulogise on the massive slab-sided kurpers which are abundant here. There is some great bassing, with the best at Lake Mutirikwe (previously Kyle) and Lake Poole. Contact the nearest tackle shop for local details. Many Zimbabweans cross into Mozambique at Mutare for the superb bass of Lake Chicamba.

Transport and facilities are reasonably good. Kariba, Deka Drum on the Zambezi, Nyanga and Lake Mutirikwe are favourite fishing locations. Some rivers are inclined to reduce to pools during the dry season (May through October). The best time for the Zambezi tigerfish is late October and early November. Tiger fishing is available at all times on Kariba Dam.

Botswana

This politically very stable country offers some of the best angling camps in the world, both

The Nicklaus River at Trout Hideaway in Mpumalanga, South Africa. Trout Hideaway offers prime still-water and river fly-fishing, with bird and game viewing and with hiking and mountain bike trails as well.

The Motete River near the new Oxbow Lodge in Lesotho. The crystal-clear rivers of Lesotho, full of wild-bred fighting rainbows, are set like silver veins amidst breath-taking scenery.

Troutbeck beauty in a gathering storm at Nyanga in Zimbabwe. (Photo: Don Lort)

This Mozambican girl holds a fully inflated puffer fish just taken from a drag net.

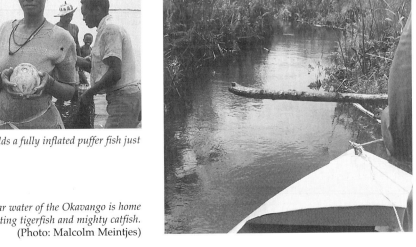

The crystal-clear water of the Okavango is home to huge kurper, fighting tigerfish and mighty catfish. (Photo: Malcolm Meintjes)

7

Dragonflies are extremely common in Africa, and their nymphs are possibly the most important food source of many African fish. This common red one is Trithemis kirbyi *of the family Libellulidae, sunning itself on bankside gravel.*

inside the Okavango and right up to the northern border, with excellent fishing for tigers, catfish, kurper (some of the best in Africa), and Kafue pike. Fishing can be undertaken throughout the year, but the summer is the best. October and November are the best months for tigerfish.

Opportunities for fly-fishing are excellent. Most bush locations are well aware of the fly-fishing potential and can offer excellent advice. Take your own tackle and flies (especially specialist tiger flies). Transport is by plane (most people fly into the major fishing camps) or by 4x4 on awful roads. A boat and a guide are recommended to navigate often complex waterways full of wildlife, some of it dangerous. The

Lake salmon and lake trout abound in Lake Tanganyika in Tanzania. (Photo: Charles Norman)

best advice is to camp only in officially approved camp areas, as people still manage to get eaten by lions from time to time.

Mozambique

This recently war-torn country is once again opening up for the angler after a lull of many years. Mozambique offers superb coastal and estuary fly-fishing. Inhaca Island and the Bazaruto archipelago are both set up to cater for the fly-fisherman both inshore and deep-sea. The camp on Bazaruto Island is a fabulous location to work from. Superb surf fly-fishing is available almost everywhere.

The mainland fisheries for tigerfish and other species are still almost inaccessible, and best left off the itinerary for a few years yet. Some of the very high country central Mozambique streams at one time had good stocks of trout in them, but no one has been up there to check them out for many years ... I wonder? The jewel in Mozambican freshwater fly-fishing is the Cabora Bassa Dam in the north-west, on the Zambezi. There are plenty of tigerfish here and excellent kurper as well. October and November are the best months.

Central Africa

Central Africa comprises a huge geographical area, much of which is inhabited by primitive peoples and very poorly equipped for transport and communication. Some countries are easier than others; some are politically unstable and best avoided.

Zambia

The upper Zambezi is best accessed via Zambia, and several good fishing camps have been constructed there in the last few years. Recommended months for fishing the north of Zambia are August and September, when there is little rain and the air is still warm and pleasant. The rivers run clear at this time, which helps fly-fishing. It is a good idea to port a rooftop boat or dinghy since many waters are hard to get at from the side. Some rivers may be reduced to pools during the dry season (May through October).

Zambia is reasonably easy to move around in

8

with a 4x4, but travel at night may be dangerous. It pays to plan well and to be sure that enough fuel and spares are carried. As with most of these Central African countries, it is recommended that a full medical kit is taken. Some of my friends go so far as to take their own blood with them! Many areas are badly fished out, and very little is done to control the rape of the rivers.

Malawi

Malawi is Rift Valley lake country, and at low altitudes is hot (and wet during the rainy season). Lake Malawi holds something like 225 species of fish, a few of which (mostly kurpers and yellowfish) are very suitable for fly-fishing. There is excellent largemouth bass fly-fishing in several impoundments around the country. The Murchison Falls offer good tiger fishing. The Zomba plateau offers trout fishing in the local streams. The trout are small and wild, but excellent challenging sport. The season extends from September to May.

Tanzania

From an angling point of view this country is still largely unexplored and unspoilt. Some places are difficult to access and a 4x4 is essential. Most unstocked high-country rivers have nothing but small *Barbus* species in them; tigerfish are restricted to the low-level rivers. There are very large catfish species in Tanzania, and plenty of kurpers. Kigoma is the centre for fishing Lake Tanganyika, which has tigerfish (both normal and Goliath), and also contains the fabulous 'sagala' (a species of Nile perch), which is known to reach 50 kg. There is also a popular sport fish, one of the kurpers, known as yellowbelly, which can be great on the fly rod. Many small species will come to the fly rod, and excellent light fly rod fishing can be enjoyed. Take your own tackle and medical supplies.

Trout fishing on the slopes of Kilimanjaro sounds quite magical and mysterious. Moshi, Arusha and Mount Meru are the centres. The best season is from November to January, though it is likely to be very wet as a result of the rains; second choice is June to August, when the weather is much more amenable.

Fly-fishermen and other anglers have begun to explore the unspoilt coastline of Tanzania and report superb fly-fishing opportunities. A coastal road structure exists, but this is definitely 4x4 country. For the most part, the best accommodation will be under your own canvas. This as yet unexploited coast offers potentially the best surf and estuary fishing anywhere on the continent. It is becoming well known as the great coast for kingfish and barracuda. From October to March the sea off Dar es Salaam, Latham Island, Mafia Island and the Pemba channel is famous for big-game fishing for marlin, sail fish, tunny, wahoo and others

The Democratic Republic of Congo and Angola

These countries together comprise a massive area of tropical Africa. The only reason they are treated together here is that neither are currently desirable locations, either because of instability, or war, or because they are just too plain risky.

Angola was at one time the favourite location for South Africans seeking Atlantic tarpon. There is no doubt that some of the river mouth areas, where shallow waters are commonly found, had populations of huge tarpon up to 100 kg. As far as I am aware, nobody has been up there and thrown a fly since the early seventies. Bonefish was also reported in those far-off days, although they are more common further north (Cameroon northward), and also on the East African coast.

The Congo river system is quite polluted in the lower reaches, but fairly clean in the wild

Cuda on fly in the surf? This one was taken on a Natal Halfbeak fly at Cocaterie on Isle St Marie, Madagascar.

9

areas further upstream. This is one of the world's great rivers ... it is enormous, and full of fishes of many species. Many of these are good fly-fishing quarry. Access, however, is both difficult and unreliable. The only anglers I have met who regularly visit (perhaps once a year) have their own plane. They usually team-up with other groups (usually professional moth catchers), and share the rigours of the overland part of the trip with these very well-equipped adventurers. But this is not for the faint hearted, and hardly to be recommended. Stories of wonderful tigerfish and kurper on the fly are the norm, the fast deep reaches of the rivers being the most productive. Good tigers are taken from the tail end of fast pools. Slab-sided kurper of several species inhabit deep reed-fringed areas, and are taken deep with sunken fly lines. This is the true home of the Goliath tigerfish, a quarry worthy of any fly-fishermen.

Indian Ocean islands

These are mostly resort locations and include Mauritius, Réunion, the Comoros, Maldives, Seychelles, and Madagascar. Madagascar is the exception, in that tourist development has not yet reached a high state of finesse. As a result, the fishing is still superb ... definitely my favourite island location. The rivers and even the never-ending paddy fields are full of kurp-er, but the main attraction is the saltwater fly-fishing. Nosy Bé on the north-west coast is per-haps the best known location. Not so well

Ivan Bampton and a typical small stream trout taken on a Kenya Bug fly from a small river in the Mount Kenya area. Not visible, behind Ivan, is a high voltage fence ... to keep the elephants away!

known and great for queenfish, barracuda, kingfish, and huge garfish in the surf, is Isle St Marie (Nosy Boraha), just off the east coast. The best fly-fishing coincides with the cyclone sea-son, which begins in February and lasts a few months. Hotel Cocoterie in the extreme north of this little island has one of the best beaches in the world and is the place to stay ... your wife will love it too!

Madagascar has one other surprise in hand, and that is a surviving population of rainbow trout in the central highlands ... yes, I couldn't believe it either, but there you are!

All the Indian Ocean islands offer first-class deep-sea fishing. On many, the reef fishing is a shadow of its old self as a result of over-exploitation, but reef techniques still produce good fish. The deep-water side of the reef is most productive and anglers fishing deep with weighted flies often get into a really big fish. In my experience the gamefishes such as kings, queens and barracudas will herd prey fishes onto the shallow side of the reef at dawn and at dusk, providing often easily reachable explo-sive fly-fishing from the shore at these times.

Eastern Africa

In this area I have included Kenya, Lake Victoria, Uganda, Ethiopia, Sudan, Rwanda and Burundi. Many of these countries are blessed with high mountainous country replete with clear, clean streams. Some of these were stocked with trout by British or French colonists, and naturally breeding populations survive in surprising places, together with those supported by the more usual 'artificial stocking'.

Kenya

Kenya offers plenty of good trout fishing, with some real 'glass case' locations in the high country around the Aberdares and Mount Kenya. Along with South Africa, Kenya is con-sidered 'real' trout country, and much of African fly-fishing lore originates there. A gov-ernment licence is necessary to fish for trout, and you may also need a permit from the landowner. Fishing for trout takes place all year round although many places become difficult

A forest waterfall in Kenya. The Gatamayu River is famous for its large trout and for its spectacular wildlife.

to reach as well as difficult to fish during the rains of April and May. Nevertheless, many fine fishes are taken during this time, usually between spates. The Gatamayu River to the north of Nairobi is world renowned. There are also excellent trout still-waters, and many rivers within easy driving range of Nairobi. All are fairly strictly controlled, and pre-organised permits are a must. Several Kenyan still-waters around Nairobi offer good largemouth bass fishing. For many years Lake Naivasha in the Rift Valley was famous for its bass. Lake Victoria is described below.

The lower altitude rivers are full of catfish and kurper. Other good fly-fishing quarry include various indigenous carp and *Barbus* species. Some of the yellowfish get really big, and there are many species to provide good sport. A yellowfish of considerable repute is the 'rhino fish' which grows to 30 kg and is found in the Athi and Tana rivers.

Northern Kenya offers the angler a chance to get to grips with mighty Nile perch of up to 100 kg. Lake Turkana, which is most easily reached by plane from Nairobi, is considered one of the dream waters of the world, with huge fishes of many species, including tigerfish and Nile perch, in its waters.

Coastal fly-fishing off Kenya is fabulous, and the opportunities are limitless. Many anglers from around the world fly into Mombasa for a stay at Hemingway's and a shot at the big marlin. Hemingway's is also the gateway to deep-water gamefishes on the fly. Coastal fishes include huge kingfish, barracuda, bonito and tunny.

Many fly-fishermen take a plane from Nairobi to Lake Victoria. This huge inland sea, bounded by Uganda, Kenya, and Tanzania, is one of the most splendid freshwater fisheries in the world. Anglers operate out of reasonably comfortable island accommodation equipped with boats and guides, and pursue giant Nile perch and tigerfish with all manner of methods. Fly-fishing is an accepted method these days, and the world fly-caught record Nile perch is from this inland freshwater sea. Nile perch were introduced to Lake Victoria and are not a naturally occurring species in this water. Many smaller species provide excellent sport on light fly tackle.

Uganda

Apart from Lake Victoria (discussed above) there is good fishing at Lakes Edward and Mobutu which both produce tigerfish, kurper, catfish, and other species which attack flies with gusto.

Unknown to most is the existence of a viable brown trout population in the Ruimi River on the eastern slopes of the Ruwenzori Mountains of western Uganda, a legacy of past settlers. The boundary river, the Suam, was stocked with rainbow trout.

Fishing is possible all year, but April and December are rainfall months and are best avoided. Take your own flies and tackle.

Ethiopia and Sudan

I have met Kenyans who use helicopters to get into the high country just north of the Kenyan border. Reports of unspoilt brown trout fishing in the Bale Mountains well south of Addis Ababa are mouthwatering. Nevertheless, with lots of political instability and banditry, I would view this as high-risk, high-adventure fly-fishing.

There is said to be a self-sustaining population of rainbow trout in the Sudan high country (they can handle warmer water than brown trout), but I have never met anyone who has actually been fly-fishing in Sudan.

Rwanda

There were once trout in the clear highland streams of this small, war-torn country. Look for the gorillas and perhaps find the trout. How-ever, at the time of writing, this is not the place to be, and remote mountain forests would obviously be unsafe.

Northern Africa

Most of this area is desert with very little fishing available. The Atlas Mountains in Algeria are the only part of Africa where indigenous brown trout are to be found, and are also the only place in North Africa offering fly-fishing of any note. They are difficult to get to, and the authorities warn travellers to beware of banditry. Frankly, if I were to go that far for a trout (and I live in Johannesburg), then I believe I would prefer a couple of weeks in Europe. The trout in Algeria are fished for with dry and wet flies. Local flies often use a spot of purple in the dressing.

The fearsome teeth of the tigerfish have been known to pierce copper spinner blades ... no place for unwary fingers.
(Photo: Malcolm Meintjes)

Western Africa

This region is still the dark continent as far as fishing, and especially fly-fishing, is concerned. The rivers and still waters support several species of yellowfish, kurper and catfish, and one would assume that the potential for fly-fishing is good. I strongly recommend (and this applies to all of the remote countries) that you appoint a good tour operator to drive you around, to provide translation services, and to pre-book accommodation and transport. In all the less well-developed African countries, a good guide backed by an established and reputable tour operator can be the difference between a miserable failure or a superb fly-fishing holiday. However, apart from delivering you to the shores of chosen lakes and rivers, he is unlikely to know anything about fly-fishing. Nothing is lost by watching native fishermen who often fish for sporting fishes and generally know where to find them. A few enquiries and some cigarettes will often produce just the information needed.

The Kafue pike is primarily West African, and gives great sport on the fly. The Alestes (see Chapter 9) are found in West Africa and offer good sport for evening fly-fishing. Fighting yellowfish inhabit many rivers along with catfish, and Nile perch also have a distribution extending throughout West Africa.

The western African coast is better known than its interior from a fishing point of view; indeed, the potential for the fly-fisherman in countries north of Angola is superb. From Congo to Senegal the river mouths, estuaries and surf are full of sporting fishes. Some areas are heavily exploited by commercial fishermen, but in general there are far more unspoilt areas than on the Indian Ocean coastline. Fishes to look for include Atlantic tarpon, bonefish, European barracuda, elf (*Pomatomus saltatrix*), long-tailed kingfish, cob, springer, various snapper, bonito, various mullets, garrick and others.

HEALTH AND SAFETY

Safety

Some African trout streams flow through deep canyons and forests, where an accident may befall anybody. It is very advisable to warn family or friends of your intention to embark on a trip into any wild place, and also to give a time by which you intend to return. At least then, if anything goes wrong, help is at hand. In similar vein, the really wild places should be entered only with company. If you break a leg on your own, it could be disastrous and very likely deadly. Exposure is a real threat to the unwary – many of the difficult-to-access waters are places which are warm in the day, but subject to massive temperature drops or rolling fog at night. Adventuring into these places justifies a small back pack with extra clothing, instant food such as chocolate, and some 'still work when wet' fire lighters. These may well save your life in the event of an accident.

In Africa, one should always be prepared for the odd mishap. Possibly the most harm you are likely to experience is at the sharp end of a tigerfish's dental array. Never handle a tigerfish without gloves, and even then with the greatest of respect. Should a tigerfish succeed in lacerating you, you must immediately attend to the wound. Wash the wound and dry it, then apply mercurochrome. This is a fine antiseptic and obtainable almost everywhere in Africa. It is easy to use, and comes in a small, easily packed container. Once back in 'civilisation', get a doctor to check the wound.

Some of the attendant wildlife can be a bit exciting as well, and top potential nasties amongst these are hippos and crocodiles. Never take either of these for granted, and always treat them with the greatest respect. Crocs and tigerfish have a mutual understanding about ecology, so if you are into a good spot with plenty of tigerfish, you can be almost sure that somewhere a crocodile will be watching you. Now, if he's a big one, you may be ringing dinner-gong noises in his small brain. Any croc over 2,5 metres could think of you in this way. In the main it is unlikely: given the choice, a nice catfish is a better option than you are. However, if he's really big, and he's hungry, you will need to be careful. The danger occurs on the shore, since crocs will leave you alone in a boat. A big croc is an exceedingly powerful and mean beastie. He can knock a large unwary animal off a rock, and is even more accom-

This fishing resort on Bazaruto Island in Mozambique offers comfortable accommodation, excellent food and fabulous fly-fishing.

plished at sneaking up from below and taking his shorebound prey in a lethal lunge ... and this he can accomplish with creatures much bigger than man! So stand back from the edge, keep off exposed rocks, and stay alert.

Angling lore has it that at one of the Zambezi fishing camps the proprietor would catch, at night, a metre-long croc, which he would place on the bar, tickling its stomach every time he walked past to keep it quiet. To the clientele (who were not in on the story) the crocodile looked stuffed, and the proprietor chose not to enlighten them. When his victims had had a few too many, however, and a suitable innocent was seated near the comatose crocodile, the tickling would stop and the reptile would obligingly wake up in a foul mood. Tail lashing and jaws snapping, it would stalk off into the night in an explosion of hastily vacated furniture, breaking glass and unrepeatable expletives from the retreating anglers. Once it was gone and several extra drinks had been gulped down, everyone thought it a great joke.

Hippos are another potential hazard, but one easily minimised by keeping away from them. A bad-tempered one can be a problem to a small boat on the water, and they are exceptionally quick on land. Mothers with young calves are very aggressive. Certainly keep away from their territory at night, they are extremely dangerous in the dark! They won't hunt you down, but react to you being in their space.

Finally, most anglers, and that includes the indigenous fishermen who stand up to their waists all day in croc-infested water, never have any problem with the wildlife. You too may fish for years and years unscathed, so long as you are aware, and keep awake. In fact, you should be much safer than you would be crossing the street in a big city!

Health

Bilharzia

The scourge of eastern Africa is bilharzia. This disease is parasitic on man, and uses one of the freshwater snails as a host during its development. At some stage it becomes free-swimming in the water and is able to penetrate the skin through any small wound or opening. Urinating in the rivers by rural populations is the main source of re-infection. It occurs only in rivers flowing into the Indian Ocean – but it occurs in all of them. The simplest remedy is not to wade, and if you do, then wear boots. Symptoms are headaches and drowsiness, which can occur some weeks after exposure. Bilharzia is easily checked for, and positive cures are available. However, if left untreated it can do considerable damage.

Malaria

This dreaded and deadly disease is prevalent throughout low-altitude Africa. One must, and I repeat, *must* take the proper precautions in malaria areas. Only a fool ignores malaria, and nothing in the wild is more capable of separating you from your life and your fishing. Regular medical updates are published by all the African health authorities, and these should be sought out and perused prior to departure. Your travel agent usually has such information available. A common error is to return home thinking, 'Well, I didn't catch malaria', and immediately stop taking anti-malarials. It could be fatal! Follow the instructions to the letter ... never miss a single dosage for the entire period of treatment, even if it continues weeks after your return (and it nearly always does).

Various sprays and applications help prevent mosquitoes from biting. It is important to use these: if you can prevent getting bitten then you are well on the way to winning. Mosquito nets are a must, and you are advised to spray them with mosquito repellent prior to sleeping. I also spray my elbows and toes ... they always seem to rub up against the net with the consequent possibility of getting bitten.

After many years of catching butterflies in tropical jungles and fishing in remote malaria-infested areas, these precautions have kept me free of the disease. But one should not be complacent. I know the slightest slip-up could result in infection, and I do my best to be careful.

Rules and regulations

Some African authorities will confiscate your car and your tackle for fishing without permits, so check that you have your permits stored in a waterproof bag in your pocket. If you have a permit, but do not have it with you, you may still earn a stiff fine. Check the regulations of the water which you are fishing – many have special rules of their own! These could apply to maximum hook sizes, or whether hooks are allowed barbed or not; some lay down a maximum allowable tippet size, some operate 'catch and release rules' or variations thereof, and finally, there will always be limits on minimum fish size and on the number of fishes allowed to be taken. In some countries, taking fish over the limited amount is regarded as theft (a criminal offence), so check the limit rules carefully ... African jails can be unpleasant. Some waters even lay down rules on acceptable flies (there are waters that only allow traditional patterns; some of them, stupidly in my opinion, ban modern lure flies and Boobys).

CHAPTER 2

GETTING STARTED:
TACKLE AND ACCESSORIES

If you knew everything, you would still have to learn how to fish.

Don Lort

So, your best friend, your boss, your husband, the book you have just read, someone or something has convinced you that fly-fishing is a life enriching experience. The time has come to spend some hard earned money to get started ... what do you do? Or, perhaps you are already fly-fishing, but nothing seems to be working right. You do your best, but the line just won't go where it should. You hardly ever see a trout and when you do it bolts at the sight of your fly. Or, maybe you have been fishing for years with a few good friends, even perhaps on your own. You get a few fish, but you feel you could do much better. This chapter is for you.

This book shares quantities of know-how (and even a few secrets), but unless you start right and have a feel for what you are doing you will never be a consistently successful fly-fisherperson. As in all things, a good base is an opportunity to build great results. In this chapter we

will look at the essentials, the things that *must* be right, and even if you have been fly-fishing for a while, you may well find something here that will turn the scales in your favour.

Fishing tackle is in essence functional; it should do a job, do the job well, and be reliable. However, humankind cannot help but impose fashion, good looks, and one-upmanship on functionality, and things are thus often not what they seem. When acquiring what is essentially a working tool, one should be wary of over-embellishment. The core items needed by a fly-fisherman are a rod, a reel, a fly line or two, some leader and tippet material, flies, a net, and a few other accessories. These include essentials like outdoor clothing and a hat, scissors, floatants, fly boxes, and a priest.

Another useful item is a sound philosophy on personal impediments. Some people will stumble along the banks of their favourite water weighed down by a bulging fly-fishing waistcoat and a back-pack weighing kilograms and containing everything but the kitchen sink. Great heavy bank-shaking footwear or waders and another small bag with lunch and flask complete the picture. How horrendously uncomfortable and inconvenient! Nevertheless, some feel that it takes all this to create the correct image (or should I say illusion?) Unless you look as though you have everything, how can you possibly be an expert? But the very best fly-fishermen carry very little; they are highly mobile, they are quiet, and like the wildlife around them their preference is to melt into the

All you need to carry?

scenery. They would prefer you not to know they are there! They are efficient, and the best things they carry are water lore and knowledge. Somewhere between these extremes of minimal and maximal impedimenta is everybody's comfort zone. Most of the good anglers I have met carry either a light fly-fishing waistcoat or a couple of moonbags. Few ever wear waders, but they do wear drab clothes. They carry one fitted-up rod, a net, priest, polarised glasses, a small bag of essentials, and that's all!

The prime philosophy for successful fishing dictates, as its first precept, that 'the fish must not know that you are there'. Your aim is to prevent the fish from forming associations of danger, which for a fish, includes man. You need to be as near invisible as you can get, and you need to move slowly and quietly. Do this, and you will see fish that most fly-fishermen walk by and never see. You will quickly learn things that others never learn, and you will catch fish!

That's the ultimate aim, but with many public waters there is nowhere to hide. Anglers stand in rod-waving rows separated by a non-verbally agreed annoyance factor, and the fishes vanish like wraiths. Even here, you can overcome the problems. You do it by standing back from the water and by learning to cast further; also by knowing about the feeding habits of the fishes, their likes and dislikes, and the way they view the world. With the right abilities and knowledge, even on crowded public waters, one can build and carry through fish-catching strategies that work.

Our aim, then, is to get everything as right as we can; to make sure our equipment is functional, to develop a good understanding of water lore, to learn to be stealthy, and to acquire productive fish-catching skills. We will start off by analysing the basic needs of tackle and casting. Other chapters will discuss the fishes and the strategies for catching them.

RODS

The first essential is to acquire a *properly balanced* outfit ... without this balance you will be unable to cast well, and you will certainly not be able to cast accurately. The other result of badly balanced tackle is that it causes fatigue,

and as a result of tired muscles and a need to compensate for poor performance, the angler develops bad casting habits. Poorly balanced tackle is probably the commonest reason for frustration and eventual loss of interest.

If you look at any modern fly rod you will find written somewhere on the butt a set of letters and numbers, usually in the form 'AFTM 6/7' or similar. Occasionally, it is abbreviated to '# 6/7'. There may well be only one number, such as 'AFTM 4'. These numbers indicate the rating of the rod – the correct line size which the rod is matched to cast. You would be correct in assuming that if the rod says 'AFTM 5', then you should buy an 'AFTM 5'-sized line to match it. If the rod has no number on the butt – *don't buy it*.

AFTM stands for 'American Fishing Tackle Manufacturers' and it is a standard code of weight for the first 30 feet of any fly-fishing line. You will notice that it is measured in imperial, not metric, units. The weight of the line in the standard tables is measured in grains (not in grams).

Thus an AFTM 4 rod is designed to cast an AFTM 4 line of which the casting length weighs precisely enough (in this case, 120 grains) to get the best performance from the rod. If you put an AFTM 2 line on such a rod, the line will not weigh enough to get the rod working. If you put an AFTM 9 line on the same rod, the line

AFTM CODE	WEIGHT (grains) first 30 feet of fly line		ACCEPTABLE WEIGHT RANGE (grains)
1	60		54–66
2	80		74–86
3	100		94–106
4	120		114–126
5	140	Most	134–146
6	160	commonly	152–168
7	185	used	177–193
8	210	sizes	202–218
9	240		230–250
10	280		270–290
11	330		318–342
12	380		368–392
Note: 437,5 grains = 1 ounce = 28,4 grams			

Fly line AFTM weightings.

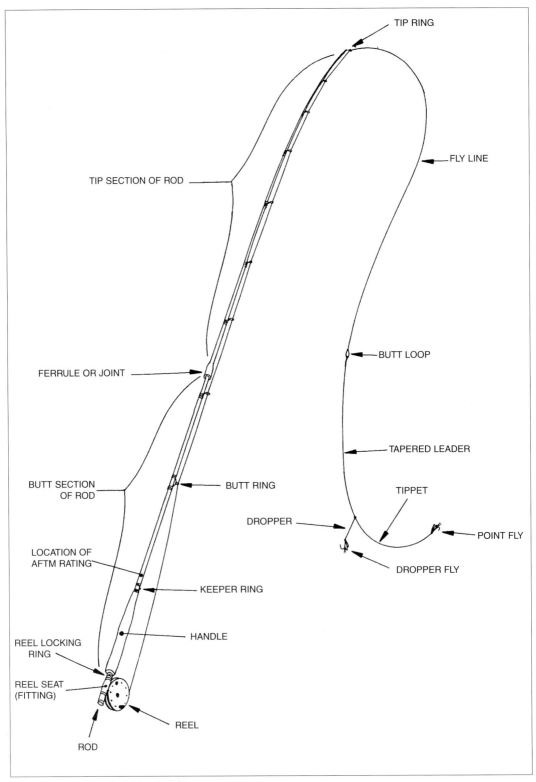

TIP RING

FLY LINE

TIP SECTION OF ROD

BUTT LOOP

FERRULE OR JOINT

TAPERED LEADER

BUTT SECTION
OF ROD

BUTT RING

TIPPET

DROPPER

POINT FLY

LOCATION OF
AFTM RATING

DROPPER FLY

KEEPER RING

HANDLE

REEL LOCKING
RING

REEL SEAT
(FITTING)

REEL

ROD

Fig. 2.1: Assembled rod, reel, line and flies.

will be too heavy. The rod will fail to impart the necessary energy, and may even break under the excessive load. Some rods, known as broad spectrum rods, may give a broader range of line size. Typically, 'AFTM 6 to 8' or 'AFTM 5 to 9' would be examples of this. These are rods especially designed to cast a range of fly lines. Such rods are an attempt to design two rods into one, and inevitably they lose out on performance as a result.

The often-found split number, such as 'AFTM 6/7' (these numbers are separated by a factor of 1 only), does not indicate broad spectrum or a potential fall-off with respect to performance. The number difference here refers to two different types of fly line, both of which suit the rod: the first number is the best weight for a 'double tapered' fly line, the second number is the best weight for a 'weight forward' fly line. For the beginner, the double tapered fly line is more forgiving and easier to cast. It is also more cost effective in that when it is worn it can be turned around and the other end will perform as a new line (effectively two for the price of one). The weight forward line demands better casting ability, but it will cast further. And, of course, once the working end is worn you will need to buy a new one. Most experienced anglers opt for the weight forward choice.

Thirty years ago I attended an advanced casting clinic and was horrified to hear the instructor say to the angler next to me, 'That's a fine rod sir. If you stick it in the ground, you could grow beans up it! Perhaps you should borrow one of our rods before the lesson starts.' The luckless chap had a cheap glass fibre rod which was as floppy as a tank aerial, and quite hopeless for serious casting. I clutched my Bruce and Walker Ultra-light fervently, thanking the good fairy of fishing that I had read an article by Dick Walker on rods before purchasing mine. My rod was good then, but it would stand up very poorly against the advanced technologies of today. So what do you look for when buying your rod?

What size rod?

In Africa you can fly-fish for just about everything with just three rods, but assuming you are new to fly-fishing, and this is your first rod

ever, you still need to know what to select. Fly rods can cost a small fortune – the best are very expensive indeed. But the performance difference between the best and those that are 'quite suitable' is not that great. The difference in price, however, can be considerable. Another problem that you may well face is the bad fishing shop salesman – who doesn't know his facts, is very pushy, and uses a few buzz words – we have all met him. Some of the better shops employ top-grade experienced anglers, but not all of them do.

Ignore the really cheap stuff, and start off by looking at rods in the medium price-range (often as much as three times cheaper than top brand names). The big serious tackle shops all carry a range like this; many of them import rod blanks (a blank is a rod prior to finishing and whipping) and custom-build a range of rods just for this sector of the market. Your rod will need to be chosen for the task in hand, and different rods are recommended for trout, bass, saltwater, and so on. So be sure of what you intend to do with your rod.

The following three rods would be an ideal all-Africa set, enabling you to fish for most species in most places. Bear in mind, however, that the specialist angler may well choose a rod specific to the species he is hunting. As you progress and learn about rods, you will also learn to be finicky about the rods you use; with experience you will undoubtedly settle on a rod which is just right for the task in hand. The following, then, is just a guide.

All-round trout, yellowfish and bass rod

Most people start off fishing for trout in dams, with the odd day by a river, and are usually looking for an all-round compromise. For them, a fast-action AFTM 7 or 8 rod of 9 feet length would be adequate for the task. The same rod would do for small gamefish such as bass and yellowfish.

The size 7 rod would be most useful if you are also intending to do some occasional stream fishing for trout. The size 8 rod would be the better choice if your eventual aim is long-distance casting in big waters, with perhaps a day now and then after bass or barbel.

Many experienced anglers fly-fishing for trout carry an AFTM 5 or 6 for nymphing and dry fly-fishing, their second rod being an AFTM 8 for fishing bigger flies and casting long distances. The AFTM 5/6 is usually 8 feet 6 inches, and the AFTM 8 is in the range 9 to 10 feet long.

Tigerfish, catfish and saltwater rod

Tigerfish anglers, those fly-rodders after catfish, and the saltwater angler going for estuary and surf would look for a rod of a minimum AFTM 8, and more likely AFTM 9 or 10. This rod would need a fast action for distance and accuracy, but this would be moderated by the need for a powerful butt action to tame high-speed powerful fishes. Many of these anglers use shooting head casting techniques, of which more later.

Stream fishing for trout, kurper, perch and bluegill

If your affirmed choice is for stream fishing, or for the smaller gamefishes, you may well choose an AFTM 4 or 5 rod of 8 to 8 feet 6 inches length. Length of rod is a personal thing. Tall people can manage quite well with short rods. I am not so tall, and I find a long rod helps me maintain a high back cast as well as giving me greater control over fish in weedy edges. However, if your favourite stream is very bushy and overgrown, a shorter rod will be much more useful.

Super-light tackle

You will come across anglers who consider anyone not using an AFTM 2 or even 1 rod to be inadequate. This is absolute nonsense. There is no need whatsoever for such light tackle; in fact it is not recommended. These gossamer rods are designed for mountain and moorland streams such as you might find in Europe; open streams where a big fish is never more than 20 cm long and where there are few snags. In Africa, where trout and other fishes are of good size and powerful, these rods are not recommended. Powerful fishes cannot be turned or controlled with these featherweight wands. 'But that's sporting', you say. I am afraid it's not! Fishes breaking off and having to swim around with flies and lengths of nylon in their jaws is not sporting. Perhaps an acceptable counter-argument is the need to present tiny size 22 flies on a gossamer tippet. Frankly, I can do that very well with an AFTM 4 outfit, and so can most beginners after a few months.

Rods for ladies and youngsters

Ladies can handle rods up to AFTM 7 or 8 without a problem once they have learned to cast correctly. Most of the fly-fisherwomen I know fish streams with AFTM 4 to 6, and the big still waters with AFTM 6 or 7 outfits. Small children are not really co-ordinated well enough until about seven years (although there are exceptions). A small boy or girl over this age should start out with an AFTM 5 rod. They need the extra strength of the 5 because there will be a 'rough treatment' factor, but not any more weight than that. At 12 they can handle AFTM 6 rods and by 13 or 14 they can master bigger rods for surf and tiger fishing.

Buying a rod

Let us assume that the choice has been made. Your decision may be for an AFTM 7 rod, 9 feet 6 inches in length (most rod manufacturers still use imperial measurements), which will reach a good distance and provide reasonable accuracy. Naturally, the rod's ability to perform the latter two functions depends on your skill, but all the skill in the world will still depend on a good rod. The things you will be looking for are:
❏ material
❏ action
❏ dampening capability
❏ finish
❏ fittings
❏ price.

Material

Rods are manufactured from five major materials. These are:
❏ split cane
❏ glass fibre
❏ graphite (various combinations of resins and fibres)
❏ Kevlar
❏ boron.

Examples of rods in different materials (top to bottom): split cane, glass fibre, high modulus glass fibre, composite graphite, high modulus graphite, boron, Kevlar, woven 100% graphite, Kevlar whisker, Kevlar/graphite composite.

The first two are no longer considered really suitable for fly-fishing. In the past, they both held sway at different times. The oldest of these technologies is split cane, which was surpassed by fibreglass in the sixties. Split cane, with its soft, slow, sweet action, is still admired and enjoyed by traditionalists and lovers of fine workmanship. It is also heavy, however, and needs considerable care to prevent splitting in most African climates. Its only true advantage is its ability to resist twisting, and as such cane provides very accurate casting capability for small stream work.

Glass fibre is reasonably light and can be acquired in stiff fast-action blanks. However, its dampening is very poor, it is not as efficient at storing energy (thus it casts less well), and it is heavy compared to graphite.

Kevlar and boron both came into eminence in the eighties. Boron was a very expensive material, lightweight and very desirable. I still have a boron fly rod which performs very well, but it is not as good as the latest graphites. Kevlar (probably better known for its use in bullet-proof vests) came and went, and was usually offered in conjunction with fibreglass or graphite. It can cost up to two or three times as much as graphite, and consequently it was eventually surpassed in the marketplace.

Our choice, then, distils down to the modern graphite fibre resin combinations. Some of these are extremely good. Technology moves on rapidly, and it seems to me that new graphite materials continually appear. Today's mid-range graphites are excellent value for money. Most offer lightweight, good casting performance and excellent dampening. The mid-range graphite rods of today are actually far better than the top rods of only eight to ten years ago. Rods such as the Crossfire range sold in South Africa, and other mid-range offerings by Orvis, Shakespeare, St Croix, Daiwa and Silstar, to name a few, are all acceptable. If you want to spend lots of money then Sage, Hardy, Scott, Thomas and Thomas, Orvis, and Loomis all offer superb rods, all of them available in Africa, though easier to get in some countries than in others.

Rod action

Check the rod type by looking at the 'envelope' of the rod's action. The envelope describes the rod movement from one extreme to the other. It

21

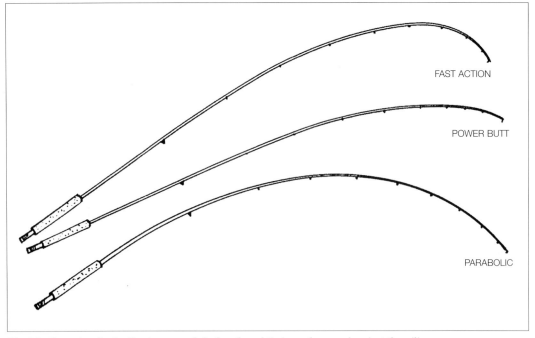

Fig. 2.2: Examples of rod action types revealed when the rod tip is gently pressed against the ceiling.

sounds formidable, but it's not. Hold the rod parallel to the ground and loosely flick it from side to side. The shape of the action will immediately be apparent. The point at which the two sides of the envelope cross over illustrates the position in the rod where the action changes from slow to fast.

If the cross-over is near the tip (a quarter to one fifth of the rod length) and the envelope thin, then the rod is 'tip actioned' ... it will be a fast rod, capable of casting long distances. This fast tip actioned rod is what you want. Thin envelopes also suggest powerful butt action, and a medium thin enveloped rod with the action cross-over one third from the tip (i.e. nearer to the butt) would indicate a good saltwater, tigerfish or barbel rod. Such a rod will have sacrificed some casting ability for fighting power. A slow-actioned rod will display the cross-over nearer to the butt, and a wide envelope. This will not cast as well.

Another method of assessing 'action' is to press the rod tip gently against the ceiling. This reveals the curve of the rod. The fast tip actioned rod will bend largely near the tip. The butt actioned rod for the surf will bend at the

tip as well, but more so, and the bend will move deeper into the butt. A soft parabolic action (such as you might find in a South African carp rod) will bend equally all the way through.

Dampening

At this stage of the selection process, you will have chosen the desired AFTM rating, the desired rod length, the action you require, and you will have narrowed it down even more to accommodate the depth of your pocket. Rod dampening is the only major factor left. Dampening becomes very important if you have aspirations to achieve distance casting – and, to a lesser extent, if your aim encompasses accuracy. Spurious vibrations brought on as a result of poor dampening can cut down casting distance drastically.

Rod dampening is simply checked in the shop by holding the rod by the handle and giving it a smart flick, and then counting the number of vibrations before the rod tip stops moving. A glass fibre rod may vibrate 15 times or more before it stops ... at the other extreme a good Sage may stop after two or three movements. A rod which stops vibrating within six movements is acceptable – the nearer to zero vibration, the better it is.

Rod fittings and fixtures

Fittings and fixtures are very much a matter of choice, but it is worth remembering that single leg rod rings have less effect on the originally designed action of the blank than double legged rod rings such as snake rings. Every whipping wound onto the rod stiffens the action.

A good locking reel seat is essential. The reel should be held as near to the butt end of the rod as possible. To achieve this, the screw reel fitting (also known as a winch fitting) must push the reel towards the butt end, and not towards the handle. This means that the screwed ring which tightens the reel is nearest to the cork. For big gamefishes and for saltwater, positive or double reel locking is mandatory, and a double screwed locking ring is essential. Saltwater rod fittings must be salt resistant!

A cork handle is very much better than any sponge one. Don't forget to remove the protective plastic handle wrapper which comes on many new rods. If you leave it there, the cork may go mouldy. A cork extension butt below the reel fitting is essential on the heavier (AFTM 9 and above) rods.

I prefer a matt finish on my rods, and I am very much against embellishments such as gold whipping and any other flashy finishes. If your rod was a gift, and is good in every respect except for a flashy finish, you can rub the flash off with toothpaste. Fish see this flash and it scares them.

Rod tubes

The extra cost of a rod tube (they are not always supplied with the rod) is a good investment. If you travel by air to other African countries, take note that the chances of your rod going into the hold are high. Once there, it will not survive without a strong metal rod tube to protect it from falling suitcases and other abuse.

Testing rods

Some shops offer a test casting facility, and if they do, you must take advantage of it. Take a whittled-down choice of three rods, and make

Examples of rod rings (eyes) (left to right): triple leg butt ring, snake ring, single leg ring, double leg ring.

the final choice at the casting facility. If you are a beginner, the shop owner can demonstrate for you; or, if you prefer, take an accomplished casting friend along.

REELS

In fly-fishing for trout and other small species, the function of the reel very seldom goes further than providing a storage location for the fly line. However, when fishing for big gamefishes in saltwater, the reel becomes a very important part of the tackle, and is a fighting tool in its own right. There is more information on reels for fighting big league fishes in Chapter 10. Very big trophy trout may also get you fighting on the reel, and certainly the odd yellowfish will. If this is likely to occur, then you must choose your reel very carefully.

In principle, for trout fishing choose a reel which is as light as possible. Graphite and magnesium are the lightest materials, but many good lightweight reels are available in aluminium. I am a great believer in buying reels all of the same type to fit a particular size of rod. This is preferable to buying spare spools for different fly lines, but more expensive.

Despite what you may be told, the reel does

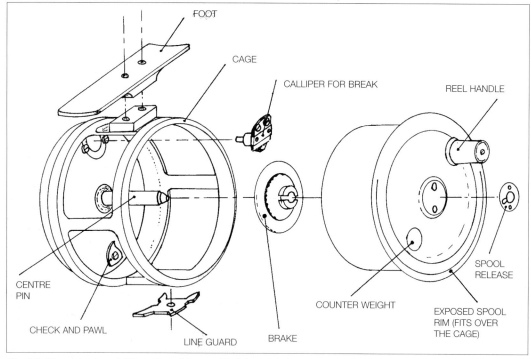

FOOT

CAGE

CALLIPER FOR BREAK

REEL HANDLE

CENTRE PIN

CHECK AND PAWL

LINE GUARD

BRAKE

COUNTER WEIGHT

SPOOL RELEASE

EXPOSED SPOOL RIM (FITS OVER THE CAGE)

Fig. 2.3: The parts of a reel. When the reel is assembled the spool rim encaps around the cage. This gives the angler a large measure of control over fighting fish as a result of the exposed rim. Types with the spool rim inside the cage are less useful.

nothing to balance the rod. You would find casting easier if it were not there. There are, however, some important things to look for when buying a new fly reel, and these are discussed below.

Spool gap

This is the clearance between the spool edge and the reel frame. In very poor reels it is an obviously visible gap. If this clearance is too great, the line will get trapped or even jammed behind the spool causing all sorts of problems ranging from oil on the line to being snapped off by a fast fish. Some reels (for example Hardy) are very precisely machined. Others have enormous gaps (some big name reels are guilty of this).

Rim

No reel is worth having that does not have an exposed rim which can be used to control the reel when fighting a fish. Palming the reel to act as a break is an essential requirement. Caged reel spool rims are of no use to the fly-fisherman.

Centre pin bearing

The 'bearing pin' that the spool revolves on should be rigidly mounted and strong. If it can come loose or can bend under pressure, then it will do so just when the biggest fish you have ever seen is on the line. The result is a major jam-up and immediate breakage of the line.

The small release clip and mounting plate that hold the spool release mechanism (situated on the face of the spool) must be solidly built. There should be minimal in-and-out movement of the spool. The better reels are often adjustable in this respect.

Audible check mechanisms and drags

Check mechanisms should be made with metal. Plastic check pawls wear quickly. Good check mechanisms can be set for either right- or left-hand wind, and should also only operate when line is pulled off the reel and not when it is wound in. Many modern reels have clutch (or drag) mechanisms designed to wear the fish down. These should be smooth in operation, they should even work when the reel is wet (some don't), and quite obviously they should never jam. The wrong materials here could melt or fuse as a result of a run from a fast fish. I prefer disc brake mechanisms in my big-fish fly reels. They cost more, but they are worth it for the peace of mind.

You will not find all of the above attributes in trout reels (although there are exceptions), but in saltwater reels they are essential. To a large extent, these, and sheer size, explain the very high cost of saltwater fly-fishing reels.

The only other area of potential weakness is the reel foot, which is used to mount the reel on the rod. Patently, this should not be able to come loose.

Capacity

This is not so much a fault area as a potential mistake. You must buy the correct size of reel. The reel is of no use if the line won't fit on it! All reels are coded to take certain sizes of fly line, and most have some spare space for 50 (or more) metres of backing. Remember, you are after the smallest reel that will hold your line and some backing. A too-large reel is just extra weight, and, additionally, the fly line will be wound onto a too-small diameter, thus causing unwanted coiling in the line at a later date. NB: large spool reels are purposely used in shooting head fishing and in saltwater. These will be dealt with in later chapters.

Dacron, or some other non-stretch braided line, is best for backing. Dacron is designed for other forms of fishing. In fly-fishing it is only used as a 'filler' or backing. There is more on this in Chapter 10.

Fill the spool so that the line is within 2 to 3 mm of the spool edge when full. The better lines are supplied with a small self-adhesive label with the line code on it. Stick this to the flat spool side normally hidden within the reel, and even years later you will know without a doubt what line is on what spool. Many lines are similar in colour, and it is difficult to assess the line AFTM rating by sight.

Spool balance

Most modern reels designed for lines over AFTM 7 have a counterweight opposite the reel

Fly-tying is the other side of fly-fishing. The really complete fly-fisherman masters both the fishing and the tying. The keen fly-tier can tie flies anywhere! Here the late Don Lort ties a fly destined for bass, a Yellow Woolly Bugger, on his car door.

handle (incidentally, one reel handle is sufficient). This counterweight balances the reel in a high-speed run, thus preventing vibration and consequent overheating of the centre bearing pin. On some of the older reels this counter-weighting can be achieved by epoxying a couple of small coins to the spool, on the side opposite to the handle (but same face).

By now, you have the information to acquire the correct rod for the fly-fishing you have in mind, and you also have sufficient knowledge to purchase the smallest and lightest quality reel of the correct size to hold the desired line. Having made these purchases, the next objective is to correctly load the reel with its line.

FLY LINES

The fly line is a specially tapered length of thick line which enables you to perform the art of casting without the need of additional weight. At first glance, the fly line shelf in any fly-fish-

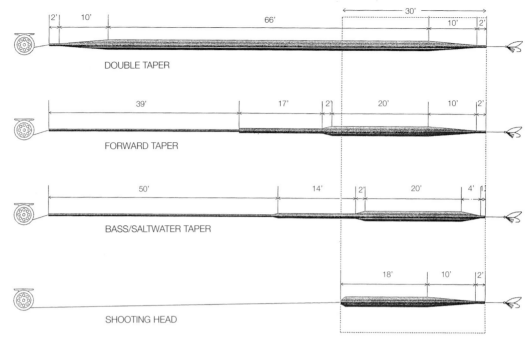

Fig. 2.4: *Typical fly line taper profiles. Exaggerated for the purpose of this illustration. The above lengths are in feet.* (Credit: Steve Barrow)

ing shop is awesome. There is a confusing and seemingly complex range of fly lines to choose from. However, as with other components in fly-fishing, the fly lines are in fact arranged in a logical classification which is laid down to a world-wide standard.

The dealer usually lays out the fly line boxes in such a way that all the box labels can be seen at once. All these labels carry a code which tells you everything about the line (everything that is, except its quality). This code is divided into three fields of information. Typically, and in this order, it defines the type of *taper* in the line, then the *AFTM size* of the line, followed by the *line characteristics* (does it float or sink?). They follow the format DT 5 F – which would be a double taper (DT), AFTM 5, floating (F) line. Similarly, WF 7 S is a weight forward taper, size AFTM 7, sinking fly line.

The most common taper and density codes are as follows:

Taper codes
L Level line, no taper
DT Double taper (tapered at both ends)
ST Shooting taper (a single taper cut to

30 feet, the correct AFTM length, commonly called a 'shooting head')
WF Weight forward taper concentrated at the casting (front) end, also known as a rocket taper.

Density codes
F Floating line
S Sinking line (up to six different sink rates, usually nominated by a type number, e.g. type IV)
I Intermediate density (slightly denser than water)
F/S Sink tip (the tip sinks, the rest floats).

Specialist tapers are available, such as 'bug tapers' (for casting poppers and surface lure flies), 'saltwater tapers' (designed to turn over big bulky flies), 'tarpon tapers' (for butt powered rods and big flies), 'big-game tapers' (for marlin and other huge fish), and so on.

Lead core fly lines
In the sinking line category there are some very fast-sinking lines known as lead cores. These are covered in later chapters – they are essential

fly-fishing equipment, but should not be used by beginners. Because of the high density and thinness of these lines they can cut through clothing (and flesh) if used incorrectly. But lead core lines are quite safe in the hands of an accomplished caster. Tungsten dust impregnated lines are a good substitute for most lead core applications.

Shooting heads

These are used by casters who are competent with the double haul method. They allow greater distances to be achieved by the caster, and also require less effort to cast as a result of reduced false casting. Refer to Chapter 4 for more information on shooting heads

Beginners' lines

If you are starting fly-fishing for the first time, your line requirements are quite straightforward. All you need is a floating line and a medium-to-fast sink line. Buy full-length lines and not shooting tapers (remember, shooting tapers are only 30 feet long).

The 'double taper' lines are the most suitable for learning to cast. They roll out better and they are considerably easier to use for the essential casting technique known as 'roll casting'. You can graduate to weight forward and shooting tapers at a later stage.

Most shops offer a 'spooling service' for a small fee. They will run the backing onto your reel and knot the fly line to the backing. Ask them to put in a loop at the leader end of the fly line as well. You must tell the shop whether you are a right- or left-handed winder. If you fail to do this, you may find yourself at home (or bankside) unwinding and then rewinding the whole line. The correct winding side is the opposite to your handedness. If you are right-handed you should wind left-handed, keeping the best hand for the rod.

Fly line coloration

Line coloration is a subject that has been explored in depth by some researchers. Their findings are that floating fly lines should always be dark in colour. The usual manufactured light-coloured lines show up as bright

Selection of fly lines by Cortland, tapered leader and pin reel for holding line clippers.

lines on the water surface, and even flash in the air before landing. Both of these effects scare fish. Unfortunately, almost all floating lines are supplied in white or some other light colour.

The solution is simple. Buy some cold water dye (I like to use Dylon), read the instructions, and immerse the line in the dye for five minutes. That's all it takes. Preferred colours are deep olives and browns. You can also camouflage your line by coiling it and placing masking tape every 5 cm or so. Dye this, and, when it is dry, remove the tape and put new masking tape over the dyed areas. Then re-dye in another colour. Olive and brown give a good result.

Some of the floating fly lines are sold in fluorescent colour – usually yellow, orange, or pink. Leave the last 5 cm of the leader end of the line out of the dye, and you will end up with an easily seen indicator which will help detect tiny takes. This is quite useful for the over-forties whose sight is perhaps not as good as it was, especially at dusk.

It is essential that deep-water lines are very dark coloured (deep greys, browns and black are best). The exception would be for fishing in fairly new sand or gravel pits where a sand-coloured line might be advantageous. Mid-water lines (the slow sinkers) are best in dark blue or green. Certainly, some of the off-the-shelf intermediate density lines are far too light, and must be dyed darker.

Line quality and care

Cheap fly lines are nearly always a poor investment. Fly lines are subject to great stress, high speed impact, and all kinds of extra abuse from the learner caster. Even in the hands of good casters, fly lines still have a hard life. Buy the best you can afford – some of the top lines, if properly cared for, will last for many years (compared with a few weeks or months for cheap fly lines).

Avoid lines with 'memory' (unscrupulous dealers may try to palm these off onto the beginner). 'Memory' manifests as coils in the line which never go away, even if you stretch it. The presence of these 'memory' coils makes it difficult to perform the proper retrieving technique. This in turn adversely affects the number of takes you get, and hence fish.

Good brand names like Cortland, Scientific Anglers, Hardy, and Masterline are all reliable. A small pamphlet on line care comes with each new line. Don't throw it away – keep it somewhere, and regularly attend to your lines. Store them in a cool, dark place out of the sun. Floating lines benefit from a rub down with a weak detergent every two or three trips. Rinse the line afterwards.

Non-stretch lines

These are usually fast-sinking fly lines with Kevlar cores. Because they have no stretch (some floating lines can stretch up to 40 per cent or more) these lines provide an 'in-touch' sensitivity that is superb. Every little tap and knock of the fly can be felt. More feeling equals more fish, and that is certainly my experience with these lines. However, because there is no stretch you must build some into your rig. This is best done by assembling the leader and tippet from soft stretchy nylon rather than the hard narrow-diameter lines usually sold for this purpose. Soft wrist-flick strikes are normally quite adequate to set the hook with non-stretch fly lines. A hard strike often causes a break-off.

Non-stretch lines should never be used when trolling with flies, even with stretchy tippet material built in. Most strikes will result in an instant break at the tippet – very frustrating. Rather use the usual fast sink or lead core lines for this.

KNOTS, LEADERS, TIPPETS AND FLIES

Rod, reel and line are to hand. Next, to catch fishes we need to attach a fly to the extremity of the line in such a way that we do not frighten them – in fact, just the opposite! Our aim is to properly present the fly in such a way that the fish is convinced that it is food, or worthy of his attention ... so much so, that he takes it!

Knots

The ability to tie a few basic knots is essential to all kinds of fishing. In the following paragraphs sufficient knots are described to handle most eventualities. Throughout the book these knots will be required to build leaders and rigs for the many methods subsequently described. Here are knots to join different lines for various situations and knots for attaching flies.

The butt loop and the nail knot

Attached to the business end of the fly line should be a small loop, usually of monofilament nylon line or braided line, with a breaking strain of more than 10 kg. Begin by attaching a length of 10 kg monofilament nylon line to the end of the fly line. The most useful knot for this job is the 'nail knot'. This is a little fiddly at first, but becomes much easier with practice.

Once the nylon line is nail knotted to the fly line, the butt loop can be tied into this nylon using a 'figure-of-eight loop' knot. Some authorities refer to this loop as a 'butt', or 'butt loop'. This butt loop is usually placed about 10 cm away from the tip of the fly line. The butt loop will save you from having to cut the fly line back every time you need to replace the leader, a course which could eventually result in destruction of the forward taper of the fly line. With the butt loop present, you simply join a new leader to it with a standard 'double loop knot' – no need to cut the fly line or to re-nail knot the leader!

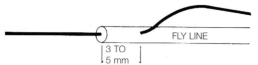

1. Make a hole in the fly line with a darning needle. Warm the needle with a gas flame until the needle moves freely – don't overheat. Take a sharp razor and slice the nylon line for a sharp point. Thread the nylon line through the hole.

2. Wind the nylon around the fly line five times. Bring the end back and lay it alongside the fly line.

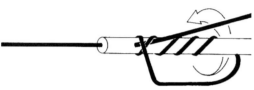

3. Turn the nylon back over itself, making sure that the free end is poked through each turn. It helps to hold each of the turns about to be made under the thumb. The arrow indicates the direction of the back turns. You will eventually back turn all the previous five turns. The 'first' back turn looks like this.

4. When all the turns are used up, carefully tighten after moistening. When everything looks neat, pull the knot up tight. Optimally, use fly tying silk to whip the joint and coat with pliable varnish. Trim the end close.

Fig. 2.5: The four stages of tying the nail knot.

The figure-of-eight loop and the double loop

This is not suitable for big-game fish, but ideal for trout and small freshwater quarry. Now, tie another 'figure-of-eight loop', but this time in the thick end of the leader. The figure-of-eight loop is accomplished by doubling the line into a loop, then passing the doubled line over and around itself one complete turn, and then tucking the doubled line through the loop so formed. Apply some saliva for lubrication, and gently tighten the knot. The knot looks like a figure-of-eight as it tightens.

Having formed the loop in the leader to your satisfaction, pass the leader loop over the butt loop at the end of the fly line, and then pull the leader up through the butt loop – this is the

1. First make a loop.

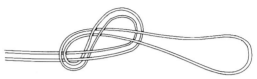

2. Then pass the loop around itself and back through the loop thus formed.

Fig. 2.6: The figure-of-eight loop knot.

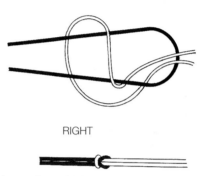

RIGHT

1 Joining two figure-of-eight loops. It may seem obvious, just looping one over the other and pulling the tail end through, but there is a right and a wrong way of doing this.

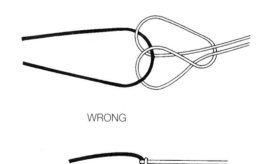

WRONG

2. The incorrect one will cut through if stressed.

Fig. 2.7: The double loop.

'double loop'. Pull everything tight: if done properly, the result looks like a reef knot. Because there are two interlocking loops it cannot come apart, and the result is very strong. When the time comes to change leaders, the two loops are simply pushed together and then they separate easily. These knots can cause a

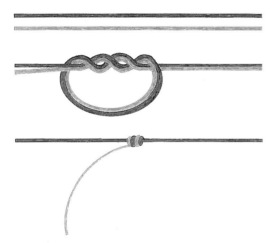

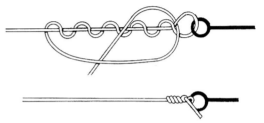

Thread the line through the hook or swivel eye and twist it four times around the main line. Then thread (or tuck) the line through the first loop formed next to the eye, and then again through the last loop just formed. Moisten the knot and tighten with a steady pull.

Fig. 2.9: The standard tucked clinch knot.

Fig. 2.8: The four-turn water knot.

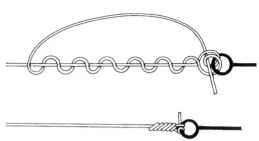

The improved version of the standard tucked clinch knot, much publicised by Berkley and again by ABU, is known as the 'double clinch' and tied as in the figures above. Breaking strength is around 90 per cent in this knot.

Fig. 2.10: The double clinch knot.

wake when retrieving fast with a floating fly line. This can be simply overcome by treating the knots with detergent.

The four-turn water knot
I love this knot, it is one of the few 99 per cent breaking strain knots, which makes it very useful. This is a knot for joining nylon monofilament lines, and it is very much better in this respect than any of the other knots ususally given in fishing books. The only comparable knot is the 'double grinner' knot which was devised by Richard Walker. One of the four-turn water knot's attributes is the way a dropper lies back against the line, rather than sticking out at right angles as in the blood knots. Good books on fishing knots are readily available for those wishing to explore the subject in greater depth.

The four-turn water knot is an excellent, simple knot for making up leaders and for tying on the tippet. Lay the two lines next to each other and form a loop with them. The two lines together are then passed through the loop four times. Tightening this knot requires great care, ensuring that neither end is able to slip.

The tucked clinch knot
The most commonly used knot for tying on the fly is the tucked clinch knot (also known as the tucked half-blood knot). This is a high strength knot and is very reliable. Saltwater and other fish with teeth need a different system for

attachment and this is dealt with in the appropriate chapters.

The surgeon's knot
This is a very simple knot for joining dissimilar materials, such as braided wire and nylon monofilament. It is an extremely useful knot

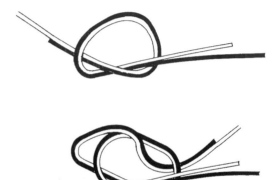

Fig. 2.11: The surgeon's knot.

where wire tippets are needed for fish with sharp teeth such as tigerfish, elf, etc. It is also useful for nylon monofilament lines with a greater than usual difference in thickness.

The surgeon's knot is a simple double overhand knot in which the two lines are held alongside one another and then formed into a loop. The two ends are then passed through the loop twice. Lubricate with saliva and then pull the knot tight very slowly. Take care not to allow any of the ends to slip or become loose. Trim the excess ends right back to the knot. Breaking strain of this knot is around 70 per cent.

The Albright knot

With this knot one can tie monocore (single strand) wire and braided wire to nylon. In large applications it will even tie braided wire to monowire. A useful knot for thick diameter nylon monofilament shock tippets. It is very popular with saltwater fly-fishermen. When fly-fishing out at sea (blue water), where larger than usual diameter monowire may be used, it is normal to tie a hay-wire loop (see Chapter 10) at the end of the wire to prevent the possibility of any slippage through the knot.

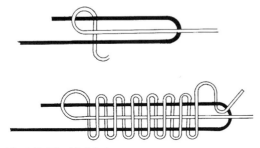

Fig. 2.12: The Albright knot

In normal surf and estuary fly-fishing, tiger fishing, and similar wire tippet situations, this is a very reliable knot with a breaking strain of around 85 per cent of its weakest component. It is thus worthwhile learning. A minimum of twelve wraps of the nylon is recommended before tucking it through the wire bend.

The double grinner knot

Invented by Dick Walter and named after his son, this is one of the finest knots for joining two ends of nylon monofilament. It can be used

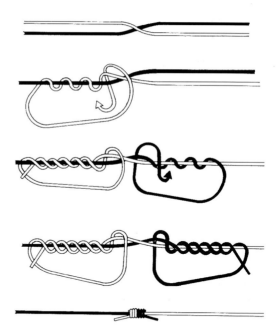

Fig. 2.13: The double grinner knot

anywhere in the line since the ends do not have to be pulled through the knot (as in the four-turn water knot, for example). It has a breaking strain of about 98 per cent even when used with dissimilar diameter nylons.

This knot is difficult at first, but in fact is quite simple to tie once you try it. Nolan Owen-Johnstone, Ron Clay, the late Don Lort, Sean Pare and others all use this knot for making up tapered leaders, for which it is excellent.

Knotty hints

Most knots break as a result of a line shock suddenly and unevenly causing tightening inside the knot. This in turn causes stretch and squeezing which breaks the line below its normal strength. Knot tightening should be done carefully, but positively. The knot should be so tight that coils cannot suddenly tighten. Knots must be pulled up carefully and evenly. If one coil is slightly looser than another, or unequally pinched, it will break under sudden stress.

Saliva is a great lubricant for knots, but it is known to attack nylons. This doesn't matter at the waterside, but if you are making up leaders at home, wash the knot in water before putting it away.

All knots should be trimmed very closely for fly-fishing – little bits that stick out soon catch up line during casting, leading to major tangles. Leaders and tippets that coil up (usually as a result of storage in packages or on reels) can be straightened by pulling the line through or against a rubber eraser. Fancy leather pads are also sold to do this job.

Leaders

The leader is the length of tapered nylon between the fly line and the fine line (the tippet) which is attached to the fly. The thick end of the leader is attached to the fly line via the butt loop. The purpose of the leader is twofold. Firstly, it enables the fly to be attached to a fine line which holds the fly and which is as invisible to the fish as possible. Secondly, it enables good presentation because, if properly designed, the leader unrolls nice and straight at the end of the cast (rather than ending up in a heap).

Knotless tapered leaders

The knotless tapered leaders are rated in two ways: (a) by the breaking strain of the thin end of the leader, and (b) by the old 'X' system. The 'X' system arose in the past when leaders were made from animal gut. The 'X' indicates the number of times the gut was drawn through a die, which in turn determines the diameter of the line.

The higher the 'X' number, the more times it was pulled through the die, and hence the finer the line became. A 5X leader is considerably thinner than a 2X.

Leaders are available in both matt and shiny finishes. Matt finish is by far the most useful, the elimination of flash being very important to the fly-fisherman. If necessary, you can remove unwanted flash by rubbing the line between your fingers with toothpaste.

Home-tied leaders

Ready tapered knotless leaders can be purchased right off the shelf. I find them rather pricey these days, and often make up my own knotted leaders from Maxima chameleon nylon. Below are three tried formulae for making your own:

	Monofilament length	*Diameter*
(a)	1,20 m (48 ins)	0,35 mm
	0,50 m (20 ins)	0,30 mm
	0,45 m (18 ins)	0,26 mm
	0,55 m (22 ins)	0,24 mm

In Maxima, this gives approximately 2,7 kg (6 lbs) breaking strain point.

(b)	1,20 m (48 ins)	0,35 mm
	0,375 m (15 ins)	0,30 mm
	0,30 m (12 ins)	0,26 mm
	0,30 m (12 ins)	0,22 mm
	0,55 m (22 ins)	0,20 mm

In Maxima this gives approximately 1,8 kg (4 lbs) breaking strain point.

(c)	0,65 m (26 ins)	0,40 mm
	0,60 m (24 ins	0,35 mm
	0,55 m (22 ins)	0,30 mm
	0,45 m (18 ins)	0,26 mm

This shorter leader is for casting into rough water against the wind. It gives approximately 3,2 kg (7 lbs) breaking strain point.

Braided leaders

Another choice available for the fly-fisherman is braided leaders. These are also tapered, but because they are made of braided nylon they are very visible. They are also very expensive. Their greatest advantage lies in their improved ability to turn over (i.e. unroll at the end of the cast), which is a decided advantage for the beginner when casting. They come in all sorts, from floaters to fast-sink types. I know of some skilled trout nymphing specialists who believe strongly in these thick-looking leaders. Many see their true worth as sink-tips (obviously using sinking braided leaders attached to floating fly line). A sinking braided leader will also help get your fly down when using a super-fast sink fly line.

The floating types float very well and turn over a dry fly beautifully. Many still-water fly-fisherfolk like to use them for static dry fly-fishing (a method which leaves the fly to lie with no retrieve). They are also useful in very confined situations such as you find in heavily bushed and treed streams, because they turn over in the smallest of spaces. However, I have to admit to a resistance to braided leaders for fine work. I am not happy with their visibility – very shy trout can be scared by them.

Nolan Owen-Johnstone, who lives in Malawi, invented a system for building almost invisible, just buoyant, tapered braided leaders. He used lengths of hollow braided floating fly line backing (specifically, the type manufactured by Masterline). He would thread various diameters of this line (various breaking strains, if you prefer) into each other, thus forming a taper. By removing single strands from the braid he was also able to change diameter, and with that and the various sizes available, he had a very flexible building system. When tensed, the braiding holds itself and does not slip. A touch of flexible glue (such as Pattex) will ensure that they stay together. These home-made braided leaders work very well.

Tippet

At the end of the leader you will tie on another length of line which is known as the tippet (in some literature it is also referred to as the 'point'. To be quite precise, the 'point' is in fact the fly end of the tippet, and the fly tied there is sometimes referred to as the 'point fly'). The choice of tippet size can be crucial, and may well decide whether you catch fishes or not. The general rule is to use as fine a tippet as you can, but this is dealt with in depth in following chapters. As a basic indication, tippet size (diameter) can be related to fly size using the following rule of thumb:

Divide fly size by four and then add one.

Example: Fly size 12 divide by 4 = 3
           Add 1, gives tippet size 4X.

Some fishes, because they have sharp teeth, need wire tippets.

The diameter of the tippet end of the leader and the diameter of the tippet itself should be nearly the same if possible. It is considered dangerous to have a difference of more than 0,2 mm in the size of the two joined lines when using blood knots, but this not so critical with the four-turn water knot, which will still tie up lines differing by a factor of 2. Even so, one should attempt to match diameters of leader and tippet as closely as possible.

Long tippet and leader combinations

For most fishing, a tippet of half a metre length is sufficient. However, experienced fly-fishermen (usually those imitating small nymphs with leaded flies in clear deep water, and using floating fly lines), may go up to tippet and leader combinations in excess of eight metres. These very long tippet additions are best tied using a heavier (0X) knotless tapered leader, continuing the taper into the tippet with three changes of line diameter of not more than 0,02 mm. Such long leader/tippet combinations do not turn over at all well, but once the fly has sunk through the deep water, they are easily retrieved.

Such long tippet set-ups are the exception, and in African waters tippets (this is excluding the leader length) longer than two metres would be unusual. A two metre tippet with a three metre leader might be a handful for the beginner caster, but no trouble to the experienced angler.

Tippet materials

Today there are many companies offering ultra-fine tippet materials. These are nylon lines which are very thin for their breaking strain when compared with standard monofilament lines. Be warned that some of these super-fine materials are disasters waiting to happen. They have the breaking strain claimed under a steady load, but if shocked (as they usually are in the strike and the take of a fast fish), they break at a much lower strain. I avoid these super-fine lines, and in fact prefer to use standard monofilament lines, or (when really pushed) an in-between product. Most fly-fishermen know about these ultra-fine tippet materials, so if in doubt about which brand to buy, ask an experienced angler. Very good products are manufactured by Maxima and are ideal for starting out.

Nylon lines are bound by a relationship between diameter, breaking strain, and hardness of the line. Because of this, lines with a low diameter and high breaking strain must be harder than normal fine lines. Thus they kink more easily, break under sudden shock, and are harder to knot satisfactorily. What can be worse than studying and stalking a trophy fish, getting him to take the fly, and then getting a snap-off at the strike?

Fine lines are very important in terms of getting takes in very clear conditions, but that broken-off trophy fish is now much wiser, harder to catch, and more easily frightened than he was. I once took a 5 kg rainbow on a 1,5 kg Maxima tippet, and because of its stretch and anti-shock properties that tippet maintained its real strength throughout the 25 minute fight that ensued. It was also thin enough in very clear water to fool that big fish.

Tippet materials are best in pale browns for surface or near-surface fly-fishing. For deeper fishing, I prefer the camouflaged lines for tippets.

Tippet dangers

When fishing it is the tippet which picks up most of the small wind knots. Wind knots must be removed immediately – if the knot cannot be undone, you must remove the knotted line and retie the fly. Wind knots cause drastic reduction of breaking strain, and are the chief cause of many lost fishes.

Teeth, even the small teeth of stock trout, can cause abrasion of the tippet. After every fish, check the tippet carefully for wear, and replace if necessary.

Droppers

Droppers are extra flies tied onto your leader/tippet combination. In Europe, you are allowed three flies in most places, but most African countries' regulations limit you to two flies maximum. This is usually (but not always) handled with a point fly and one dropper at the tippet/leader join. The four-turn water knot is superb for dropper attachment.

There are some specified methods which call for droppers (such as the chase rig, and 'over-the-front' fishing), but droppers are not recommended for newcomers to fly-fishing – they can cause all kinds of tangles when learning to

cast. One must also remember that in any water with an abundance of snags (such as is always found when hunting largemouth bass) the flying dropper (or point fly if the dropper was taken), may catch up in a sunken snag and cause the loss of a fish. My use of droppers is entirely limited to trout fishing in clear water, or in water with soft weed only.

From a casting point of view (not from a strategy viewpoint), it is easier to cast if the heavier fly is tied on the point. This helps turn-over. Droppered end rigs should not be used when casting into the wind.

Flies

Flies will be dealt with in depth in later chapters on fly-fishing techniques and different species of fish. Additionally, Chapter 13 lists flies which are favourites with experienced fly-fishermen, giving the method for using the fly together with the pattern detail for tying it.

Fly-fishing chemistry ... sinking and floating

Bulky flies may need to have all the air squeezed out of them before they will sink. Leaders which won't sink should be treated with detergent or a home-made sink putty. The putty is made by mixing Fuller's Earth (obtainable from your chemist) with washing-up liquid, and then kneading this mixture into a soft putty. The line is simply pulled through the putty. This is a very important thing to do. It may seem obvious, but I have several times spoken to anglers apparently doing everything right, only to discover that their fly is still on the surface because the leader fails to sink. The trout, down deeper, have no idea that the fly is there!

Flies can be made to sink faster (especially useful in rivers and fast-running water) by squeezing a small piece of 'lead putty' (obtainable at fly-fishing shops) onto the fly head. In Kenya especially, the flies are very often weighted with a more than average amount of lead incorporated into the pattern. Some of the Kenyan fly-fishermen also tie in a short (50 mm) length of fast-sink line just behind the fly ... I think this is rather too obvious, but there is no doubt that it works!

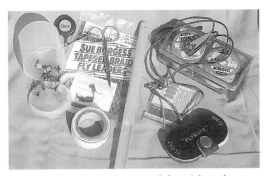

Handy items for the fly fisherman (left to right and top to bottom): pill box for dry flies, pin reel and scissors, braided knotless tapered leader, plastic marrow spoon, tippet line dispenser, nail clippers. Then: PVC tape to guard against line cuts, sight bobs bite detectors, fluorescent tubing bite detector, flymate line chemical applicator.

Line care chemicals (left to right): braid sink, silicone line grease, dry fly powder, line sink, line conditioner, Mucilin quick sink, and (bottom) Hardy dry fly floatant aerosol.

Author's favourite fly box by Wheatley: note rounded corners, firm-fitting lid, non-corrodible construction, light weight and pocket-fitting size.

A

B

It is very important to have sharp hooks in every kind of fly fishing, and especially so when pursuing hard-mouthed species like the tigerfish. (A) The thumbnail sharpness test: if the hook slides across the nail it is blunt. (B) The correct way to sharpen: pull the hook point down almost into the stone – it is incorrect to push the hook away from the stone.

Diatomaceous earth, as used in the older swimming pool filters, can also be worked into a putty and rubbed into braided leaders to form a sinking leader.

Dry flies should be proofed with a silicone spray and allowed to dry before use. It is para-mount that a proper dry fly spray is used – tent waterproofers and other sprays with paraffin in them should be avoided. An excellent mixture which will proof flies for a long time can be made up at home from grated white candle wax, silicone grease, and carbon tetrachloride.

Polarised sunglasses make an amazing difference. On the left, normal light; on the right, polarised light. Polarised light, by considerably reducing surface reflection, reveals the trout.

Mix it outside to avoid inhaling the fumes. The fly is simply dunked in this lot and allowed to dry. With a preponderance of fishing with Duckworth's Dargle Delight dry fly in South Africa, I usually keep a few of these proofed flies with me, pre-dunked and dried, in an empty film spool container.

Mucilin was the favourite proofing agent for some time (I haven't used it since the fifties), and some still like it. We always used Amadou (a dried fungus) to dry the flies proofed with Mucilin. Today, anglers can buy drying powders into which the fly is dipped and is immediately dried.

Another aid to dry fly-fishing in streams (especially at dusk) is various kinds of 'sight improvers'. These small fluorescent devices are usually self-adhesive and are stuck on the line just at the butt loop. My favourite is undoubtedly the fluorescent putty which can be kneaded onto the line. This is very effective – I like the fluorescent orange and yellow since these are the most visible.

ESSENTIAL ACCESSORIES
Sunglasses
Polarised sunglasses are a must for fly-fishing. They cut down glare and reflection, and enable the angler to see into the water. Very often you will see fish and other underwater life through polarised glasses which you may otherwise miss altogether. However, perhaps the most important advantage of sunglasses, or any kind of glasses, is the protection they afford to the eyes. Casting can be a fickle business, especially on a blustery day. Protect your eyes!

Priest
This device is for administering the *coup de grâce*. It has no other use. Many kinds of these are available at fishing shops and every fly-fisherman should carry one. However, I am an advocate of the 'catch and release' philosophy. I like to put fish back to grow bigger and to fight another day. However, things can occasionally go wrong – perhaps the hook is embedded in a gill and the fish bleeds, or some other mishap may occur. Some anglers like to keep their fish, and then the fish must be killed. This is what the priest is for. A sharp blow to the centre of the skull kills the fish instantly. That's a lot better than leaving it to gasp its last on the bank as the sun slowly dries its gills. Everyone must learn how to use the priest properly, and the best way to do this is by watching an experienced angler.

Nets
There are many kinds of landing nets, and much depends on what kind of fishing you are involved in. A much larger net is used to land a 15 kg barbel than you would need for pan-sized trout.

Small wooden-framed clip-on nets are ideal for small stream fishing and for float tubing. Metal-framed nets would not do for float tubing because they sink if they come loose.

A stronger metal-framed net with wide mouth and deeper net is ideal for large trophy trout, yellowfish and bass, or for fly-fishing in estuaries out of a boat. You need a big strong net for a big fish. The wading style net with a long handle has its uses for catfish in the shallows and for tigerfish, but it would get in the way on a boat, or when walking through thick brush. Flip-up nets can go awry, and they usually do it when you least want them to, so be careful of these.

The net mesh should be soft! Hard netting and its knots damage fish by rubbing off the slime and causing damage to scales. A damaged fish returned from one of these nets will almost certainly die from later fungal infections. Wire-meshed nets are simply barbaric – no one who cares about fishes would ever consider using one. They cause immense epidermal damage, especially in crowded nets. Knotless mesh nets are now available which are totally harmless. Fishes lifted out with these nets can be returned undamaged.

Using a landing net

When using a net do not swipe at the fish, because there is a very high chance that you will break the fine tippet or, worse, get part of the hook ensnared in the net. This can be a real problem when willing helpers want to net for you. If the person is a non-angler, he will almost certainly take a swipe at the fish, and may well cause you to lose a fine specimen. Unless you know that the person is an accomplished angler, always net the fish yourself.

The correct way is to lay the net in the water ready for the fish. Do not move the net yet: sudden movement may frighten the fish. Also, if the net is left still, there is always a chance that the fish may see it as a refuge and dive straight into it. The right way is to wait until the beaten fish is pulled over the net, and then lift the net gently. If the fish is unexpectedly large, lead the fish into the net head first – do not lift the net until at least two thirds of the fish is in. Very large fishes should be lifted by grabbing the mesh – a straight lift may break the net handle.

Releasing fishes

Kill your fish quickly if you intend to keep it. Otherwise treat it with care, and return it to the water as quickly as you can. The best and most simple way to return fishes is to use barbless hooks, and simply tweak the hook out without removing the fish from the water. Most trout

fisheries are going to be 'barbless' by the turn of the century! If the hook is barbed, the fish can still be released easily, by removing the hook with a pair of artery forceps or pliers. A barbed hook can easily be rendered barbless by rolling the point in a pair of artery forceps or pliers. The barb normally breaks off without damaging the point.

Fishes are very vulnerable to damage from handling. They should never be put down on dry soil because of the damage to the slime layer. Wet plastic is satisfactory for photography, and the process should be done as quickly as possible. If you must handle a fish, do it only

Correct way to return a fish: wet the hands and return the fish with head up-stream, taking the weight at the head and the tail and gently lowering the fish back. Never throw or drop a fish back in the water.

This photograph illustrates how the angler avoids supporting the fish's weight by the stomach, by locating his hands under the head and tail. (Photo: Steve Barrow)

with wet hands! Fishes should be held carefully, the most common mistake being unnecessary pressure on the body. Never hold a fish up by the gill plates for photography unless it has already been killed – it will not survive this treatment. Many people are surprised to learn that a fish out of water is a very delicate creature that is easily hurt. The returned fish may well swim off, but bad handling could cause death hours or even days later. Fishes should be cradled forward of the visceral cavity without pressure on the gills (if you hold the soft stomach area by mistake, essential organs such as the heart are easily crushed) and held with the other hand at the tail root. The fish is then care-

fully lowered, on an even keel, into the water. The fish should never be squeezed.

Ideally, the fish should swim off. If not, you may have to get some oxygen going into the gills, by moving the fish gently backward and forward in the water. As mentioned, handle fishes only with wet hands, and take care not to dislodge the slime.

Fishes are a valuable sport resource, some say too valuable to be caught only once. In the years ahead, the importance of 'catch and release' will increase. Kill enough for yourself and no more; return the rest. Do this and our fishery resources will last much longer for the future enjoyment of all.

CHAPTER 3

TO THINK LIKE A FISH

Everything should be as simple as possible, but no simpler.

Albert Einstein

I well remember as a small boy being told by my father: 'If you want to catch a fish, then you must think like a fish.' I still believe that to be one of the most fundamental rules for catching any kind of fish. However, in order to think like the beastie, one first needs to know how he perceives things, and then to know his likes and dislikes.

Don't be misled by the numerous fish hunting books which expound upon the intelligence of uncatchable monsters, or those stories in which a superbly intelligent trout outwits a whole angling club for uncountable years, before a five-year-old with a brick (and sufficient where-withal to drop it off the village bridge) ends an era of awe-inspiring dominance. If you need a

real comparison, a mature fish probably has less intelligence than the average farmyard hen. His 'thinking' is either instinctive or based upon the experiences of his life – and if these experiences have included encounters with man or his fishing tackle (the flash of a rod, or perhaps the sting of a rejected fly), then he is likely to be more difficult to catch.

All fishes have behaviour patterns which are specific to their own species. They have preferred ecological niches, preferred food forms, preferred ambient conditions and so on. The angler has to learn about these and allow for these specific idiosyncrasies when formulating his strategy.

In this chapter we will look at the fish's senses,

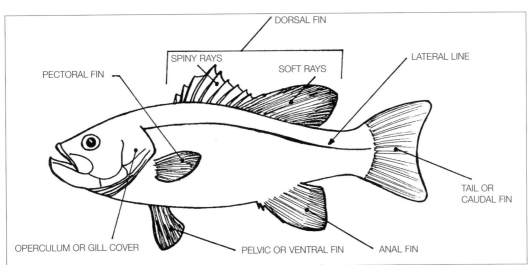

Fig. 3.1: The parts of a fish.

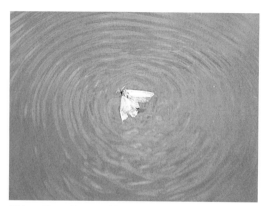

This swift moth trapped in the surface is sending out low-frequency vibrations, clearly visible in the surface as waves. Nearby fishes easily pick up this 'sound' with their lateral line sense.

and then we will examine the water conditions around our quarry, and what these conditions mean to him. Armed with this information, in addition to our own individual experience and knowledge, we will then be in a position to put on our thinking caps, and to start 'thinking like a fish'!

THE SENSES OF FISH
Vibrations

In the world of human beings this is what we call 'sound'. The noises of our world (and these days one tends to think that there are far too many of them) are all vibrations of differing frequencies and volume. A fish's ears differ from those of a mammal, but it can still hear well enough! The fish has no cochlea and no external

or middle ear. It does, however, have an organ made up of semi-circular canals containing small stones called otoliths whose movement is used to control balance. These otolith earstones are very interesting, since they build themselves up annually with layers of calcium carbonate which can be used to determine the age of a fish.

There are differences between what we are able to perceive, and what the fish can perceive. Our fish cannot hear the high vibrations which we easily sense: it's doubtful that he could hear whistling, or even normal conversation. He is, however, marvellously attuned to the clicks and grunts of the underwater world, all of which sounds we are normally entirely unaware of. Additionally, the fish has the edge over us in his ability to sense low-frequency sounds and pressure changes through his lateral line ... these at levels which we are totally insensitive to. The consequence of this is that we must constantly make an effort not to announce our presence by making what are, to the fish, loud noises in this low-frequency band.

When I was a child, jumping and running anywhere near a fisherman was an absolute taboo, a lesson that was soundly impressed on me by a keen and knowledgeable angling father. If we needed to pass by another angler, whether we knew him or not, we would always give a wide berth, and tread softly. This creeping about was always secretly rather fun as a kid, but it is in fact quite important. The lesson was very worthwhile! Just understanding that a fish can

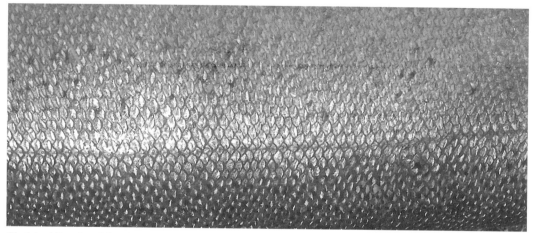

The lateral line of a rainbow trout.

sense your presence without having to see you is a very useful thing to know. Many a fish has ended up in my net that would surely have vanished had I not been treading softly. You will often see anglers stomping around a water, rod in hand, and bemoaning the fact that there are no fishes – the fishes, in fact, went elsewhere the moment they detected the heavy footfall of the angler. This same angler will probably never actually see cruising fishes – fishes which the quiet angler is constantly seeing, and often catching. In fly-fishing, the opportunity to cast a fly to a cruising fish is very often a sure way to catch him. Thus one cannot be careful enough. Soft footfalls and silent movement are important components of every good fly-fisherman's strategy.

This 'feeling' of footfalls and other very low-frequency vibrations (knocking the sides and bottom of a boat is another example) is detected by the fish not so much with his ears as with his lateral line. The lateral line is a marvellous organ which is sensitive to low frequencies, to pressure changes, and to changes in a self-generated electrical field (more on that later). We have no comparable sense organ. The lateral line is normally a continuous line along each side of the body, but in the African kurpers it is in two portions, the anterior being higher on the body than the posterior line. The lateral line is not just there to warn the fish of foot stomping anglers. It will also warn him of the beat of an otter's tail, or the approach of other enemies. It can inform him of the struggles of a wounded fish, or a sick creature nearby ... perhaps an easy prey. In just the same way, it will also tell him that the fur or feather fibres on a fly are vibrating in the near vicinity, and hopefully he will think that is easy prey too.

The problem of sound in boats is in fact more serious than heavy footfalls. The average boat is an excellent sounding chamber, and every little knock and scrape is 'felt' by fishes nearby. This is perhaps the biggest drawback of boat fishing, but with proper care it need not be a problem. However, proper care is essential! Nothing is more frustrating than a noisy angling partner in a boat, especially if you are yourself taking great care to be silent.

Hi-tech instruments for the fly-fisherman. Left to right: Color-c-lector lightmeter, pH meter, echo-sounding fish finder, barometer, thermometer.

Carpeting a boat can go a long way to help. Today, nylon fronded carpet is available which is easily washed, and which does the job well. It goes without saying that soft-soled shoes are essential in boats. The sounds made during conversation are mostly reflected off the water, and those that do penetrate the water are too high frequency to bother fishes.

Taste and smell

These are the so-called chemical senses, and smell especially is very well developed in most fishes. Some catfishes can apparently detect some substances in the amazing proportion of two parts in one million parts of water. That is better sensitivity than most laboratory instruments! With this super-sense, any fish is well equipped to hunt down food by scent. However, the sense of smell is also a very important defensive device in the fish's self-protection system, and a sense much underrated by anglers.

Substances such as suntan oil, nicotine, mosquito repellent, outboard oil and petrol are all potential danger signals to a fish. Also, don't be deluded into thinking that because you don't smoke, all is OK. This is not so! Human skin contains a substance known as L-serine which smells pretty awful to a fish. It's not enough to just take care with baits, lures and flies. The simple action of running the line through your fingers (we all do it) can easily transfer enough L-serine to the line to keep fish away. The best cure is to wash your hands with a bar of soap three or four times a day – especially if you smoke, or are swopping fuel tanks. Watch out for grease or oil being transferred to your line – this often happens just after a reel service.

It's strange but true that human saliva has been known to be attractive to catfish. Perhaps we should start spitting on all our Mrs Simpsons before presenting them to the barbel? In the UK, somebody has proven that human urine is attractive to the saltwater bass. As a consequence, secret pre-baiting ceremonies can be witnessed all over the British Isles in high summer as the bass come inshore. Hopefully, it won't catch on in Africa!

Plastic worms are an example of the tackle trade cashing in on the fish's superb sense of smell. Plastic worms are usually sold with a thin layer of aromatic oil over them – fruit smells (e.g. grape, strawberry, etc.), liquorice, night crawler (the American name for a garden worm), and so on. You would be wrong to see the prime purpose of these scents as fish-attracting (although some obviously are). The main purpose of these scented oils is to mask the smells from one's hands. Many keen bass fishermen store their plastic worms in a smear of these oils.

Some European fly-fishermen dip their flies in sardine or pilchard oil, an act considered 'not done' by most fly anglers, and which comes very close to ground baiting. Their reasoning goes along the same lines as the plastic worms above. However, should they fail to get all the oil out of their flies, I imagine it would quickly spread and ruin all the other flies in their fly box. Trout appear to have no objection either to the traditional Mucilin floatants or to the modern silicone waterproofing floatants. However, do make sure that any floatant (liquid or spray) does not contain paraffin as its solvent. The usual carbon tetrachloride or trichloroethylene solvent is fine, since it evaporates before it gets to the fish.

Touch

Touch is one of the fish senses most anglers give no more than a passing thought to. However, realistically thinking, every lure or fly which a fish goes for is touched by a fish's mouth somewhere. Remember that the fish expects to feel

something alive, with the correct texture of the creature he thought he had just caught. The fish's sense of touch operates better when the ambient temperature of the water is reasonably high, as in summer. In winter, he may feel nothing of your fly or lure.

It could well be, then, on a warm day when the bass are spitting out the lure, or the trout are quickly rejecting the fly – both of which manifest as 'coming short' – that you need to change not the pattern, but the texture of your lure or fly. Perhaps the trout fly should be changed to one with a plastozote (plastic foam) body, or alternatively a full-bodied (18 feathered) Walker's Killer may be the answer.

Sight

More seems to have been written about sight and the effect of light and colour on fishes than

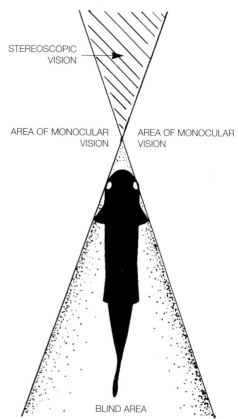

Fig. 3.2: The fish's vision. Because the eyes are in the side of the head, binocular (stereo) vision is restricted to a small area ahead. The spherical lens gives 180 degree vision.

The log provides an unusual degree of comfort. But here the author fishes well hidden by surrounding reed beds, quite invisible to the fish. (Photo: Ron Clay)

about any of their other senses. This is probably because sight is the least understood, and at the same time the most important, of a fish's senses. However, much research has been done, and today the angler can acquire a very useful understanding of the way light affects the life of a fish.

Fishes have almost 'all-round' vision, with some additional, but very slight, stereoscopic (three-dimensional) vision. Conversely, we humans have very well-developed stereoscopic vision which is complete through our whole visual field.

Sport fishes all have extremely good vision. Of great importance is that they are apt to ignore slow movements, but respond actively to any kind of rapid or jerky movement. Obviously, it's best to keep out of sight, but this is not always possible. Stalking a fish requires total control of movement. Hence, no sudden movements of arms or head and no heavy footfalls is the rule.

Water refracts light, which causes some interesting effects. The fish's ability to spot an angler is thus to the fish's advantage in some ways, and to the angler's in others.

The fish's window

This refraction (or bending) of light entering the water produces a field of vision above the fish commonly known as the fish's window. Around the edge of the window the light is distorted, becoming less distorted towards the centre of the window, until vision is quite clear directly above the fish. This 'window' moves with the fish everywhere he goes. It gets smaller as he nears the surface, and larger as he sinks away from it.

The fish's limited forward field of stereoscopic vision is used to measure distance, especially when assessing or pursuing prey. Monocular vision from the side means that the fish is quite unable to measure distance from any object. It is, however, very sensitive to sudden movement in this area. Immediately behind is a completely blind spot.

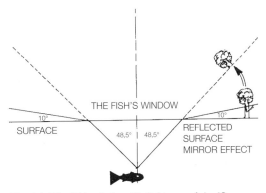

Fig. 3.3: The fish's window. No light rays of significance enter below ten degrees to the horizon. Note that the fish sees the tree as if it were on a steep incline.

Typical difficult African mountain stream fishing, with crystal-clear water and little cover. The angler must keep down, move slowly, and dress drably. (Photo: Don Lort)

Fishes appear to have greater light-gathering power than we do, not in the way of a cat's eye, but because of the effective aperture of the eye. It's as well to remember that a fish can see considerably better in murky light than we can. However, in achieving this, it loses out in depth of field vision. It is effectively short-sighted! No fish sees at distance very well; *The Game Fishes of Africa* (1952) states that no fish, even in the clearest conditions, can see further than ten metres, though modern research with sharks tends to demonstrate much greater acuity than that.

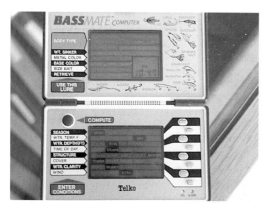

A computer designed for the bass angler tells him the best lure and tactic for the prevailing conditions.

As mentioned above, a trout feeding on flies just centimetres above him will probably have objects in the edge of his 'window' out of focus, and would have trouble spotting an angler purposely keeping fairly low. However, the deeper the fish is (subject to water clarity), the better he will see you. An angler walking along the bank and making no attempt to keep low will be spotted by every trout in the stream. Bankside vegetation helps a lot to eliminate the outline of the fisherman. Keep low, try to keep between the water and the bankside vegetation, move slowly and softly, and you are half-way to catching your fish.

Colour

Many game-fishermen will have experienced those days when kurper will only hit a red Mepps spinner, and fly-fishermen will remember times when trout only want green flies and bass ignore all artificial worms except those coloured fire-tailed blue. It is a very real and commonly occurring situation, and thus of great importance. The visual powers of fishes, the effect of depth on colour, and the effect of murky water are not the only considerations. Other factors include colour preferences – fishes

Depth	Colour						
Surface	Red	Orange	Yellow	Green	Blue	Violet	Black
3 m	Rusty	Orange	Yellow	Green	Blue	Violet	Black
6 m	Brown	Rusty	Yellow	Green	Blue	Violet	Black
10 m	Sepia	Brown	Cream	Green	Blue	Violet	Black
13 m	Black	Sepia	White	Green	Blue	Violet	Black
18 m	Black	Black	Grey	Grey-green	Blue	Violet	Black
21 m	Black	Black	Black	Grey	Deep-blue	Violet	Black

The effect of water depth on colour.

are annoyed by some colour combinations and contrasts, and yet will ignore others; then they avoid certain intensities of light one day, and apparently couldn't care less the next; they react to fluorescents in different ways, and so on. In the USA, you can actually buy a dedicated boat dash-mounted computer to sort out all the variable information, but this is not really necessary. We shall examine each aspect in turn, and you will see that it all slots together quite well.

Effect of water on colour

Sunlight is composed of the seven rainbow colours. As the light penetrates the water, the water filters these colours out, different colours at different depths. The warmer reds, oranges, and yellows are filtered out first, and in that order. Greens, blues and finally purple/violets are the last to go, until in really deep water all colour has disappeared. What all this means is that the fish, under the water, does not necessarily see the same colours that you see in the clear air above.

As an example, your orange-tailed fly could well appear to a deep-down trout as a grey-tailed fly. A Yellow Matuka fly may appear as greyish white, and a red fly which you have just cast into a deep hole looks black to the trout watching it. If the fly colours are fluorescent (actinic colour), the effect will be different again. The table above illustrates the phenomenon as it applies to ordinary colours (here assumed to be spectrally pure colours, which they probably wouldn't be in real life). The water is also assumed to be clear. Green water would tend to emphasise orange and red colours rather than blues and greens. Brown peat-stained water can

be pitch black with no light at all as little as five metres down – yellows show up well in the shallows of this. Muddy water obviously cuts all light out much more rapidly.

The colour along the top of the table is the one you see in the air. The colour underneath this is the colour the fish sees at the depth indicated on the left.

This effect of increasingly deep water is accelerated in murky water. Likewise, the more suspended matter in the water, the faster the colour loss. A red fly will appear black only one metre down in very coloured water. However, do not forget that a naturally coloured fly will obey the effect in a way that the fish is used to, whatever the clarity of the water. A natural coloured fry fly, frog fly, or insect fly will change in colour as it sinks down, in the same way that the natural fry fishes, frogs, and other denizens of the water do ... maybe one should copy that?

Colour combinations

You can easily see from the colour change table above that the very popular deep-diving bass plugs finished in red and white will appear either black and whitish grey, or black and grey at great depths. The American red and white Parmachene Belle fly works in the same way. The reason these contrasting colours work so well in water of varying depths is not due to the colours, but rather due to the always present contrast effect. At depths below three metres the red has already changed to brown. Colour contrasts are easily detected by fish, and this is one of the reasons that sluggish trout, and also bass, in deep and cold water will often go for a colour contrast lure or fly, and yet ignore a self-

Colour combinations	Fly examples
Red and yellow	Micky Finn
Red and white	Parmachene Belle
Fluorescent signal green and black	Viva
Orange and gold	Whisky fly
Fluorescent pink and black	Sweeney Todd

coloured lure or fly. These colour contrasts are often referred to as 'attractor colour combinations'. Typical examples of good attractor colour combinations are illustrated above.

All these colour combinations are also commonly available in the top bass plugs and in other lures – it's not just fly-fishermen who have discovered them. There are many more, but these are the most commonly encountered.

Bright colour at depths
To present bright colour to a fish in really deep water, one is forced to work with either blues or violets. Violet is, and has been for a while, the best-selling plastic worm colour in the USA. It's a good all-rounder, and one of the reasons for its amazing success is that it always has colour at any depth. It is always somewhat surprising then that violet is so scarce in fly patterns. In fact, it is almost totally unknown in Africa in anything but bass flies. Opportunities certainly exist for the fly designer to produce a whole range of deep-water flies using blues, purples and violet. The Purple Tadpole Lure and the Purple Dragon 'O' Nymph are the only African flies of this type at the time of writing. Black, for the same reason, is also a very popular deep-water fly colour. Strictly speaking, black is a total absence of colour, but what is meant here is that it shows up rather well both in very deep water and in the shallows.

As regards fluorescent colours, one theory is that since the fish is better equipped to see at the high-frequency violet end of the spectrum, the ultra-violet component of the sunlight causing the fluorescence, as well as the fluorescence itself, are possibly both readily visible to the fish. If this is so, the fish will see things with a fluorescent component as being much brighter than they are to our eyes. Not only this, but since the fluorescence and the ultra-violet are at the high-frequency end of the spectrum, they will also be the last to be filtered out by deep water. It follows then that the fluorescent effect should be apparent in deep water. The most useful colours for very deep conditions in still-water impoundments should be, in theory, fluorescent violet and fluorescent blue! Unfortunately, both being dark colours, they do not fluoresce well.

Recent discoveries with respect to the rainbow trout's ability to see in ultra-violet light have shown that as the fish ages he slowly loses this faculty. Very big trout have probably entirely lost their ability to see in ultra-violet light, so the advantages of fluorescents are somewhat diminished in big trophy fish.

Fluorescents in practice
Perhaps one should think of the fluorescent effect as something one mixes with other colours – which would be a convenient explanation for the fact that you can have fluorescence with lots of different colours. Unfortunately for the theory of fluorescent violets and blues at great depth, dark colours seem to mask the effect – with black, fluorescence is completely masked out. Paints and dyes in fly-tying materials and plugs are only really bright with the lighter colours such as yellow, chartreuse or lime-green. Additionally, for the best results, fluorescence needs a white or silver undercoat to reflect back on itself. In conclusion then, your really bright light-coloured fluorescents will continue to fluoresce under the water, but depending on the extent to which the base colour is changed by the depth (as in the table of depth colour change on the previous page). White may indeed be the best deep-water fluorescent of the lot, and experience tends to support this. Some evidence also suggests that ultra-violet light is inefficient at penetrating deep tinted water, and that water has to be crystal clear for it to really work.

The fluorescent effect cannot take place without sunlight, or at least the UV component of sunlight. It will work fine with filtered sunlight such as on a cloudy day, but as soon as darkness comes it ceases. Remember that, because of the refraction of light in water, darkness underwater comes sooner than it does above in the fisherman's world. Once the sun gets down to around ten degrees above the horizon, the fish's world is already in darkness.

Response to preferred colours

In terms of response to colour, all fishes exhibit a strong attraction toward red. It also has a peripheral attraction to them in that they quickly spot red even if it is on the very edge of their vision. Even though fishes do 'see' the colours at the high end of the visible spectrum extremely well, they 'react' to colours at the low end of the spectrum best. The violets of their world are much brighter to them, but the reds are most interesting. That, at least, is one theory, but not one I really like.

I believe they go for red for no other reason than that it is common to very many of their preferred foods – the red gills of a small fish, the colour of bloodworms, and so on. Many of the very successful lure flies exhibit a spot of red in their make-up – now you know why! Orange, and to a lesser extent yellow, are also attractive to fishes. The Micky Finn fly in red and yellow combines two of the most attractive colours together with the added effect of contrast. The result, a very deadly fly!

In conclusion, it would appear that white fluorescent colour is the most attractive fluorescent for deep flies, and red or orange fluorescent for the shallow flies. Mid-water flies appear to be best served by green and yellow fluorescents.

Key colours

Green is common in natural foods, especially in insect nymphal stages, and on a larger scale in animals such as frogs. Fishes easily associate food with green, and the inner glow of the living green insect is best copied with fluorescent green. Combine this fluorescent green with the contrast of the silhouette colour black, and the deadly colour combination of the Viva fly has been formed. This colour combination is also very effective in plugs and in plastic worms.

Colours such as green and red, looked at in the context above, are often referred to as 'key colours'. The concept of incorporating spots of key colour is an essential component of good lure and fly design.

It does not necessarily have to be a bright fluorescent colour – the key colour in the Highveld Dun fly is the soft olive of the body. With tiny daphnia, the trout become switched onto the daphnia colour (usually orange), and in some buzzer pupae the tiny spot of red haemoglobin may be the 'key colour'. In the Yellow Panacea fly it's the yellow colour of the wing that switches on the predators, and so on.

It should not be forgotten that 'key shape' can also be important, such as in the body shape of the fully dressed Walker's Killer fly, or in the shape of the Buzzer patterns.

At any time the 'keys' of colour and/or shape can bring an aggressive attack from the fish. This may be a normal response as a result of preoccupied feeding on a food form which also exhibits the keys, or it may be pure belligerence which would perhaps not normally have happened had the 'keys' been absent. The importance of key shapes and colours is thus a very real concept in fly-fishing.

In the USA, Dr Loren Hill did extensive experiments on fish colour preference, and discovered that the attractiveness of certain colours changed in accordance with ambient light conditions. As a result of his research, he produced a meter which he marketed under the name of 'Color-c-lector'. The meter measures the light intensity at any chosen depth of water, and converts this information onto a dial which indicates the best lure colour to use in the measured conditions. The unit is popular in the USA with bass anglers. Some plug and lure manufacturers have gone so far as to produce a range of coloured lures or plastic worms that exactly match the colour indications on the Color-c-lector dial.

Finally, all this analysis should not be seen as reason to forget that the fish itself is primarily concerned with the natural prey and its natural colour! It is my belief that the clearer the water, the more important it becomes to use natural-coloured lures. The core of imitative fly-fishing is a combination of using the natural colours of the originals, with slight exaggeration of the key colours of these creatures.

Fish memory of fly and lure colour

Experiments carried out in Germany showed that fishes not only have good colour vision, but are also quickly able to learn to detect specific colours. Once learnt, they remember the colours for some time, and are quite capable of associating the colour with food, or alternatively, with danger. They do not think about these things; these reactions become part of their habitual behaviour. If they associate, say, purple with danger, then the next time they experience that shade of purple they will flee. Perhaps this should be taken with a pinch of salt, but on the other hand it does conveniently explain why fishes develop an aversion to particularly heavily fished lures and flies. As an example, there are many examples of an effective new fly pattern becoming ineffective after intensive use of the fly for one or two seasons. Perhaps the many 'pricked' fishes and other escapees are enough to form a group association of fear attached to the pattern?

Bright light

Fishing under the African sun is almost always best with a soft breeze under a cloudy or milky sky. You can fish shallow, you can fish obvious lies and holding spots, and you can expect to catch fish. However, on harsh bright days (especially in mountainous areas), it becomes much harder, and with good reason.

Fishes, as we all know, have no eyelids. It is very important to understand what this means to a fish! Bright light is disturbing to all creatures with sight (the very sensitively sighted creatures experience real pain from intense light), and this is especially so if the creature is unable to control the light. Fishes (they all have no eyelids) are in this situation. What this means is that fishes will move away from bright light, either by going deep or by moving into shade – whatever is the area of greatest comfort. This is why the knowledgeable bass fly-fisherman casts to the shady side of a stump or bush, and why the stream fly-fisherman concentrates his efforts on the deeper pools and against the edges of thick weedbeds on a sunny day. Effectively then, don't expect to find feeding fishes in the shallows on bright days. This is not a rule carved in concrete – not at all! If a preponderance of a favourite food form is in the shallows, then fishes will sometimes ignore the discomfort of the light to feed on them. Gamefishes hunting small fry are a typical example of this behaviour.

It has been said that if you lower a white object into the water on a bright day and measure the depth at which it disappears, then twice this depth will represent the upper limit of where the fishes will be. There could well be something in this, because it certainly improves results on bright days to fish at and below this depth.

There is a simple device called a Secchi disc which limnologists (water scientists) use to measure water clarity. It is nothing more than a disc divided into quadrants painted alternate black and white. This is lowered into the depths, at all times maintaining a horizontal position. As above, you watch the disc until it disappears, and then measure the depth (this is done by premarking the string at regular intervals). This depth is noted, and then the Secchi disc raised until it reappears, and the depth noted again. All it tells you is how clear the water is – it's up to you to decide what to do with the information. As a measurement of clarity it is interesting to record the results in your fishing diary; after a while you will usefully be able to relate it to fishing methods and their success. In the USA, it has been shown that bass prefer to be at depths where 20 per cent or less of the light penetrates, as measured on a bright day.

A bass has no eyelids, and will thus avoid bright light whenever he can. He usually does this by going deeper.

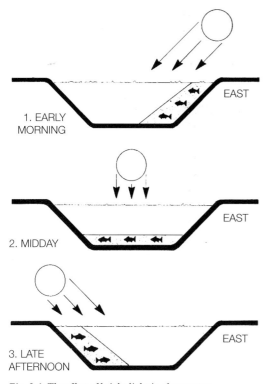

EAST

1. EARLY
MORNING

EAST

2. MIDDAY

EAST

3. LATE
AFTERNOON

Fig. 3.4: *The effect of bright light in clear water.*

wind in the rippled water, against shadowed banks, and so on. Figure 3.4 shows how light penetration changes during the day. Fish the eastern shallows in early morning, and the western shores in the afternoon. Fishes will move into all the shallows as the light level drops, but they will be on these shallows the longest!

Electrical fields

Slightly more than half of a fish's brain is devoted to the sense of sight, which gives a fair idea of its importance. However, it has been shown that fishes with their eyes blacked out (fishes that cannot possibly see) are still capable of hunting down their prey. They achieve this mostly through their lateral line sense organ. This wonderful organ, in addition to its vibration-detecting capability, is also able to sense nearby objects through a change in a weak electrical field generated around the fish. Some authors have referred to this as a kind of 'radar'. In practice the fly-fisherman takes advantage of this by using long-hackled flies, which when retrieved slowly apparently produce weak subsonic vibrations making it easier for a fish to find the fly even in pitch black conditions (as an example, refer to the Woolly Worm patterns). In any event, the mere presence of an object (such as a fly) can be detected by the lateral line radar as the object moves through the electrical field. Both trout and bass find objects they cannot see, and they do it with considerable ease as a result of this extra sense through the lateral line.

ENVIRONMENTAL FACTORS

Many environmental factors can motivate fishes into either action or inactivity. When selecting the best place to fish it is important to have some idea of why a fish prefers one spot to another. We have already looked at the effect of light as an environmental factor, but there are other very important considerations such as temperature, pH, dissolved oxygen content of water and availability of food.

Additionally, at certain times of the year, the desire to breed will modify fishes' 'normal' behaviour. When breeding, fishes are usually easy to find because of their very strong preferences

The Color-c-lector mentioned under Key colours electronically converts this clarity information (from its own sensor) directly into the best lure or fly colour for the prevalent conditions. However, water clarity and light levels change constantly throughout the day. The angler would need to take several measurements during a typical day.

In many African locations where light intensity can become very high in summer (especially on the South African Highveld at altitudes of 1 800 to 2 100 metres, and in Lesotho at up to 3 500 metres), this matter of bright light will have a great impact on fishing! It is especially important on still days with no ripple to break up the light. Tactics have to be carefully thought out. The prime objective is to work out where the fishes might go – where can they find a place, say at noon, where most of the bright light is filtered out? Wherever this place is, it will also have to meet the fishes' other requirements, as described elsewhere in this chapter. Under weed beds or lilies, in deeper water, in the shadow of stumps, rocks or trees, down-for certain areas or structures, and for their attraction to requisite environmental conditions.

Food availability

As a good general rule, the assessment of where a fish can most easily find food is a 'must be done' exercise. However, the other three factors mentioned above may individually, or collectively, cause a fish to cease feeding altogether. If he has ceased feeding, you may have to appeal to some other instinct such as aggressiveness or territoriality to get him to strike. He may move right on to another feeding area and a different type of food because of uncomfortable changes in the immediate environment; or he may move on because the food form (fish, insect, or whatever) which he is eating has moved elsewhere. This 'migration' of food forms and of fishes can become an almost regular daily activity among some of the fish species that fly-fishermen pursue. Both the food forms and the fish are affected by the same factors, and both look for comfort zone environments.

Temperature

Fishes, like humans, have preferred comfort zones. However, unlike us, they cannot change their environment, and thus the environment controls their actions to a very great extent. The fish is cold blooded, and in consequence his body temperature is virtually always the same as the temperature of the water he swims in. We, on the other hand, are warm blooded, which gives us great independence from the temperature of the air around us. The point of this is to realise that we must not think of the effect of temperature on fishes in human terms.

The fish, whether he likes it or not, has to react to water temperature. If possible he will move to an accessible comfort zone. For example, in very hot weather a fish will prefer deeper cooler spots, and in winter he will keep away from the cold edges of the dam and head for the warmer deeps.

Dissolved oxygen

Temperature has a far more profound effect on environmental conditions than would first appear to be the case. The amount of dissolved

A waterfall on the Lunsklip River, South Africa. Malcolm Meintjes into a rainbow trout which has taken advantage of the higher oxygen content of the waterfall pool on a hot day. There are many such locations in Africa ... the stuff that dreams are made of! (Photo: courtesy Malcolm Meintjes)

oxygen in the water is directly proportional to temperature, and this factor can mean life or death to a fish. Other factors also affect dissolved oxygen content, and these include barometric pressure, wind, and currents. All fishes will move rapidly away from oxygen-depleted water. In fact there is sufficient motivation to move on even when the dissolved oxygen content in one spot is only slightly less than in another.

The effects of dissolved oxygen and temperature manifest in different ways with differing species of fish. The preferred feeding range for trout is quite different to that for tigerfish or bass. The survival temperatures for trout are different to those for barbel. In fact, even two closely related species such as the rainbow trout and the brown trout have different tolerance levels to high temperature. Carp will feed very actively at 18 °C, trout like 13 °C, and largemouth bass are happiest at 21 °C. However, all these species actually feed through a 'band' of temperature – for example, largemouth bass can be found feeding through the range 8–26 °C.

The amount of oxygen dissolved in water

Float tubing before the storm. A typical African summer storm brews in the distance. Heavy hail and tremendous winds will ensure the end of the fishing for the day as a result of plunging water temperatures. (Photo: Don Lort)

decreases as the temperature rises, and eventually it reaches a level which kills fishes through asphyxiation. The species vary in their reaction to this. Trout, for example, are exceedingly uncomfortable at 29 °C and will die at temperatures around 31 °C. Most freshwater fishes would be in severe trouble at this upper temperature. At the other end of the scale, very low temperatures also affect fishes – they become torpid and their physical ability to extract oxygen decreases. Fishes become reluctant to move in such conditions, but will still feed if the food item is slow moving or easy to catch. So long as the energy to be expended in getting the food is less than the energy contained in the food, then the fish will probably take it. However, most anglers would not be trying to tempt fishes at extremes of temperature. Most of us would be much more interested in fishing in the good feeding range of the fish. Trout are excellent quarry in cold conditions, very often coming strongly to the fly, whereas largemouth bass can be quite difficult to catch in extremes of cold.

Deep water

In very deep water it is quite possible for pockets of water to form which are totally depleted of oxygen. These are obviously deadly to fish.

Oxygen meters are available which can detect these dead areas as well as the oxygen-rich areas of water. These dead areas form under the thermocline which is found only in the deepest African waters, and is a somewhat rare occurrence. Most African deep waters are well able to support life, and are adequately oxygenated throughout the season. Since many species (e.g. bass and kurper) head for the deeps during winter, it is always worth searching the bottom with a fly and a lead-core line at this time.

Sudden temperature changes

Violent thunderstorms, often precipitating hail even in the hottest times of the year, mean that Africa's waters are subject to rapid changes in temperature. Temperature changes in the thin atmosphere of the high country are also inclined to be sudden, with consequent fast and possibly fatal changes in the temperature of the upper layers of water in still impoundments and lakes. A fairly common event in many high-altitude African waters such as on the Highveld is the winter kill-off of kurper that have been caught-out in the shallower areas of a dam or lake during a rapid fall in temperature.

On one occasion I was fishing Jericho Dam in South Africa in the company of Lynton Buller

51

Swartwater Dam. In this high altitude lake, the inflowing stream can affect pH, temperature and oxygen content. The deeper water of the stream bed may also attract fish. Such places are usually 'hot', and worth a cast.

and my two sons. We got trapped in a really nasty hailstorm – the kind that turns everything white instantaneously. For an hour after that storm, dying yellowfish could be seen all over the surface. Needless to say you can't catch fish in those conditions. Although that was a truly drastic temperature drop, any fast change of even only one or two degrees will put fishes off the feed. Temperature will also affect the size of food items which will interest fishes, and the speed of movement of natural food items. Both these factors are of importance to the fly-fisherman. In extreme conditions, most strikes at the fly are likely to be rather gentle affairs.

Obviously, combinations of sudden temperature change followed by bright light (as occurs frequently after thunderstorms) can make things very difficult indeed. Either one of these phenomena could demand a switch to deepwater techniques. If both occur together, you had better start scratching the bottom structure and searching deep holes.

Slow temperature change

Temperature change over a period of a few days, especially if the change is within the nor-mal temperature feeding band, is not likely to bother fishes at all. In fact if the change is moving towards the preferred temperature, then the fishing is most likely to improve. It's not what they are used to, but rather sudden changes which really cause fishes to go off the feed.

Environmental niches

All fishes have a definite niche in the ecology of their dam or river. All the gamefish that one might aspire to pursue in Africa are predatory to some extent – some very much so! Some will hide in the aquatic jungle or the bottom rock structure in order to ambush their prey. Others are opportunists roaming at high speed, and surprising and chasing down their prey. Others, such as a nymphing trout, may hold station and sip down passing prey; or perhaps they may cruise slowly through a surface insect hatch, taking food here, there and everywhere. Many species can adapt to all these different modes of hunting, depending on the ambient conditions. The angler needs to know as much as he can about these fish habits in order to have any chance of presenting the fly correctly to the fish.

The Jukskei River just outside Johannesburg. It looks beautiful, but apart from a few catfish has no fishing to offer.
Destroyed by pollution, a fluctuating pH, abstraction and rubbish, it is a sad reflection on the authorities in charge.

Acidity and alkalinity

One subject that many anglers prefer to ignore is that of pH. 'Complex scientific stuff,' they mumble, turning the page and moving on to more familiar issues. In fact it is not that complex, but it is very important, and I trust that you will bear with me as we explore this subject, which has a significant effect on the behaviour of fishes and thus on your ability to catch them.

Scientists measure the acidity or the alkalinity of waters over a logarithmic scale of 0 to 14. There are special instruments which measure this pH and give a numeric reading directly indicating the state of the water. A reading of pH 7 (the centre of the scale) is neutral (neither acid nor alkaline): the pH of distilled water is 7. If the water is acid the reading will be below 7 – hydrochloric acid has a pH of around 2; if alkaline the reading will be above 7 – my tap water reads at about 8,2. You may well have seen somebody measuring the pH of their swimming pool, or perhaps their aquarium, using a chemical indicator kit. This simple kit provides a crude method of measurement, unfortunately nowhere near accurate enough for use as a fishing tool. The problem is that the pH scale is logarithmic, meaning that the scale of readings is increased tenfold (normal scales are single-fold) for every similar scale division. The angler can purchase fairly sophisticated electronic pH meters which can be mounted on the dashboard of a fishing boat, and which continually and accurately monitor pH as a boat travels. Obviously, this is an ideal big-water solution.

The whole of the fish's environment is affected by pH, and make no mistake, fishes care a great deal about their local pH level. In humans a slight change in the pH of our blood can make us very sick indeed. In fishes a too high or too low pH in the surrounding water can be fatal. At lesser extremes, the fish has an acceptable range of pH within which he is fairly comfortable. And, just as with temperature, the fish will always orientate towards comfortable pH zones or areas. Most of the body fluids in fishes have a slightly alkaline pH in the range 7,6 to 7,8. Water in this range would logically be most comfortable.

Ideally, the first thing an angler should do on arriving at the water is to check pH. The best pH zone will be the best area for fishing. You can then start narrowing things down by checking

Angelo Komis, fly-fishing for yellowfish, takes advantage of an inlet stream on the Vaal River. Such streams can change pH and oxygen content. (Photo: courtesy Angelo Komis)

temperature and other factors, and then arriving logically at the very best hot spot for fishes. What is important in this analysis, is that you will have arrived at your conclusion from a fish's point of view.

From the foregoing, you will have realised that pH know-how is very important to the still-water angler. However, electronic pH meters are not cheap, so what then? Well, there are a few guidelines which help, but if you really want to get to grips with pH, then a meter is the answer.

Guidelines on pH

The pH level of a given still water is very often related to the kind of soil beneath the water. You can get a good idea of this from the surrounding soils. A water impoundment built on chalky or part-chalky soil will incline toward alkalinity. Conversely, peaty soils, or where the dam has been flooded over vleis or marshes, will probably cause the water to tend toward acidity. Most farmland flooded by water will average around the neutral or slightly alkaline pH reading of 7 to 8. Brown-stained but clear water is often the result of a peaty bottom, and consequent acidity. Very clear water with a tendency toward a

bluish tinge is often slightly alkaline. Such alkaline waters very often have a rich aquatic plant life, high concentrations of insects and other fauna, and fast growing fishes.

Rainfall is acidic, and in parts of southern Africa, where the authorities seem more concerned with productivity than the cleanliness of the air and water which our children will inherit, it is often very acidic indeed! Good rainfall, then, is most likely to lower the water temperature, increase the oxygen content, and simultaneously lower the pH level. The pH will be particularly affected around dam inflows a few hours after rain. The consequent effect on the fishing will vary depending upon the normal conditions. If the water is normally on the high alkaline side, and has been suffering from high temperatures for a few days, then the increased oxygen and the normalised pH may well bring the fishes onto the feed in a big way. Alternatively, an already acid water which becomes more acid as a result of the rain will probably have its fish population put right off feeding.

Under 'normal' conditions, the inflow of a stream or river into a dam may cause a differ-

A farm dam needs to be carefully assessed with respect to the effects of weedbeds, inflows, temperature, depth, locations of food and so on. A choice of location based on analysis usually means more productive fishing.

ent pH over an area adjacent to the inflow. Depen-ding on the volume of inflow, the area affected could be large or small. The same can apply in running water where a tributary joins a river.

A dam or any large stretch of water such as a broad slow river (and you find these throughout Africa in the dry season), may exhibit different pH all over it (a dam almost always will). This affects your choice of fishing area, since the fish-es will go to the most comfortable area, and within that area they will move to the best feeding spots. Since the various food forms also have preferences for 'comfortable pH', the food forms and the fishes will in any event most likely converge on the same area. This movement of food forms in response to varying pH levels is possibly the most important motivator in the fish's choice of location, and is also the prime trigger for bringing him onto the feed. We have all come across the situation where fishes are feeding well and providing good sport in one area of a water while elsewhere nothing is being caught at all. Much of this can be due to the living plants and their contribution to the background pH in their area.

Choosing a spot using pH guidelines (without a meter)

When making your fishing decisions, weigh the effect of the water-plants against your previous assessment of the background pH. The plants, releasing oxygen in daylight and carbon dioxide at night, will raise the alkalinity of their sur-roundings during the day and, conversely, raise the acidity during the night. The daytime plant effect through the release of oxygen will stop as soon as the light is gone; likewise, the night-time effect will still be apparent in the first one or two hours after dawn, until the light is actu-ally on the water. The results which you may then expect are:

❏ in a water which normally tends to acidity, weedbeds will be attractive to fishes during the day;

❏ in a water which normally tends towards alkalinity, weedbeds will be attractive to fishes at dusk and for the first hour or two of dawn.

Looking at this from the opposite point of view, if you are already aware of the fish move-ments around the weedbeds in your favourite water, then you can work out an indication of the background pH.

Decaying vegetation, normally a condition associated with late autumn and winter, causes a small increase in acidity in its immediate area. Since this is a shallow area phenomenon, you can expect fishes to move off the shallows into deeper water if the water is acidic. Conversely, in alkaline waters, as soon as the sun warms the shallows, the fishes may well become active there.

Usually, when I am out fishing with a friend, the first thing we do is try to find the best pH area – i.e. the nearest to the comfort zone (purely by observation, as I don't have a meter). Once we have that nailed down, we then start to eliminate areas progressively on the basis of temperature, structure, and light effect. We end up with a preferred fishing area which we then explore thoroughly. Occasionally we get it wrong, but on average we do very much better with our fishing because of this exercise, and I am convinced that it makes a big difference to our results.

Atmospheric pressure

This has a little-understood effect on fishes. However, it has been written about by authorities like Ray Webb and Barry Rickards in their book *Fishing for Big Pike*. Over a period of years these remarkable anglers kept detailed records of all prevailing conditions during their fishing trips. Eventually they noticed a correlation between atmospheric pressure and good or bad fishing days. What they discovered was that any sudden drop in barometric readings caused a complete lay-off by the fishes – nothing was caught when a depression passed over the area! Within hours of the pressure dropping, the fishes would cease to feed. Next day, with the depression having passed on and the barometer rising, the fishes would be back feeding again (at a lower level perhaps), and within two days they would be feeding naturally. This observation applies to all species of fish.

Atmospheric pressure affects all water surfaces, and the theory goes that below the water, the fish's lateral line becomes dysfunctional as a result of the rapid pressure change. In consequence, the fish is deprived of an important

hunting and defensive sensory system, and finally he becomes inactive. A few hours later the fish adjusts to the change, and begins to return to normal functioning.

Cold fronts contribute to fish inactivity and to the breaking up of shoals of schooling fishes. With the cold front, the depression is accompanied by a sudden lowering of light levels subsequent to the cloud build-up. This seems to especially affect fishes like largemouth bass, which often retreat into heavy structures and weedbeds in fairly shallow water under these conditions. They will sometimes take a spinner or plug, but do not usually react well to flies when they are in this inactive state.

The moon

The moon has long been known to affect fishes. We have all seen the moon tables in the angling press portending to list the best fishing days and the best times. I wonder how many people know that many of these tables are compiled by astrologers who base their tables on the passing of the moon through the heavenly constellations. They are little more than fortune telling!

Many anglers have noticed that daytime fishing when the moon is full is definitely not so good. The effect is particularly noticeable with rainbow trout. For many years I have heard anglers saying: 'They feed at night during the full moon, then they're not so hungry during the day – that's why we can't catch them!' However, almost nobody ever attempts to test the theory. I suppose the fly-fishermen of Africa are not too keen to cast in the dark, as they expect huge unseen bird-nests to develop in their casts and tippets.

Well, one night with the full moon cascading silver moonbeams across the water – we decided to try it. We used shortened leaders, big black silhouetty flies, and we went fishing. Result: we caught and returned plenty of moonlight feeding rainbows. In New Zealand a whole discipline on night fishing with flies has developed – special flies and techniques provide their fly-fishermen with great sport on moonlit nights.

CHAPTER 4

BASIC CASTING TECHNIQUES

'You won the competition? What did you do?'
'I cast a fly into a cup under a table about 20 yards away. They didn't believe me, so I did it again!'

Ron Clay, visiting Europe

As a casting instructor for many years, I have always been amazed at the mystique that some people spin around fly-casting. I have met people who honestly believed that they could never master casting because they were working-class folk, some who thought it impossible because they had little strength (usually women), and some who thought it was no different to tennis. I have met some who had been as keen as mustard on fly-fishing for 20 years and could cast no further than ten metres. At the other extreme, our local vicar read one magazine article and went straight to the water and started double haul casting to 35 metres (some might say he had divine inspiration). The truth is, everybody can cast a fly line – they just have to learn the correct way.

Two of the casting instructors at Trout Hideaway in South Africa learnt to cast from an article I wrote in the early seventies in *Tight Lines* magazine. With no personal instruction (I only met them years later), they managed all by themselves, and both are extremely competent casters today. The moral is, that it can be done from a book! Nevertheless, a casting course is highly recommended, and every aspirant fly-fishing person should attend one if possible.

BEFORE YOU START

Chapter 2 explains how to go about setting yourself up with a balanced outfit. This is the essence of fly-casting: without a balanced outfit you should not even attempt to learn casting.

The wrong outfit will force you to try and compensate for its inadequacies, which will result in bad technique – technique that can never work properly. Bad habits will be formed, and these may take years to correct later. Quite apart from the bad habits, the fly-casting will never be good – incorrect technique may tire you quickly, wind knots become a major problem, and without correct technique you can look forward to little accuracy and many other problems. If you know what goes wrong and why, then you can correct it, and this is where instruction is invaluable. The importance of a balanced outfit plus casting know-how cannot be over-emphasised.

Some say fly-casting is an art form ... and perhaps it is. Flicking a tiny fly under a bush, so accurately that it drifts down over a fish without skating, is indeed artistry. Predicting the path of a rising fish, and casting to the spot where he will be in ten seconds ... that is also artistry. Casting 45 metres out with a tungsten cored line, to drop your fly into an old river bed ... that's skill. Reaching the third wave at the edge of a reef just where the queenfish are harrying fry ... that's also skill. I could go on, but the point to be made is that fly-casting at its best is both artistry and skill! You could say that the skill can be learnt and the artistry comes with experience, as a bonus.

Accident prevention

In the early days of your fly-fishing it is advisable to use barbless hook flies – these are much easier to remove in the unlikely event that you do get impaled. I use them all the time anyway, since they are easily tweaked out, and are much better for releasing fish. On some waters, barbless hooks are compulsory. Generally speaking, accidents from casting only occur as a result of distraction or unexpected gusts of wind.

Keep a watchful eye for passers-by when casting. Often they are non-anglers and have no idea of what a back cast is, or how easily they can get hooked-up. An angler passing by should always shout 'passing', and would in any event be wise enough to wait for the cast to be completed before passing.

A brief history

Up until the late 1930s, 'classical' casting was considered the standard method, and was the only acceptable method throughout the fly-fishing world. Classical casting is unfortunately limited by its own restrictions, and as a result the world record cast stood at 22 yards (20,1 metres) for a very long time. So restricted by convention were the fly-fishermen of those days, that no one dared to improve methods. 'It is simply not done, old chap ... you learn to cast with a folded copy of *The Times* under your elbow, and that's the only acceptable way!'

In the 1930s and 1940s, the foundations of classical stream fly-casting began to be rocked from two directions. One was the opening to the British public of vast still-waters for trout fishing. The other was happening far away on the west coast of America, where anglers were fishing rapidly descending fast deep streams and rivers for steelhead trout (sea-run rainbows). Fishing deep in fast rivers demanded long casting techniques, and this was reinforced by a growing interest in competitive casting. A man called Marvin Hedge introduced a new casting method, and simultaneously smashed the existing fly-casting records. With his technique, casts of double the old record were achievable, and more importantly, they were achievable by the average fly-fisherman.

Public awareness of long-distance casting in Britain was promoted by Tom Ivens in his classic work *Still-water Flyfishing*, first published in 1952. The simultaneous opening of the big reservoirs in Britain meant that by the early 1960s, most still-water fly-fishermen in the UK could reach out to 35 yards (32 metres) and were competent 'double haul' casters. The fly-fishermen learnt about a new basic casting method called 'sweet casting' (a method unrestricted by under-arm newspapers) which could give him much greater accuracy and largely improved overall capability. Adding two hauls to this cast upgraded it to the 'double haul', and the caster was then easily able to achieve very long accurate casts. The new casting was here to stay!

Casting schools

When you apply to join a casting school, make sure the instructor can teach you in the modern style ... steer very clear of classic casting schools. If the instructor doesn't, or can't, teach double haul, stay away and invest your money elsewhere and more wisely.

The normal process of casting should first teach fly-casting without the hauls. The techniques of the hauls, although discussed in the early stages of learning, are added later. However, be careful, the 'double haul' cannot be added to classical casting methods – if you have already gone the classical route, you will need to re-start, to clean up bad habits, and then learn the relaxed easy method of basic sweet casting from scratch.

Where do shooting heads fit in?

A shooting head is nothing more than the first 30 feet (just over 9 metres) of the fly line designed to match (balance) your rod. This cut-off portion of fly line is attached to a thinner 'shooting line' which allows the short fly line to fly out when released. Because the shooting head is the exact weight for best performance of the rod, and because the shooting line flies out so easily, greater distances are achieved than when using a full fly line.

It would be a foolish beginner who tried to learn from scratch with a shooting head. Once you have learnt the basics, you can certainly go for it, but the 'double haul' should be regarded as part and parcel of shooting head casting. By all means have the shooting head method in mind as a target to work towards. If your aim is to fish the salt, this technique is essential – long-distance casting in the surf can make a huge difference to your catch at the end of the day.

Not everyone believes in shooting heads, and I can think of two superb fly-fishermen who use full fly lines for all their fly-fishing (including the sea). I use both shooting heads and full fly lines. I would never use a shooting head on a trout stream, but I might well do so on a large river. I prefer the full line for floating line nymph fishing and for dry flies on still water. I much prefer the shooting head for casting long distances over deep water, for working a lead core, and for surf and reef fishing. Where public waters are heavily infested with fly-fishermen, I enjoy the greater distance I achieve with the shooting head, since it allows me to fish water away from the shore disturbance. Shooting heads are easier to handle on boats; and for Nile perch, tigerfish, and catfish, the shooting head is my choice.

It's the method that counts
When I first started fly-casting instruction in 1972, Ron Clay used to come along and help. He would often demonstrate that sweet casting was a function purely of technique and timing. His favourite way to demonstrate this was to perform 30 metre casts with a metre length of broomstick (which had a staple hammered in one end for a tip ring). Later, in the mid-1980s, Murray Peddar would often assist me. Murray could produce 25 metre casts without any rod at all, making a loop with his fingers for the tip ring and using his arm as the rod. Today, Steve Barrow demonstrates 30 metre casts lying face down on the ground – all very mind-boggling for the students. The fact is that these casters are all masters of timing, and masters of the sweet casting method. Their understanding and practice of the principles of casting is so good that they can cast under the worst conditions imaginable (it doesn't get much worse than no rod at all!).

Getting ready to cast
Before you commence, especially if this is your first attempt, put on some protective clothing – a waterproof waxed-cotton fishing jacket is more than adequate. Wear glasses or sunglasses (best are the wrap-around types), wear a hat, and turn up your jacket collar to protect your neck. Tie a small piece of wool to the end of your leader ... NOT a hook, or if you prefer you can snap the point and the hook bend off of your fly, and use that.

Adopt a stance at roughly 60 degrees angle to the bank (assuming you are casting straight out). Pull off about 20 metres of line and lay this at your feet. You can put a piece of plastic down if necessary, but try to choose a clean place with short grass and not thick bankside vegetation. There is no reason why you should not start off on your lawn, or a nearby sports field – you do not have to be by the water. Keep away from rocks and sharp stones!

Hold the rod in your best hand with your thumb on top of the rod handle. Hold the fly line which is hanging from the butt ring in the other hand.

ROLL CASTING
Roll casting was developed as a method for lifting sunken lines out of the water. Sinking fly lines are very resistant to being lifted off, so much so that you can very easily break your rod in the attempt.

Roll casting as a method of lifting off sinking fly lines at the end of a retrieve, or even before, is thus an essential skill.

Roll casting to start the sweet cast
Roll casting is also very useful for starting the sweet cast itself. Roll casting enables you to lift the line from the water, and to lay it out in the air before you, ready to go straight into the back cast. If this is done in one smooth motion, the line need never touch the water during the casting process. Many experienced fly-casters regard the rolling-out of the line, followed by one smooth back cast, and then a single forward cast and release (all in one smooth motion, resulting in a 40 metre cast), as the ultimate in double haul casting.

Since the roll cast is used to start the sweet cast, it is important to learn the technique before starting to learn sweet casting.

The roll cast.

Roll casting as a stand-alone casting method

Roll casting can stand alone as a casting method in its own right. In a method known as 'shot-gunning the pockets', the fly-angler works his or her way through the stream, casting into every trout lie (pocket) of water. This is normally performed wading, but can be done from the bank. Every cast is a roll cast, simply and easily done. In this way the angler can search out the whole stream, exploring every likely trout or yellowfish lie. Since roll casting does not require a back cast, this is a wonderfully useful method on tiny, overgrown streams where back casting is impossible.

I often fish waters with very high but fairly open bankside vegetation. Very often any attempt at a back cast would put the fly straight into a tree. Walking the banks, and roll casting right across the river (sometimes 20 metres wide) has put a lot of trout my way.

In summary, roll casting is an essential skill to teach in any casting school. It is extremely useful in its own right, and is absolutely necessary for retrieving sunken lines and for starting the sweet cast itself.

How to roll cast

It is easiest to learn the roll cast with a floating fly line on water. Grass presents quite a high resistance to the line and makes the cast unrealistically difficult. Lay the line out in front of you as if at the end of a retrieve – this would mean approximately nine metres of line is in front of you (see Figure 4.1(A)). This is simple to assess with a shooting head, since the join between shooting head and shooting line reaches your hand at exactly the right distance. With a full line you will have to estimate this nine metres. In any event, it is not a critical length, and a bit more or less will not affect the cast.

Hold the line firmly in the non-casting hand, so that it cannot slip through your fingers. Raise the rod slowly, which will have the simultaneous effect of fishing the retrieve almost to your feet (another bonus) and forming a curved loop in the line between water and rod tip. Use a smooth unvarying speed for this part of the action. Bring the rod past your ear (see Figure 4.1(B)). Just as the line reaches your ear, punch the rod sharply forward, still keeping the rod vertical (see Figure 4.1(C)). The line will slide out of the water into a circular loop which will

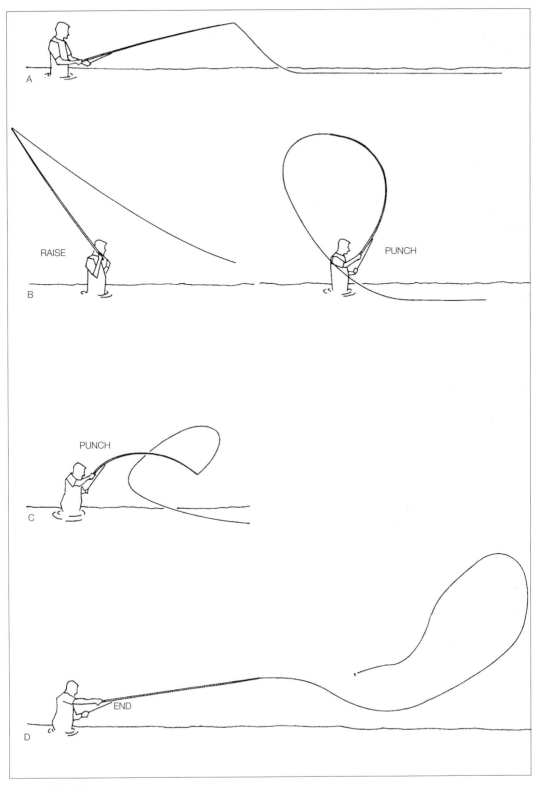

RAISE

PUNCH

PUNCH

END

Fig. 4.1: *The roll cast.*

unfold into the air before you. Depending on whether this is a stand-alone roll cast or the prelude to a sweet cast, you will either allow the line to straighten and settle on the water (as in the stream fishing mentioned previously), as in Figure 4.1(D), or you will whip it into the commencing back cast of the sweet cast. The line can be made to unfold higher by leaning the rod just a little back from the vertical during the punch

Direction is achieved in the roll cast by leaning the rod either right or left for the direction you require. You can quickly achieve proficiency with the roll cast with minimal practice.

Having got the roll cast working with a floating line, try it again with a sinking line. Allow the line to sink well down before commencing the roll cast. The line will appear to slide out of a hole in the water. It comes off very easily! If you try just lifting the line, you will find it difficult. You may even break your rod.

Having acquired the simple technique of roll casting, we will use this method for getting the line into the air to start learning sweet casting.

SWEET CASTING – THE RULES

Sweet casting is the basis of good casting method ... looked at another way, it is the double haul without the hauls. Utmost among sweet casting principles is that it should be a very relaxed business, and it *must* be easy. It does not require great muscular effort or strength. Nevertheless, you may get tired when beginning. If you do, stop immediately and rest. Tired muscles spawn bad habits, so keep relaxed. If you are working hard, then you are doing it wrong. Always relax and think about what you are doing. In this section, I will highlight the kind of things that go wrong and what to watch out for. So, when you are by the water and problems arise, think about your cast, and you will soon realise what the problem is.

Problem handling

In order to get your casting right you will need to approach problems one at a time. For example, you might decide to work on your wrist flick (and only your wrist flick) until you are satisfied with it. Then you can move onto other problems (still one at a time), such as wrist

twist, back cast timing, and so on ... always one at a time! The other essential is to practise regularly, but keep the sessions short. Twenty minutes every other day for six weeks would turn you into a competent caster.

Some days you will feel that you are battling and that everything is going wrong. Such days may even happen years after you have learnt to cast. The reason is nearly always tenseness – you have forgotten to take it easy, you are trying too hard, using muscle power to get distance instead of technique. Give it some thought, relax, take it easy, and you will find it all starts working well again. Sometimes we slip into a frame of mind where it's us against the fish and the water – almost a war, and of course that is quite wrong! Fishing is an enjoyable and relaxing sport offering opportunities not only to catch fish, but also to relax the mind, and enjoy nature and the beauties around us.

Before we commence practical sweet casting, we shall first examine the rules of casting and their implications.

The rules of sweet casting

❏ *Rule 1:* The aerialised fly line should not exhibit slack, or show ripples or waves.
❏ *Rule 2:* Throw tight loops.

These two rules control all of fly-casting, and the aim is to apply them to our own casting. It can take some time before you get close to manifesting them in your casting, and you would have to develop into a perfect caster before they were completely obeyed. Nevertheless, they set the objective for all fly-casters, and the perfectly smooth flow of efficient casting loops is what we strive for.

The implications of Rule 1

Let us first have a look at Rule 1, and see what this means to the caster. It is the basic and most fundamental rule. A lot of bad casting occurs as a result of the back cast being full of waves and kinks which result from incorrect technique. The energy which the caster imparts to the line is thus largely wasted, because all these aberrations (waves and kinks) have to be removed by the energy in the rod and line before the forward cast can commence. As much as 70 or 80 per cent of the imparted energy can be wasted in the removal of waves from the back cast. If you are false casting, the rule will also apply to the false forward casts, and each one of these wavy casts will waste available energy. This waste of energy means that not much is actually applied to the cast itself, and the result is a poor cast.

Slack line causes exactly the same problem, only worse. An awful lot of energy is wasted on tightening-up and removing slack line from the system. In a really bad case of slack, you can waste all of the available energy with a no-cast result. Awareness of the necessity to eliminate slack and waves is the single most important part of becoming a better caster! This wasting of energy is why many people cannot cast a fly line. The classical casting method which rigidly keeps the elbow in one position actually causes slack – just one of the reasons why classic casting is so limited.

The appearance of waves in the cast is actually an indication of what the rod tip is doing. It follows that if we control the rod tip we can control the waves. These are the common causes of waves in casting:

❏ *Twisting the wrist*
Wrist twisting is the most common casting error, but one which is easily corrected by observation. Many a struggling caster has discovered that this was the only error! In bad cases, correction of wrist twist can put 50 per cent or more onto the distance achieved. It is also the most common error occurring in self-taught casters.

Watch the reel during the cast. It must remain in the same plane throughout, not tilting or moving towards either side. Twisting the wrist (even minimally) causes the rod tip to circle, which in turn puts waves into the line. Twisting the wrist is also the major cause of wind knots in tippet and leader. And later, if you aspire to shooting head casting, twisting the wrist can cause major twisting in the shooting line, which in turn causes major knots in the shooting line (terrible things to undo) during casting.

The need to turn the wrist in the cast is a natural one, which is why it needs attention to get it right. As the arm moves, it tries to turn, sometimes only a little. This is a fault which is exaggerated if the caster is inclined to sweep or stick his elbows out away from the body during the cast. The moral is: keep everything in the same plane. It doesn't matter which plane, so long as you stay in it. Good casters can perform casts in any plane, which is especially useful for casting under bushes and for fishing in tight situations.

❏ *Twisting the body*
There is a very natural tendency to turn the body in order to watch the cast. This sometimes causes wide circling motions at the rod tip, causing waves to develop which are often quite large. Because of the plane that the waves develop in, they are often difficult to see. Many casters are often unaware of the existence of these waves. Whatever you do during the cast, you must once again remember that the rod must stay in the same plane of movement. Obviously, twisting of the body will move the rod out of that plane.

Overcome this problem by looking back over your shoulder instead of turning the body. This is another error that, once corrected, can make a major positive difference to one's casting.

❏ *Sudden stops*
A sudden stoppage of the rod will cause the rod tip to vibrate, which in turn sets up waves in the cast. This can come about as a result of two eventualities. The first is poor dampening of the rod (refer to Chapter 2 for more information); the second is the sudden stop of the rod.

Poor dampening causes the rod tip to continue vibrating after the rod has been stopped by the caster (for example at the end of the back cast). These vibrations, in turn, set up waves in the line. These unwanted vibrations are a function of the quality of the rod. Good rods vibrate far less than poor ones, which is one of the reasons why purchases should be made very carefully.

The other reason for lingering vibrations is the sudden stop of the rod itself, which occurs because the caster has failed to 'drift' out of the

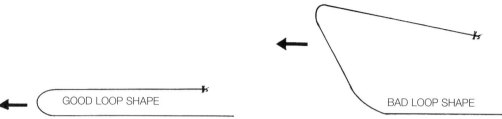

Fig. 4.2: Casting loop shapes. The correct narrow casting loop, which cuts through the air; and the bad large loop, which stops the line from straightening on the back cast or achieving distance on the forward cast.

stop. In classical casting, the student is taught to stop the rod dead at the end of the back cast. In sweet casting the rod stop is still there, but the caster, immediately after the stop, relaxes the rod and allows it to drift further back. This drift stops the rod from vibrating. When done correctly it is almost impossible for the observer to see the transition from the stop into the drift.

The drift is very important in sweet casting, since it also removes waves generated in other ways. However, it is not possible to put the drift into the back cast unless the back cast has been performed reasonably well. Thus, most beginners will develop the back cast as well as they can before advancing their technique and learning the very important drift. The drift is easily learnt, and is a natural step in the development of casting.

The implications of Rule 2

Big sloppy loops will slow the back cast down as a result of wind resistance, thus preventing the build-up of power in the rod. I have seen loops so bad that they are unable to penetrate the air at all, and the whole anticipated back cast simply collapses behind the caster. These huge loops result from bad timing and, more importantly, insufficient application of the wrist. No cast can work unless power builds up in the rod. This stored power or energy in the rod is imparted by the moving line. The weight of the moving line, and the momentum in it, put the power into the rod.

Tight loops in the casting process can cut through the air with great ease. A good tight back or forward element of the cast can cut through the teeth of a gale force wind. The rod stores up maximum power as a result of the fast-moving line, and hurls the released line through the air. The line speed comes from the rod, not from your muscle (although muscles obviously play a part). The adding of the double haul technique to the basic cast is, in fact, nothing more than a method of increasing line speed.

In conclusion, aim for tight loops in the cast. Tight loops produce casts that penetrate the air. These loops also ensure that maximum energy can be applied to the rod, and hence to the cast. Common causes of unwanted large loop development are:

❏ *Sweeping the rod*

Tight loops are generated by applying rapidly increasing power to the rod at the right time. This is achieved through accelerating wrist snaps (or flicks). If these wrist snaps are missing from the casting technique, the caster will try to put power into the cast some other way, and this always manifests as a sweeping of the rod. This sweeping is always accompanied by a 'whooshing' sound from the rod. Because the rod fails to power-up, the caster tries to move the rod ever faster and faster, which in turn causes the 'whooshes' ... but with no power available in the rod, the cast can never work. When casting is performed correctly the rod is almost silent; the only sound one hears is the whistling of the line through the air.

The correction of this problem is achieved through practising your wrist movement. Get the 'wrist snaps' right, and the rod will cease to sweep. A very useful tip is to cast your mind back to childhood and remember the action needed to flick a ball of mud off the end of a stick – this movement is identical to the 'wrist snap' in casting.

□ *Rod tip path*

The path of the rod's tip can be likened to a paint brush on a ceiling. Even though the rod itself, as a result of loading, bends in opposing directions during the cast, the tip of the rod must move in a straight line. This straight line movement, coupled to wrist power snaps, is what makes super tight loops in casting. The rod should never be moved from its intended path.

The commonest cause of rod tip dropping (not to the floor, but from its intended path), is the application of extra effort at the end of the cast. The caster tries harder, consequently he pushes the rod forward much harder than he should, which in turn produces a downward movement of the rod. The rod tip drops and the net result is the opening of the loop – that is, the loop gets bigger and the cast gets shorter. This is probably the second most common cause of poor casting.

The same effect can be caused by attempting the back cast over a high object such as a river bank. The necessary high upward-sloping back cast forces the caster into a change of slope for the forward cast, with the result that the tip loses its ceiling and a huge rolling loop develops. The loop often causes the fly to catch up on the line, resulting in a huge tangle. The delivery is also very splashy and fish-frightening. Expert casters are able to handle this second situation by changing the slope of the ceiling precisely at the maximum extension of the back cast. However, this requires a finely developed sense of timing. 'Steeple casting' is a method which deliberately uses this 'change in ceiling' technique in order to cast in situations where high cliffs and similar structures are right behind the caster.

SWEET CASTING – THE PRACTICE

It is essential to understand that in sweet casting you are not limited to movements of the

Fig. 4.3: The correct grip for sweet casting and for the double haul cast.

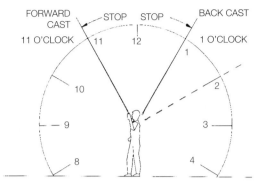

Fig. 4.4: Clock face positioning.

forearm as in classical casting, which restricts movement to pivoting at the elbow. Sweet casting allows and even encourages use of all arm and shoulder muscles to achieve the desired results. Punching the rod during forward casts is quite acceptable, and many sweet casters seeking distance will pull the rod right back during the back cast.

Clock face positioning

The fly-caster will form an easier understanding of the casting movements if we compare their positioning to a clock face. Imagine a clock face with its centre some 30 cm to the side of your casting arm, with your rod hand at the centre, and the rod as the hour hand. The whole controlled basic casting movement takes place between 11 o'clock and 1 o'clock. In the back cast the rod is stopped at 1 o'clock, and in the forward cast it is stopped at 11 o'clock.

Applying power

The movement which gives sweet casting its power is the wrist flick (also referred to as the wrist power snap). This movement is an accelerating movement of the wrist, and is identical to the movement used to flick a ball of mud off of the end of a stick. A stock whip also uses a similar movement. Some instructors liken this accelerating movement to a hammer driving in nails.

Cast components

The back cast (see Figure 4.5) consists of a backward wrist flick which is stopped at 1 o'clock, followed by a short wait as the line extends out behind the caster. When the cast has straight-

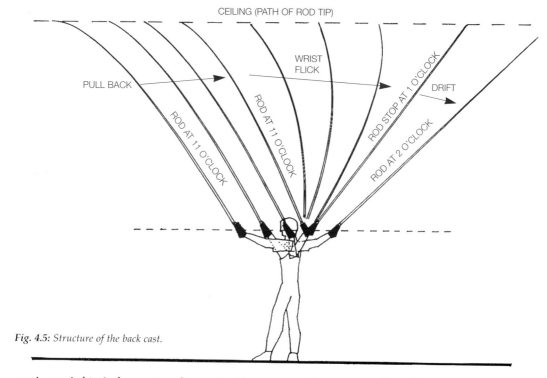

Fig. 4.5: Structure of the back cast.

ened out behind the caster, the caster then moves the rod forward (see Figure 4.6) and performs a forward wrist flick which also has a stop, but this time at 11 o'clock. Once more the line will extend, but this time in front of the caster. When it is fully extended one can then perform another backward accelerating wrist flick, once again stopping at 1 o'clock. This can be repeated many times, simply aerialising the line backward and forward. The entire movement can be quite slow (it need not be fast, because the rod is doing all the work). Provided that the wrist flicks accelerate into the stop positions, and that you wait for the line to straighten out between each back and forward movement, you will soon be able to keep the line in the air. Casters commonly do not wait for the back cast to straighten – but you must! If you have this problem, wait just a split second longer than usual, and make yourself do it repeatedly until it becomes reflex. 'Whip cracking' noises are also indicative of not waiting long enough on the back cast.

Problems arise because learner casters forget to accelerate the wrist flicks. Before they know it, they are wondering where the power went

and they start swishing the rod in an attempt to compensate. Timing and the soft acceleration of the wrist give way to brute force, the casting stops working, and everything becomes hard work!

Once you have the line going backward and forward, try letting a little line slip through the fingers of your non-casting hand at the end of each forward and back movement. If you can keep the line aerialised, you will quickly notice that the whole system, and especially the rod, appears to work better as more line is released. This is because the increasing weight of the lengthening aerialised line begins to approach the working weight of the rod, and as it does so the rod *loads up properly* and starts doing the job it was designed for.

The drift movement

The elimination of waves in the line is very important. The sweet caster has an advantage, and that is in the movement known as 'drifting'. After wrist flicking to the back stop position, allow the rod to drift back smoothly and easily. The drift absorbs rod tip vibrations and other small twists of the rod tip. It is acceptable

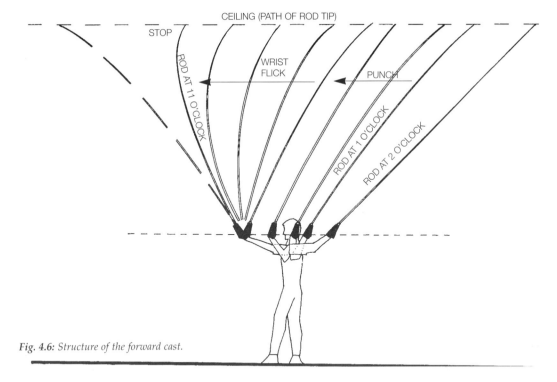

Fig. 4.6: *Structure of the forward cast.*

for the rod to drift further back than the 1 o'clock position, but not much beyond 2 o'clock. That drift takes the waves out of the line, which means that the forward cast can be immediately applied to a smooth non-wavy line. Later on when you are learning the double haul you can drift the rod much further back, but don't try that yet. It is very important to distinguish between drifting the rod back and the movement known as 'breaking the wrist' – these are quite different!

Breaking the wrist

The wrist should be firm throughout the casting movement. If you allow the wrist to collapse, the cast will be spoiled. This is most commonly observed at the end of the back cast where the angler is seen to allow the rod to fall right down as a result of the wrist no longer supporting the rod. This 'collapse' drags the whole cast down. The fly can hit the vegetation and often gets caught up, and whether it catches up or not, the rod is quite unable to power-up for the forward cast. Many casters are quite unaware that they are doing this, and an observer is often the first person to pick out the

fault. Breaking of the wrist affects people in varying ways. Both men and women can be affected by it. Some correct it immediately, others never get it right without help. The best cure is to acquire some Velcro tape and make a fairly loose loop around the extreme end of the rod (at the butt end of the reel seat) and the wrist. This keeps the rod attached to the wrist, allowing the caster to get a proper feel for the cast (which is not possible with the wrist break). Once a feel for correct casting is achieved the problem usually disappears.

Extending the sweet cast

Once you have the aerialised line moving smoothly backward and forward, you can try extending the action by using shoulder and arm muscles. From the back cast, when the line has completely straightened out behind you (parallel to the ground); punch the rod forward (still in the 1 o'clock position) culminating in the wrist flick. What happens now is that you have pre-powered the rod by punching it forward, and the power of the wrist flick is added to this power, thus giving a longer cast. Similarly, the rod can be better loaded up in the back cast by pulling (reverse punching) the rod (still in the 11 o'clock position) back, before inserting the wrist flick toward the 1 o'clock stop and drift action. As with the extended forward cast, the rod is pre-loaded by the reverse punch, and then really loaded-up with the wrist flick, thus giving it much more energy. This extension of the casting movement by extending arms and by punching and pulling the rod with one's shoulder and arm muscles gives greater distance as a result of greater applied power. The rod does all the work, provided that the caster applies the energy at the correctly timed moment.

Line release

At the end of each false cast release some line (my preference is to release line on the back cast only, but other casters release on both false casts). Eventually, enough line is aerialised to get the rod working well, and it will work at its best when 30 feet (9 metres) of fly line have been aerialised (the correct weight of line for the rod). When actually casting (as opposed to practising), one would pull off extra line (over and above the 30 feet mentioned above). As one reaches the state where the rod is working at its best, simply release the line immediately at the end of the final forward wrist flick. The loose pulled-off line will fly through the rod rings as it is dragged out by the applied momentum of the cast line. This is the time when temptation often gets the better of the learner caster, who predictably tries just that much harder on the final forward cast ... you must not overpower the forward cast! Simply treat it the same as other false casts and just release the line, then everything will go according to plan.

Remember the important potential pitfalls:
❏ twisting the wrist;
❏ sweeping with the rod;
❏ forgetting the wrist flicks;
❏ not waiting long enough for the back cast to straighten;
❏ twisting the body;
❏ overdoing the final cast;
❏ using power to compensate for lack of technique;
❏ breaking the wrist.

At this stage you will have covered all of the basic technique of the sweet casting method. You can reach this stage quite quickly. One should make a point of learning and practising basic casting away from fishing waters. The temptation to get on with the fishing, and to adopt an 'it will come naturally' type of thinking about your casting, can only lead to problems, bad habits, and poor casting ... it is also quite irresistible when faced with rising fish in front of you! Take the time to learn and practise away from fishing waters. If you can apply yourself without distraction, you will quickly master all the necessary techniques.

Splashy casting

Remember when fishing in earnest that it is very poor practice to beat the water to a froth. Each forward false cast must not hit the water – it must be aimed above the water. If your timing is correct (as it will be if you practise), the line will straighten in the air above the water and will be whipped into the next back cast before it can land on the water. Beating the water really frightens fish! If you use the roll cast properly to roll the line out of the water and into the cast itself, you should have no problem with the start of the cast. In order to avoid splashy landing of fly line and leader, try aiming for the cast to land a foot above the water – it will then settle gently onto the surface.

For many fly-fishermen, achieving the best of sweet casting is quite sufficient for their angling needs. However, the true benefits from the next step, the 'double haul cast', come not from distance as much as from being in total control of one's casting. The double haul cast can be applied in varying degrees, and because controlled power from maximum distance down to minimal distance is available, the good caster can produce incredible accuracy, and can respond in measure to almost any fly-casting situation anywhere.

THE DOUBLE HAUL CAST

The addition of the backward and forward 'hauls' to basic casting technique increases line speed and, as a consequence, the distance it will travel. Double haul casting ranges from simple

The double haul cast: (A) shows the extended back haul, note that the caster is watching the back cast by turning his head and not by twisting the body; (B) shows the full forward haul, which would be used to reach out for distance; (C) shows the moment just after release, and the line flying out in a tight loop. (Photos: Ron Clay)

A

B

C

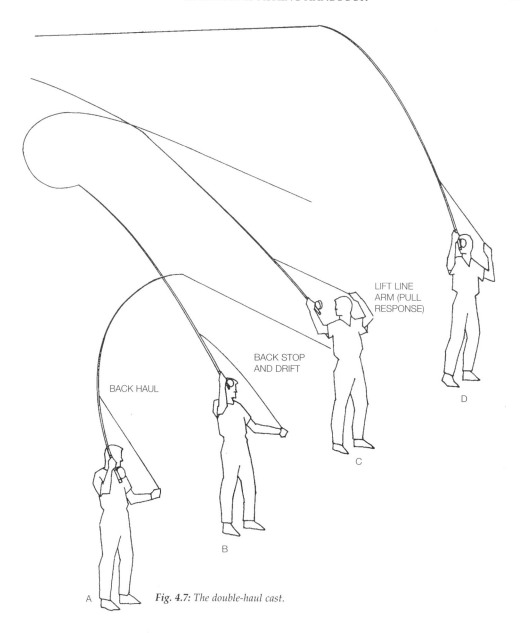

LIFT LINE
ARM (PULL
RESPONSE)

BACK STOP
AND DRIFT

BACK HAUL

D

C

B

A

Fig. 4.7: The double-haul cast.

application of line hauls to the epitome of double haul casting (which uses all the muscles of arm and shoulder), with maximum extension and speed of rod movement to achieve the greatest line speed possible.

Because things get faster, timing becomes more critical in the double haul. Common casting errors become amplified and produce even greater problems than they do in sweet casting. Nevertheless, I have never met anyone who

could not make some progress with the double haul, just as long as they really wanted to. Double haul casting is one of those activities which really benefits from practice, and like riding a bicycle, once learnt it is never forgotten.

Starting to learn the double haul

Initially, you should aim for a smoothly moving line without kinks or waves. Having achieved that, you can then start applying power and

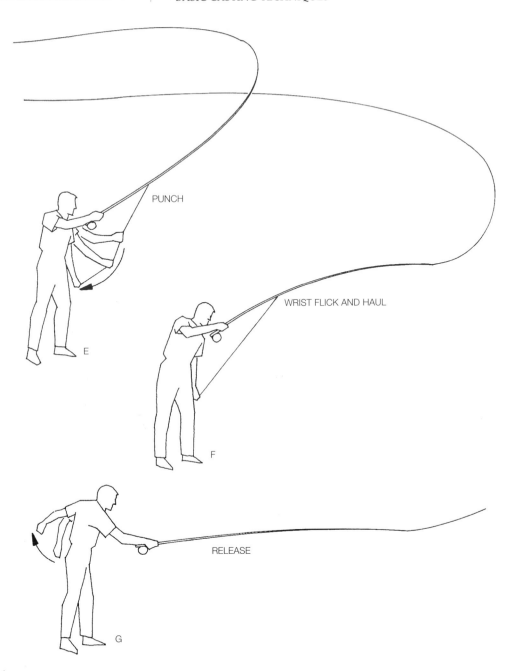

PUNCH

E

WRIST FLICK AND HAUL

F

RELEASE

G

extra speed to the hauls and rod movement. It is amazing how a very relaxed and easy double haul cast, done properly, sails out to 30 metres without any undue effort.

Some double haul benefits

When the timing is correct, when the hauls are properly placed and the cast is smooth, without waves, very little effort is required. One of the great advantages of this casting is that one can cast all day, even with a heavy AFTM 10 outfit, and yet still feel relaxed (and not even a little tired) at the end of the day ... truly a wonderful benefit.

Another major benefit of the double haul which is not so readily apparent includes improvement of effective water-time ratio. Because your line spends relatively longer time in the water (casting takes less time per cast and the fly is in the water over a much longer retrieve time), more fish will see your fly during the course of a day's fishing.

Another tangible benefit is being able to fish into the teeth of a gale – that means being able to fish in the most productive water (where others are unable to fish at all). Mastering the double haul will enable you to fish for species which you could not otherwise hope to catch (such as the denizens of the surf), and it will also give you the ability to fly fish over very deep water.

The back haul

Before proceeding, one has to assume that the caster has mastered the basics of sweet casting and has a good understanding of the mechanics of the cast as outlined previously.

The back haul is the easiest of the two hauls. The haul is added to the basic sweet back cast by holding the line firmly and simply moving the line hand in the opposite direction to the rod hand at the same time as the wrist flick is applied (see photo A on page 69 and Figure 4.7 (A) and (B)). You can think of this as simply spreading your arms. As you work at practising the back haul, you can gradually increase the speed of the line hauling arm. You will hear the line zip through the air, and you will feel the rod bending through the cork grip as the power builds up. Keep to the golden rules – they apply even more during the double haul – no waves, and nice tight loops!

A further development of the back haul is to respond to line tug. The back cast, because of the increased energy in it, will tug lightly at the line hand. Respond to this tug by allowing the line hand to drift up to the butt ring of the rod (see Figure 4.7(C)) – do not allow any slack to develop. The hauling hand is now almost in the same position as the rod hand (see Figure 4.7(D)). This will allow you, if you wish, to perform a maximum distance haul during the forward haul. Both arms are back, and they will commence the forward haul by moving forward together.

I know some casters who are quite satisfied with applying just the back haul to their casting. This comes about because the forward haul is more difficult to learn, and because the back haul alone can still cause a marked improvement in distance. Don't fall for this easy way out ... it's like getting to the winning post and then sitting down in front of the line instead of crossing it!

The forward haul

The forward haul is the most difficult component of the double haul technique. However, it is the part of the cast which gives most reward for perseverance.

The forward haul is critical in timing and release – it must be done at exactly the right time during the cast. We are dealing with split seconds here, and we are dealing with a movement that, until learnt, feels unnatural.

The forward haul takes place during the forward sweet cast wrist flick – almost simultaneously, in fact (see Figure 4.7(E)). The complete haul takes place from the butt ring position of the hand (the place where this hand ended up during the back haul), right down and back (almost straight armed) as far as you can go, as in Figure 4.7(F). The line is released at the instant of the completion of the haul, as in Figure 4.7(G). The correct release point is at the moment of maximum power. Obviously, the hauling hand has to move fast to cover all this distance in the limited time of the wrist flick. The longer and faster the haul, the faster the line speed.

The forward haul can be applied in varying degrees from tiny, almost hand length, movements to short pulls and of course to the complete haul itself. When actually fishing, the amount of forward haul will vary constantly from cast to cast in order to achieve the required effect. Don't forget – the temptation is to put in too much effort and overdo the whole thing. Another common fault is reaching forward on tip-toe, believing that this will improve the result. It will not – all it does is push the rod tip down, which spoils the cast and causes the whole line to land in a heap.

Having mastered your sweet cast, having added the back and the forward haul, and having worked at it until your cast performs fairly well ... what next?

Double haul and shooting heads

You can ...ke yet another step to improve achievable distance – not important if your happiness is always around the bend of a stream, but critical if it is found past the third wave out to sea. This is not so much technique as a modification in your current fly line set-up. The change is from a full fly line to the cut-down fly line rig commonly referred to as a 'shooting head' (incorrectly called a shooter head). A shooting head, as previously mentioned, is nothing more than the first 30 feet of the correct fly line for your rod.

Shooting line

The end of this shooting head is always spliced (usually with a nail knot in freshwater fly-fishing) to a running length (no more than 50 metres and more usually only 40 metres long) of special line which is most often a monofilament line of oval or flattened cross section. This special line is called the 'shooting line'. When the shooting head is cast, the shooting line flies out behind it. Because this shooting line is both thinner and more slippery than fly line, the line goes much further. Today, shooting lines are available in other materials than ovalised nylon monofilament. Some of these float (great for floating shooting heads); others sink. Some of the shooting lines are hollow braided, some are close braided, and some are round section mo-nofilament nylons. Most are designed to help eliminate knots during the very high-speed pick-up of shooting line which occurs during the double haul cast. Such knots can be a real and frustrating problem. My preference is for the ovalised nylons of about 10 kg breaking strain; but I find that although they last well in freshwater (sometimes for months), they have a very limited (sometimes less than a day) life in saltwater. Lighter shooting lines (not less than 5 kg breaking strain) supposedly give greater distance to the cast (although I find little difference), but you run a higher risk of the fly line breaking off. Braided shooting line (although sometimes more inclined to knot) lasts better in the salt.

For really accurate stream casting, change the grip by pointing the finger along the handle.

The shooting line is in turn knotted to the backing line on the reel. For saltwater fly-fishing, this can be as much as 200 metres in length, and is usually some form of non-stretch braided dacron line. There is little point in putting more backing on the spool, since as a result of line drag, it will exceed its own breaking strain and then break. For most other purposes (other than tigerfish, Nile perch and catfish), 50 metres is sufficient backing.

Cut-down shooting heads

You will recall that we discussed the balancing of rod and line, and that the correct weight of fly line for a rod is contained in the first 30 feet of the correct matching line. If you take the next size of line up the scale (i.e. an AFTM 10 instead of an AFTM 9) and cut off a further 6 feet (1,8 metres) of this line at the reel end, the remaining 24 feet will weigh the same as the line one size lighter. In other words, the AFTM 10 cut to 24 feet (7,38 metres) concentrates the same weight as the 30 foot AFTM 9 into a shorter length of fly line – all very logical. Such a shorter line should be more efficient in the air than a longer line of the same weight. This is in fact true, but it affects casting style by making the timing of the cast much more critical. The elements of the cast become much faster and each action takes less time. This makes cut-down shooting heads popular with skilful casters.

It is not worth cutting another 6 feet off an even higher weight line size though, because at 12 feet shorter (i.e. 18 feet) it becomes quite unmanageable.

Fig. 4.8: Tilting the casting 'ceiling' for different wind conditions.

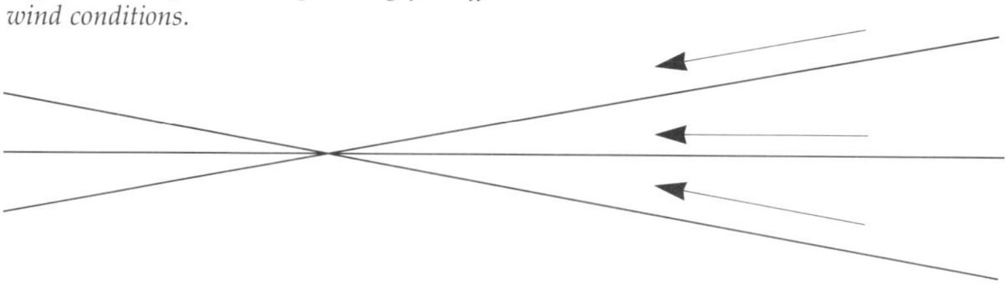

INTO THE WIND:
TILT CASTING 'CEILING'
DOWN-HILL (AIM AT IMAGI-
NARY TARGET)

NORMAL: FLAT CASTING
'CEILING'

WIND BEHIND: TILT CASTING
'CEILING' UP-HILL

The shooting head in practice
Distance from shooting head to rod tip during the cast
Normal shooting heads are quite easy to handle, and the double haul caster will find no problem with them. When you are casting, the shooting head should be out of the rings, and all of it should be in the air during the cast. The correct distance of the 'shooting head to shooting line join' from the tip ring during the cast is between one third and a full metre.

Shooting head reels
The ideal reels for freshwater shooting head casting are large diameter types such as the lightweight magnesium Ryobi 455 mg. The large diameter spool goes a long way towards reducing line coiling in the shooting line, a major problem for the shooting head caster. I make an arbour for the spool from the computer packing foam that looks like a hard pink sponge, and having fitted this, I wrap the foam twice with a covering of masking tape to prevent line cut-in. The backing, shooting line and shooting head then go on and they fill the spool to within 3 mm of the edge.

Saltwater fly reels, because of their inbuilt capacity for long braided line backing, are usually of the correct diameter for shooting head rigs, and do not require a spool arbour.

Handling shooting line
Shooting line in oval monofilament can be quite slippery when you first try to cast with it. Don't despair, the knack of holding and controlling it during the cast will come eventually. Line slippage can result in cuts to the index finger, usually right on the crease at the joint. PVC insulating tape is a fine material for protecting this finger joint without affecting mobility. It is a

good idea to wrap the tape onto the finger before commencing fishing.

When fishing, pull off the shooting head and shooting line ready for casting, and then pull off an additional two metres of shooting line from the reel to allow for the casting movement. This extra two metres will prevent you from pulling coils of line from under the piles of shooting line during the casting movement and causing unwanted tangles.

Mixing fly lines
Fly line should never be put down on top of shooting line, and shooting line should never be placed over braided backing. It is amazing how these lines manage to stick to one another during the high speed movement of the line, causing awful knotting.

Stretching fly lines
It is advisable to stretch shooting line before fishing. This action destroys the coil memory and returns the line to its normal fairly uncoiled state. In the field, an easy method is to loop the shooting line over a fence post and then walk backwards for about 20 metres dragging the line with you. Once there, pull the line repeatedly with both hands at once.

Line rafts and line baskets are good repositories for loose shooting and other line whilst fishing. These devices are covered in detail in Chapter 5.

CASTING IN THE WIND
Following winds
When you are learning to cast, there is no doubt that a wind from behind is the easiest to handle; and when you are casting in earnest, a following wind picks up the line and allows better distance to be achieved than on a windless day.

74

With proper technique, you can back cast easily into the strongest wind and take great advantage of very windy days.

Opportunities occur as wind-blown insects land 40 metres from the shore and great trout or yellowfish cruise the ripple line sucking down these food morsels. The double haul caster can reach these fishes and enjoy wonderful sport when others draw blanks. To get the best from this following wind situation, just tilt your casting ceiling upwards and aim the cast uphill (aim at an imaginary target). On really windy days with an AFTM 8 or 9 outfit, casts of 55 or 60 metres are achievable.

Facing winds

When the wind blows towards you it should present no problems. The wind blows food forms across the water and accumulates these foods in corners and along banksides. The average angler cannot cast into a strong wind, and is thus unable to reap any benefit from these feeding areas. The double haul caster, however, is just as much at home into the wind as anywhere else. Many excellent fishing days are to be had casting into a gale force or lesser wind.

When casting into a wind the caster has to pick a target spot (say 25 metres out) and cast 'downhill' to it. He does this by tilting his casting ceiling downwards, and aiming at an imaginary target. He loses out on the distance achieved, but he can still cast well enough to pick up shore-cruising fish.

Side winds

Side winds coming from the non-casting arm side are almost as good for distance as a following wind. Flatten the cast ceiling a little below the uphill slope adopted for following wind conditions. Side winds are great wind conditions to fish a sink-tip line and allow the wind to drift a nymph or buzzer imitation across the water in front of you.

Side winds onto the casting arm can be a problem, especially in a strong wind. The angler needs to be careful in these conditions, since this kind of wind is the one most likely to ensure a good hook-up in yourself. A blustery day is particularly dangerous in this respect. Needless to say, barbless hooks and sunglasses are recommended if you find yourself fishing in these conditions.

There are two ways of handling 'onto the casting shoulder' wind conditions. The first is to angle the rod over your shoulder so that the line is moving on the downwind side of your body. Some find this difficult to accomplish, but for them there is yet another way. Turn your back to the wind and cast in reverse. Yes, really – we call it reverse casting! With your back to the wind, cast as usual, aiming the forward cast over the land behind you, but release the back cast to fly out over the water instead of the forward cast. You will find, with only a little practice, that you can still achieve reasonable distance in this way.

There is yet another solution and that is to learn to cast with both hands. It is a bit of a chore, but eventually the right side teaches the left (or vice versa) what to do.

Wind and the shooting head

Very windy conditions can be a menace to the shooting head caster as his shooting line drifts about and gets caught in everything. These are, without doubt, conditions in which the full fly line is preferable. The shooting head caster can overcome such conditions to some extent in dry weather, by kneeling on the bank and piling the shooting line in front of himself, using his body as a wind shield. It is actually quite easy to double haul cast in the kneeling position, and even sitting if need be.

Line baskets are another answer, but I mistrust these in windy conditions. It is all too easy for the wind to turn the whole lot of line coils right over with disastrous consequences. In a boat, a bucket with a centimetre of water in the bottom is an ideal receptacle for the line coils, and works well in the strongest wind.

CHAPTER 5

FLY-FISHING RETRIEVES

(Overheard):

'An honest fisherman is a pretty uninteresting person.'

THE ANIMATION OF FLIES

The 'retrieve' is thought by many top anglers to be the most important component of successful fly-fishing. What they are really saying is that the imitation of the natural movement of the fish's prey, which is brought about by the 'retrieve', is more important than the imitation of the prey itself.

This viewpoint was epitomised in the works (*c*.1938) of the South African writer Kingfisher, who set out to prove that the retrieve was the 'be all and end all' of fly-fishing. In his own words, '... I felt confident that if my selected fly had been a Durham Ranger, Butcher, Baker, Candlestick-maker, or any other it would have made so little difference that I decided, as an experiment, to change my fly to something else. I glanced through a number of catalogues in trying to decide which to choose, but eventually decided to add another to the already long

Concentrating on the curve of the line from rod tip to point of entry into the water is the best way to see delicate bites. (Photo: Ron Clay)

list of flies, by having an entirely new one tied. My object was to make it as unlike the Invicta in colour as I could, and selected the very vivid colouring of a South African bird (not fly) known as the Mountain Swallow (Bee Eater).' This Mountain Swallow, as the fly was known, was designed in the traditional 'winged wet fly' style, and was tied on a no 10 down eye hook. It had both tail and throat of mixed blue and orange hackle fibres, the body was gold ribbed orange wool, and the wing was built with married blue and orange mallard slips. Having designed his awful fly, he then proceeded to fish with only this fly for the next few seasons. Kingfisher kept meticulous records, and he was able to show that he caught just as many fishes with his (he thought) outlandish fly, as he did with his old favourite flies, which were the Invicta and the Lemon Grey.

Time passed, and lo and behold the angling fraternity discovered that the Mountain Swallow was a fantastic fly ... it became a best seller in the 1940s and 1950s! At the same time, it also destroyed Kingfisher's hard proven theory. The real question is – was it the fly that was so good, or was it the retrieves (at which Kingfisher was a master)? No one has ever proven it one way or the other, and the truth is that proper imitation of the food form and proper imitation of the food form's movement are *both* of paramount importance. Get the fly right and you are in with a good chance. Get the retrieve right as well, and you are in with the best chance possible!

Retrieves are methods of pulling in the line in such a way that the fly behaves like the insect or other creature that it seeks to imitate. Most natural food form movements can be copied by just a few standard retrieves, which in turn can be slightly modified by the angler to get the required result. Throughout Chapter 13 on the top African flies, a retrieve is given for each pattern (with the exception of most dry flies, which are floated rather than retrieved). Chapter 11 on entomology also refers extensively to retrieves ... the art of retrieving a fly properly is a very essential skill indeed!

The basic ten retrieves for all African conditions are:

❏ Strip retrieve
❏ Troll retrieve
❏ Slow strip retrieve
❏ Sink and draw
❏ Float and draw
❏ Sunken line retrieve for buoyant flies
❏ Figure-of-eight retrieve
❏ Accelerating slow pull retrieve
❏ Wind drifting
❏ Static (i.e. no retrieve required).

Trapping the line against the rod. The line needs to be trapped between pulls. It must be done positively so that a taking fish doesn't end up with free line or the angler with a 'line-cut' in his finger. (Photo: Ron Clay)

Trapping the line

Most strip retrieves require that the line is trapped between pulls. That is, as each pull (or strip as they are also known) is completed, the line needs to be trapped firmly (while the hand goes forward to grab the line again, ready for the commencement of the next pull). Trapping must be done correctly: if the line slips through your fingers when you need to strike, you can come quite unstuck. Either the strike is unsuccessful and the fish gets off during the fight (or worse, never gets hooked); or the backing may slip through or over your fingers and cut you! The cut could be quite severe if the fish is very fast like a kingfish. It is quite impossible to put in a solid strike if the line is loose!

The most usual way to trap the line between each pull is to lock it against the rod handle with two fingers of the rod hand. The finger pressure is released enough between hand pulls to allow the line to run under the fingers as the hand pull takes place. This gives good control of the line at all times because (a) the fingers are

always in place and (b) they are always ready to lock the line.

Fast strip retrieve

This is the favourite retrieve of the lure fly-fisherman, and is the easiest basis from which to work out fish-imitating retrieves. You strip the line in with the line hand, trap it under the rod hand fingers, release the line (in the line hand) *while still trapped*, and then move the line hand forward to grab the line for the next strip. The process is repeated until all the line is retrieved. Strikes can come at any time.

Variations in the length of strip enable one to copy the movements of small fry. The usual retrieve for small fry might be five or six long (30 cm), fairly fast strips, followed by say ten or twelve short strips of 10 cm. Occasionally, one should pause for a few seconds and then start stripping in again.

Most saltwater fly-fishermen don't bother to vary the retrieve when fishing fry imitations, and simply strip the line in at a fast and continuous rate. Their results would improve with a little thought – saltwater fry swim in long dashes and then pause before dashing again. Four or five long (one metre or so) strips, followed by a three or four second pause, is a very effective way of copying this movement.

Similarly, the fly-fisherman fishing really deep with a lead core line and a big fly (maybe for brown trout), will also keep up a continuous-rate retrieve without variation. The length of strips for this style of fishing are usually around a metre, but they would be slower than those used by the saltwater fly-fisherman. This fly-fisherman would also improve results with an occasional pause.

Some of the rationale behind the constant rate strip retrieves is to keep the fly clear of underwater snags. However, by using lead-backed, upside-down flies, one can largely avoid this problem. A great many anglers believe that when using an aggression-generating fly such as a Micky Finn, then the constant rate, high-speed, long-pull strip retrieve is the best. Personally, I like to vary even the deepest of strip retrieves, and I certainly put variation into my saltwater retrieves. The last few pulls as the fly nears the shore are often more effective if a little extra speed is added, thus often tempting a following fish to strike.

Remember that a continuous-rate smooth-swimming fly does not result from these strip retrieves. In fact, it achieves a series of dashes. Smooth retrieves can only be achieved by the so-called 'troll' retrieve techniques; and, in a different and much slower way, by the 'figure-of-eight' retrieve.

Troll retrieve

It's happened to most of us: the last cast of the day ... just as you wind in the line, so a trout takes the fly in the most positive way. Suddenly, you wonder: perhaps I should have wound in each cast – maybe I would have caught lots more fish? We all know how effective trolling a fly behind a boat can be. And then there are the times when you are wading back out of the water, steadily going for the shore, and a trout takes the trailing fly! All of these movements

have one thing in common: the fly is moving at a steady rate – not jerky, no dashes and pauses, but at a steady rate!

Some great anglers, including Dick Walker in the UK, have ruminated on this phenomenon. In South Africa, Louis van der Westhuizen examined it, and eventually came up with a bankside retrieve which does a fair job of achieving this smooth swimming motion. We shall explore this later.

The phenomenon of predatory fish strike response to certain movements of prey has been examined in laboratory experiments. What was found was that a smooth horizontal movement certainly excites trout a lot more than a discontinuous movement. However, the best kind of movement to elicit a strike response was a smooth horizontal movement with an undulatory motion. A fly moving smoothly and in one direction, but gently undulating up and down as it goes, is very attractive to all fishes. It is this movement that Louis van der Westhuizen's troll retrieve simulates so well.

Louis van der Westhuizen's troll retrieve

In Louis's troll retrieve, the effect is achieved by thrusting the rod forward as the line is stripped in. Then, as the line is trapped against the handle and the line hand goes forward to grab line for the next strip, the rod (and of course the trapped line with it) is pulled back toward the fisherman. The whole process is then repeated. This achieves a constant pull on the line which with practice can become quite a smooth flowing action.

The undulatory effect is achieved not by the retrieve so much as by the design of the fly, which is weighted forward (i.e. behind the eye of the hook) so as to cause this movement. Strip retrieves of this kind are fast retrieves, but the same effect can be achieved slowly by using similarly up-front weighted nymphs and a 'sink and draw' retrieve. In nature these undulatory smooth movements are common: buzzer pupae do it, fishes do it, leeches do it, and so on.

Hand-over-hand troll retrieve

In saltwater fly-fishing, tiger fly-fishing, and occasionally in trout fishing, a very fast yet

The continuous troll retrieve. Louis van der Westhuizen with rod arm in the forward position of the 'troll slip retrieve'. Louis is fishing a dam in the Kamberg district of South Africa. (Photo: Malcolm Meintjes)

smooth troll retrieve is sometimes needed. Just a few years ago, the method given below was frowned upon, but is now highly acceptable, and nobody thinks any the worse of it. All you do is to place your rod under your arm, and then pull in the line with both hands – hand-over-hand. The result is an ultra-smooth, fast-as-you-like retrieve. Believe me it works extremely well! Once again the use of up-front weighted flies gives it added spice.

Many anglers think that the strike is impossible with this method, but in fact it is not. You swivel the waist to strike, at the same time hauling on the retrieve hand. The rod is then passed to the rod hand ready for the fight. This can even be accomplished without a great deal of trouble with very fast fishes such as kingfish.

What is important is that the rod is clamped under the elbow of the 'rod' hand, not the other hand! This hand should always be your best hand. If you are right-handed, then the right hand should always be in control of the rod – it follows then that your reel should be set up for left-hand wind! This is very important with gamefish, as there is no time for 'fishing rod boogie' in the middle of a fight with a fish with

the wind in its tail – you are just going to get broken if you fish like that.

We have now discussed the basic fast retrieve methods, all of which you can vary as you wish to achieve the result you require. However, in fly-fishing, and in particular in trout fishing, the slow retrieves are just as important – in fact, more so. There will also be many occasions when you will wish to mix retrieves. Simulating dragonfly nymph movement is the best example of this. These nymphs crawl along very slowly (usually emulated by a figure-of-eight retrieve), but they also use rectal propulsion to dash forward from time to time. This latter movement is usually accomplished by a shortish strip retrieve which is introduced every half minute or so into the slow retrieve.

Slow strip retrieves

Most of nature's water creatures, excepting the fishes, move very slowly. Even the fishes spend long periods hanging suspended in the water. Try watching some nymphs or other insects in very clear water, and you will see that it takes several seconds for them to cover even a few centimetres.

79

I remember an early 1960s fishing seminar at Grafham Water in the UK, where I was stunned to be told that the retrieve over 30 metres with a Black and Peacock Spider fly should take all of 10 minutes ... and then stunned again to be told after the session by Steve Stephens that the instructor was wrong – it should take 25 minutes. After all, it is simulating a snail! That indicates how very slow good insect-imitating retrieves should be: 10 minutes for a nymph over 25 metres is probably fast. Such super-slow retrieves are best covered by the figure-of-eight method, but the slow strip retrieve can achieve a great deal for the imitation of somewhat faster creatures such as damselfly nymphs.

Flies such as the Walker's Killer are well fished with slow strip retrieves, and I do mean slow. The retrieve is the same as the fast strip retrieve – you trap line in the same way, but each pull (the strip) is very slow, and generally no more than 25 cm long.

Sink and draw retrieve

I have a special memory, as a teenager in the 1950s, of sitting in a boat on a large still-water fishing the evening rise. We were fishing deep with the Mallard and Claret fly, hoping to pick up a nice brown trout (there were no rainbows in that water). Just about 40 metres away was another boat occupied by two rather elderly men, one of them red-faced and coughing a lot as he puffed on a continuous supply of cigarettes. Buzzers had begun to emerge and they were spiralling upward, caught in the soft rays of the setting sun and appearing to mingle with the smoke above these old fly-fishermen. But what was really amazing is that these fishermen were catching trout after trout, and yet we were fishless. We tried everything to no avail, and as the sun set and darkness descended, we tied our boat up at the jetty and approached these master anglers, intent on learning something from them. They were very helpful, and told us that they were fishing weighted corixid imitations and retrieving 'sink and draw' to copy the corixid movements. It was the first time I had ever heard of this retrieve, but I never forgot it, and I have caught plenty of fishes with it in subsequent years.

Plastazote Corixa. Because it floats, this fly is drawn down in the retrieve, and then allowed to float upward. (Photo: Niel Hodges)

The sink and draw retrieve is very useful for imitating anything that goes up and down in the water (such as corixids, mayfly nymphs, etc.) It is usually used in conjunction with a weighted nymph or fly and a floating line. It is exactly what it sounds like – you allow the fly to sink, and then draw it back up again with a slow steady pull prior to the next sink, and so on. There is lots of room for variation: you could let it sink for quite a long time and perhaps use several slow strips to pull it back near the surface before repeating the operation. Over sunken weed beds, as occurs often after an African deluge, you may allow only a short sink time with a consequent short 'draw'. Most takes come on the draw, but be ready for a take at any time.

Float and draw retrieve

This is a much more modern retrieve than sink and draw, and one which has really only come into its own with the advent of buoyant flies. This retrieve method is used with super-fast sink lines and buoyant flies such as the Plastazote Corixa.

The leader needs to be about a foot shorter than the depth of water that you are fishing. After casting, the fly line sinks to the bottom, and the fly floats a leader length above it. Pull the line and the fly dives down. Stop pulling, and the fly floats back up. This produces a more realistic retrieve than the 'sink and draw'. Most takes come as the fly is floating back up. This is a very useful retrieve method around weed and reed beds.

Booby, Rasputin and other buoyant fly retrieves

These retrieves, designed for fishing lake beds, are especially for use with buoyant flies which are fished right on the bottom with super-fast sink fly lines. The fly is fished on a very short leader, between 25 and 60 cm. There are, however, occasions when a longer leader might be useful (especially if you know what depth the fishes are at).

Fishing with the short leader and large (size 8 or 10) Boobys, the aim is to simulate the movement of the larger food forms such as dragonfly nymphs and small fishes. The retrieve consists of slowish long pulls, with a 10–15 second pause between pulls, which allows the fly to float up prior to commencing the next pull. You can vary the action by putting in two or even three pulls from time to time. In this way, the fly undulates enticingly along the bottom. This is a very effective method!

Most takes come as the fly is floating up, and they are often very fierce takes. Occasionally, a fish will take the fly with two soft taps (especially when using the figure-of-eight retrieve). You need to concentrate to detect this bite form, and must strike on the second tap as quickly as possible.

With smaller Booby nymphs, such as the Gold-ribbed Hare's Ear, the usual retrieve is a figure-of-eight type.

Figure-of-eight retrieve

This is a very important retrieve in the fly-fisherman's bag of skills: it is a 'must be learnt' technique if you are to be successful at nymphing. Probably more trout are taken with this retrieve world-wide than with any other.

The figure-of-eight retrieve enables the fly-fisherman to bring back the fly smoothly, and as slowly as he likes. It is used in both still and flowing water, with the slight difference that the stream fisher keeps all the retrieved line in his hand (this is known as 'figure-of-eight bunching'), whereas the still-water fly-fisherman usually drops the line coils.

Since the coiled line is always in the stream angler's hand, it is not necessary to trap the line in the usual way. However, some anglers still like to guide it through fingers loosely held against the rod handle.

Figure 5.1 illustrates the figure-of-eight retrieve. This retrieve can be done very slowly indeed, and a quarter of an hour for a single cast retrieve is quite easy to achieve. It can also be performed very quickly to give a smooth but slowish lure fly retrieve. The retrieve can also be varied by doing perhaps a few slow loops, and then a couple of fast ones.

Accelerating slow retrieve

This a hybrid retrieve which on occasion can be very deadly. I like to use it with a Porringe fly around weed beds or other structures, particularly when fishing a new water for the first time. The fly moves intermittently, first enticingly slowly, and then accelerating as if trying

(a) Take the line between thumb and first finger.

(b) Close the hand over the line. Thumb and forefinger now release their grip and move to grasp the line again at X.

(c) Lift the thumb and forefinger to draw in the line.

(d) Gather this line into the hand with the second to fourth fingers. Repeat the whole procedure.

(e) The figure-of-eight formed by the gathered line.

Fig. 5.1: The figure-of-eight retrieve.

81

to escape! The acceleration in this retrieve is thought to provide the necessary spark to get an interested but non-taking trout to strike.

Essentially, it is a slow strip with an acceleration at the end of the strip. When applied to dry fly-fishing – as, for example, when retrieving a termite imitation – it is commonly referred to as a 'twitch' retrieve.

This slow accelerating retrieve is achieved by applying the first part of the figure-of-eight retrieve (i.e. the taking of the loop) into the end of the slow strip (while the strip is still taking place), thus suddenly more than doubling the fly speed. The loop is dropped at the end of each strip.

Wind drifting

Not so much a retrieve as a method, this is a deadly way of taking fishes in still water in cross-wind conditions.

Wind drifting requires a sink-tip fly line and a long (5–8 metre) leader. The fly, usually a buzzer, is cast out and allowed to drift around with the wind. The length of the leader and wind speed need to be matched to avoid catching the bottom. Takes are usually very positive. This is a great method on bright days with a ripple on the water when not much else works.

Static fly

As the heading suggests, this is not a retrieve in the sense that anything moves a great deal – a suitable fly is cast with a sinking line and just left to lie.

Static fly-fishing is a method that carries a fair risk in Africa, in that any crab coming across your stationary fly line will almost certainly cut it. A lot of fly-fishermen in Africa handle this by using cheap trolling lead core line, which costs only cents if it is lost, something that could be a disaster with an expensive quality fly line.

I originally took to this method after seeing it used on a really stormy day with the wind pumping strongly. We fished the downwind side of the water, anchored over five metres of water, perhaps 40 metres from the dam wall, riding the waves. The flies were Viva Tadpole Lures which were cast out on Hi-D lines, and allowed to move about in the strong undercur-

rent. The crabs were not a problem in this undertow. Takes were frequent and hard, and some fine rainbows came to the net. I have used this method several times since and it has always been a winner. It is especially good on windy days on large waters.

The crab problems arise in still water when the line is cast out, allowed to sink, and just left there. One can avoid the attention of crabs to some extent by limiting the time the line is allowed to lie. Certainly ten minutes is the limit and five minutes is much safer. Static fly is a great way of fishing the Red Booby, which the trout take avidly for a bunch of bloodworms. In Africa, any Booby, and also the Suspender Buzzer, works well if fished statically.

ROD POSITIONS DURING RETRIEVES

In the books, one always reads about keeping the rod at right angles to the line to absorb the shock of a taking fish. Good advice, but often unnecessary. Many fly lines can stretch in excess of 30 per cent of their length and that kind of stretch is quite able to absorb the shock of a taking fish. Such absorption also unfortunately removes a lot of the angler's sensitivity to feeling soft takes and plucks. Couple this to more shock absorption in the rod and you may well miss many bites – you just won't feel them.

With surface takes on floating lines there is usually visual indication of a take, and the angler strikes well in time in order not to get broken off. Keeping the rod at right angles is once again not necessary.

When fishing sinking lines there is no doubt in my mind that the rod should point down the line to increase bite sensitivity. The use of Kevlar cored lines increases this sensitivity even more (they are non-stretch). Even with such non-stretch lines, there is always a bow in the recovering line and some elasticity in the leader to absorb shock.

However, I do believe that when using the hand-over-hand troll retrieve for tigerfish or saltwater gamefish, one should definitely tuck the rod under the arm so that it points upward. The shock absorption can really make a difference here, because of the inevitable delays in the strike method. In any event, in this troll

Charlotte du Toit fishing a floating line. In this situation, using a floating line on a flat calm, no line raft is necessary since the line is well controlled. (Photo: Louis van der Westhuizen)

retrieve method, the hands are in constant touch with the line, so most takes (which are nearly always fierce in this method) are felt well in time and easily sensed by the hands.

In the 'over the front' loch style (see Figure 6.2) used on large dams when drifting in a boat, one should always keep the rod up, but for a different reason. In fact, the rationale here probably applies to many dry fly situations as well. The rod, by being held up, puts a bow into the line, and this bow has to be taken out in the strike. It works just fine because taking out the bow gives just the right amount of time for the fish to turn down before the hook goes home. Too quick a strike usually results in a miss, but the upright rod ensures that this does not happen.

THE END OF THE RETRIEVE

Very often a trout will follow the retrieved fly right to the point where the fly is lifted out of the water. Slowing the fly so that it is easier to take does not usually help at all. The trout usually turns off and disappears. However, if you accelerate the fly over the last metre or two of the retrieve, the trout will often take it.

It is a very common occurrence that trout follow a fly right to the last pull, yet do not take the fly. In very clear water, you can even see the odd trout frantically searching for the missing prey, quite oblivious of the watching angler. In such a situation, the trout will often take the fly if it is simply dropped back in the water and allowed to sink.

LINE RAFTS AND BASKETS

Some people regard line rafts or baskets as essential aids to fly-fishing. However, I am of the opinion that anything that is not necessary at the time, should not be used. Consequently, I only use a line raft or line basket when it is a 'must'. By definition, rafts and baskets are different things. The 'line raft' is a device which floats on the water in front of the angler, and acts as depository for loose line (such as the shooting line used for a shooting head). The 'line basket' is usually clipped around the waist, and the angler retrieves his line into it. Many of these basket devices may be better described as line pouches.

Line raft

The function of the line raft is to stop line from sinking through the water and getting caught on rocks or weeds, or other snags. It became

83

P J Jacobs double-haul casting into the Bazaruto surf in Mozambique, after kingfish. Note the essential line basket strapped to the waist.

popular in the UK with wading reservoir fly-fishermen. These anglers are relatively stationary, very often casting continually whilst waiting for a shoal of rainbow trout to come past. The raft floats on the water in front of the angler. It is held in place by clipping it to the belt, or to a stick thrust into the reservoir bottom, or by clipping it to a 'wader's landing net' which is thrust into the mud.

The line raft is not popular in Africa. I believe this is mainly because the African fly-fisherman is very much on the move, continually trying different spots and purposefully seeking out his quarry. As such, the line raft becomes an encumbrance. Nevertheless, on a water like Sterkfontein Dam in South Africa's Free State, the line raft can be useful when wading and fishing over weed beds along the shoreline. A fly-fisherman pursuing this method usually makes a couple of casts and then sidesteps two or three steps. The raft can be dragged along slowly and used all the time, and the angler covers kilometres of bank during a full day. In this situation the line raft is certainly justified. There are many bass dams where this style of fly-fishing is very productive.

A simple but effective line raft can be made

from a sheet of bubble pack approximately two-thirds of a metre square. Tie one corner with a 25 cm length of nylon cord to a metre-long piece of dowelling, and it's complete. The bubble pack faithfully follows the up-and-downing of the waves and ripple, and very seldom turns over with consequent dumping of the line. Twenty years ago, they used to make line rafts from bicycle inner tubes with netting spread across them.

Line baskets

These are much more popular devices, and most fly-fishermen own one. Basically, it is a pouch which clips around the waist. The saltwater anglers use a larger basket (something like a supermarket basket is fine), which is in constant use. In freshwater the line basket is useful when wading or fishing rivers, and when working overgrown bankside around dams.

Freshwater pouches

The most likely problem with line pouches (line baskets) occurs when walking from spot to spot. One must always be careful to ensure that the line coils do not turn over. If they do, and you try to cast, you can be sure of a major tangle – this is especially problematic with shooting line. If you have a long walk, it is much better to wind the line back onto the reel.

There are several models of clip-on freshwater line baskets. The ones with a flat bottom are best. The type that traps coils of line in a corner of the pouch should be avoided.

Saltwater baskets

Every saltwater and estuarine fly-fisherman must have a line basket. Rocks will cut your fly line or shooting line very easily; sand will abrade it, and if it gets caught in the rush of the tide it can be very inconvenient trying to recover it. The takes you get in the salt are often very fast, and properly controlled line pouring out of the line basket is the only safe way to handle things in the first rush of a big gamefish. Most anglers fly-fishing the salt use a shooting head of some sort, and believe me, the sea has its own infinitely variable ways of messing up a shooting line which is not properly controlled!

It is very useful to install plastic spikes of some sort in the bottom of a saltwater fly-fishing line basket. These will cut down the horror of the unexpected wave which always comes along and turns over your line. Saltwater fly-fishing demands long casting and consequent high line speed. The smallest thing can cause a tangle! The most useful type of basket is a supermarket shopping basket, held around the waist with a rubber bungie such as can be acquired at most hardware stores.

Rules for baskets and rafts

A few simple rules can help a lot. Firstly, never lay fly line on top of shooting line – the two types of line stick together sufficiently well to pick up coils in the cast and cause tangles. Always pull off an extra metre of line at the reel and allow this to lie loose out of the raft or basket – this gives slack for the action of casting which might easily turn the line coils over otherwise. Never grease a shooting line or a shooting head! The grease will get everywhere, coils will stick, and the end result is frightening in its line knotting efficiency. Always stretch shooting line before commencing casting. If fishing the salt, give it a stretch every hour or so.

CHAPTER 6

TACTICS AND STRATEGIES – STILL WATER

When the wind is in the East,
'Tis neither good for man nor beast;
When the wind is in the North,
The skillful fisher goes not forth;
When the wind is in the South,
It blows the bait in the fishes' mouth;
When the wind is in the West,
Then 'tis at the very best.

J O Halliwel, *Popular Rhymes*, 1849

The information in this chapter is orientated primarily around trout. See Chapter 8 for more complete coverage of the other freshwater gamefish species, and Chapters 11 and 12 for descriptions of the food forms whose appearance and movements you will need to imitate.

Still-water tactics can be approached most easily if we examine three possible water depth environments:

❏ surface
❏ shallow and medium depths
❏ deep water.

Most still-water fly-fishing for African trout takes place in shallow and medium-depth waters. Many anglers avoid deep-water fly-fishing, thinking it far too difficult. It is in fact not difficult, but it does require a different approach, together with different flies and tackle. Similarly, very few still-water fly-fishermen deliberately fish the surface. The thought of dry fly-fishing puts them off, for some reason. In fact, still-water surface fly-fishing is probably the easiest kind of all.

For overseas visitors reading this book, perhaps a digression on terminology will be worth while. The people of Africa very often refer to still-water impoundments, even the largest, as 'dams'. In Europe, and in the USA, a 'dam' is only the wall (concrete, earth, or otherwise), that keeps the water contained, and the water itself is referred to as a lake, impoundment, reservoir or water, e.g. Grafham Water).

SURFACE TACTICS
Dry fly
Traditionally, trout are thought of as 'rising to the dry fly' as part and parcel of the mystique of fly-fishing. Trout are usually linked to running water in this picture, but in fact, still-water trout are often just as keen on the floating fly as are their river brethren. Still-water dry fly-fishing is a largely neglected form of fly-fishing – perhaps because to the man in the street it is the one aspect of fly-fishing that pertains to the old elitist school. Another possible reason for its neglect is that almost nothing is known about it. Only a very few books have ever been written on the subject of still-water dry fly-fishing, and none specifically for Africa. There is no doubt in my mind that it could easily be developed into a specialised form of fly-fishing. As such, it is rather surprising that so few fly-fishermen

work at it. Ron Clay is an avid and successful still-water dry fly angler who has landed many superb fishes with this method, but I have met few others.

Surface fly-fishing is a strategy which should not be overlooked – it can be exceedingly productive at times (sometimes better than any other method). Still-water dry fly-fishing is usually orientated around imitation of surface food forms, or it can be handled with a broad spectrum approach (unkindly referred to as 'hit and miss'), such as casting out a Duckworth's Dargle Delight (DDD) on a blind basis, and just waiting for a fish to come along and take it.

The 'hit and miss' approach can be very productive on small managed waters, but it tends to be less efficient on waters where trout can roam over vast distances. Roaming shoals of rainbows are likely to be preoccupied with a specific food form, and may not respond to any fly other than a close imitation.

Tackle for still-water dry fly

Preferred outfit for dry fly-fishing on still waters is an AFTM 6 or 7 rod with a fast tip action. My preferred length for this rod is 9 feet 6 inches. Dry fly-fishing requires great accuracy in casting, since the fly is often needed to land within a few centimetres of the fish. Twist-resistant rods such as Bruce and Walker's or Daiwa's hexagraphics are ideal. However, a good graphite rod will also do the job. For 'dapping' flies and for fishing 'over the front' from a boat, a longer AFTM 6 rod of 11 feet is more useful.

Still-water surface fishing, because of inevitable line drift and the often present need to mend lines (see Mending line, Chapter 7) in order to stay constantly in touch with the fly, demands efficient methods of fast retrieve. Multiplying fly reels, where the spool turns more than once for each turn of the handle, are the answer for this. Such reels must still pass the tests detailed in Chapter 2. The fast retrieve gearing of the spool should be carefully examined: if it looks at all weak don't purchase it!

Lines must be good for dry fly-fishing. Any line which coils on the water and refuses to straighten is a complete waste of money. Hardy makes lines with a matt finish which is ideal for

floating lines. Another excellent line which straightens well is Scientific Angler's Aircell Supreme in mahogany colour. They also last for many years if looked after. The thinnest smear of 'silicone-free' grease is recommended for lubricating the floating leader (try 'Permagrease'). After every trip, it is advisable to clean floating lines with a commercial line cleaner. Double taper lines give a better presentation of the fly, which is particularly important for dry fly-fishing.

Leaders for still-water dry fly-fishing need to be longer than the usual three metre wet fly leaders. Leader/tippet lengths of 4–5 metres are recommended for the dry fly on still waters. The extra length is best obtained by including a length of 10 kg breaking strain monofilament between the butt loop at the end of the fly line and the thick end of the tapered leader itself. Because line grease builds up into lumps on leader knots, knotless tapered leaders are preferred. Matt finish leaders and tippets are important in dry fly-fishing.

Dapping is a method which is popular on the lakes of Ireland, but has a very few followers in Africa. You use a long rod and a delicate floss dapping line with a big bushy (buzzy) fly at the end of the line. A stiff breeze to take the line out is the other necessity. The breeze lifts the floss, and by lowering the rod one is able to keep the fly dapping (bobbing on and off the surface of the water). Dapping is obviously best done from a boat, and has been tried with success on several of the larger African waters. Trout love this method, probably because the fly looks like a real one taking off and falling to the surface continuously.

Travel light when dry fly-fishing. Many fishes are spotted with a stealthy quiet approach, and many, having given their position away with a rise, need to be approached very carefully. You cannot be stealthy when encumbered by tons of tackle.

Terrestrials and mass hatches

Often in summer in the late afternoon, just before a storm or heavy rainfall, huge quantities of winged ants or termites leave their nests for their mating flight. If an off-shore breeze is blowing, many of these terrestrial insects will be blown onto the water. A fall of terrestrials (such as ants and termites) on any African trout water will result in the trout rising to them. Bass, kurper and yellowfish will also rise in this situation. At this time, as the trout become totally preoccupied with ants or termites, no wet fly ever invented is likely to interest them. The fly-fisherman is forced to resort to imitative dry fly-fishing ... the prey is on the surface and his dry fly must be there as well!

The 'ant fall' is a dry fly situation that most still-water fly-fishermen have experienced. This is the easiest situation to handle. All you need is a floating fly line, an appropriate imitation, and a properly set-up leader and tippet. The finer the tippet the better, and something like a 5X leader and a 1 kg tippet is not out of place if you are an experienced angler. If this is an inexperienced venture into dry fly-fishing, use a tippet of 1,5 to 2,5 kg. The leader should be greased for floating – or, if you prefer, use a floating braided leader. The tippet can also be greased, but the last 10 cm of tippet must never be greased. Greased line causes severe surface interference. If this distortion of the surface is right next to the fly, it will be spotted by the trout. Spray or dunk the fly in floatant and allow it to dry. Then cast out into the feeding area and wait for a take.

A similar situation arises with caenis mayflies (also called the angler's curse) which at times hatch in untold thousands, and litter the surface like small confetti. The fallen insects (or hatching caenis), get trapped in the surface film and vibrate their wings vigorously. It is difficult to imitate this movement, and the angler's only hope is a twitch retrieve with 20 second pauses after every twitch. The twitches are accomplished by short sharp accelerating pulls.

Fishing in the ant, termite, or caenis hatch situation is good for the first quarter of an hour or so, and then becomes very difficult. Each fish can literally cruise around with its mouth open, engulfing great numbers of insects. Consequently, the fish gets utterly preoccupied with the insect and the more he eats the more preoccupied he becomes, until nothing but a natural will interest him. In Africa there are many ant species, and imitations in differing sizes (from size 10 to 16) in black, red, or brown may all be required at some time. Termites, being much larger, need a size 8 imitation, usually in white or cream.

When to dry fly fish?

When the day is still and hot, and the surface of the trout dam is absolutely flat and glassy, I usually forget about dry flies. As dusk approaches, though, all manner of insects may hatch. My special joy is to find the big sedges hatching. However, the daylight and early hours of such days are often more profitably spent looking for bottom-feeding trout. The same applies on days immediately after a cold snap, or days even with a breeze when the air is very cold, and stays cold – the insects just don't appear and the trout do not rise.

Bright days with a soft warm breeze on the water setting up a ripple (even when very hot) can be rewarding with the dry fly. Very windy days in the warm months always produce some kind of surface activity, and even if trout are not seen to be rising, they will come and take the dry fly time and time again. Sometimes, on a very cold cloudy day, the sun comes out and warms the water, and then sedges or occasionally mayflies will hatch even in winter. Similarly, after several days of cold cloudy weather a sudden break in the cloud may bring on all kinds of hatches. In summer, flies will hatch on warm cloudy days with a breeze, and these can provide some of the best fishing.

On most days one will catch more fishes with submerged techniques than with dry fly – often a decision has to be made. Mostly the submerged techniques will win, but when trout are definitely orientated towards feeding on the top, then I follow suit.

Dry fly-fishing on a breezy day

Good fishing can be had on bright days with a surface breeze by fishing a non-imitative fly such as a Royal Coachman which is a general attractor pattern on the surface. Just cast out and wait for a trout to come along and take the fly. One can also use a broad spectrum imitative pattern which vaguely imitates many different insects. The best fly for this is undoubtedly the DDD (sizes 10 to 14). This fly is so buoyant that there is no need to grease the tippet at all. The Soldier Palmer Pink fly (size 8) works almost as well. You can improve your chances by fishing in bays where trout or yellowfish are seen to be working the surface. Casting to the edge of the ripple also works well. Other good places are weed beds (cast just to the side) and along the edge of reed beds. Often 'casting and waiting' with a DDD is efficient over quite deep clear water. I suspect this is because deep trout have a much bigger window than surface trout (see Chapter 3). Consequently, these trout are better able to see surface flies. They may take ten minutes or even a lot longer to come up and take the fly, but it is usually worth the wait.

If you are faced with a situation where many trout are rising around you, but are uninterested in either dry fly or sub-surface nymphs, two possibilities are high on the list. One, the trout are feeding on floating snails, and two, they are feeding on emerging insects, i.e. insects in the actual act of hatching. Fishing for these emerger-eating trout can be quite rewarding.

Wet fly-fishing in the surface and just sub-surface

A summer breeze has a predictable effect on fish behaviour, as shown in Figure 6.1. In response to the wind-induced current, fishes move upwind in shoals, both sub-surface and surface feeding. They then go down two or three metres and swim rapidly back downwind, not feeding, to repeat the cycle.

If you are fishing anchored or from the shore on the upwind side, then casting across the wind often brings the best results. However, if the breeze strengthens enough to churn up

muddy water on the downwind side, then the fishes will tend to stay there and feed on the wave-disturbed food forms. The best spots are where muddy and clear waters meet. Black or yellow flies are often best in these conditions.

If it has been blowing for several days and the abrupt muddy/clear water cline disappears, then the fishes will often be feeding close in to the shore under the muddy waves. A white fly is often best at this time for brown trout, a fluorescent yellow fly for rainbow trout and a black fly for smallmouth bass. If the wind changes, it may still take several days for the fishes to move off, no matter what the conditions become.

Wet fly-fishing in the surface is a major part of the fly fisher's armament, and fishing in the surface with nymphs and emerger patterns can be very productive. Just as with dry fly-fishing, this should be an imitative process: a little knowledge of the food forms and how to imitate them can make a big difference. For most of this in- and sub-surface fly-fishing you would use a floating line, an ungreased leader and wet flies (mostly unleaded nymphs and emerger patterns).

Emergers

When a fly is actually engaged in the process of hatching we refer to it as an 'emerger'. What happens is that the nymph or pupa rises to the surface and floats in the surface film. The shuck integument (the nymphal outer skin) splits, and the adult insect struggles free into the air. Trout are attracted by this struggling, and any insect that is slow to hatch is likely to become a meal. American literature refers to these transition (between dry and wet) flies as 'flymphs'.

An emerger pattern is fished right in the sur-

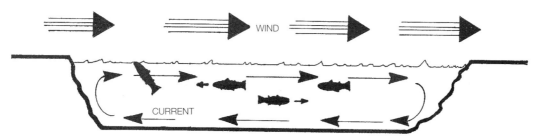

Fig. 6.1: *The effect of average breeze on still-water rainbow trout in summer.*

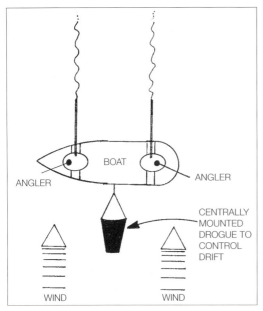

Fig. 6.2(a): *Loch-style fishing (also known as 'over the front'), a traditional 'just sub-surface' method for large still waters.*

face film. The fly is cast out and allowed to lie, with frequent twitches by the angler. Most of the still-water mayflies hatch very quickly, and as such are seldom seen as emergers. The sedges and buzzers are the insect groups of most interest here.

Conditions for emerger rises
In normal conditions insects hatch very quickly, too quickly to over-excite the trout. The conditions which cause emerger feeding sprees are those which slow the hatching of the nymphs. Examples of these follow.

In cold weather such as experienced at the beginning of spring, chironomids (buzzers) and very small sedges are the only insects likely to hatch, and because of the cold, the hatch will be slowed down and the insect's wings may take longer to dry. Similarly, flies hatching in rainfall at any time may take longer to dry out (especially the wings). In Africa, the most important

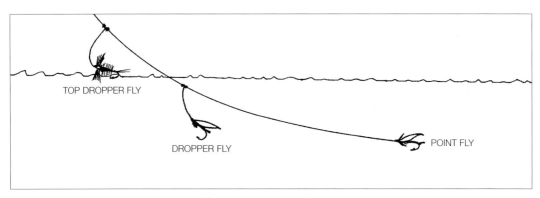

Fig. 6.2(b): *Typical loch-style presentation of flies in 'over the front' fishing.*

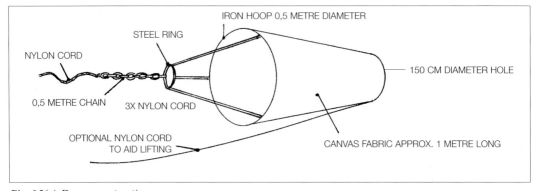

Fig. 6.2(c): *Drogue construction.*

time is probably on foggy mornings. Once again the wings take a long time to dry, and the insect's hatching time is lengthened.

Film and scum on the water surface reduce surface tension and this in turn also slows up emergence..This explains why a still, glassy surface on a hot summer's morning often brings on emerger feeding. Finally, the bigger the natural fly, the longer it takes to emerge. Obviously, during any of the conditions above, on days when big flies such as the large olive buzzer or large sedges are hatching, this provides the best opportunity for emerger fishing.

Typically, a slowed-up hatch might mean that a buzzer could take up to 90 seconds to hatch, and chances are that if it fails to emerge completely in that time it will die of exhaustion before the shuck integument is shed. By comparison, a healthy buzzer, in good hatching conditions, will probably get away in two or three seconds.

Good patterns are: Pearl Pushkin for hatching sedges; Suspender Buzzer and Claret Buzzer (with plastazote breathing tubes) for buzzer hatches; PVC Nymph for mayflies; Invicta, and Partridge and Orange for sedge hatches. These

A splendidly conditioned rainbow taken on a Claret Buzzer in 2,5 metres of water. Most African trout waters are rich in insects, producing rapid growth and great condition.

flies should be fished on a tippet lightly greased to within 10 cm of the fly. The fly should not be proofed.

Loch-style fly-fishing

Loch-style, also known as 'Over the Front', still-water fly-fishing is a very effective method of fishing the drift for trout. As the boat drifts under the controlled drag of the drogue (see Figure 6.2(a)), the angler at each end of the boat casts a shortish line forward, lifting the rod as

The author fly-fishing the vast expanse of Sterkfontein Dam in South Africa. When first visiting a water such as this, it pays to start out fishing topographically preferred spots, assessed from the surrounding structure of the dam. (Photo: Ron Clay)

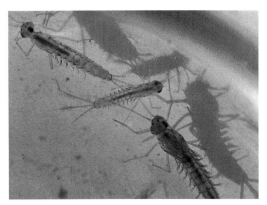

One of the African pond olive nymphs taken from a high mountain lake in winter. A favourite food of still-water trout.

When the wind blows into the corner of a dam wall, it can be a really productive place to fish.

the boat moves downwind. Rod lift-speed is controlled to give either slow movement of the flies, or a dead (no movement) presentation. As the cast is completed the top dropper fly (see Figure 6.2(b)) is dibbled attractively on the surface prior to the re-cast. Long rods (AFTMA 6 size, 11 feet or more) are used, usually with double-tapered floating line (sometimes slow sink). Most productive is drifting the wind lanes.

MEDIUM-DEPTH TACTICS

Most fly-fishermen in Africa are going to be spending a lot of their time fishing in still water from sub-surface down to a depth of roughly four metres. In some waters, this depth may be referred to as the 'deep hole', but four metres does not really count as deep. For many anglers, fly-fishing in waters at depths down to about this four-metre maximum, this is the productive zone. However, before promoting medium-depth fishing, I trust that the discourse on deep-water fishing which follows this section will encourage you to be a little more adventurous.

Methods for medium-depth waters vary considerably. If you are fairly new to still-water fly-fishing, then a very good way to approach this 'normal' kind of fly-fishing would be to read Chapter 13 on the fly patterns and how to use them. By the time you have done this, you will have discovered most of the techniques available. In essence, medium-depth fly-fishing in still waters slots into two groups, lure fly-fishing and nymphing.

You will probably be using a range of fly lines, including Fast Sink, Slow Sink, Intermediate, and Floating. Depending on where you are fishing and what species of fish you are after, you could be using rods rated from AFTM 5 through to AFTM 9.

Since all the techniques for fishing the various flies are included under their descriptions (see Chapter 13), I will not be repeating them here. Nevertheless, I feel that it would not be out of place to give some advice on what to do when approaching an untried still water in Africa. In this section I have also included some coverage of successful specific methods which can often save the day.

Assessing new still waters

It is a sound habit to survey the water from afar before walking down to the banks – and not just to check for crocodiles! It is also a very good idea to seek out as much local knowledge as one can about a place before commencing to fish it. Often the local hotel, tackle shop (very often a corner of a hardware store), landowner or even police station can supply good background information. This watching from afar actually has deeper significance. Through such observations, the angler is able to assess from the surrounding topography, the deep areas of the lake, the possible course of the feeder stream, drop-off locations, rocky strata, and so on. By observing the way the bank falls towards the edge, one can judge what happens under the water.

Tread softly and keep hidden! You just might see huge fish cruising in the clear water.

Good places to start are:
❏ Promontories, especially if they run into deep water. Fan cast around from one side of the point to the other, covering all the water with a sinking line.
❏ River beds. Explore using fast-sink line.
❏ Corners of dam walls, especially if a dirt road used during construction runs into the water. Usually best explored with a slow sinker.
❏ Gulleys. Scratch the bottom with dragonfly nymph imitations.
❏ Where rock and boulder structure are seen on the bank and are suspected of continuing under the water. I like a floating line and weighted nymph for this.
❏ Any shear structure (small cliffs) which runs under the water. Fish right against these with a well-sunk fly.
❏ Along the edge of reed beds. Fish with a floater or intermediate, or try a Booby on a super-fast sink line.
❏ Openings and channels in weed beds. Fish a weighted nymph, or try a dry fly.

Fish every one of these places that you can find. This may well take up your whole day, but it should pan out well. The same structures should be fished from a boat; if a strong wind is blowing, explore the downwind shore with a stripped lure fly. With new waters, I make a point of first visiting the downwind shore and examining the detritus at the edge. Very often, dead insects and pupal shucks can give you a good starting clue as to which imitation to use.

The method you use will depend upon what you find when you arrive. If the water is flat calm under a bright sun, you will have to fish deep. If there is a ripple and a good breeze, things may change accordingly: it may even be a good day for a dry fly, and there is always a chance of a rise in the lee shore ripple, which can be exploited with a wet Coch-y-Bonddu or other imitative fly on a slow sink line, or a long leader and a floating line.

What is much more usual in the African summer is changeable weather, and not a sign of a rise when you arrive. Or perhaps a sparse rise is on the go, but it dies out before 8 a.m. In such conditions you are not going to find your fish feeding in the surface. If you think there are daphnia in the water, you might decide to try long casts, strip retrieving an orange lure about a metre down with a sinking line for half an hour. If that doesn't work, it will pay you to start fishing the bottom itself. There are several methods open to you here. A weighted nymph fished on a floating line might be the answer, and another deadly tactic is to try a Booby (so long as you fish it using the correct method). Bloodworm imitations, caddis, snail, and deep-fished buzzer pupae may also work. Perhaps the best way to search out hot spots is to use a Mrs Simpson or a Walker's Killer fished slow and deep.

Weed beds are always worth searching along the edges with a damselfly or other nymphs. If a rise is on the go, simply imitate the hatching fly with a dry fly. If the fishes are head and tailing (see Chapter 8) to buzzer pupae, try to catch a few adult buzzers in order to select the correct colour imitation (a small aquarium net is ideal for this). Remember your aim is to catch the first trout. Once you have him, he can be spooned (see Chapter 11), and then you will have definite clues as to what the trout are feeding on.

Fishing in strong wind
Figure 6.3(a) illustrates the effect of strong winds on the movement of medium-depth still water. Drifting and current-borne food items collect downwind, where fishes wait for them. In these conditions, the angler should cast along the shore and slightly outward at an angle of 30 degrees to the shore, as illustrated in

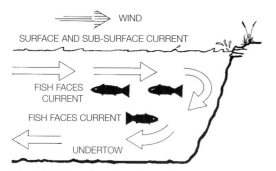

Fig. 6.3(a): *The effect of strong wind on still water.*

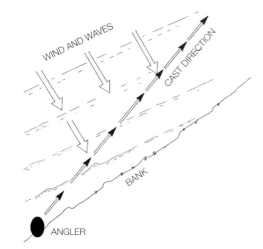

Fig. 6.3(b): *Casting in strong winds.*

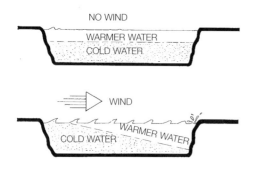

Fig. 6.3(c): *The effect of wind on still water in winter.*

Figure 6.3(b). Cast three times from each position, then take three steps along the bank to the next casting position. This method gives good coverage of the feeding fishes (they could be shallow or deep in summer, but probably only deep in winter), and puts the fly or lure across the vision of the fish, thus producing more takes.

A strong wind can cause the colder water to be pushed against the shore the wind comes from (effectively, the cold layer tilts), as illustrated in Figure 6.3(c). An angler foolishly seeking the comfort of the wind behind him and easier casting could find colder water in front of him and no feeding fish. The warmer water is on the downwind shore, and this is why fishing into the wind or across the wind on the downwind shore can be the most productive tactic on a windy day. The deeper the water, the more pronounced this effect can be. Fortunately, in Africa, we rarely suffer the complications of water layering and thermoclines, as commonly experienced in colder parts of the world. Sterkfontein Dam is an exception, and the new dams of the Lesotho Highland Waters Project, when it is finished, will also produce these effects quite markedly.

Proven methods

If you fish the preferred spots, taking into account the prevailing conditions and choosing the best method accordingly, your chances of succeeding should be good. The methods described below are not 'high finesse' methods and beginners should easily find themselves at home with them. They all work, sometimes exceptionally well.

Chase rigs

So-called because the larger fly appears to be chasing the small one, and looks intent on eating it. You can make up your own chase rigs, but the best one I know of is a Walker's Killer chasing a Steele's Taddy. The red-bodied Walker's Killer is on the point and is size 4. The size 10 Steele's Taddy is no more than 10 cm from the Walker's Killer and is on the dropper. For this dropper, use a four-turn water knot, which is strong but also lies back nicely. The retrieve is a very slow strip with occasional accelerations. The fish usually takes the Steele's Taddy.

Leaded nymph

There are a large number of these that you can use, but I find one in particular very deadly, and thus I recommend it as a start-up method on a new water. The fly to use is a weighted

A 5,52 kg (12lb 1oz) cock rainbow taken by the author from a deep corner of Kiepersol Dam at Trout Hideaway in South Africa.

Typical Canadian deep-water fly, flasher bar and diving planes.

Montana Nymph with a 'fluorescent chartreuse thorax'. Fish it on a floating line on a 3–5 metre 3X leader. Let it sink well down, and then retrieve using a figure-of-eight retrieve. The retrieve is a slow strip with 10 to 15 second alternative waits between each strip.

Booby flies

These are great flies to search unknown waters with. They are extremely effective, especially in medium-depth water (although they also take plenty of fishes in deep water). If the weather is cold use a Yellow Booby; if warmer, use a Viva Booby. In winter, when trout are attempting to spawn, an Egg Booby can be absolutely deadly for large fish. Use a very short leader of no more than 25 cm, and fish with a super-fast sink or lead-core fly line. Strike absolutely every touch and tap.

Lead-backed tadpole lure

These are very deadly, perhaps the deadliest of all. Fish on a sinking line to suit the depth. The deeper it is, the faster the line sink rate should be. Fish this fly with a troll strip retrieve right on the bottom. Takes are often very fierce, and a 1X leader is recommended. The most effective all-round pattern is the Viva Tadpole Lure.

Bottom-fished Olive Woolly Worm

Steve Barrow has developed this method to perfection. Use a size 4–8 Olive Woolly Worm on a fast sink line. The fly should be lead-backed. Allow the fly to sink well to the bottom and then retrieve with a deep 'sink and draw' retrieve.

DEEP-WATER TACTICS

Landlocked salmon are included here because not only are they very inclined to live in the deepest part of our still waters, but they also behave very much like deep-water trout.

Deep-water fly-fishing by definition excludes most rivers and streams in Africa, and with the exception of deep pools in the big rivers is primarily orientated towards still water. Shallow pans and lakes are also not suitable for deep-water tactics, and such waters are generally well served by dry fly or floating and intermediate line tactics. By 'deep water', I refer to water of depths greater than 3 metres down to as much as 40 metres. Below the 40 metre level, fly-fishing tactics become extremely difficult with standard equipment, and perhaps one should consider exploring such depths with a down-rigger.

Flashers and flies

On the western coast of Canada, many anglers fish with down-riggers with a big fly attached as the lure. A down-rigger is a device which is fixed to the rear of a boat and which, by means of a heavy weight which can be lowered to the required depth together with the angler's fly (or lure), enables the angler to troll in very deep water. These big flies are often up to 15–25 cm long, and are commonly tied in fluorescent colours with a lot of built-in flash from luminescent or Mylar tube bodies, and Flashabou wings.

The fly is preceded, a couple of metres up the leader, by a shiny metal device called a 'flash-

Fig. 6.4: *Comparative sink rates of differing density fly lines.*

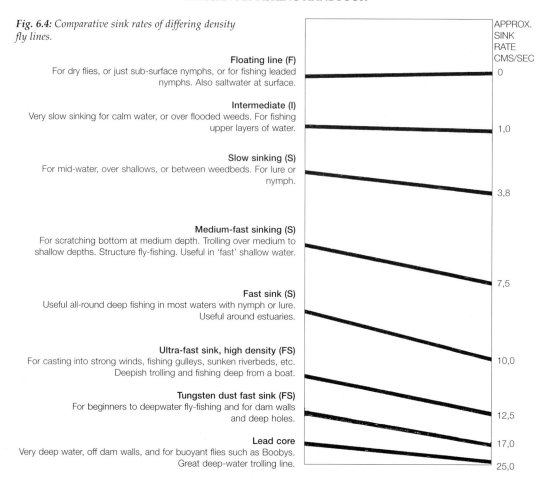

Floating line (F)
For dry flies, or just sub-surface nymphs, or for fishing leaded nymphs. Also saltwater at surface.

Intermediate (I)
Very slow sinking for calm water, or over flooded weeds. For fishing upper layers of water.

Slow sinking (S)
For mid-water, over shallows, or between weedbeds. For lure or nymph.

Medium-fast sinking (S)
For scratching bottom at medium depth. Trolling over medium to shallow depths. Structure fly-fishing. Useful in 'fast' shallow water.

Fast sink (S)
Useful all-round deep fishing in most waters with nymph or lure. Useful around estuaries.

Ultra-fast sink, high density (FS)
For casting into strong winds, fishing gulleys, sunken riverbeds, etc. Deepish trolling and fishing deep from a boat.

Tungsten dust fast sink (FS)
For beginners to deepwater fly-fishing and for dam walls and deep holes.

Lead core
Very deep water, off dam walls, and for buoyant flies such as Boobys. Great deep-water trolling line.

APPROX. SINK RATE CMS/SEC

0

1,0

3,8

7,5

10,0

12,5

17,0

25,0

er'. The flasher is a thin, highly chromed, bent bar about 20 cm long. It doesn't spin (although it is attached with swivels at each end), but rather oscillates and waves in the water, sending out flashes and vibrations which attract the salmon and steelhead trout in the deep fjords where this method is used. This 'flasher rig' is worked deep down, either with a down-rigger (as described above), or alternatively with a special diving plane (the Pink Lady diver is a popular one), designed for this job.

Such methods are helped enormously by the use of an echo sounder which enables the angler to thoroughly work a chosen bottom contour. The only claim such a method has to fly-fishing is that it uses a fly to catch the fish. But, there is no fly rod casting in this method, the usual rod being a three metre medium action spinning stick. This disqualifies it as a

genuine fly-fishing method. However, I mention it here because the African Rift Valley has some enormous ultra-deep lakes which are virtually unexplored in terms of super-deep fly-fishing. The 'fly and flasher' method certainly works in these waters. It has also been used with success in South Africa's very deep Sterkfontein Dam.

Why go deep for fish?
The answer to this could fill a book in its own right! A curt answer might be that fishes go deep for food; but some species simply prefer it there. Some may develop a fixation for bottom foods: the brown trout, which has developed an almost exclusive diet of snails, is such a fish. Others like to stake out territory at the bottom, and spend their lives there. Perhaps more compelling reasons are those afforded by environ-

mental changes and the movement of food forms. Bright light and intense cold can force fishes to move to the bottom. In Africa, the sometimes constant high-altitude bright sunlight can force some fishes into an almost permanent bottom-dwelling life.

Light and food are in fact the prime motivators, and these are the factors which are most pivotal in forcing fishes to a deep-feeding lifestyle. This is just as well for the fly-fisherman, since his tactics are all orientated around presenting something which looks like 'dinner' to the fish.

Insects and other food forms inhabit either the bottom or weed beds and other structures. Even in the deepest of waters there will be something living in the bottom mud and ooze, something which a fish will perceive as food. The gills of a trout are not equipped to filter bottom ooze, and trout are most unlikely to feed head down in great depths of water. However, carp, moggel and other species will feed in this way. Trout will be hunting dragonfly nymphs and small fishes and they will take snails and nymphs off gravel and rock bottoms. For the most part, the fly-fisherman's job is to imitate these creatures with feather and fur, and to present the fly to the fish in as natural a way as possible.

In African waters, whether they are trout waters or waters where the angler is hunting other species, there are great opportunities for deep-water fly-fishing. Many fly-fishermen never give the deep water and its special requirements a second thought, and as a result they miss out on all sorts of possibilities. Some of my very best fishes have come from deep water, and there have been many days when only deep-water tactics paid off.

Even before we start fly-fishing in the deeps, we are presented with a problem of applied geometry. If the water is say 25 metres deep, and you can cast perhaps 30 metres, simple arithmetic tells you that the line will go straight down to the bottom and your retrieve capability is only a measly 5 metres before the fly starts lifting off the bottom. Fairly obviously then, the ability to cast to a fair distance (at least 35 metres in this case), is pretty essential.

The aspirant deep-water fly-fisherman is strongly advised to attend a clinic and master the basics of the 'double haul' casting technique. This skill will give most fly-fishermen the ability to reach out to 35 or 40 metres. If you have a real aptitude for it, you may easily reach 50 metres with a lead-core line outfit.

Lines for deep-water fly-fishing

In order to take advantage of the longest casts possible, all my deep-water lines are shooting heads. The ideal fly line for this is one which sinks very rapidly – the faster the better. There are a few options, each with its own merits:
❏ lead core
❏ tungsten dust
❏ ultra-fast sink Kevlar cored
❏ ultra-fast sink.

Lead core

The lead core line offers the fastest sink rate and is cheap to make which is an important element in Africa where crabs often snip through and ruin any fly lines lying on the bottom. The constant loss of expensive factory-manufactured lines can be a bit wearing on the purse and the patience, thus cost is a high priority. The lead core also has a relatively low elasticity, which means it is acceptably sensitive to bites. High-stretch lines diminish sensitivity to soft taps and knocks because of their elasticity – they absorb these important touch signals! However, lead core lines are not suitable for beginners ... make a casting mistake with these lines and you could be scarred for life. Apart from inflicting serious cuts, lead core lines are also demanding in terms of timing in the cast. The cast timing is fast because the lead core is generally shorter than usual. This is easily mastered if you are an accomplished caster, but difficult for a newcomer to the double haul technique. In my opinion, it is hardly worth going below an AFTM 9 with a lead core outfit; from this point of view it forces you into the big rod league.

From a fishing point of view the lead core line is a real bottom hugger: you can be sure that your line is right where you want it, whether you are fishing buoyant or leaded flies. So, if

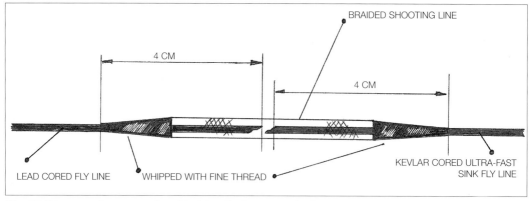

BRAIDED SHOOTING LINE

4 CM

4 CM

LEAD CORED FLY LINE

WHIPPED WITH FINE THREAD

KEVLAR CORED ULTRA-FAST SINK FLY LINE

Fig. 6.5: Diagrammatic representation of the join of lead core to Kevlar fast-sink tip.

you are an accomplished caster, the lead core is first choice. It offers the fastest sinking rate as well as the real advantage of being cheap to make up. You have the choice of buying a manufactured lead core line such as Kerboom (and these are great lines), or you can make one yourself from trolling line, or you can ask your local tackle dealer to make one for you.

In the 1950s, before modern lines were available, we made up these lead core lines from a standard saltwater trolling line, which consisted of a lead wire core, encased in a braided nylon outer. This braid-covered line was rough to the touch and rather heavy. It came in only one thickness. It was so heavy that in those embryonic days of the lead core, we used to cast it with carp rods – not even the biggest salmon fly rod could handle this line. In spite of its drawbacks, we managed to catch plenty of excellent deep-feeding brown trout with it. Today, things have improved considerably, and there is now a plastic-coated trolling line with a thin lead core which is much more suitable. However, it is still somewhat heavy, and one has to work between an AFTM 8 and AFTM 13.

The most popular size is made up to match an AFTM 9 rod, with AFTM 10 being popular with saltwater fly-fishermen. For my AFTM 9 line, I cut a length of lead-cored trolling line of exactly 19 feet (5,85 metres), and splice to this a further 6 feet (1,85 metres) of ultra-fast sink Kevlar-cored line. I use the remaining untapered end of a weight forward ultra-fast sink

line which has previously been cut down to form a shooting head (normally most fly-fishermen cutting their own shooting heads throw this cut-off untapered piece away). This combination shooting head turns over well during casting, and can be cast long distances with ease. It is also very sensitive when it comes to bite detection.

My saltwater AFTM 10 line is made up of 24 feet (7,4 metres) of lead-cored trolling line. For the salt, I leave out the tip of Kevlar line. The saltwater line is subject to much more abuse, and the attentions of much harder-fighting fish. In the salt, one cannot allow any form of potential weakness in the line. In spite of being utterly level with no taper, the lead core shooting head can still be cast long distances. Line turn-over is not good – it may even be splashy – but when fishing great depths in saltwater this is not important.

The splice of the lead core to the Kevlar line is accomplished with a short length of braided backing line, or any other hollow braided line. I slip this over the forward end of the lead core and over the Kevlar line tip (to join them); then whip finish each end of the braid, and finally work Pliabond or some other flexible adhesive into the joint. Never use Superglue for this job; it becomes brittle and eventually snaps off. Once the Pliabonded joint described above is dry, you can then needle knot the Kevlar line tip to a 10 kg monofil butt loop (for attaching the leader). Refer to Chapter 2 for detailed information on the knots used here.

Tungsten dust

The Tungsten dust lines are also very fast-sinking lines, and although not as quick sinking as the home-made lead core, they are certainly acceptable. These are quality lines with properly designed forward tapers, and are consequently much safer to cast than the lead core. A good caster, with a powerful fast taper rod, will probably get the lead core to go further, but not that much further! Tungsten lines are slightly more stretchy than a lead core, and therefore are not as sensitive when it comes down to bite detection. In terms of sink rate, they are generally faster than any of the normal 'fast sink' rated lines. They are excellent lines for the beginner who wishes to get into Booby fishing, but not as good as the Kevlar core lines for other deep fly-fishing.

Ultra-fast sink Kevlar core

These lines will not sink as fast as the tungsten line, but they are almost totally non-stretch and thus they offer great bite sensitivity. For handling lead-backed flies for deep fishing they are great, and the excellent bite sensitivity certainly pays off. However, I do not like these lines for fishing bottom buoyant flies like the Rasputin or Boobys. I find they are simply not dense enough for that job. They are a trifle expensive in terms of getting snipped off by crabs (I know, I have lost lots of them), but if your purse can handle it, these are great lines for fishing down to the 12 metre level. Below that, I still prefer the lead core. Just a note about these Kevlar cored lines: never use them for deep trolling! Because of their non-stretch capability, every fish that hits a trolled fly on these lines will break off.

Standard ultra-fast and fast sink

These lines are not, in my opinion, in the running for fishing depths greater than five metres. Above this depth they are very useful. The big problem with these standard sinking fly lines is stretch. One can miss a lot of very delicate bites with these lines, particularly when a long line is cast, as is generally the case with deep-fished flies. On some days, especially in cold water, such sensitivity is extremely important. Most of

This 4,24 kg (9lb 2oz) rainbow hen was taken by the author at Trout Hideaway in South Africa, using an Egg Booby fly on a lead-core line in 25 metres depth, in the middle of winter.

these lines cannot handle the buoyant flies, excepting the very small Booby nymphs. They also require a great deal of patience. Compared with a lead core line, these lines sink painfully slowly, and consequently they use up a great deal of valuable fishing time.

Leaders

For the most part, when trout fishing in still water with the deep fly, I find that an 0X tapered leader on my AFTM 9 lead core is perfectly adequate. However, there are times, especially when the fly must be right on the bottom (not a few centimetres off it), when an impregnated braided tapered sinking leader is best. In early season, when fishing lead-backed Viva Tadpole lures and similar flies, these braided leaders do seem to improve results. Length-

This brown trout of 4,1 kg (9lb 0oz) was caught by the author at Trout Hideaway in South Africa. It was taken from 12 metres of water on a Leaded Olive Steve's Caddis.

wise, I never exceed a leader length of three metres for deep-water fly-fishing with the lead core. A leader of only two metres is perfectly adequate for most fishing.

A dark-coloured line is best for the tippet. At one time I used to dye my tippets dark brown using a ten per cent solution of silver nitrate which turns the line brown on exposure to sunlight. Today you can buy ready-coloured brown nylon monofilament lines for the job.

The chances of striking into a really good fish are higher when deep-water fishing, and thus a tippet must be chosen to suit the fish you might expect to catch. I seldom go below 2 kg for my tippet, usually about 3,5 kg, although at times (when fishing an especially snaggy bottom with big fish), I can go up to 5 kg. Boobys have their own special leader and retrieve requirements, and you are referred to the detail on the Booby in Chapter 13.

My preferred knot for joining leader to tippet is the 'four-turn water knot' (see Chapter 2). I am not too happy with the common bloodknot, which can pinch softer lines and reduce the strength of the knot to below 50 per cent of its original breaking strain.

Fly considerations

Flies for deep-water fishing are usually weighted, the main exception being the buoyant flies such as Boobys. The weighting style of deep-water flies is important. Most weighted nymphs are weighted with a few turns of lead wire around the thorax, but what we need is deep-water flies that are weighted along the back. The reason for this is that not only does the fly sink quickly, but it also rides point up! With lure fly patterns, it is usual to weight them by tying thickish (16 SWG) lead wire along the back of the hook shank, before tying on the pattern itself. With nymphs and small flies, the usual method is to tie lead foil (e.g. from a wine bottle) along the back. This is rolled up before being tied into the dressing.

All these deep-water fly weighting methods will cause the fly to swim upside-down, and the dressing should thus also be tied on upside-down. Upside-down flies are of course much less likely to get hung-up on the bottom,

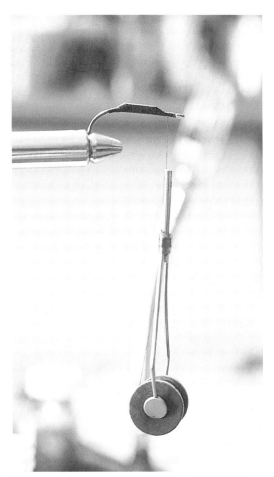

It is useful to tie-in the lead weighting on the back of several hooks before tying on the dressing ... a sort of production line. This photo shows the lead wire after binding the silk. The silk is always varnished at this stage.

a very important consideration when bottom fly-fishing.

An alternative method which does not require weighting is to use a 'keel' hook. Once again, the dressing goes on upside-down, but the keel hook is not weighted. Unfortunately, keel hooks do not hold well, and are guilty of forming a hole in the fish's mouth where they penetrate, especially after a long fight.

In Chapter 3 you can read up on colours for deep-water fly-fishing. In essence, lure flies for deep water (i.e. flies that are not deliberately imitative) should have considerable colour contrast built into them. Combinations such as yellow and red, white and red, white and black, and violet and white, can all work well. Pure violet or purple flies with fluorescent blue in the pattern are also effective. Flies such as these are generally strip retrieved.

Fishing with largish nymphs, crab and fish imitations is the best way to go. Dragonfly nymph imitations are possibly the most effective of all. One should not forget the blood-worm-imitating flies when fishing deep – deep-water fishes often browse on these. Retrieves for the imitative flies should be designed to come as close as possible to the movements of the original food form.

Fishing a new deep-water location
Always attempt to take advantage of some bottom feature, if at all possible. Depressions in the bottom, old roads and ditches in flooded waters, cliffs, drop-offs, points of land, old river beds, rocky areas and gravel bottoms are all potential hot spots. Anywhere with an underwater structure such as rocks is always worth a good search.

Strip off shooting line, and make a long cast out over your chosen spot. Allow the line to sink right to the bottom. How do you know it's on the bottom? Well, you can make several casts, each time counting down until you get to the bottom; or much more simple, cast out and then watch the line. As the line sinks, it will tighten under its own weight. But the moment it hits the bottom, the line will suddenly go a little slack. Remember that it is the end of the shooting head nearest to you which has caused this effect, so you must still allow a little more time for the leader and fly to touch bottom. A count of 15 should be adequate to cover that.

Keep the line trapped against the rod handle throughout the sinking period – don't put the rod down! Quite a few takes come as the fly is sinking, and you must be ready to feel these and to strike instantly.

Now that everything is on the bottom, commence your retrieve. Most bottom takes are fairly fierce affairs, but you may feel some very soft plucks, often hardly detectable. Point the rod down the line so that you are in constant touch with the line itself throughout the retrieve. As soon as you feel anything at all, strike! The strike should be firm, and normally you will feel the tugging of the fish straight away.

CHAPTER 7

TACTICS AND STRATEGIES – STREAMS AND RIVERS

Fish say they have their stream and pond;
But is there anything beyond?

Robert Brooke

When you approach a still water the immediate problem is often that of locating fishes in the vast expanse before you. But when you walk along the banks of a stream or river, you know there are fishes – and what's more, you know more or less where they should be. River trout and other river denizens have habits related to food and the environment which are a good guide to where they will be holding. However, although the

A misty morning on the Sabie River, dead drifting a nymph in a fast run. (Photo: Don Lort)

fish's 'lie' may well be easier to pinpoint in theory, the stream will probably require quite different skills, perhaps different flies, certainly a different approach to retrieves and line control, and you will need to be much more careful about keeping out of sight.

The good stream fly-fisherman 'reads' his river – he 'knows' the good lies, but he 'reads' on a basis of study of fish habits and his own experience. You will need to 'know' about rivers, about stream insects, and about accurate casting. You must be observant, and you will also require much greater mobility than when fishing still waters.

HIGH-COUNTRY STREAMS

Since much of Africa is tropical and far too hot for trout, the mountains and high escarpments are the only suitable areas (with the exception of the Cape in South Africa). Some of these high areas are fairly barren, like English moorlands, but many streams and rivers are in areas where lush high-altitude rain forest flourishes. Others are in areas where the local vegetation is high-country thornbush. In South Africa, many streams are densely infested with invasive plants such as wattle and gum trees. In the Cape, the vegetation is temperate, but nevertheless can form quite heavy bush in places.

African trout streams are usually quite narrow, rarely exceeding ten metres across in the high country and very often less than half of this. Some broad rivers in KwaZulu-Natal in

Keeping well back from the water's edge is a good way of keeping hidden. (Photo: Don Lort)

South Africa, especially those rising in Lesotho, carry trout in the higher reaches, and these are often wide, fast-flowing shallow rivers. A great many of the African trout streams and rivers pass through rugged scenery, cutting through rocky gorges, and some are difficult to access. Streams tend to fall fairly rapidly from high country, and many are blessed with deep pools, rapids and falls and gurgling runs, enough to delight any fly-fisherman. Fishes can grow to 5 kg in some of these streams, but are unlikely to exceed this. Many of the preserved stream fisheries commonly carry fishes of 2–3 kg offering a high standard of fly-fishing.

Good casting skill is a great asset when fishing rivers which are often densely vegetated, and an ability to stalk one's fish certainly pays off well. Because of the vegetation and the rough nature of the water, it is usually fairly easy to approach fishes, and excellent sport is available to the careful angler.

LOWLAND RIVERS

Many of the fly-fisherman's fishes are creatures of tropical streams and rivers. Most of these are jungle-edged slow-flowing rivers, often in areas of high rainfall. Movement along the banks is often hindered by high, dense vegetation, and you frequently have to search for openings suitable for casting a fly. The great slow-flowing African rivers are full of fishes, many of which take the fly readily. Temperatures are usually high all year round and accompanied by high humidity in the wet season. Torrential rainfall is not unusual.

Areas with rapids are prime fishing locations, and often rocky outcrops provide good fishing spots. Fish at least four or more metres back from the river's edge to reduce problems with crocodiles, keep to camp at night and don't wander the banks in darkness.

CASTING CONSIDERATIONS ON STREAMS AND RIVERS

The roll cast, which we covered under basic casting technique in Chapter 4, is very useful in any situation where a back cast is not possible (which, in Africa, tends to be most of the places one fishes). Five to 15 metre casts are quite possible with the roll cast, and this kind of distance

African trout streams are commonly hidden in thick vegetation, demanding careful and accurate casting, but the fishes are often trophy-sized and well worth the effort.

is adequate for most stream situations. (Distance with the roll cast is achieved by releasing extra line through the line hand, as the unrolled line flies out.) I have often roll cast across a weir with a wet fly, and picked up trout in the eddy on the opposite side of the stream. Those fishes were quite unaware of my presence, and trees were growing thickly right behind me. No back cast technique could possibly have worked in that situation.

Wading upstream, where bush and trees are hemming you in, and roll casting into likely holding spots as you go, is an excellent method for wet fly and nymph fishing. The Americans call it 'shot gunning' the pockets (the pockets being the holding spots). One can work kilometres of bushy stream in this way. Roll casting is not really suitable for dry fly (although some try it) because it tends to drown the fly even when using a floating line. My preference is for a slow sinking line and either small woolly worms or nymphs. These are retrieved with figure-of-eight bunching, or slowly strip retrieved into a line basket.

Not so well known is the roll cast's ability to free stuck flies from rocks and trees. Very often (though not always), a roll cast applied to the fast-held line will release it and allow your fly a new lease of life, instead of having to be broken off.

Dry fly anti-skating techniques

Avoiding 'fly skating' is the single biggest problem the stream-side dry fly-fisherman has to contend with. Ideally, the fly should drift downstream without unnatural movement, because once it begins to skate across the surface, it is highly unlikely that any trout will take it. Casting across a stream ensures that the downstream-drifting line will be affected by varying flow rates along its length, resulting in a belly forming in the middle of the line. Because the line is moving at different speeds along its length, it begins to drag the leader and tippet across the current and causes the fly to skate. Many anglers have worked on the problem of presenting a fly with no surface skate, without much success – it is a conundrum as old as river dry fly-fishing itself – but there are ways to get the most from a cast before the fly starts skating.

Reach casting

Reach casting is one of the preferred methods, and is accomplished as follows. The angler makes his cast, but just before the fly lands, he quickly lays the rod over (in the upstream direction) from the normal vertical position to an almost horizontal one. This throws an upstream bow into the line, which has to be taken out by the stream before the fly starts to skate. It thus gives the angler more skate-free time for the fly to float over the waiting fishes – these vital extra seconds before the skate commences is often all that is needed.

The reach cast is easy to control, and with practice the caster will be able to perform 'curved' casts to match whatever obstacles he meets in his fishing. Following the floating line down the current with the tip of the rod is recommended in order to keep in touch and in control.

The 'reach cast' is, to my way of thinking, the best of the slack line casting methods, and the one that I use the most. More skate-free drift is achieved than by the other methods described below, which in turn means more fish! Reach casting also gives the accomplished caster opportunities to throw curved casts (since this what the upstream line bend really is), and to reach quite difficult spots as a result. As you learn, you will be able to put the 'reach line curve' into the cast right at the leader, or, in varying measure, anywhere through the cast.

Mending line

'Mending line' is a method of controlling the line so that you remain in touch in the best possible way. You mend the line either to control unwanted loose line or to pre-empt drifting of the line (and thus also to prevent bowing in the line and consequent fly skating) as a result of the changing current. It is aimed firstly at keeping the fly where it is wanted without causing it to skate, and secondly to extend this skate-free period as long as possible.

There are several 'mends' available, but most

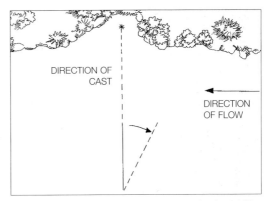

Fig. 7.1: Reach casting – just before the fly lands, quickly lay the rod over in the upstream direction. A great method for extending skate-free fly drift.

important is a technique called 'reach mending'. Reach mending consists of pushing the rod forward at the beginning of the drift, then as the fly drifts by, the rod is slowly pulled in and then pushed out again as the fly drifts down to the end of its swim. This is also a useful technique for fishing wet flies when cast across the stream.

Another 'mend' commonly used by dry fly-anglers is the 'coil flick'. Put simply, during the drift down of the line, a loose coil of the floating fly line is flicked upstream. This coil of free line augments the skate-free drift time already achieved by the upstream bow created by the reach cast. Initially, the angler will find it diffi-

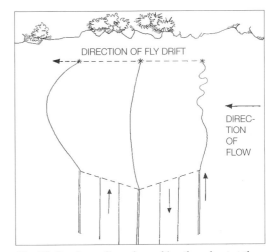

Fig. 7.2: Reach mending – by pushing the rod out at the beginning and end of the drift, and pulling it slowly inward during the drift, the fly will maintain skate-free drift longer.

This angler, reach mending in good cover, cannot be seen by the fishes in the clear water. (Photo: Don Lort)

cult to avoid dragging the fly during the mend, but in time and with practice it can be done.

You can turn over the bow in the line (caused by the mid-stream current) by an upstream flick of the rod tip. The downstream bow lifts and turns over, becoming an upstream bow. The flick should be gentle: too much applied energy will drag the line towards the caster and cause the fly to skate.

Don't forget that developing an ability to 'mend' your line can make up for many casting deficiencies. Many successful anglers who are perhaps poor casters owe their success to highly developed line mending and line control skills.

Slack line casting

Most other methods for delaying skating involve casting a loose line onto the surface of the stream. The current then has to remove the waves of slackness from the line before dragging the fly, hence giving precious time for the fly to float down without skating. The aim of the slack line cast is to put more line onto the water than is actually required to reach the target. The easiest (but not the most satisfactory) method for the beginner is to watch the forward cast straightening out in the air, and then, just before it finally straightens, pull back on the line hand. This causes the cast to come up dead, and the line falls slack and wavy onto the surface. Casting slightly uphill increases the effect and makes even more slack available. This method is quite crude, allowing little control and making accurate distance achievement (and any other accuracy) very difficult. However, it is a starting point.

More slack can be generated by flicking the rod backward and forward (vibrating the tip), and allowing loose line to move up through the rings and onto the water. It is as well to remember that too much slack lessens control, and makes the strike more difficult.

An alternative, more advanced, slack line cast method is to hold a spare loop of line in the line hand, and release it late at the end of the cast. It is a method that needs more skill and good timing, and must be based on good sweet casting technique. Done properly, it can put the slackness near the end of the floating fly line and into the leader where it is most needed.

Using the backdrop of the bank and a rock on the upstream side, this angler is invisible to the fishes upstream. Sideways casting, using the stream for the back cast, is a good method in such heavily bushed conditions. (Photo: Don Lort)

Wet fly casting

For wet fly casting where bankside vegetation is no problem, properly executed sweet casting (see Chapter 4) is all that is needed. The better your accuracy and your ability to put the fly down quietly and in the right place, the better you will perform.

Occasionally, the need will arise for a long cast, and then your ability to double haul cast will really pay off. Perhaps the need is to cast into a tributary or over a wide pool – perhaps, as in Cotton's adage from the 1600s, 'to fish fine and far off'.

Stream casting puts many other interesting demands on the fly-angler. In many situations, an ability to keep the plane of casting low is very useful. Casting under bushes and tufts of grass is an obvious example. Being able to do this, and to cast accurately into almost any situation ('right on the button', as they say), is an enormous asset.

Mending the line (keeping in direct touch) is often just as essential in wet fly-fishing as it is in dry fly-fishing. Fishing 'across and down' requires good mending skills. As well as the

'mends' described above, the wet fly-angler will usually mend his line in the cross-stream drift (such as might be required in dead drifting a nymph) by raising and lowering the rod as the fly drifts by. When the fly is allowed to drift down at the same speed as the current, this is known as dead drifting.

DRY FLY-FISHING

Moving upstream, casting upstream as you go, generally gives the best results. Perhaps the main reason is that the fishes are lying with their heads upstream, and an angler approaching from behind them is less likely to be spotted.

Upstream dry fly

Fly skate can be kept to a minimum when casting upstream with a dry fly. You can figure-of-eight or slow strip retrieve into a line basket (or keep the line coils in your hand) to keep in touch until the vagaries of the current eventually cause the fly to skate. The drawback is that the tippet will have to pass over the fish before the fly, and this may spook the fish. To minimise disturbance of the surface film, make sure

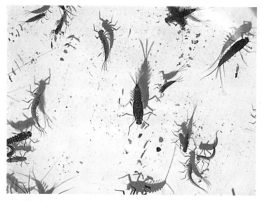

A single sweep with an aquarium net in an African trout stream produced this assortment of mayfly nymphs.

the last few centimetres of tippet are not greased. In bright sunlight, the shadow of the tippet can easily frighten a feeding trout, and then the angler must position himself so as to cast across-stream to the fish, thus avoiding the drift of the tippet shadow.

Preoccupied surface feeders and mayfly rises

Most trout holding in the current will be examining everything that passes overhead on the surface. Trout spend their whole lives picking and choosing, and they can be pretty good at it, too! Some days, they are so selective that they can drive you mad with frustration. You can see the fish, perhaps a fine specimen, rising regularly to the fly – he may even be unafraid of your tippet and fly – but consistently ignoring it. This usually occurs when they have been feeding on a specific life-form for some time (very often some kind of mayfly), and have become totally preoccupied with it to the exclusion of all else.

Choice of fly

It may be possible to utilise the 'key colour' approach (see Chapter 3), and capitalise on a colour feature of the food form, but in general 'matching the hatch' with a good imitation is going to be the best avenue. Some anglers believe that one should only use winged patterns in very clear water on bright days. The winged patterns seem to be more precise imitations for these conditions, and the hackled only flies will often be ignored. Good flies for African

preoccupied hatches include the Greenwell's Glory, Mooi Moth, Pale Olive Dun, Grey Duster, Adams, Highveld Dun, and Black Gnat.

You should endeavour to examine the rise carefully, checking for bubbles after the rise. The fish may appear to be surface feeding, but absence of bubbles means that it is really taking near-surface nymphs or slow hatchers (emergers). If so, you can put on a correct nymph imitation and solve the problem. Other problems arise as a result of poor presentation. The mayfly duns which may be hatching will sit with wings cocked riding the surface. If your fly is poorly proofed and sitting halfway into the film it will be ignored. Conversely, the trout will ignore the well-cocked dry fly when it is feeding on emergers. Observation is the key: time spent watching can be very fruitful.

Mixed rises to mayflies

It is worth remembering that mixed rises occur from time to time: the trout take a dry fly and then an emerger or two, perhaps another dry fly and more emergers, and so on. In these rises they usually eat more emergers than hatched duns. This is important because emerger fishing is likely to produce more fishes for the angler.

The feeding preoccupation described above occurs commonly, but in most African rises the fishes are happy to feed on anything floating by that represents food. In Africa, fishes are much more likely to feed on terrestrial insects than are their European and American counterparts. Rises brought on by hatching aquatic insects, although not uncommon, are seldom as frequent or intense as European and American (temperate and Arctic) hatches.

Terrestrial insect feeders

Terrestrial imitations can be very effective, and general imitations such as the DDD will catch in most rises. African trout will eat almost anything alive. As an example, Lesotho trout are often found with mice and lizards in the stomach contents, and many African trout frequently eat frogs. More usual is a taste for beetles, grasshoppers, crickets, caterpillars, moths, and of course ants and termites.

Beetles and grasshoppers

Grasshoppers and beetles are taken in a big way at the surface. The various floating hopper imitations, floating imitations of beetles such as the dry Coch-y-Bonddu, and DDD are taken enthusiastically. In Africa, there are huge populations of diverse species of grasshoppers and locusts. Compared with similar insects in the northern continents, hopper populations are often massive in Africa. Trout, yellowfish, and many other species feed on these insects to a very large degree, and in a 'no apparent rise' situation, the fishes will often come up for surface-fished hopper imitations.

Streams flowing through grassland will have the heaviest 'fall' of grasshoppers, but there are also plenty of species in wooded and bushy areas. Grassland stream trout will nearly always show a hopper or two in stomach contents. Hopper imitations work best when cast next to the bank, or even twitched from the bank into the water. A slow surface twitch retrieve sometimes livens up a hopper imitation. Deer hair hopper imitations such as trimmed Muddlers and Joe's Hopper can be greased to ride high in the water, and these appear to be the most effective imitations.

Sedges and buzzers, and dry fly imitations

There are a great many sedge species in African rivers. They can hatch at any time of the day, generally small ones first and larger species as the day progresses. The adults can be imitated with the Henryville Special, Goddard and Henry's Sedge, and Walker's Sedge. At a pinch the DDD will work as a sedge imitation. My favourite when big sedges are coming off at dusk is the Soldier Palmer Pink. The small long-horn sedges, which are the major part of the daytime sedge hatches, normally hatch near the edge of the stream. Trout rising to flies under overhanging grass tussocks and low bushes are usually feeding on these. A small size 14 or 16 Henryville Special works well in this situation.

Buzzers are infrequent hatchers in daytime hours on streams, although they will hatch all day in still water. The medium-sized (size 12) orange and silver buzzers hatch in large numbers just before and after dusk. Small olive and

A dark pool under an overhanging tree holds several trout. These trout were rising to terrestrials, and a drifted grasshopper imitation proved to be their downfall.

pale amber buzzers will hatch as well. In streams, the trout feed mostly on the nymphs, which require wet fly imitations, but on occasion they rise well to the adults, and a size 14 Buzzer will often prove effective.

Grass beetles

In African grassland there is a small shiny golden brown beetle which reaches almost plague proportions towards late summer. These are avidly taken by trout. Small (size 16) dry Coch-y-Bonddu and Red-tag Palmer dry flies, together with Beams' Brown Woolly Worm wet fly, are readily taken for these beetles.

Beetles tend to be more important than hoppers in bush and forest country.

Attractor dry flies

You arrive at the water as it sparkles and tumbles in the sunlight. There is no apparent rise, it's a cold day and the solar powered grasshoppers are dormant. However, you know the fishes are there, and the question is, what is the tactic for today? This scenario can be the time to use large (size 8–12) attractor dry fly patterns such as Royal Coachman, Bi-visibles, and fluorescent Tup's Indispensable. They work well on riffles and tumbling water, and will sometimes be taken by a trout when nothing else (wet or dry) will move the fish. There is a certain fascination in watching them bob along on the waves, a fascination that explodes into excitement at the take of a rising fish. A large well-proofed Soldier Palmer Pink (size 8) fished on the surface in rough water will often take good trout and yellowfish. Two weeks after the first rains is a really good time for attractor dry flies. The fishes are hungry, swimming in well-oxygenated water, and the big insect hatches have not yet begun.

WET FLY-FISHING

When fishing with dry flies to rising trout, the fly-fisherman knows where the trout are, and where he should cast. Everything is clearly seen as a result of the rises. However, when wet fly-fishing to fishes below the surface this is not the case at all. The angler needs to be able to 'read the river' to find the fishes. Reading the river is the single most important skill the stream-side wet fly-fisherman can develop.

Reading the river: holding spots

Fishes choose their lies based on certain criteria, namely availability of food, safety and economy of effort. They need to be able to hold position relatively easily in a lie where plenty of food drifts by, and where they are able to spot danger and escape from it. Trout and other fish 'lies' have all these properties in varying measure. Often the better the lie, the larger will be the fish in it. If this fish is caught, the next largest trout in the pool will move in and take over. Remembering the location of good lies can stand you in good stead, and over the seasons a good fly-fisherman may take several good trout from a good 'lie'.

Knowing the criteria fishes use to choose their holding spots (lies) means that the angler can do the same. In any stream the following offer potential to meet requirements: boulders on the bottom, sunken trees, depressions, overhanging bushes, reeds and tussocks, deep-water runs, rocky cliffs plunging into the water, divisions in the stream, eddies, confluences, undercut banks, the edge of drop-offs, and so on. The ability to 'read the river' is nothing more than the ability to recognise all of these places and to assess their potential to hold fishes. A very large part of the river has no fishes in it at all, so why waste time casting into barren areas? The place to fish is always into the trout's chosen lies.

The skilful wet fly-angler works his way along

Small trout, such as this wild-bred rainbow parr, take flies greedily. They grow into big trout and should always be returned carefully by tweaking out the hook. Ideally, they should not be handled. Note the parr marks on the side.

the stream, casting into all the likely lies. Such an angler, working the holding spots with the correct flies and retrieves, will be consistently successful. And, wherever this angler goes, the same techniques (the water-reading skills) will work!

Depressions in the stream bed, fast runs

Fishes like to lie in river bed depressions with the current passing overhead. They will hold in such spots even in exceptionally fast water, tilting upwards to take morsels such as nymphs as they wash past.

In streams with runs of waterweed separated by channels, such depressions may hold several trout. Many nymphs and small creatures lose their hold and are swept along in the current until they can settle again. Small fishes will also hang suspended in the current, safe in the weedy retreat. But if they drift out of the refuge they may be taken. Upstream casting into the runs and 'dead drifting' (drifting at the same speed as the current) near the bottom is the way to fish these.

Depressions in open, fast, shallow water (fast runs) very often hold trout, and should not be ignored. In the water which I fish, many trout of 2–3 kg are taken in such places. Very careful observation usually reveals their presence, but they are hard to see in the ripple of running shallow water. A shift in colour, a shadow crossing the bottom, the flash of a turning fish – these are the giveaways.

'Across and down' is a favourite way to fish such spots. Many anglers fish them blind, quite indifferent to the position of the trout, relying

Trout match their background very well and often give their position away only because they move. The moral: watch each pool carefully for a few minutes before fishing. (Photo: Don Lort)

on achieving water coverage by persistent casting. However, even for these anglers, awareness of fish lies can make a big difference. Careful observation and consequent efficient coverage of the river may also save you from hooking a lot of scavenging parr which often swim in shallow water.

This is the accepted scenario for traditional wet fly patterns, and many, such as Mallard and Claret, Teal and Red, Guinea and Red, work well. There are very few stoneflies in African rivers, and they are hardly worth imitating, but alderflies (toebiters in the Cape), swimming nymphs and heavy cased sedges live in such water. Imitative patterns work very well, and a study of the local insects and appropriate imitation pays off. Various Stick Fly patterns and Hot Spot nymphs imitate sedge larvae, and the ascending pupae of sedges can be nicely imitated with a Pearl Pushkin. Toebiters and dragonfly nymphs have many suitable imitations in the Killer patterns and Woolly Worms.

These imitative flies can be fished downstream as well as up, and a good downstream technique is to keep in touch with the fly in such a way that the fly is always downstream of tippet and leader. This is done by drawing the rod back just before the fly hits the water. Then as the fly drifts down, the rod is gradually lowered to keep pace with the current – done properly the fly is presented first, before the leader, a good technique for 'leader shy' fish.

Boulders

These are perhaps the best known holding spots. Trout are able to hold well in quite fast

currents by taking advantage of the current dispersion caused by a large rock. One rock may be home to two trout – the expected trout lying downstream of the boulder (perhaps a metre or less back), and another in front of the rock where the water divides.

If possible, the upstream cast is best, but many rocks can only be reached by casting across the stream. A 'reach cast' followed by an upstream loop mend is one way to handle this. Normally, the current is fast and the fly will quickly be swept away. As a result, the fly must get down quickly and a weighted fly is obviously preferable. I often use lead putty on my flies, varying the amount to suit the situation. It is not necessary to cast right into the hole behind the rock – the fish is used to darting out and grabbing his prey quickly. Nevertheless, an accurate cast close to the rock is needed. You will probably not need a retrieve, but in a situation where everything is easily controllable, either a dead drift with a nymph, or a darting retrieve with a lure fly is preferable.

Where the current is somewhat less fierce and a retrieve is possible, use a very slow dead drift retrieve. At the end of the retrieve use the 'induced take' method, which will often be just the ticket to get the fish to take. Do this by raising the rod so as to add speed and life to the fly. It goes without saying that in order to perform this properly, good line control (being in touch at all times) is essential.

Where there are a lot of rocks, there will be trout associated with several of them. You are very likely to scare the others when you hook the first one, so try to choose the 'best' rock, the one that you think holds the biggest fish. Very big rocks, with depressions behind them, often hold several trout.

Bank lies

There are many lies where a slight change in the bank structure holds a feeding trout. An indentation in the bank, or a slight projection with quieter water behind it, are the most common. Trout will hold in these spots even in very fast water. Most such lies are in fairly shallow water, and in fact the deep ones will probably hold many small fishes. The bigger fishes seem

The white flash of an open mouth indicates a trout taking food. Often this is the only indication that a trout has taken a fly.

tion, and these lies are usually associated with slower water. The fishes (often several) hold under the bush, feeding on the insects which drop out of it and whatever else drifts past. They also benefit from the seclusion of the bush and its shade.

Many of these spots are in ripple-free, relatively slow water. Sometimes they hold a good fish, but they are very often hard to cast to. Sideways casting can sometimes get a fly under the bush, but the bush may actually touch the water and then this is impossible with a dry fly and floating line. Most of these places are successfully fished by drifting a wet fly down with a sinking line into the lie using the current. The slow retrieve of nymph-imitating flies is often successful, but use fine tippets, a slow sinker, and good imitative patterns for success.

to enjoy the larger structures of this type, often next to extremely fast water.

Very accurate upstream and across casting is required to get the fly into the correct spot in fast water. Aim to get the fly just above the lie, right next to the bank itself. These fishes are often taking drowned terrestrials, and a proofed Muddler Minnow on a slow-sinking line often works well.

Bush lies

Some of the bank lies are commonly formed as a result of tough plants (especially some of the grasses) growing out from the bank and rooting in the mud of the river. The other common kind of bank lie is caused by overhanging vegeta-

Sunken and partially sunken structure lies

After the early summer rainfalls, all kinds of debris can be washed down the streams and rivers. The undercutting of banks together with softening of the earth causes whole trees to fall in. These floating structures (as a result of rotting and stream water permeating the wood), eventually sink and come to rest. All kinds of other debris come up against them and a raft of floating material is formed. Impenetrable (to a fly cast) thickets of timber can accumulate in this way, and many a trophy trout will take up home in such places. To catch them one normally has to appeal to their more aggressive feeding instincts.

Watch carefully: eventually the trout will either swim right out of the tangle, or, at least, will approach the edge of his sanctuary. A stripped fish imitation, such as a Catlet Muddler, will often seduce him into a follow into open water and an eventual take. The other opportunity is a dry fly drifted past. In real life, he would have to stick his nose out of his sanctuary to nab floating flies. Sometimes, with the right current, it is possible to drift a fly under the hiding place, but you may well get hung-up. A take in a lie like this needs a sideways strike and haul to have any chance of success. The fish would have to be hustled out before he realised what was happening.

This raft of twigs and detritus has accumulated in the branches of a sunken tree. A trout of 2,6 kg (5 lb 12 oz) has taken up residence and fell to a Catlet Muddler drifted under the raft.

These debris-type holding spots always demand a fair amount of stealth if you are to succeed, and you may have to spend a good deal of time waiting and watching for the right opportunity.

Cliffs and very deep runs

These are the favourite locations for trophy fishes. The hard rock of the cliff concentrates the current, which in turn gouges out deep runs right against it. Darker water here can signify runs which are metres deep. For some reason (and I suspect it has to do with the need for a long cast right across the stream, together with skilful line mending and having to fish deep), these spots are ignored by many fly-fishermen. In dry winters, these cliff-edged swims are often the best bet for a fish. Their main attraction to me is the way in which big trophy fishes hug the bottom in these runs, feeding on crabs, dragonfly nymphs and small fishes, with consequent rapid increase in weight.

In some rivers one can wade to the edge of the deep run and cast upstream with a fast-sinking line, but the fishes are very likely to spot you doing this. The other problem with the upstream cast is that it may reach you before the fly has a chance to sink!

The correct method is with a super-fast sinking line such as a tungsten dust cored line. This should be cast downstream and allowed to sink right to the bottom. It will take longer than usual because of the current pushing against the sinking line and tending to lift it. Nevertheless, if the line is dense enough it will get down. Use a short two metre leader/tippet of at least 2 kg (these are big fishes) with a Viva Tadpole (size 8 or 10). Retrieve with small twitches and an occasional short strip. Takes are normally very positive, but they may be light (like a slight hang-up in weed) in the cold months. I have seen 5 kg trout (browns and rainbows) taken from small streams in this way. The nature of these lies often means that the downstream cast can only be made by wading at the top of the pool. Take care on gravel-bottomed runs – it is easy to slide in, and it may prove very difficult to get out again.

Where the drop-off is into water of a metre or

A

B

C

A montage showing holding spots in a river. (A) Stream bank lies. (B) Rocks and clump lies. (C) Fast water lies.

113

A deep dark pool on the Matibamatso River in Lesotho.

barren Lesotho high country, and there is almost no bankside vegetation to hide the angler at altitudes of 3 000+ metres. It is consequently rather difficult to keep out of sight, and these deep pools are an extremely welcome feature, since their depth helps the 'keeping low, treading softly' angler to stay hidden.

Some of these pools hold a good head of big wild-spawned rainbows, and an occasional brown trout up to 3–4 kg. During the day they are best fished (almost like still-water fisheries) with fast-sink lines and Walker's Killer, Mrs Simpson, or Hamill's Killer (all size 8). The Viva Tadpole and the Red Setter are also effective in size 12. In the evening, good hatches of orange buzzers can occur in these deep pools, together with hatches of large sedges. A dry fly will often score, as will surface-fished nymph imitations. An effective near-surface fly in the Lesotho summer evenings is the orange Hot Spot Pheasant Tail Nymph at size 12. Some of the Kenya streams also have good deep pools which fish well with the Kenya Bug (size 12), and weighted Killers.

Reed beds

Reeds can stand all along the bank of a river, or grow out into the water at a point or confluence of streams. Trout like them: they don't seem to enter the reeds like bass might do, but will hang along the edges of the beds waiting for insects to fall in. This seems to be a favourite pastime in autumn, just as the reeds begin to go brown.

Where the reeds are growing against a gravel bed, the trout will sometimes bottom feed, rooting out nymphs next to the reed stems. An upstream cast with a leaded Olive or Brown Nymph may connect with these feeding fishes.

In summer the bright green reed stems sometimes form unexpected lies where the current is strong, normally at the tail of a pool or the edges of a tumbling rapid or weir. Indentations in the reeds in the strong current may hold fishes, but often these are small ones unable to compete for more effective lies in the mainstream. At a confluence, the reeds often grow out into the water, sometimes with an eddy to one side of the stand of reeds. These spots with turning water nearly always have a fish in resi-

less depth, the fishes are likely to be along the edge of the drop-off, next to the shallow water. These fishes see extremely well, and need to be approached very cautiously. A thorax-weighted Gold-ribbed Hare's Ear on a light tippet and floating line will sometimes take them, but line flash and shadow can be a real problem. A slight ripple helps enormously. If you frighten one fish, they all seem to know, and you may as well rest the pool and carry on to the next run. These fishes are often hanging above a gravel bottom and a good hatch of mayfly could be on the cards, in which case a dry fly is the answer.

Deep pools

In Lesotho streams, small waterfalls (and occasionally big ones) tumbling into a deep eddying pool are a common sight. In other locations they are rarer, but still occur frequently enough. Lesotho is wonderful in this respect, and it is not altogether unusual to find three or four such falls and pools in every kilometre of stream. The water is crystal clear in the almost dence, and are always worth a cast or two with a size 10 Woolly Bugger.

Eddies and pockets

Eddies are seen by many anglers as the key spots in the river. Although they often hold trout, some of the holding spots discussed previously produce better fishing. Nevertheless, these pockets of circulating water are always worth a cast or two, and fishes of 1–2 kg will often take up residence in them. They are perhaps the commonest trout lies and almost every pool will manifest one or more kinds of eddy.

The best eddies are those at the inside bend of a river (some refer to this as the eye of the pool, hot spot, or just plain 'inside eddy'). The current sweeps past the inside corner, creating an almost dead spot around the bend. Water will spin slowly in this eddy and much foodstuff will be captured in the whirling current. The very best of these have the added advantage of a bush above them, and often these hold a very good fish. Big trout like shallow eddies of this type, and are often easily seen by the careful and stealthy fly-fisherman. Such eddies also occur at bridges and small promontories. The bridge type is often eulogised in English fly-fishing literature as the home of the elusive 'monster'.

There is often an eddy at either corner of a weir, and at a confluence there may be several complex interacting eddies. Small trout often inhabit the former type, but the latter can be home to some good-sized fishes.

Confluences are always worth fishing thoroughly. There is a very nice one on the river I fish, with a huge wattle hanging over it. Reeds grow on the confluence point and a large elodea weed bed grows on the opposite side of the incoming tributary. The bottom is deep and rocky. Many fine fishes live in this confluence pool, and in the crystal-clear water they can be quite difficult to fool. A stealthy approach from

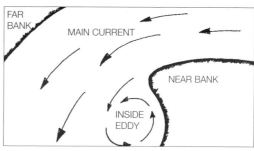

Fig. 7.3: The inside eddy.

An eddy revolves at the edge of a small weir. Several good fishes have been taken where the white water meets the edge of the circulating eddy.

downstream, casting as you move upstream, and searching the pockets, sometimes produces a good-sized fish. But if one of those fishes sees you, that pool is dead for hours and nothing will incite them to take.

Stream fishing is a stealthy business which calls on many skills ranging from casting to entomology, and a good understanding of fish senses and behaviour. It can be very rewarding both in terms of fishing and in terms of enjoying the natural world. There is very little to match the sheer joy of stream fishing with a fly rod, and even the hardened saltwater fly-fisherman relishes the opportunity to be 'at one' with the gurgling, ever-changing brook. A good fish from a small, overgrown, crystal clear river is a great achievement, one to be proud of, and one to be savoured again and again.

CHAPTER 8

RISE FORMS

If circumstances lead me, I will find
Where truth is hid, though it were hid indeed
Within the centre

William Shakespeare, *Hamlet*

The fly-fisherman walks the shadows of the fish's world like an astral wraith; only slightly seen, always disappearing, often deadly dangerous.

From the angler's world of crystal-clear air, the glassy surface of the water is the edge of a mystery. The shadowy existence of fishes is glimpsed and savoured, its revelations hard won, its secrets only slightly understood. The magic kingdom of the fishes ends at the surface, an atom-thick barrier in which only the rise forms and the shards of changing light tell stories. The 'rise' is a key to fish behaviour, a key which we can see, examine, and unravel. The rise, then, is a very important clue to the activities of the creatures behind the barrier, and we would do well to learn as much about it as we can, since such knowledge is the basis of nearly all dry fly and surface technique strategy!

In a study of rise forms, some understanding of the behaviour of light, and also of the vision of fishes, becomes important. The reader is ad-

vised therefore to study the following information on rise forms in conjunction with the information given in Chapter 3. The detail of fly-fishing responses to specific rises is given in Chapters 6, 7 and 11. However, where appropriate, and for reasons of clarity, some basic information on strategies is also supplied here.

TROUT RISES

The trout and its rise forms have been the basis of study by many fly-fishermen, and the subject has been covered in many books on fly-fishing. It can be regarded as the cornerstone of imitative dry fly-fishing, in that the dimpled surface of a river or lake is the doorway to often rewarding surface fly-fishing. I say 'surface' fly-fishing deliberately, because the angler's response to a rise might be one of several – it may be dry fly-fishing, or fishing in the surface film, or fishing perhaps just a few centimetres under the surface.

Learn about rises, and your chances of choosing the correct tactic and the correct fly will improve, and so will your success rate. The rise type will not usually tell you exactly which fly pattern to select, but it will tell you a lot about the feeding pattern behind the rise.

Still-water trout rises
Head and tail rise
The 'head and tail' rise is one of the better known still-water rise forms. It is usually seen in a calm surface, or in a slight ripple. Most

The head and tail rise, seen here in a slight ripple.

A ring rise ... time for a dry fly? (Photo: courtesy Trout Hideaway)

often seen at dawn or during the evening, but can also be seen throughout the day at times, especially if conditions are still and foggy.

The fish moves upward with a slight ripple, and breaks the surface with the dorsal fin and the tip of the tail. Sometimes the back too is exposed. The action is a kind of silent porpoising and is quite unmistakable. Yellowfish rise in the same way at times. A leader made up as suggested in the information on buzzer flies (see Chapter 11) should be cast out and retrieved slowly with a figure-of-eight retrieve.

When the wind is blowing and a wave is running, this rise can be hard to see and you will need to watch closely to spot it. All you will see is a slight shimmering disturbance and a small flattening of the wave where the rise occurs. If you are lucky, you may just see the back of the fish. Such conditions are best examined with binoculars (the small collapsing back-packer's type is ideal), which makes such rises a lot easier to see!

The head and tail rise is usually a good indication that the fish is feeding on buzzer pupae suspended in the surface, or moving just below it prior to hatching. Once the buzzers start to actively hatch, the rise form may change to a condition where the trout produce bow waves and swirls without breaking surface. A commonly seen phenomenon is a small calm patch suddenly appearing in the ripple. What has happened is that the trout are deeper, and are now taking the buzzer pupae as they near the surface. This only happens in really heavy hatches. If there is a wave running, a good method is to drift a buzzer around with the cross-wind. If there is a flat calm, change to a sink-and-draw retrieve on an intermediate line.

Occasionally, sedges will start to hatch with the buzzers. The sedges may well continue to hatch after the buzzers have ceased. You can easily identify the change with binoculars, they magnify fly detail well, and shorten perspective. You may not observe any change at all from shore with the naked eye. Use the same tactics as for the buzzers, but change the fly to a Pearl Pushkin, or a Longhorn, or perhaps an Invicta. The trout will often continue to rise in the same way, even though the food form has changed to sedges.

Rather more rarely, trout will rise to floating snails with the head and tail type of rise. Keep it in mind for those days when none of the insect-imitating flies are working in a good rise.

117

A rise in the ripple. A stiff breeze has flattened the rise, making it harder to see.

Ring rise

The appearance of surface insects causes its own rise forms, and the rise is similar whether they have just hatched or are terrestrials which have been blown onto the surface. The most commonly seen rise form is the ring rise. Usually, one hears a quiet 'plop', followed by concentric rings moving out from a centre. These rings are not so easily seen in a ruffled surface during a breeze, but the experienced angler can usually pin-point such a rise even in really rough water. The ring rise to big insects such as daddy-long-legs, large sedges, or moths is often more decisive, with a louder 'plop' and larger concentric rings.

Very big fishes taking insects from the surface do not necessarily make a larger or more energetic rise. However, they often make a different sound ... more like the last water going down a sink drain. This noise has directed me to many a good fish at dusk in a heavy hatch.

A trout leaps for an airborne insect.

Sometimes, almost with the last cast, when it is very hard to see in the gathering dusk, a big brownie will leave its lair and start to feed. This big fish's 'down the drainhole' sound gives him away! The second-largest rainbow caught at Dullstroom, in South Africa, was taken in just this way. The angler heard the 'down-the-plug' rise sound, cast his buzzer, and eventually landed a beautifully conditioned 7lb 9oz hen.

Furrowing

Trout behave in a specific way during mass hatches. I refer here particularly to the enormous hatches of caenis mayflies (otherwise known as 'Angler's Curse'; for more information see Chapter 11), and also to some of the really big falls of flying ants or termites. The trout start off by feeding on the caenis nymphs as they come up to hatch, and then start taking the odd emerging dun as they begin to appear on the surface. Eventually, there are so many flies hatching that the trout simply cruise around with their mouths open. They suck in the nymphs like a vacuum cleaner, making bubbling noises as they go. The fish's head is often visible at this time, as it makes a small bow wave on the surface. It is this action which I refer to as furrowing. (Yellowfish and kurper will also rise in mass hatches of small flies.)

In this rise type there is a chance that you can enjoy good sport at the beginning of the rise, but once the trout starts furrowing there is generally no way that he will prefer your fly to such a bounty of naturals!

Leaping and splashing

Sometimes the trout leap clear of the water, often splashing wildly as they land. It is this noisy fall-back into the water which can be heard some distance away. This action is sometimes brought on by trout taking dragonfly adults hawking above the surface. But, much more commonly, it is in reaction to egg-laying female sedges fluttering across the surface. Interestingly, this behaviour is usually in response to smaller species of sedges.

Trout will also leap when ants or termites are falling on the water, but generally only when they are falling rather sparsely. The small brown grass beetles, which are so common in summer in the high country, will also sometimes cause the trout to leap. Good flies for these 'windborne fall' situations are Coch-y-Bonddu, Black and Peacock Spider, and the Black Ant. A surprisingly effective method is to strip retrieve a Black Lure just under the surface on a floating line.

The jumping often takes place on a lee shore at the line where the ripple commences. This is where wind-blown terrestrial insects are most likely to land in a breeze. The trout soon find them, and often concentrate in the ripple, making it a productive target area.

Swallows are often the first to know about an imminent hatch of flies, and often give advance notice of the hatch by queuing up on a fence or on telephone wires.

Still-water tailing

Trout and many other fish will occasionally take to browsing shallow bottoms for snails and insects. They will sometimes pick snails off the rocks and boulders along a dam wall. They will also feed over gravel bottoms in shallow water, where they are inclined to look out for dragon-fly and caddis larvae. Such feeding is usually accompanied by swirls and odd sightings of vertically held tail fins. The fishes are head down when feeding like this and often heavily preoccupied. However, they will take a passing Pearl Pushkin or a Long Horns fly drifted along the bottom.

Winter – the close-in ring rise

This is difficult to describe, and a purely African phenomenon, I suspect. Throughout high-country winter, in the first hours after a frosty dawn, the trout cruise the very shallow margins feeding on small olive corixids rendered torpid by the previous evening's frost. The corixids are found in water of less than half a metre depth, and they hang suspended usually between half depth and the bottom. The trout swim in and take a mouthful as they turn at the margin. The result is a broiling ring rise which is often quite noisy ... there will usually be several going on at any one time (see Chapter 6 for the fly-fishing method).

As the water's edge warms up in the sun, the trout move out to deeper water. A hatch of deep-olive bodied, dark brownish winged mayflies often coincides with this outward movement. The trout respond to this with the normal ring rise (see opposite).

Small fry herding

The herding of small fry is usually associated with brown trout, but rainbows, kurper and yellowfish also do this. It is often a very noisy business as the fishes swirl, splash and bow wave about. At times, the sound can be heard up to 50 metres away! The surface disturbance is considerable and is often augmented by leaping fry going in all directions. In these circumstances any good lure fly (my personal preference is for a Polystickle) will be taken.

Running water trout rises

Rises in running water are very different in most respects to those in still water. The angler is also at an advantage in that it is a simple job to catch the insects with a small aquarium net and identify them sufficiently to put up a matching fly.

It has been said that you can identify the food of a stream trout by the rise form. The rise, it is said, differs in subtle ways for the differing insect types. I somehow doubt it, but GEM Skues, in the earlier part of this century, tells us that some of the English blue-winged olive duns are risen to with a characteristic kidney-shaped rise. However, observation leads one to believe that this is not the case at all ... so what does one believe? The truth is that there are several different rise forms in rivers, and the fol-

A splashy rise to a large sedge.

lowing are worth noting. At least with these rise forms, one can tell more or less what the cause is, and can then take the appropriate action.

Running water ring rises

These are the most commonly seen trout rises. They are rising with a distinct whorl of ebbing rings and a clear, but slight, sipping noise. The slower the water speed, the easier this rise is to discern. In fast water, the rise rings die away quickly, and if there is a ripple as well, all you may see is a brief cross-wise ripple at the point of rise.

Most often this is a rise brought on by mayfly duns, and is always a good time for some dry fly-fishing. The fishes are usually ready to take anything floating by, and are not preoccupied with mayfly duns of a specific kind. They will probably rise in the same way to any terrestrial bug that comes by.

Sucking noise rises

Now and then you may observe a rise in running water which makes only the tiniest of surface disturbances, but is accompanied by a clear sucking noise. If you could observe the fish's station carefully you would find that he is holding just under the surface (hardly moving), and sipping insects from the surface quite confidently. The rise noise is usually very noticeable, and since there is not much to see, one must often locate the rise position by ear. A rise of this kind is very often directed at spent mayfly spinners (see Chapter 11 for more information on these) which are stuck in the surface film and cannot move. The same kind of rise may occur in response to nymphs which have failed to hatch, and also to a steady stream of 'stuck in the film' terrestrials, such as you might come across on a windy day. This rise form often indicates a situation where the fishes will rise freely to the dry fly, and a Sherry Spinner may well give a really good day's sport.

Splashy rise

A really splashy rise with little ring development generally indicates the rise of a small trout. However, on those occasions when sedges are hatching on the stream and buzzing along the surface, big trout strike at the moving flies. Often the trout are moving at good speed, causing quite considerably splashy rises. Such rises are usually evening phenomena (although they can occur at any time from mid-morning), and can be easily handled with a dry Goddard and Henry's Sedge.

Erupting rise

Almost like a submarine surfacing, the fish pushes itself upwards in the water, and all the dorsal body surfaces from shoulders to tail fin become visible simultaneously. This kind of rise is indicative of a preoccupied trout which is critically scanning each food item drifting past. This trout hangs just below the surface and is normally concerned only with a single species of mayfly dun. This fish is so preoccupied that he will ignore all other species of flies, and most artificials as well! The answer here is matching the hatch really well, but this can make for frustrating fishing.

Flashing

Not strictly speaking a 'rise', but rather more an observation. It occurs over stony bottoms in streams when trout are rooting-out shrimps and nymphs. It needs clear water, and the angler normally sees the action repeated many times. The flash of the trout body indicates that the trout are taking nymphs from rocks and stones. The trout brush the nymphs off the rocks and stones, and appear to turn or twist on their sides at an angle to the bottom ... this action causes the characteristic flash.

Tailing

If you ever see a 'V' shape (point upstream) appear in the river and then die away a few seconds later, you are looking at a tail fin! Occasionally, you might spot the tail as well, but most often not. The trout are grubbing for caddis, snails, and nymphs by standing on their heads in shallow water. This is an easily missed stream rise form, unless you remain observant. The usual response is to fish a dead drifted nymph imitation with a sinking line.

Bubbles after the rise

In the event that bubbles follow a rise, you can be sure that the fish is feeding on surface insects such as duns and sedges. As the fish sips from the surface, he inevitably takes in some air, and this is released from the gills as the fish turns down. An absence of bubbles indicates a sub-surface feeder which may be picking up ready-to-hatch nymphs as little as a centimetre below the surface.

OTHER RISE FORMS AS AN INDICATION OF FISH SPECIES

In Africa many more fishes than just trout will rise to a fly. One of the problems for the fly-fishing beginner in Africa is in recognising a rise, and in being able to interpret its meaning. We have already examined the trout rises, and we will now explore rises by other fish species as a means to identification and a pointer to suitable tactics.

Bass

Bass are inclined either to erupt from the surface in dashing powerful jumps, or, quite the opposite, they rise so gently as to simply dimple the surface ... they are quite capable of taking prey from the surface in absolute silence with but the slightest ripple to mark their passing. Usually this tiny dimple of a rise is followed by an oily swirl as the bass turns down. This oily swirl results from the fish sinking a foot or so before turning. On occasion, bass make a characteristic kissing sound as they rise to small flies. Bass often rise to insects in a flat calm (unlike many other fish), and they are very active at the surface just prior to thunder storms. The bass rise is usually to larger prey, so they are most easily taken by using surface flies such as poppers, imitations of sedges and

The big mouth of a bass. Largemouth bass can easily engulf large floating food forms. Nevertheless, rises are often almost ripple free. (Photo: Don Lort)

moths, mouse imitations, etc; and by casting these near to structures such as lily pads, weedbeds, or reeds.

Kurper (or tilapia)

Kurper as most anglers call them, or tilapia (or bream, as they are called in some parts of Africa) very often rise to insects. Usually when they do, there will be several of them at it. Kurper have a distinctly small rise with a splashy centre. An easy rise to recognise once you have seen a few.

Carp

Carp are often taken on wet flies in Africa. I have never come across a carp that was caught on a dry fly. Carp sometimes jump clear out of the water, landing with a tremendous splash, or they come half way out only to slide back down again. At such times they are easily recognised. Occasionally, they porpoise just as trout do, but the large easily visible scales and the bronzy-blue colour always give them away.

Yellowfish

The rise form of these very important fish is rather 'trouty' at first glance. However, the yellowfish are much more aggressive, and very often the rise shape in streams is parabolic in shape as a result of the faster forward movement. In the main, the trout and yellowfish rises are very difficult to separate because they have rather similar feeding habits. Also, the yellowfish turns after taking the insect in virtually the same way as a trout does, thus generating the same circular ring rise. Yellowfish spend a lot less time at the surface than trout do, but at times they will rise heavily all over a water. They are much more inclined to take large prey at the surface such as frogs and fallen baby birds – something trout seldom do.

On occasion the larger yellowfish species can be seen chasing fry. The fry skip across the surface with a bow wave surging after them. The bow wave is all that you see of the yellowfish.

Barbel (or catfish)

Barbel, also referred to as catfish, are usually associated with a messy rise, often with an accompanying 'gloop' sound. The gloop occurs as a result of the barbel exercising its rudimentary lung. The rise is always followed by a separate surface disturbance as a result of the fish turning down with a powerful beat of its tail. This rise form is fairly typical and easily recognised once you have seen a few.

Barbel will take drowning birds, mice, and other things from the surface, but seldom insects. Their usual reason for rising is in fact to take in air, which they do fairly frequently.

Grass carp

These rather special fishes of Chinese origin have been introduced into many trout fisheries for the sole purpose of keeping the weeds down. They browse heavily on the weeds and appear not to disturb the trout one bit. The grass carp are rather fond of surface activity, and, because of their often impressive size, they have caused many a beginner to experience unwarranted excitement and excess adrenalin at the 'huge fish rising over there'.

The grass carp love to bask and sport a bit in the shallows in the evening, but they are usually easily identified by the large triangular dorsal fin which often shows at such times. Another give away is large 'furrows' of water as the fishes move around with their powerful tails. Grass carp are occasionally taken on flies, often foul hooked, but sometimes fairly hooked in the scissor. Such captures are the exception rather than the rule, and I have never heard of one taken on a dry fly from the surface. The

A fly-caught mud mullet. Mud mullet, or moggel as they are also known, are often taken on flies. This specimen fell to a Whisky Fly fished on a lead-core line.

grass carp are magnificent fighters on fly tackle, as anyone who has caught one will tell you!

Mud mullet and other mudfishes

Members of the mudfish family are essentially bottom dwellers, but on occasion some of the species rise to flies, and can provide excellent sport since they are all great fighters. They generally rise in a very splashy manner reminiscent of a small fish. The splash is caused by the tail fin as they turn down. Watch closely, and you may even spot the often greyish tail.

Frogs

Possibly the commonest non-fish rise you will come across in African trout waters is the good old platanna. The 'plattie' is not normally rising to an insect, but is actually coming up for a gulp of air. His snout just breaks the surface and a rise ring is formed ... sometimes if you watch carefully you may see the snout break surface. That is the one giveaway; the other is the weakness of the rise ring. There is also absolutely no sound in these froggy rises. Frog rises are very

An African sculpin or water turtle hooked by a carp rig.

common, and you must learn to recognise them if you do not wish to waste time casting at something you do not want to take your fly. Many beginners are unaware of frog rises and spend much wasted time casting at them.

Turtles

If you see a snout come up in an almost ripple-free rise, and then stay put for anything from seconds to several minutes; you are watching a water turtle.

CHAPTER 9

AFRICAN FRESHWATER FISHES

Men who like a spice of danger, even in their fishing, will go far afield and into lonely spots.

B Bennion, 1923

So much is now known about the various fishes that can be caught on a fly, that specialist groups are forming everywhere. In Africa, there are fly-fishermen specialising not only in trout, but also in other fishes such as catfish, yellowfish, kingfish, and so on ... they are what the British call 'specimen hunters'; they eat, drink and sleep their fishing!

Since the various trout (although exotic), are the most popular of the species pursued with the fly rod in Africa, some information on their history will not be out of place here. The fly-fishing methods used for the other inland species, and for saltwater species as well, all originated in trout fly-fishing, and while they may have changed a great deal for some species, all fly-fishermen (no matter how well-versed in the methods for their selected species) have a lot to gain by acquiring the basic fly-fishing methodology from trout fishing strategy and technique.

TROUT AND SALMON

The brown trout *(Salmo trutta)* is the best known of the indigenous salmonids of the northern temperate regions of Europe and Asia. Long before Europeans ever heard of the rainbow trout, the 'brownie' was passionately hunted by the fly-fishermen of Britain, and colonists lost no time in attempting to introduce this much-loved fish into the far corners of the world. From the damp, sometimes icy land of its birth, it spread to lofty mountains overlooking steaming jungles thousands of metres below, to island paradises such as New Zealand, the continental vastness of Australia, the snow and fire of Tierra del Fuego, and many other distant lands. As Isaac Walton so aptly said centuries before, in 1653, *'the Trout is a fish highly valued, both in this and foreign nations'*.

The first attempt to introduce brown trout into African waters was in 1875 with a shipment to South Africa, but all the ova were dead on arrival. Not until 1890 was a successful attempt made, by John Parker. These were hatched in Natal and the fry released into three eastward-flowing streams. In 1895 the first adult browns were stripped by one John Scott in the Cape Province. Scott devised a method of sending trout by post throughout South Africa, and they eventually arrived in the then Transvaal and Orange Free State.

Rainbow trout *(Oncorhynchus mykiss* syn. *Salmo gairdneri)* were first introduced into the Cape in 1897. Rhodesia (Zimbabwe), Nyasaland (Malawi), and Basutoland (Lesotho) all imported trout from South Africa between 1900 and 1930. Kenya went ahead on its own, and the first batch of mixed brown and rainbow trout was imported there by Ewart Grogan in 1905 from the UK. Several other stockings followed from both the UK and South Africa. A hatchery was set up in Kenya and from there Uganda and Tanganyika (Tanzania) both received stockings. Ethiopia received its first trout in the 1950s.

Trout and salmon are essentially cold-water species which during the last ice age were able to spread through the seas and up the rivers of North America and Europe. They need well-oxygenated water, and are thus naturally restricted to cooler, fast-flowing rivers and colder, deep, still waters. They are more susceptible to dissolved carbon dioxide than most fishes and are unable to survive in polluted or stagnant water. The high temperatures of African river estuaries, and the seas themselves, ensured the non-survival of anadromous (sea running) fishes and attempts made in the late 1800s to introduce salmon into Africa consequently failed. The opening of the enormous high-altitude Lesotho Highland Water Scheme offers an opportunity to introduce salmon and trout which could run the cold rivers to breed, and then return to this great cold-water impoundment to feed, as if they were in an inland sea. There are certainly precedents for this in other parts of the world, where major sports and tourist industries have grown from such endeavours.

Most of the African rivers and streams into which trout were introduced held little competition other than indigenous yellowfish. Many of the larger species of yellowfish were missing from some streams, and the trout quickly carved out a niche for themselves, living well on the local insects and the indigenous small fishes. Where other competing species existed, trout still did well, and with artificial stocking have more than held their own.

The salmonids are fairly primitive bony fishes, well adapted to surviving in a range of environments. They are carnivores, capable of handling a wide range of food forms from fishes and mammals to insects and worms. They are extremely active, capable of a fair turn of speed, and able to jump from pool to pool on fast-moving rivers. Salmonids can accelerate from rest to a speed of 20 knots almost instantaneously. They all have well-developed senses and have excellent vision and vibratory sensing systems.

Brown trout are known to grow to maximum weights of around 20 kg in the great lakes of Scandinavia. Rainbows have been recorded to similar sizes in the USA. Both species attain weights of 6 kg or so in Africa. Although fish of

A series of rearing ponds at Sabie in South Africa. Fishes from here are destined for the table.

7 kg have been reported, they have never been recorded.

In Africa, brown trout manage to breed successfully in both still and running water. Rainbows also manage to breed, but very much less successfully. In Lesotho, there are plenty of self-sustaining fisheries, which because they are subjected to low angling pressure may well survive for ever without re-stocking. However, these are the more remote rivers. The easily accessible rivers tend to have far less viable fish stocks. In the rest of Africa, most fisheries need regular re-stocking in order to survive. The fact is that in most trout fisheries in Africa, the trout survive only because of man. Thus, a fairly sizeable hatchery and fish growing industry has sprung up, especially in southern Africa.

Some of the hatcheries are exporting both fishes and ova. They also serve a large hotel and fishmonger industry, and to a lesser extent supply living fish to the sport fisheries. Today, the

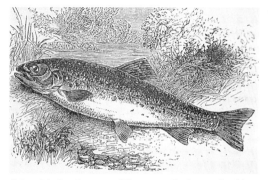

Interest in trout grew rapidly among the 'upper class' in nineteenth-century Britain. This engraving of a brown trout is from the year 1840.

Rearing cages at Swartwater Dam in South Africa. This large operation produces fishes for sport at one of Africa's prime fly-fishing venues.

great majority of fishes reared by these establishments are rainbows. The browns (and to a much lesser extent landlocked salmon and brook trout) are far less common, and are reared for sport only. Rainbows are hardier than browns, but perhaps more important for the fishmonger industry is that the rainbows grow faster and develop saleable protein much more quickly.

Mixed fisheries of browns and rainbows are returning, and it is now fairly easy to find fishing locations with both species. Because of slightly differing habits and temperature preferences, the two species provide a broader spectrum of sport, one often feeding when the other is uninterested. Browns grow big and are excellent in deep-water fisheries. They fight differently, the rainbow being a flashy, leaping fighter compared with the brown, which jumps less often and is a dogged fighter more likely to seek out snags than a rainbow. Whatever the comparisons, they are both great fighters on light fly tackle.

The rainbow trout is now the best known of the trout species in Africa, and if a water has only a single species of trout it will almost cer-

tainly be rainbows. Rainbow trout come from the Pacific coastline of America, and like the brown trout have been introduced into rivers and still waters in many corners of the world. When introduced to a water, rainbows disperse more rapidly than brown trout and will fill up the far niches of a river much more quickly than browns. Brook trout disperse even faster! Additionally, rainbows are more tolerant of high water temperature, and in this respect are more likely to survive in borderline temperature situations. The lifetime of a rainbow is shorter than the brown trout, but because of their fast growth rate and prowess as fighters, they are more popular.

Brook trout *(Salvelinus fontinalis)*, also known as brook charr, have not been successful introductions in Africa. They require colder temperatures than the others, and have difficulty competing with the larger rainbows and browns. They may perhaps still be found in a few streams (the Blyde in South Africa is one), but are hardly worth seeking out as there are no records of brook trout being caught in recent years.

Although several attempts have been made to

introduce anadromous Atlantic salmon *(Salmo salar)* to Africa, they have never been successful. None of the sea-running trout introduced into Africa have ever successfully managed to survive the run to the sea and the return, and thus steelhead (sea-run rainbows), and sea trout (sea-run browns) are unknown in Africa.

The 'landlocked salmon' *(Salmo salar)* is specifically similar to the anadromous 'Atlantic salmon', having the same structure and virtually identical taxonomic characteristics, and is regarded by many as a superior freshwater gamefish to the trout. They originate in the USA, where several populations are known, often with slight differences in appearance, and are known to exist in both river and still-water systems.

In Africa, they have been introduced at Trout Hideaway in South Africa, and are also known from a river in the same area. Landlocks are autumn spawners, and need cold-gravelled areas at river and tributary mouths, with swift water flow, if they are to be successful. They are known to reach 10+ kg, but a trophy specimen is generally considered at around 5 kg, with 1,5 kg a good average size.

The wild landlocked salmon in the waters of Maine in the USA start life as insect eaters, and end up feeding on minnows and other small fish. As a result, streamer-style flies and other fish imitators are considered most useful. Flies like the Gray Ghost were originated in Maine for the landlocked salmon, from whence these flies spread to achieve world-wide fame.

The landlocks like deep, clear water, and tend to stay down throughout the hot months of the year. The most useful method is to strip lures deep down on a lead-core line. The Catlet Muddler is a very good fly for African conditions. However, they are also partial to wind-blown terrestrials, and will often come up from the deeps towards dusk, and rise to insects in the smooth surface of the lee shore. Dry fly-fishing with the Chicken or the Soldier Palmer Pink can be very successful.

The landlocked salmon is a fast fish, often fighting at great speed with spectacularly energetic leaps. Indeed a superb target for the fly-fisherman.

Salmon in Africa? Yes indeed! This landlocked salmon was photographed at Trout Hideaway in South Africa, where these fish are proving to be great sport. (Photo: Adolf Nicklaus)

TIGERFISH

Catching the mighty tigerfish with the fly is surely the most exciting kind of freshwater sport fishing around. Not only are you contending with the pound-for-pound freshwater champion fighter of all time, but you are doing it in the finest way too! The only parallel to this kind of heart-thumping excitement is saltwater fly-fishing for ocean battlers like sierra and small sailfish. Today, there are a great many anglers who fish for tigerfish with the fly, and the 'hunting of the water tiger' is practised not only by the fly-fishermen of Africa, but also by a steadily increasing stream of overseas visitors. Tigerfish are ready takers of flies, and are particularly good in the early morning and late evening. Hugh Copley, in *The Game Fishes of Africa*, was moved to write *'They ... seem to exist simply to try conclusions with the angler'.*

Tigerfish *(Hydrocynus vittatus)* have several local names, such as kibebe (Lake Tanganyika),

A fine brace of tigerfish from Jedibe in the Okavango, Botswana. (Photo: Malcolm Meintjes)

Geoff Taylor with a record tigerfish from Jozini Dam in South Africa, at the very southern limit of tigerfish distribution. (Photo: courtesy Geoff Taylor)

lokel (Lake Rudolf), tsage (Nigeria), manda or binga (Democratic Republic of the Congo). Distribution is from the Lower Nile across to Senegal and Niger, and south to Angola and northern South Africa. They are in Lakes Victoria, Tanganyika and Rudolf (Turkana), but not Lake Malawi.

There is another huge tigerfish in Africa, found primarily in the River Congo system, and also possibly in the higher reaches of the Zambezi. Photographs from the Democratic Republic of the Congo of 40 kg specimens taken on dead fish bait are fairly common, and this fish is said to attain 60 kg. That's a daunting picture when one considers the dental array of this fish. Goliath tigerfish *(Hydrocynus goliath)* are magnificently powerful fighters, and a big one would strain any fly-fishing outfit (even one designed for tarpon) to its utmost limit. I have come across stories of spinner-caught specimens, but have never heard of one taken on the fly. So, if you can get into the tropical Congo basin, here's your chance to achieve something new ... if your tackle can survive it.

Tackle for tigerfish
Rod
My favourite rod for tiger fishing is a 10 foot AFTM 9 saltwater surf fly rod, i.e. something with good butt power, together with a reasonably fast tip, and consequent casting ability. The nearest thing on the UK market would be a salmon/sea trout rod. However, before you

rush off to buy a saltwater USA product, do ensure that tip speed hasn't been sacrificed for butt power completely, as you might find in a tarpon rod. I like an extension butt on these rods and the best single leg rod rings you can find. These must be good; otherwise, if you intend to use the same rod in the salt, then sand and grit abrasion will quickly destroy cheap rings. A good salt-proof double-locking reel fitting is a must. This rod can also be used for big trout in still water, for bass, for the salt, and for catfish and Nile perch – effectively, a good all-round big-fish rod!

Reel
In today's world, there is no doubt that a disc-braked reel is the answer, and, for good value, little beats the System Two. These are great reels, but beware, don't allow the brake system to get wet, because it will cease to work effectively. There are plenty of other makes on the market, most of which also work well.

If your interest is light tackle (plenty of tigers are taken on AFTM 6 outfits ... plenty are also lost), the smaller System Two is still the best choice. This disc-braked reel, like the tigerfish rod, will double-up for the other species of big fish as well.

Lines
I load my tiger reels with 200–250 metres of Dacron backing of 12 kg breaking strain, and knot this to 50 metres of shooting line, which in turn is knotted to the shooting head itself. For those who do not like shooting heads, just nail knot a full-length weight forward fly line to the backing.

The best shooting head for tigerfish is a cut-down weight forward line. I like to take an AFTM 10 line and cut it back to 24 feet to match my AFTM 9 rod. The timing of the cast is faster, but it allows long-distance casting in restricted areas, and because of the short back cast, more freedom from hang-ups in the shrubbery ... both useful advantages on jungle-edged rivers. I find a fast-sinking line to be most useful for tigerfish. I also carry a lead core for really deep water, and an intermediate line for small tigers over shallow water. The double-haul casting technique is an essential skill for fly-fishing for these gamefish.

Leaders

Because of the 'heavy' design of most tigerfish flies, smoothly tapered leaders are not necessary. I use a simple design consisting of two metres of 0,4 mm Maxima Chameleon at the line end, knotted to one metre of 0,32 mm. I do not bother with swivels for joining the tippet, since the tigerfish often strike these, and then bite straight through the line. I like to use a simple surgeon's knot, or an Albright knot, for joining the leader to a wire tippet. A method favoured by some is to form a loop in the wire and crimp it. The leader is then joined to this loop with a tucked clinch knot.

Flies

The range of Tigger flies (see Chapter 13 and plate 2), were specially designed for tiger fishing a good many years ago by the author, and have proven themselves all over the African continent. There is still some discussion on whether built-in wire tippets or attached wire tippets are best ... I prefer them built-in. There are modern variations to these flies incorporating fluorescents and Krystal Flash components, but I have honestly seen no proof that tigerfish are impressed with these additions. The truth is that a tigerfish will take any fly if he's in the mood ... the Tigger series simply presents him with a fly designed to sink fast, to hook him, and to survive the mill of his teeth.

The hook point of a tigerfish fly *must always be needle sharp* – the tiger's mouth is bone hard, and it is one of the most difficult fish to get a good hook hold in (especially from the comparatively soft strike of a fly rod). Check the point every five or six casts by running it over your thumb nail ... it won't slide if it's sharp! Penetrating this bony mouth is much easier with a small hook than a large one. A size 6 does the job well, and you will seldom need anything larger.

Most flies other than the Tiggers cannot survive a tigerfish's first strike, let alone the fight that follows. By all means try a trout fly or two, but don't forget the steel wire trace! The tiger-

Irving Stevenson with a big Kariba tigerfish taken trolling a copper-bodied Tigger fly. (Photo: courtesy Irving Stevenson)

fish will usually strip the dressing, and spit back a piece of bent wire, because normally that is all that is left! Some saltwater flies, if dressed on Inox hooks and epoxied at every stage (especially the glass minnows), will survive a fight with a tigerfish. Some of these flies work well, but even they are often destroyed.

Hooks

I don't have much faith in mass-produced commercial flies intended for tigerfish. It is far better to contact the factory or your custom fly-tier, and have your Tiggers especially tied up for you. Instruct them to glue every stage of construction carefully, and specify clearly the hook that you want the fly dressed on. Some anglers send their vice-checked hooks in with the order. Vice-checking checks the 'temper' of the hook steel and about 20% of hooks fail this test. To do this, put the hook in the jaws of the fly-tying vice and tweak the hook. If it bends, reject it. This business of hooks is critical. You need a normal shank (never a long shank) flat forged hook with a low-profile barb. To emphasise the importance of it, I repeat that the hook must be exceptionally sharp, and the size range only from 2 to 6 – nothing larger. If you learn to tie your own flies then you will get exactly what you want, and that is the best way of all.

Finding tigerfish

The best water condition for fly-fishing for tigerfish is clear water. You may have to keep low and creep about, but if you do this, and you wear polarised sunglasses, you may well spot the tigers. You can then cast directly to them.

Tigerfish in rivers are usually easy to find since they have a strong preference for well-oxygenated water, such as you find in deep water at the end of fast runs, or, better still, at the tail-end of rapids. The best structural scenario is perhaps where the river flows over shallow water, and then out and over deeper water. If the water is actively flowing and streaming about, then so much the better! A good rocky bottom, with occasional large rocks breaking up the flow, is also a good area. Big tigerfish like to patrol deep drop-offs, particularly where a deep cliff-like structure drops several metres to the bottom. You can often find such structures on the bends of rivers.

I was once told by a native fisherman on the Zambezi that tigerfish like to move about in loose shoals, and that they follow a fairly consistent beat, with preferred spots and pathways. This may explain their sudden appearance and disappearance from obviously good spots. Consequently, if you are sure of your chosen spot, then chances are that if you persist, the tigerfish will eventually turn up.

In still water, such as you will find at Kariba, Jozini Dam and other large waters, locating tigerfish is somewhat different. Typical areas to search are:

❑ Areas where there are unusually large numbers of crocodiles. This usually indicates large numbers of catfish, which the crocs feed on. In turn, the catfish are there because there is plenty of food for them. Tigers don't quite pick the teeth of crocodiles, but they are not averse to darting in for bits of loose flesh from the crocodile's meal.

❑ Areas with sunken trees in water 3–5 metres deep, where there are usually plenty of kurper or mudfish shoals.

❑ Promontories. Moving fish are forced to swim close as they go past. Rocky points are the best.

❑ Underwater islands.

❑ Submerged rocky and gravel-bottomed areas. These attract fodder fish as a result of high insect populations.

❑ Sudden drop-offs and underwater cliffs: tigerfish patrol along these.

❑ Old stream and river beds.

If you see large shoals of small fish (such as kapenta on Lake Kariba), then fish these areas. A favourite method of finding tigerfish on large stretches of water is to troll with a spoon or spinner until you get a strike. You then fish the area with flies. If you have an echo sounder, the five metre contour is usually productive.

Playing tigerfish

Fighting a tigerfish on fly tackle is a heart-in-mouth business with explosive activity which results in many tigerfish escaping. Most of these fish are lost on the 'jump' either because of too light a strike, with consequent poor penetration of the hook, or because of slack line during the jump.

Just as with trout, one should 'bow' to a leaping fish. In other words, keep in touch with just enough pressure to ensure that no slack develops, and always keep the rod tip (which should be kept well up at the commencement of a leap, bowing down as the leap develops) towards the fish. Loose line may be smashed by the tigerfish falling on it, it may be cut by his teeth, or the hook may fall out if the least amount of slack is present. An extra-hard haul on the line hand simultaneous with the strike (which should be sideways to improve the chance of a scissors hold) will often drive the hook home. Some fly-fishermen like to strike three or four times, although I am of the opinion that multiple striking can cause a hole to form in the mouth, which can do more harm than good.

The tigerfish fights with all the power and energy he possesses, and for a while he will prove to you that he is the greatest fighter in freshwater. He will eventually burn out, and then (if you have still got him at that stage) he becomes a pussycat ... easy to tame! Remember, be very careful of tigerfish's teeth and remove the hook with artery forceps or pliers.

YELLOWFISH

There are many species of yellowfish in Africa. Most of what is written here is specifically

A superb fly-caught still-water smallmouth yellowfish, taken by Ken Jessop using a Black Panacea fly at Sterkfontein Dam in South Africa.

intended for the smallmouth yellowfish *(Barbus aeneus* syn. *holubi)*. However, these instructions will work just as well for other species of yellowfish.

A growing band of fly-fishermen specialise in yellowfish, and who can blame them! The yellowfish is pound for pound probably three times stronger than a rainbow trout. It takes flies well, and is every bit as much fun to catch. The smallmouth yellowfish grow bigger than trout (up to 10 kg), and fair-sized specimens around 3 kg are fairly common in many African rivers and still waters. Other species can reach 25 kg. There are huge specimens to be found in many of the larger African still waters, one of the best waters being Sterkfontein Dam in South Africa.

Most yellowfish are taken in rivers, but the 'yellows' of large still waters are perhaps the biggest specimens one could hope to find. Most streams and even small brooks hold a good head of yellowfish, and they can provide sport just about everywhere. Streams that flow into large still waters are perhaps the easiest places to catch yellowfish.

Yellowfish in streams and rivers

Favourite river types for the fly-fisherman who is after 'yellows' are the bigger rivers with lots of rapids and fast runs, and with deep pools here and there, such as one would find in the Vaal River in South Africa. Generally speaking, such fishing is reserved for those months when the water is running clear; generally from April to November in southern Africa (the opposite months in countries above the equator). When the river is running thick and muddy after the

The inflow stream at Sterkfontein Dam, probably the best yellowfish water in Africa.

131

Fly-fishing for great yellowfish in small streams is wonderful sport. (A) The strike (B) Surging into another pool (C) Circling (D) Ready to land. (Photos: Joe Joannou)

rains, artificial flies are difficult to see and the fish do not respond well. Small streams have an advantage at such times, since they clear relatively quickly (sometimes within a day, on dam inflow streams). The big rivers may not clear at all, throughout the rainy season!

For searching clear water (and yellowfish are generally best found by sight) a pair of polarised sunglasses is essential. Yellowfish in rivers like fairly shallow (wadeable depth) clear water, and are often easy to spot. However, don't ever forget that if you can see them, they

can see you too, and you must be cautious in your approach. You will also need a good pair of non-slip waders, or alternatively 'tackies' (plimsoles) and jeans, as the South Africans prefer. Try to carry everything in a small fly-fishing waistcoat. The going can be tough, and you don't want to be encumbered with lots of equipment.

When fly-fishing for yellowfish, remember that they are a cautious fish and you will achieve very little by walking along the bank in full view, or by standing and casting in one spot all day. If you wish to catch 'yellows' you must hunt them in their lair! It is a great advantage in yellowfish fly-fishing to locate your fish prior to fishing, and this may mean diligent and careful low-profile searching. Keep down, keep quiet, and move slowly.

Yellowfish like fast-flowing water over a gravelly or shingle bottom, with a preferred depth of no more than 1–1,25 metres. The very best spots are such runs with interspersed rocks, and with water grass or other aquatic vegetation on either side of the run. Big fishes often hang in the current under the weed or in drop-offs behind the rocks. Watch carefully and a fish will reveal itself as it moves out in the current to take a passing morsel. Yellowfish will travel several metres in clear water to eat a passing fly, and you may see your fly simply disappear before your eyes as a yellowfish engulfs it. On broad shallow areas, yellowfish will hold station in any bottom depression, even if the water is fast. In this respect their behavioural patterns are similar to rainbow trout.

You should work your way upstream. If the fishes are there, then sport will be good. Yellowfish will take even in very cold water. Do not give up on a fish without several casts – he will eventually take the fly, and will often be more accommodating than trout in this respect. A soft strike will hook him, but you must get your loose line onto the reel as quickly as possible, and play the fish off the reel. You may be forced to jump over rocks and other obstructions during the fight, and you cannot do this with metres of line lying around. A line basket may be advantageous on rocky rivers.

If you spot a fish in larger pools, cast across and dead drift the fly down. On hot days, the yellowfish like to move into well-oxygenated water if they have the choice. Then you will find them in fast, often white water near the base of rapids – anywhere things get churned-up and bubbly.

Yellowfish takes are often gentle affairs. You may see the fly disappear, or perhaps just a gentle straightening of the line. You should always watch the line very carefully, since any untoward movement is likely to be a take. Just now and then, you may get a violent pull.

Yellowfish can be hard to see in the ripple and boil of fast-moving water. Nevertheless, spotting yellows is the fastest way to improve results, and careful stalking pays off. (Photo: Angelo Komis)

Yellowfish in still waters

Yellowfish in still waters respond very well to the same tactics and strategies used for still-water rainbow trout. In general, yellowfish prefer shallower water, and often cruise the edges of large impoundments rising to flies in very much the same way as trout. They can often be spotted by walking the banks quietly.

Yellowfish are also very fond of cruising in reed-fringed bays, and can usually be found quite close to the reeds. They are quite sociable in still waters, as compared with the often solitary existence of large specimens in rivers. The big ones tend to swim in shoals of less than five individuals, whereas the smaller specimens may be in shoals of up to 20 or more.

The best approach in these bays is with a boat. Drift into the bay quietly, and watch the surface carefully. The presence of the yellowfish shoal is

A largescale yellowfish taken on fly by Rodger Kennard. (Photo: Angelo Komis)

This 17+ kg largemouth yellowfish was taken from the Vaal River by John Southey of Douglas, South Africa. (Photo: courtesy John Southey)

given away by rises ... rises which are often fairly small and quiet, and which do not indicate the true size of the fish responsible. A 7 kg yellowfish will often rise with a small rise rather like a stockie rainbow! The approach must be very quiet. Even electric trolling motors are known to scare them off.

My preference is for an intermediate density fly line and a tippet of not more than 2,5 kg. Thick line scares yellowfish perhaps more than it does trout. However, one has to weigh the incredible strength of the first rush of a hooked 'yellow', and then there's those reeds! My favourite fly for this method is the Black Phantom retrieved in a slow strip retrieve, just below the surface. On warm summer evenings good sport can be had with a dry fly, and my favourite pattern is the Soldier Palmer Pink. This should be cast out in the vicinity of the fish and left to rest with an occasional twitch.

Trophy largemouth yellowfish are often taken trolling with big flies such as Lefty's Deceiver. There is no doubt that a lead strip tied under the fly during the dressing helps prevent these

big flies from twisting and spinning. The leader for this pursuit needs to be at least 5 kg. Flies of some 8–10 cm length are most successful. A flying hook added to the fly is said to improve the hooked fish to strike ratio. The best patterns imitate the local small fishes. A proven one is grey over green on top, with white sides and underbelly interspersed with strands of pearlescent Krystal Flash. Painted eyes and a red lurex throat complete the dressing. (This fly has not yet been named.) Troll with a lead-core fly line or similar, over the five metre contour.

Tackle for yellowfish
Rods and reels

A specialist outfit for smallmouth yellowfish in rivers might be an AFTM 7 or 8 rod with a semi-parabolic envelope – something with plenty of power in the butt to stop a powerful fish. The rods built in the UK for sea trout meet the specification. You do not need a rod with a fast tip and distance casting ability for rivers, although such a rod will be adequate if that is all you have. The pools are usually small, and the requirement is to stop the fish from getting into rapids or other rough water. The so-called 'split-cane' copies (i.e. graphite or Kevlar hexagonal rods) are ideal for the job. The same reel as you use for trout will be adequate; just ensure it has an exposed rim for controlling runs. For still water, an AFTM 8 or 9 outfit with a shooting head is recommended.

Lines

A slow sink and a floating line will meet just about all your stream fishing requirements. Yellowfish are often very receptive to the dry fly. Certainly, a slow sinker will be the ideal line for most of the shallow pools, where you can use weighted flies if you need to get right on the bottom. The leader should be tapered, but not too light – yellowfish are very strong, and you will often need to hold them hard. I find a 1X to be safe, but I sometimes go down to 3X if the fish are line-shy. Anything lighter will ensure you get broken as you try to turn an irresistible yellow dynamo from the rocks!

Flies

Yellowfish flies have been distilled over the years to just a few favourites. Yellowfish can be taken on anything, but the following wet flies definitely work well:
❑ Black Phantom
❑ Peacock Beams' Woolly Worm
❑ Theo Van Niekerk's Yellowfish Fly (commonly called a TVN)
❑ Mrs Simpson.

The following dry flies are also worth having:
❑ Daddy-long-legs
❑ Chicken
❑ Duckworth's Dargle Delight (DDD).

There is no doubt that the successful yellowfish anglers are the ones who are good at finding the fish. Fly-fishing for these golden fighters requires, more than any other branch of fly-fishing (excepting perhaps trout), a very careful approach. Do this right, and they are easy to catch. Mess up, and you may never catch one!

CATFISH (family Clariidae)

There are many anglers who wouldn't give any kind of catfish the time of day. Well, they just don't know what they are missing! Most of the African catfish are great fighters – a good one can run well over 100 metres in its first rush! But perhaps their best advantage is that they can be found everywhere in Africa.

The barbel (or sharptooth catfish as the scientists call it) (Clarias gariepinus) is the best known African catfish, with the huge vundu (Heterobranchus longifilis) being the ultimate monster for the freshwater fly-fisherman. The latter are common in the Zambezi and northwards at weights of around 50 kg, and have been recorded on bait up to the 150 kg mark.

Catfish of the family Clariidae (which includes barbel and vundu) have a rudimentary lung, which enables them to survive in oxygen-depleted water and also to live through drought and other low-water conditions. It is this lung which often gives them away to the watchful angler, since barbel need to return to the surface now and again for a gulp of air, a process often accompanied by a clearly audible 'gloop' noise.

Barbel and vundu are not the handsomest of beasties, and I guess the disgust they generate in some people has a lot to do with their appearance. Nevertheless, they are exceptionally fine eating, and a true sport-fish in every sense of the word. The little beady eyes, the long mobile whiskers, the huge flat head and grey, mottled, eel-like smooth skin; all these generate a picture of some loathsome animal. Top it off with his ability to walk on his pectoral fins, and it is perhaps understandable that not everyone loves him. But, under this grey exterior beats the heart of a warrior. He will fight weight-for-weight as long and as hard as any fish; not in a dashing way, but rather with power and determination.

A big barbel specimen is a worthy adversary for the most skilled fly-fisherman. A battle with a comparatively small barbel of 10–15 kg could take half an hour or longer, and then you might well not win! This is a big fish on a fly rod, and most anglers report 4–7 kg as being far more usual. The barbel are fishes with pure mean

Louis van der Westhuizen, pioneer of fly-fishing for catfish in Africa, here with a 10,2 kg barbel from Hartebeestpoort Dam in South Africa. (Photo: courtesy Louis van der Westhuizen)

A younger author (1970) with a small vundu of 27 kg, taken with a size 2/0 Mrs Simpson at the Msuna fishing camp on the Zambezi River. (Photo: John Bridges)

power; they are likely to smash your line, and even your rod if it is a poor quality one.

Seasons and location of barbel

The best times of the year for barbel are spring and early summer, and again in autumn. Some fly-fishermen pursue them all through the warmer months in the high country below the equator, and all year round on low-altitude still waters. The fly-fishermen of South Africa pursue their barbel only in still water, and almost nobody tries to find them in rivers. This is due partly to the fact that barbel can be easy to find by sight in still water, but are very difficult in rivers; and partly to the necessity to pass the fly very close to the barbel for any real chance of success.

Barbel are located by wandering the shores of a suitable still water until they are spotted. The area we want to fish will be fairly shallow (less than a metre deep), and easy to wade. Often the best areas are bays of a quarter to as much as

three hectares in extent. The clearer the water the better, and the best time is the last month preceding the rainy season (when most waters are clear). You can still catch them in muddy water, but it is far more difficult.

Common signs of barbel activity are rises (accompanied sometimes by the characteristic 'gloop'), swirls and bow waves. Barbel tend to congregate over a chosen area, and you are looking for shoal activity rather than the actions of a single fish. Once these areas are located it is usual to find them in the same place, year after year.

Methods for barbel

Once you find the barbel, try to cast to them initially without wading. If you must wade, then do it extremely quietly and very slowly. First, spot a likely fish and try to cast no more than a metre in front of it – the nearer the better. Retrieve the fly so that it almost touches the fish as it goes by. The barbel will usually turn and

Nearly as big as its captor, a huge fly-caught barbel.
(Photo: Louis van der Westhuizen)

A morning's work: these barbel were taken with a Lady Purple fly from a dam near Rustenburg in South Africa.
(Photo: courtesy Louis van der Westhuizen)

engulf the fly with great confidence. Set the hook with a hard wrist strike, and then watch out for fireworks.

Tackle for large catfishes

This is not a game for light tackle, and the AFTM 9 or 10 rod described for tigerfish will do the job well. I like to use a virtually complete saltwater rig with a disc-braked reel. A slow-sinking line or intermediate sink shooting head is ideal. A tippet of 7–8 kg is recommended to have any chance of turning a barbel or vundu from a sunken tree.

The suggested entire leader is two metres of 10 kg Maxima, knotted to a one metre of tippet. No wire trace is needed. The big flies which are used turn over by themselves. Complicated tapers are not necessary.

Flies for large catfishes

Most of the flies used are big and gaudy, designed to grab the attention. They all need to

be tied on strong hooks (the salmon irons by Partridge in the UK are recommended). The following patterns are popular:
❏ Lady Purple (also known as the Church Window Fly, a form of Mrs Simpson)
❏ Pink Panther
❏ Orange Barbel Zonker
❏ Yelland's Kurper Fly.

Usual preferred sizes are 2 and 4. In my experience the Lady Purple is far and away the best. The retrieve is not critical, and a fastish fairly steady pull works well. The various troll retrieves are very effective.

KURPER

Kurper (also known as bream or sometimes tilapia) are among the most popular angling fishes in Africa, and rightly so! They are tremendous fighters, and fairly plentiful too. Very often they attain a respectable size. They are renowned for their superb taste and the ease

A vleikurper taken on a Catlet Muddler. Vleikurper have been introduced into many African waters as a food fish for other sporting species, and their geographical distribution has been greatly enlarged.

with which a boneless fillet can be cut from the fish. Fried fresh kurper fillets take a lot of beating, and barbecued with lemon and butter sauce they are utterly delightful even to the fussiest of gourmets.

Most cichlids (the family kurper belongs to) are mouth-breeders, with one of the parents guarding and protecting the young, providing a secure retreat in the parent's mouth. At this time, they are very aggressive to intruders, yet not actively feeding (a natural precaution which patently protects the young from their normally voracious parents).

There are hundreds of species of cichlidian mouth-breeders in Africa, some large enough to fly-fish for, and many too small to have any significance for the fly-fisherman. All the larger species respond to the same techniques of fly-fishing. The trick is to locate the species you want to fish for, and then to go for it.

Just a word of warning. Kurper have sharp spines in the dorsal fin. I find the best way to

This redbreast kurper weighed in at 1,2 kg, which is a good size for this small fish.

handle them is to use a wet rag or piece of towelling sufficiently thick to protect one's hands from the spines. Hold the fish with the rag, along the back.

Of the smaller species which are taken regularly on the fly only the vleikurper (also known as the banded tilapia) *(Tilapia sparrmanii)*, a lovely olive-green fish with a scarlet edge on the dorsal fin; and the redbreast kurper *(Tilapia rendalli)* are likely to come to your attention. A 1 kg specimen of either of these would be a good one.

The vleikurper is popular for stocking bass ponds as fodder fish, and consequently it can often be found outside of its natural range ... you might find one anywhere!

The larger members of the family are the true sport-fishes. Some of them can reach 5–8 kg, and give terrific sport on a fly rod. Included among these are:

❑ Blue kurper *(Oreochromis mossambicus)*, also known as mgwaya or Mozambique tilapia, extremely popular in South Africa; distribution from KwaZulu-Natal north to Kenya.

❑ Threespot bream *(Oreochromis andersonii)*, also known as njinji or three-spot tilapia; found from Angola to Gabon, across to the Victoria Falls and the Zambezi.

❑ Nembwe *(Serranochromis robustus)*, also known as sengwa or tsungwa in Lake Malawi, olive bream, or yellow-bellied bream ... probably the best of all for fly-fishing!

❑ Thinface bream *(Serranochromis angusticeps)*, also known as thin-faced tilapia or thinface largemouth; found from northern Botswana and the Zambezi northwards.

❑ Green happy *(Sargochromis codringtoni)*, also known as green bream, with similar distribution to the thinface bream.

❑ Yellow-belly *(Boulengerchromis microlepis)*, also known as mucupi, in Lake Tanganyika.

❑ Black kurper *(Oreochromis nigra)*, also known as black tilapia or ngege, in Lake Navaisha and the Athi river system in Kenya. Comes well to a small red fly.

Fly-fishing for kurper is an all-year-round pursuit in the more northerly and equatorial countries; in the south it is a summer sport only.

Still waters with standing timber are good locations to find kurper.

Malcolm Meintjes with a fine blue kurper. (Photo: courtesy Malcolm Meintjes)

The magnificent nembwe, also known as yellow-bellied or olive bream, can provide great sport for the fly-fisherman. This one from the Okavango weighed 2,6 kg, but bigger specimens exist. (Photo: Malcolm Meintjes)

They have a somewhat mixed and seasonal diet, many occupying themselves with silk-weed and algae towards the end of summer (a diet which unfortunately taints the flesh). The rest of the time they are carnivorous – the blue kurper is especially partial to this mixed diet. The more northerly kurper species tend to be more aggressive and more carnivorous.

Locating kurper

Like most fish, kurper are not spread about like currants in a bun. They swim in shoals within which most of the members are of similar size. Catch one of half a kilogram, and the chances are the next one will be the same weight. These shoals are constantly on the move, but if they find a productive feeding area they may stay for hours or, exceptionally, even for days. Sometimes a shoal of bigger kurper will come along and drive off the smaller ones, then all of a sudden you start catching bigger fish – once again all of the same size.

As the shoal individuals get bigger and older, more and more of them die off. Attrition reduces the shoal until, after many years, the shoal will reduce to one or two enormous individuals ... these are the huge specimens which are caught from time to time. Really big kurper are only ever caught in ones or twos, never in large numbers!

In still water, kurper prefer a depth of 2,5–4,5 metres. They have a decided liking for a gravel or stony bottom, and love structures such as rocks, reeds and sunken trees. They can nearly always be found among standing timber, where a lake has flooded as a result of levels rising. They prefer submerged bushes, which is a pity, since it is difficult to fly-fish amongst these, although the effort once made, is usually rewarding. Ideally, the water should be as clear as possible for fly-fishing.

Kurper will feed in shallow water in certain conditions. Particularly good are the freshly flooded grass game trails which result from a typical rainy season deluge. These trails are especially good if they are fringed by tall grasses. The rhinoceros trails at Loskop Dam, in South Africa, used to be fabulous for big blue kurper on the fly after a downpour. White flies and the Ivory Nymph are good patterns for these.

Another shallow-water event involving big kurper occurs at the end of summer when they will herd shoals of small fish into the shallows, every now and then making a concerted slashing attack. The result is very noisy splashing with small fry jumping everywhere. Kurper are very easy to take with a Polystickle fly at such times.

Drifting

Some very big kurper have been taken in African waters by drifting down with a boat. The tackle used is an AFTM 9 rod with a lead-core line. Initially, wind-drift down the four metre contour, steering the boat with the motor, or dipping the oars. If there is no activity, try the six metre contour. I like to use a black fly for this. If the lead core continually hits bottom, change to a fast-sink line. Kurper seldom hook themselves, and you will need to hold the rod and strike at the first touch.

Standard tackle for kurper fishing

The preferred outfit is an AFTM 6 fast tip-action graphite rod, and a fast-sink fly line. Set it up just as you would for trout fishing, i.e. a tapered 3X leader and a 2 kg tippet. You can safely use the same reel as you would use for trout. I like to use weighted flies for kurper, since there is no doubt that the closer you are to the bottom, the better the fishing becomes. Small Stick Flies, Peacock Beams' Woolly Worm, and Gold-ribbed Hare's Ear work well. Occasionally, they strike aggressively at bright flies such as Micky Finn. Plenty are taken on small (size 10) Polystickles.

Dry fly

Occasionally, usually at the beginning of summer, kurper will feed on the top. Their distinctive splashy rises are easily recognised. Use the same rod and reel, but this time with a floating line and a greased size 14 Duckworth's Dargle Delight (DDD). There is no need to grease the leader with this fly. Cast it out and just leave it, but watch carefully – sometimes they take the dry fly without any surface disturbance!

BASS

In Africa, the basses are as well-loved as the trout. Most bass anglers are into lure fishing in its various forms, but there are quite a few fishermen who specialise in taking bass on the fly. So effective is fly-fishing for bass, that some clubs have even banned it as a method for competition ... how stupid can you get? If someone has the skills and the knowledge to win a competition with flies, against all the lure techniques available, then he has won because he deserved to!

Bass often coexist with trout in high-altitude African waters. Although the fisheries managers usually panic over the bass, they normally have little effect on the trout (which in the main are too large at stocking size to be attractive food for bass). Such mixed fisheries often provide superb sport. The Invicta club water in South Africa is such a place, and the bass and trout there are splendid!

There are three introduced bass species in African waters, all of them indigenous to the United States. These are largemouth bass (*Micropterus salmoides*), certainly the best known of the three; smallmouth bass (*Micropterus dolomieu*), the best fighter; and spotted bass (*Micropterus punctulatus*), a rather small bass which is very rare in Africa.

The largemouth bass is distributed throughout the geographical range of this book. It has become established by introduction, but has become so successful in some countries that it has spread into lakes and river systems where it was never introduced. Largemouth bass were initially introduced into the Cape from stock bred in the Netherlands in 1928. There are excellent bass waters in South Africa, Zimbabwe, and Kenya. Largemouth bass are scarcer in other African countries, but are generally present somewhere.

There is a fast-growing subspecies of the largemouth bass known as the Florida bass (*M. salmoides floridianus*), which has been successfully introduced into several African waters. Most of these locations are in KwaZulu-Natal and Zimbabwe. Where the two types mix, i.e. in waters which already had largemouths before the Floridas were introduced, the slow-

Ken Jessop, master bass angler, with a good largemouth bass of 2,7 kg from Morgenstand in South Africa. (Photo: Geoff Taylor)

er-growing subspecies usually takes over as a result of genetic dominance.

The smallmouth bass is more or less restricted to South Africa, where it is fairly common. It was introduced in 1937, and has been very successful in some waters, especially so in the south-west Cape where it has long since been declared unwelcome by the authorities because of its impact on indigenous fish. It is a superb fighter, and many South African anglers in Gauteng, Mpumalanga and Northern Province regard it as the top inland sport fish.

The spotted bass occurs only in South Africa's KwaZulu-Natal and the Cape, in very few waters. It is best known in Midmar Dam in South Africa. It was introduced in 1937 to enhance fishing in turbid waters, but has not been a successful introduction.

Tackle for bassing with the fly

The most useful rod for this is something with enough backbone to turn a fighting fish only

Ron Clay and a fine brace of smallmouth bass, male and female.

feet from his lair. With bass, the structure he hides in can be anything from a sunken tree or bush, to sharp-edged rocks – this stopping and turning power is very important! Once again we are back to our standard 'big fish in Africa' rod – the same rod we use for tigerfish and catfish – an AFTM 9 with lots of stopping power in the butt.

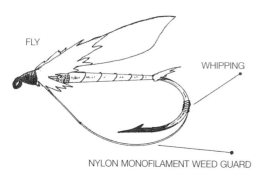

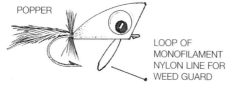

Fig. 9.1: Weed-guarding flies and poppers for use in structure.

Even when dry fly-fishing for bass, you are still faced with the problem of hustling the bass out of cover. Dry fly-fishing for bass usually means poppers, or hair frogs, or similar – all big flies which need power to drive them through the air and out long distances. And where do you cast them? Right into the middle of lily-pads, weedbeds and the like! You need the power. That bass has to be 'horsed' over the weeds before he knows he's even hooked – and it takes a mean rod to handle that! Once again, just as you did for tigerfish, you need to team the rod up to a reel with a decent disc-operated brake system. You will need a selection of lines with different sink rates, and also a floater.

There are a great many specialist bass flies about, and many trout flies are also excellent for bass. Some of the best, and the strategies for using them, are described below. It is a very good idea to build weed guards into bass flies. This makes them far more useful, since you can cast them into structure without such a high probability of losing them (although you will still lose some). The weed guard has to be built in during the actual tying of the fly. You can get these custom tied, but it is of course much better if you do it yourself.

Tactics and strategies for fly-fishing for bass

Smallmouth versus largemouth bass

Most summer largemouth bass taken with the fly rod are caught in shallow water, usually near some suitable structure such as rocks or weedbeds. It is mostly a waste of time fishing open water for largemouth bass. You may get the odd one, but they are the exception, since largemouth bass are exceptionally strongly structure orientated. Smallmouth bass, in comparison, are predatory wanderers. They are more opportunistic feeders, and although they like structure nearby they are not strongly tied to it. Consequently, the smallmouths can often be taken in open water. It follows then that a lighter outfit (an AFTM 7 or 8 rod with a standard trout reel) is adequate for these fishes.

The smallmouth is in fact a much harder fighter than the largemouth. In terms of its fighting prowess, I would put a good smallmouth (say

142

Lily pads in a farm dam. For many bass anglers lilies are like nectar to a bee ... irresistible! The pads often hold magnificent bass. You need to hustle them out quickly ... if they get around the stems, or into the roots, they'll be off.

2 kg) next to the tigerfish in fighting ability – they are mean fighters, and are both fast and strong. Generally speaking, the same techniques that catch deep-water rainbow trout will also work for smallmouth bass. The bass is an ambushing predator, a true carnivore. You must offer something worthy of his attention, and present it as closely as possible, or right into, the structure that is his home.

Bass certainly take aquatic insects, and they are not at all averse to dragonfly and damselfly nymphs, or to the larger sedge pupae and larvae. They are very partial to the odd terrestrial. However, the use of small insect-imitating flies (such as buzzers and mayfly nymphs) is not recommended in summer conditions, since this is likely to prove attractive to large numbers of small fingerling bass. In general, the larger flies are more effective, but you have to fish where the larger bass live.

Shallow water

Our definition of shallows for bass fishing is water of two and a half metres depth, or less. This then includes all the shore line weed beds and lilies, reed beds, and shallow water rock structure.

In summer there will be large numbers of bass in such areas. They will be suspended, gently finning to maintain station. Their tails are in the structure, ready to thrust them forward at any likely meal that comes past. The bass hangs there, suspended in his jungle of weed or brush, or hovering between rocks. He surveys a good few square metres of territory which he regards as his larder. If his suspicions are not aroused, he will eat anything that ventures close enough.

The bass can be motivated to strike for three main reasons:
❑ it is simply food that attracts him;
❑ he will strike at anything considered competitive for food in his territory;
❑ he gets angry with creatures which persistently invade his territory.

All these motivations can be taken advantage of by the fly-fisherman as follows:
❑ copying food is an imitative process (just as in trout fishing, but often with much larger flies);
❑ territory violation could be achieved by using a small fish-imitating fly (another predator);
❑ anger can be stimulated with contrast attrac-

143

tor flies such as Micky Finns, Snot Tadpole Lures, Vivas, and the like; or by repetitively presenting the same pattern time after time.

Small bass have as their biggest predator their own parents, and indeed any bigger bass. Naturally, they tend to congregate where there are no big bass, i.e. open shallows, very shallow weedbeds, and often over structure-free clay-bottomed areas. If you catch one small bass, then move on – there will be lots more small ones there, but no decent-sized ones. The big bass will only be found in water deeper than half a metre (down to very deep), and then only over rock structure, standing timber, flooded brush, old roads and ditches, drop-offs, weedbeds, water lilies, and so on ... always structure orientated!

In winter at high altitudes, when it is very cold, the metabolic rate of the bass slows down and his habits change. He moves into deep water, and can no longer be found in the shallows except during a spell of exceptionally warm days. In that event, he becomes more active, and, if he gets warm enough, he will return during the middle two or three hours of the day to the shallows to hunt whatever he can find. The water in winter is always very clear in southern Africa, since this is the dry season. The water edge will be low, and often easily waded. There is no weed structure left after the frosts, and so the bass will either roam in an opportunistic fashion during these warm hours, or he will be found near standing timber or rocks. Generally speaking, the angler will be more successful if he keeps moving, covering as much water as possible. Make three casts and step sideways a few steps, three more casts, and so on. You cover lots of bank in this way.

On these warm winter days, you should attempt to make the flies as noticeable as you can, without overdoing it. You are fishing in bright sunlit clear water, so super-garish flies are out. On the other hand, warm-water colours will not work either, so you are reduced realistically to yellow flies, but not contrast attractors like the Micky Finn. Rather try the Yellow Panacea, the Tanager, or the Yellow and Gold Frog Nobbler. Use lightly weighted small flies

(size 10), and retrieve them fairly slowly in accelerating pulls on a floating line. You want to get them moving at sufficient pace to keep them just above the bottom. This is not a method that you will get many chances to implement, and in some years there may be no opportunity at all. However, when conditions are right, some good sport can be had in this way.

Wading or boating?

Most bass anglers in Africa tend to be totally boat orientated. There's nothing wrong with fly-fishing from a boat, but often they miss a lot by not wading. It is always advisable to wear waders in African waters because of the ever-present threat of bilharzia, and also because in some countries (especially the northern ones), leeches can be a problem.

Working one's way through lilies, thick weedbeds, reeds or sunken grass is great fun. It can be done quietly and effectively. Wading gives you the opportunity to see more fishes than by any other method. Very often, as long as you are slow and quiet, fishes will present themselves quite close to you. In the course of a few hours, you can work hundreds of metres of bankside structure by making three casts, then taking three steps, three casts, three steps and so on. A line raft is a useful accessory for this type of fishing. Fishing dry from the shore may also be productive, but nine times out of ten, wading the structure will be more successful. Don't forget, fish keep close to the weeds or whatever structure is there, and not the open water!

Boating tactics for shallow water

The usual boating method is to home in on some shoreline structure, or perhaps some shallow-water structure picked up on the echo sounder, and then to anchor up (or hold position with an electric trolling motor). You then proceed to search, casting the fly so as to cover the structured area thoroughly. Possibly more bass are taken on the fly this way than any other.

It is important to cast right to the edge of the structure, or (with weed-guarded flies) right into the structure. The retrieve should produce

PLATE 1

1 Murray's Mouse
2 Dahlberg Diver (grizzle)
3 Deerhair Frog
4 Black Water Pup

5 Basic Bug
6 Giant Shimmy Leach
7 Deer Hair Popper
8 Sandal Foam Popper

9 Dahlberg Diver (yellow)
10 Rubber Leg Deer Hair Popper
11 Eel Fly

PLATE 2

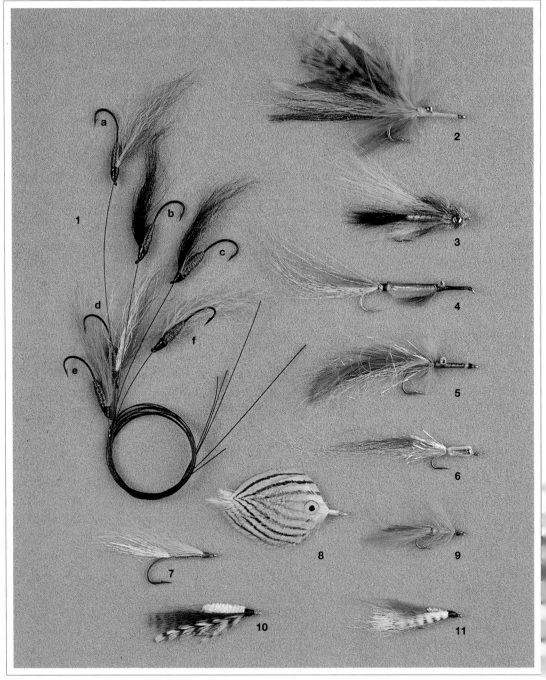

1 Tigger Flies
  a Micky Finn Tigger
  b Zulu Tigger
  c Chris's Tigger
  d Parmachene Tigger
  e Whisky Tigger
  f Vleikurper Tigger

2 Jansen's Halfbeak
3 Blue Silversides
4 Natal Halfbeak
5 Tom Lentz's Needlefish
6 Salty Bead Eye
7 Murray's Irish Blonde
8 Moonfly

9 Pink Shrimp
10 Lee Cuddy (African version)
11 Bonefish Special

PLATE 3

1 Hulley's Sprat
2 Snapping Shrimp
3 Green Crazy Charlie
4 Orange Crazy Charlie
5 Brown Glass Minnow
6 Chartreuse Glass Minnow
7 Clouser's Deep Minnow (red and yellow)

8 Clouser's Deep Minnow (chartreuse)
9 Sosin's Peach Blossom
10 Monteague's Bonefish Minnow
11 African Tangler
12 Calamari
13 Fry Fly
14 Kent's Rainbow Mohawk
15 Argentine Blonde

16 Franke-Bell Bonefish Fly
17 Big Mamma Parmachene
18 Yelland's Kurper Fly
19 Saltwater Booby

PLATE 4

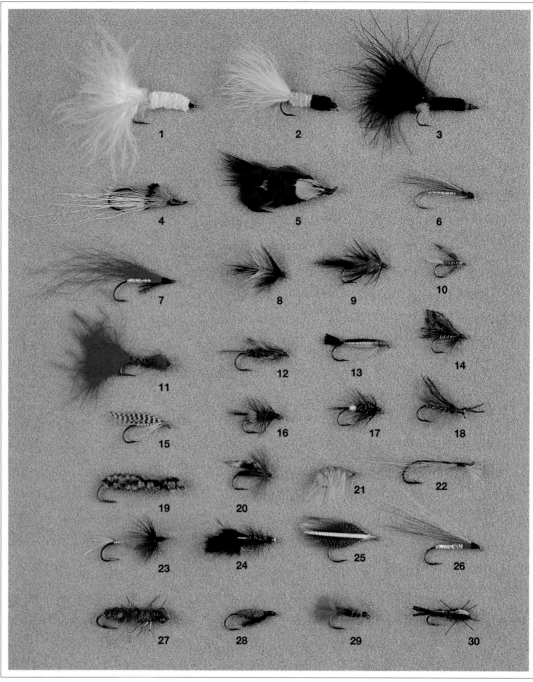

1 Snot Tadpole Lure	12 Emerging Nymph	23 Jalan
2 Cyril's Choice	13 Vleikurper Polystickle	24 Woolly Bugger (peacock, with bead
3 Viva Tadpole Lure	14 Alexandra	head, blue tail)
4 Pink Panther	15 Jindabyne	25 Tanager
5 Lady Purple (Church Window)	16 Beams' Woolly Worm (original)	26 Micky Finn (South African version)
6 Vleikurper	17 Beams' Woolly Worm (green butt)	27 Peddar's Dragon
7 Dullstroom Orange	18 Dark Ferash	28 Sandy Sedge
8 Sunset	19 Terry Ruane's Dragon	29 Adolf
9 Orange Fuzzy Wuzzy	20 Kom Gouw	30 White-gloved Howdy
10 Little Red Wing	21 Golden Shrimp	
11 Digger's Red	22 Green Mamba	

PLATE 5

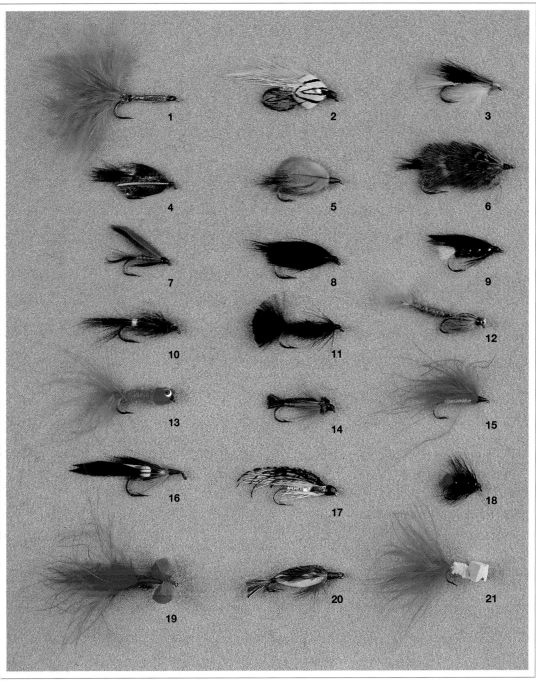

1 Frog Nobbler (orange and gold)
2 Gray Ghost
3 Mike's Secret
4 Walker's Killer
5 Hamill's Killer
6 Mrs Simpson
7 Mountain Swallow

8 Black Phantom
9 Viva
10 Wolf's Woolly Worm (WWW)
11 Thom Green Leech
12 Wiggle Nymph
13 Puppy (orange)
14 Jersey Herd

15 Marabou Whisky
16 Anhinga and Gold
17 Baby Rainbow
18 Zulu
19 Red Booby
20 Rasputin
21 Egg Booby

PLATE 6

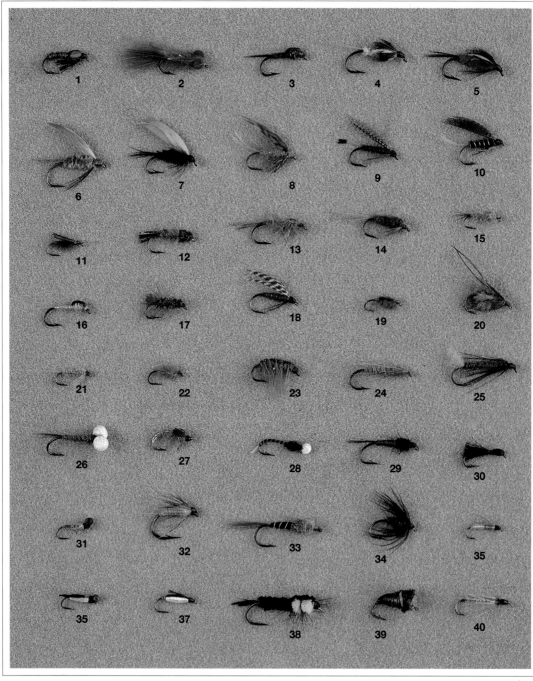

1 Hot Spot Nymph
2 Red-eyed Damsel
3 Pheasant Tail Nymph (PTN)
4 Walker's Nymph (yellow)
5 Walker's Nymph (red)
6 Machadodorp
7 Black Gnat (wet)
8 Invicta
9 Mallard and Claret
10 Connemara Black
11 Olive Corixid
12 Iven's Brown and Green Nymph
13 Gold-ribbed Hare's Ear (GRHE)
14 Leptophlebia Nymph

15 Don's Nymph
16 PVC Pond Olive
17 Red-tag Palmer
18 Teal and Red
19 Dick Walker's Chomper (olive)
20 Green Longhorns
21 Nymph of Feather Fibre (olive)
22 Green Duster
23 Walker's Shrimp
24 Steve's Caddis (orange)
25 Caddis Stick (olive)
26 Olive Nymph Booby
27 Pearl Pushkin
28 Suspender Buzzer

29 Charcoal Nymph
30 Steele's Taddy
31 Barney Google
32 Ivory Nymph
33 Theo van Niekerk's Yellowfish Fly (TVN)
34 Black and Peacock Spider
35 Porringe
36 Kent's African Beetle
37 Silver Corixid
38 Montana Nymph
39 Cliff Henry's Floating Snail
40 Silver Phantom

PLATE 7

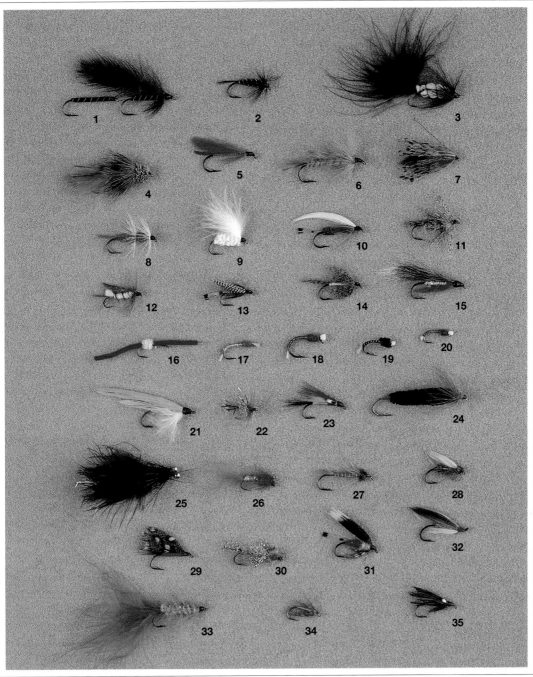

1 Black Lure
2 Kenya Bug
3 Foam Fly (Viva)
4 Olive Marabou Muddler
5 Whisky Fly (original)
6 Parson's Glory
7 Orange-aid
8 Red Setter (African version)
9 White Death
10 Royal Coachman (Streamer)
11 Herbst's Toe Biter
12 Joe's Hopper

13 Peter Ross
14 Carter's Pink Lady
15 Carp Fry
16 San Juan Worm
17 Olive Buzzer Pupa
18 Claret Buzzer Pupa
19 Black Buzzer Pupa
20 Red Buzzer Pupa
21 Texas Rose
22 Duckworth's Dargle Delight (DDD)
23 Chorus Girl
24 Steve's Dragon

25 Bathtub Special
26 Malcolm's Joseph
27 Hugh Huntley's Damsel
28 Swazi Queen
29 Guinea Fowl and Red
30 Don's Dragon
31 African Belle
32 Silver Doctor
33 Olive Woolly Bugger
34 Partridge and Orange
35 Hilliard's Special

PLATE 8

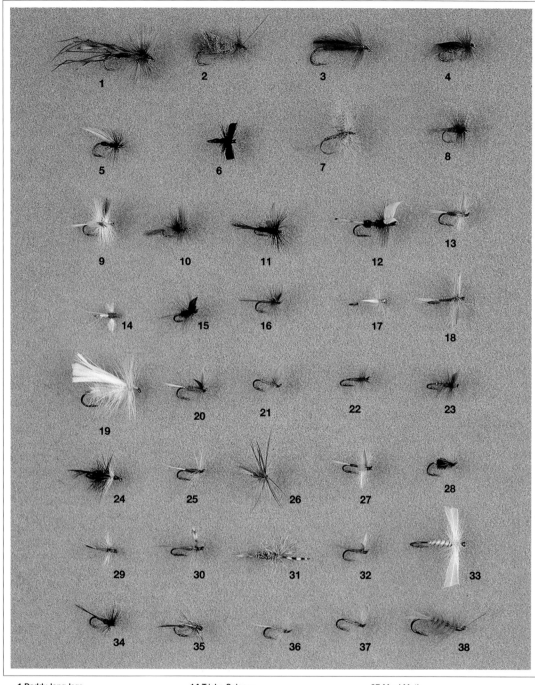

1 Daddy-long-legs
2 Goddard and Henry's Sedge
3 Dick Walker's Sedge
4 Henryville Special
5 Black Ant
6 Whoulston's African Black Ant
7 Komis Dullstroom Dun
8 Dark Hendrickson
9 Cream Dun
10 Dark Cahill
11 Black Gnat
12 Royal Coachman
13 Blue Dun

14 Tricho Spinner
15 Troutbeck Beetle
16 Orange Quill
17 Pale Olive Adult Buzzer
18 Holsloot Spinner
19 Dick Walker's Chicken
20 Blue-winged Olive
21 Greenwell's Glory
22 Olive Dun
23 Whickham's Fancy
24 Black Bi-visible
25 Sherry Spinner (hackled)
26 RAB

27 Mooi Moth
28 Coch-y-Bonddu
29 Grey Duster
30 Adam's
31 Caribou Spider
32 Highveld Dun
33 Kent's Termite
34 Sepia Dun
35 Grizzle Hackle
36 Tup's Indispensable
37 Hackled Greenwell's Glory
38 Soldier Palmer Pink

Fabulous smallmouth bass structure with cliffs plunging into the depths; many other predatory fish species also love this kind of structure.

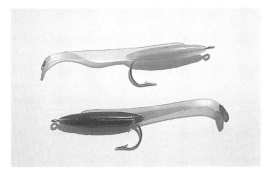

Rasping at the edge of acceptability: plastic Waggler Flies ... are they flies, or not? The bass don't mind, they love them!

These sunken willows are ideal structure to cast around and into for a trophy largemouth bass.

Clear some of the deck structure, and the average bass boat becomes an excellent platform for fly-fishing. (Photo: courtesy Ken Jessop)

Charles Norman, a well-known writer on African sport fishing, displays a couple of largemouth bass. (Photo: courtesy Charles Norman)

145

the right movement associated with whatever one's fly is supposed to copy. I prefer a slow-sinking fly line for this work, and a three metre leader tapered to a 4 kg tippet. You will need at least this strength of tippet to pull the fish away from structure.

The worm-imitating fly patterns (such as Giant Shimmy Leech and Eel Worm) are exceptionally good. The Woolly Buggers are also great flies to start working an area with, and another personal favourite is the Viva Tadpole Lure. In Kenya, flies imitating leeches are very effective (they also work well in other places). Try Thom Green's Leech. All these flies are on the large side, and are good flies for big bass.

At the beginning of the season, or when minor temperature drops (1–2 degrees) take place, then orange flies perform well. Good patterns are the Whisky Fly and the Dullstroom Orange. These should be retrieved at a medium pace for best results. Bass tend to bite very gently after a temperature drop, and often the take feels just like a hang-up in weed. The best course is to strike everything that feels even vaguely suspicious. Vicious temperature drops are best handled with the Micky Finn, but bass are notoriously hard to catch after an African hail storm (which has a devastating effect on water temperature). In fact, you will probably catch just as much if you go home after one of those.

Preoccupied feeding – imitative methods

Bass are not often thought of as preoccupied feeders, and especially not so in the light of insect eating. However, preoccupied feeding on insects among African bass is much commoner than you might think. They will very often feed on one type of insect, especially if a good hatch is in progress. They can get so preoccupied that they will actually ignore all other types of food (and hence all other types of lures and flies). This behaviour is seldom associated with tiny insects (such as caenis mayflies), but is fairly common with the large sedges, damselfly and dragonfly nymphs, daddy-long-legs and termites. So, if you find yourself in the middle of a perfect day, when absolutely nothing appeals to the bass, start looking at the insects!

Good flies for imitation of the hatching sedges

are the Invicta and the Pearl Pushkin. The Caddis Stick is a good one for imitating the sedge larvae. Flies around size 8 or 10 are most useful.

For damselfly imitation use the Red-eyed Damsel (the Olive version is very useful), and for dragonfly imitation, try Terry Ruane's Dragon. An intermediate sinking line with a 3 metre tapered leader and a 3 kg tippet is about right. The daddy-long-legs and the termites are imitated with dry flies.

Sometimes, when the damselflies are hatching in profusion, the bass are tempted to leave their structure. They will even ignore the (usually hated by bass) bright sunlight to get at them. The retrieve for these damselfly nymphs (that works best for bass) is a slow hand-over-hand troll retrieve.

Trolling the shallows for bass with flies

There are more effective things to troll than flies, when it comes to bass. However, there are times, and these are usually days which are hot with a slight surface ripple, when trolling with flies can be very effective. None of the fly rod surface poppers and bugs are worth trolling: only wet flies seem to work. A slow-sinking line with a short (2,5 metre) leader is preferable, and a tippet of at least 5 kg to avoid breakage. Steve's Dragon and the Vleikurper are good flies on sunny days, and the Olive Marabou Muddler can be good on cloudy days. All flies used in trolling should have weed-guards. This can save the frustration of picking off weed throughout the day.

The best trolling speed is slow, either with an electric outboard or rowing gently. Hold the rod and point it down the line for increased bite sensitivity. Rods are lost trolling for bass. If you do have to put the rod down (maybe you are on your own, and you have to steer as well), hook the reel over the seat edge or somewhere to ensure that mister bass doesn't send it whizzing over the back. Set the reel drag just hard enough to prevent over-runs; if you set it too tight, you may get break-offs. Never lock the reel, or lock the line over the reel handle. Non-stretch Kevlar-cored fly lines should not be used for trolling, as they cannot absorb the shock of the taking fish. Something always gives – usually the tippet.

Places to troll are along the edge of weedbeds, close in to deep banks, near overhanging bushes (sometimes difficult), through flooded grass (with weed-guarded flies), along drop-offs, and also zig-zagging past promontories (slowly working deeper and deeper). If you pick up a fish, try the same spot again. There are often a few fish around a good feeding spot.

Spot and drift casting

This is a definite upward graduation, from simple trolling to serious fishing. Dragging flies around catches a few fish, but working areas as you go is more productive.

If the wind is right, and it usually is somewhere, it is possible to drift and steer your way down kilometres of bank on large dams. Simply by using the outboard as a rudder, you can drift in and out of bays, and follow the line of the bank without having to use power. If the wind is not suitable, however, you will need a partner to row, or you can use an electric motor to power yourself along.

The aim, as you drift along, is to cast into small bays and openings in the structure. Cast to the shady side of logs, rocks and stumps. Get the fly working under willows and other trees by casting to the side of the tree and allowing the boat to pull the fly under the tree as you drift past. Most of the time you will cast across and ahead to your target so that the drift of the boat does not over-accelerate the motion of the fly. At all times, try to imitate the correct motion of the creature you are trying to copy (fish or insect).

Control of the depth at which the fly swims is achieved by selection of differently rated sinking fly lines, and also by the option of leaded or unleaded flies.

Dry flies

Poppers

Bassing with floating flies is a much broader concept than dry fly-fishing for trout. Bass dry flies include poppers of various kinds, Dahlberg Divers, Frogs and many others. Bass are also frequently taken on standard dry flies such as sedge imitations, daddies and termites.

Poppers small enough for fly-fishing come in several types. Some have solid cork or foam bodies, some deerhair. They often include such embellishments as rubber legs and moving eyes. Some are 'popping' poppers, others are simply floaters with no popping capability (such as the Basic Bug and the Frogs). There is a huge range of choice in colour and types, but most of them work, whatever their colour might be. My personal preference for fly-fishing is the smaller (up to size 4) deerhair-bodied types.

Sometimes a bass will sip a popper down so quietly you won't even know it has gone. At other times, your heart will miss a beat as a great bass takes the popper in a noisy shower of spray. I once had a popper taken in mid-air before it even hit the water! Popper fishing is a great evening pursuit when the water is glassy surfaced and dimpled by the odd moving fish. At such times, it is great to cast at these movements and other fish signs, and then to wait, with every nerve as taut as a guitar string, for the take ... great stuff!

Many believe that small deerhair poppers are taken for moths – the bigger ones for small birds, or bats, or even mice. The consequence is that fly rod poppers are available in a wide range of sizes. In spite of this, there is no doubt that the smaller poppers are the most effective (and, fortunately, they are much easier to cast). For popper fishing in holes in weedbeds, it is essential to use types with weed-guards fitted.

There are no hard-and-fast rules about popper retrieves. I have known a popper to sit motionless on the water for 20 minutes and then get

The Basic Bug, a simple deerhair popper.

The best way to release a bass is not to remove it from the water at all. Simply slip the hook out while the fish is still in the water.

sucked in by a bass so slowly and silently that nobody noticed it had gone. On another day, a bass will chase a sputtering popper for metres, and still not take it. If there is a standard retrieve then it is the American 'sit and gurgle' routine – just let it sit for 20 seconds, and then twitch the rod tip to make it gurgle. Let it sit again, repeat the gurgle, and so on. Most takes come while the popper is sitting. Another popular retrieve is 'aggressive splashing' which is achieved by metre-long pulls, with longer in-between waits. Your popper can be fished right over weeds, through grass, and around logs. This kind of 'poppering' often produces some spectacular surface fishing over shallow water.

Diving poppers

These are used in the same way as the standard popper types, but they have the added advantage of integrating a diving movement into the popper action. These poppers have a deerhair collar which causes them to dive. They are named Dahlberg Divers after Larry Dahlberg from the USA, their inventor. To get the best action, hold the rod low while retrieving. Light twitches make it pop, and good pulls make it dive. When there is no retrieve, it floats up enticingly to the surface.

Ants, termites, and DDDs

How lovely are those warm summer evenings with flying termites fluttering everywhere! Bass love them and almost any reasonable imitation will score. The bass will leave their normal cover to eat termites, and this is the one time when a lighter outfit (such as an AFTM 6) can be used. The same applies to big falls of ants. The usual method is to cast out and let the fly sit, with an occasional twitch to liven things up. If you see a bass rise, cast to where you think he will be in the next few seconds, and wait for the take.

There are times when a dry fly cast into the structure of a sunken tree or at the edge of a lily bed can tempt a big bass that has refused to go for anything else. Most of us know of one or two uncatchable specimens upon which nothing works.

Try approaching very quietly, then flick out a DDD, and just let it sit there. Proof the fly well, because you may wait half an hour without anything happening. Watch it very carefully, because the take when it comes is often almost invisible – the fly simply disappears!

Deep-water tactics for bass on the fly
Deep-water winter bass

Bass are found at all altitudes and are able to survive in considerably warmer water than trout. The low-altitude bass are only moderately affected by the changing seasons. However, as the coldness of the high-altitude winter night grips the water, sending the temperature plummeting to 7–10 °C, the cold-water bass respond by changing their behavioural patterns.

The cold-water bass migrate to the deeps, and there they group together in loose pockets in depressions or deep holes in the bottom. They are semi-torpid much of the time, lazily finning to maintain position. If a likely food morsel comes past, they will go for it, but only if it is moving very slowly (easy to catch) and only if it comes close. They are not interested in expending energy, and certainly not in chasing anything.

The best way to catch these fishes is to use a contrast attractor fly pattern such as the Micky Finn. The fly needs to be fished on a lead-core line right on the bottom, and the angler may have to do quite a bit of searching to find the bass pockets. If you get one bass, cast again to the same place because you may well get several before they lose interest. Takes will be the gentlest of pulls, just like getting hung-up in weed. So, strike everything that's even a little suspicious.

Deep-water summer bass

To get involved in deep-water summer bassing, a fish-finding echo-sounder is an absolute must. Bass are totally structure orientated, and, unless you find deep water structure, you will not find bass. Easy structures to pinpoint without the echo-sounder are roads and ditches, even old fence lines and hedges. Just follow them by line of sight from the point where they enter the water. Similarly, cliff-like structures and rocky outcrops very often indicate underwater structure.

Sunken buildings, quarries, underwater islands, submerged woodlands and plantations, river beds, and other structures show up well on the sounder. All these are good locations. Most of the food forms of interest to the bass at these depths will be fish, crabs, or large insects such as dragonfly nymphs.

The food fishes will probably be members of the carp or barb families, small catfish and mudfish. Flies such as the Viva Catlet Muddler, the Purple Tadpole Lure, Mrs Simpson, and the Black Lure are all good patterns for this work. Another very good method is offered by the Booby Flies and the Rasputin.

You will require a super-fast sink or a lead-core fly line to operate in deep water. A short 2 metre leader with a 5 kg tippet is recommended, or a very short leader of 25–50 cm for the Booby method.

Ordinary non-buoyant flies are best tied weighted along the back, so that they swim upside-down. The addition of a monofilament weed-guard is advantageous.

Largemouth bass in rivers

Flash floods, which often come with the terrific downpours of the African rainy season, have washed out several bass impoundments over the years, and then dumped the unsuspecting

A good bass holding spot on the Vaal River.

fish into the nearest river. This is a process which has occurred often, and as a result, there are now rivers in Africa with self-populating heads of largemouth bass. Perhaps the most famous for largemouths is the Vaal River in South Africa. Smallmouth bass have also spread into some of the smaller South African rivers in the Mpumalanga high country.

In the long, almost still stretches of the Vaal River, the largemouth bass can be approached with the same philosophy and tactics as one would use in still water. However, the bass in the Vaal River have now spread into the fast water below the artificial barrier of the Vaal barrage, and are established in the fast-flowing sections of the river. Most of the rivers where bass are found in other parts of Africa are also fast flowing.

Flies and tackle for rivers

The flies used in the faster-flowing rivers are mostly streamer types, of which the Vleikurper, the Catlet Muddler, Black Panacea, and the Whisky Fly are the most popular. However, the killer-type patterns, of which the Mrs Simpson and the Black Phantom are considered the best, are also very effective. I still stick to my AFTM 9 outfit for bass in big rivers, but on very overgrown streams where a shorter rod is necessary, I opt for an 8 foot 6 inch AFTM 7. I do not believe that it is necessary to use extra large flies for river bass, and confine myself to hook sizes from 6 to 10. The retrieve is a fishy style strip retrieve for the streamers, and long medium-paced pulls for the killer patterns.

Bass often take flies very gently, and the fly-fisherman will improve results by using non-

149

stretch Kevlar-cored fly lines. These are much more sensitive for gentle bites. The other important tip is to always ensure that there is a bow in the line between rod tip and the water. You can watch this bow carefully for gentle lifts and twitches (which so often occur with largemouth bass taking flies).

Smallmouth bass in running water

Smallmouths are quite different to largemouth bass when in running water, and actually very similar to rainbow trout. In fact, if you fish for them as if they were trout you will be successful. Just as with rainbow trout, they like to hold behind rocks and other obstructions which provide relief from the ever-present pressure of the current. From these lies, they can dash out and grab passing food. Largemouth bass will also do this, but the main criterion with them is to find places where there is both structure and almost minimal current, e.g. slow eddies with fallen trees, or weedbeds. Smallmouths will hold in depressions in the river bed, but not their largemouth cousins. The smallmouth bass is in fact well adapted to flowing water, whereas the largemouth bass is not!

The best method is to work upstream, working from likely lie to likely lie. Cast ahead of the target so as not to scare the bass. Start your darting fish strip retrieve just before the fly reaches the hot spot. Upstream fishing is my preferred approach, but many anglers prefer to fish 'across and down', believing this to be easier. Fishing across and down is often the only way to drift a fly underneath a log, or perhaps under an overhanging bush.

A line basket is essential for stream fishing, and it will save lots of the frustration which can occur with drifting lines. If you do not have the line basket, you will be forced to keep the spare line in your hand, and this is best done either with hand-held-loops, or with figure-of-eight bunching. Remember, fish the productive water only. Don't bother with open water totally lacking in structure.

NILE PERCH

Most of the members of the family Centropomidae are marine fishes, but the genus *Lates*, which contains the Nile perch, is found in several of the northern freshwaters of Africa. The true Nile perch (*Lates niloticus*) abounds in Lakes Albert, Kioga and Rudolf, and in the Nile system. It has been introduced into Lake Victoria. It can reach weights of 100 kg, but a specimen of 50 kg is considered a good fish. Undoubtedly a splendid challenge for the all round fly-fisherman!

Lake Tanganyika has three similar, but smaller, species which are collectively known as 'sangala'. Although smaller, they still reach weights of 50 kg. These are *Lates mariae*, *L. augustifrons* and *L. microlepis*. Of these *L. mariae* is considered a deep-water fish. The others are usually found inside the 8 metre depth contour. All the Nile perches have males which are much smaller than females.

The Nile perch and the sagala are voracious predators, and feed on any small fish they find. They are especially fond of kurper, and even take tigerfish. Bait anglers use dead fishes as big as 30 cm on their rigs, whereas the spin fishermen like spoons of 10–15 cm. For the fly-fisherman, it is usual to tie on big Lefty's Deceivers (approximately 15 cm long), or Surf Candy, or large Seaducers ... all saltwater patterns! For the latter two you will need flies some 10–12 cm in overall length. It is advisable to use a short steel trace because the flies are often taken by tigerfish, which will bite the fly off if it is tied to nylon. On the other hand, you get more strikes from both the sagala and the Nile perch with nylon tippets!

On occasion, the Nile perch will take poppers from the surface, and a large (size 2/0) Dahlberg Diver works well. The usual gurgle and dive retrieve works well (one short slow pull followed by one fast pull, and then a five second wait). Sometimes just let the Diver sit on the surface – takes are usually fierce.

The AFTM 9 fly rod outfit, previously recommended in this chapter for tigerfish, is adequate for Nile perch, but some anglers like a rod as large as AFTM 11 for punching out those big flies. A straight untapered leader of 8–15 kg pale green Maxima is adequate. At times, you will be able to find the Nile perch by spotting surface activity. You can then cast directly at

After the battle, this mighty Nile perch is returned alive to the water. (Photo: Charles Norman)

them. I prefer this method, but most fly-fishing anglers prefer to troll the flies using lead-core fly lines. The troll speed should be very slow – less than a slow rowing speed, as the big flies may cause severe line twisting if trolled too quickly. There is no point in putting in a swivel, since small tigers will hit these with gusto, and then cut through the line. All you will feel is a jolt, and then everything is gone!

It is most important to keep hold of the rod when trolling – these are big fish, and they will have not the slightest trouble in whisking your beautiful expensive rod straight over the back of the boat!

A big Nile perch will strike hard, and will immediately run anything from 50 to 100 metres. Once this run is over, he will usually start 'tail walking', shaking his head violently to throw the hook. He may well repeat the run and the tail walk operation, but will then settle down to a slogging match, requiring lots of rod pumping to get him in. Unfortunately for the fly-fisherman, Nile perch often sound straight to the bottom, and then it becomes almost impossible to pump the big ones up to the surface on the relatively soft fly rod. However, if you are near the bank, you can often run your Nile perch into shallow water (slowly with the boat), and get him up that way. Very often, as you try to slip your mighty Nile perch over the net, he will react by performing a last, and totally unexpected, tail walk, often successfully throwing the hook and having the last laugh!

The tarpon fly rods manufactured and marketed in the USA are ideal for Nile perch. These rods are capable of pumping a big fish up to the surface, since their design incorporates a great deal of power in the butt of the rod. They do this by sacrificing distance casting ability, but it is a worthwhile sacrifice in the case of the Nile perch. There are specially tapered fly lines designed for tarpon fly rods, and these are well worth investigating if you choose such a rod.

Fly colours are not all that important, although there is a school of thought which suggests that the olives, yellows and silver of the naturally occurring kurper give a better fly. Similarly, blue-backed Lefty's Deceivers with

The magnificent sight of a 'tail walking' Nile perch. Once seen, never forgotten! (Photo: Charles Norman)

an orange body and a silver throat hackle, imitating small tigerfish, certainly perform well.

COMMON CARP

The carp *(Cyprinus carpio)* was introduced into the South African Cape with UK stock in the 1700s, with a serious introduction in 1896. This was not a primary, but a second-level introduction (it was in fact not indigenous to the UK either). The immortal words of Sir Richard Baker sum it up:

Hops and turkeys, carps and beer,
Came into England in one year
round about the mid-1500s, I think.

Because of the very warm waters in Africa the carp has done very much better here than it does in most European countries. Wherever it gets a foothold, the inevitable consequence is a population explosion, which generally ruins most sport fisheries. It is a particular nuisance in bass fisheries. This arises as a result of the carp's uncanny knack of muddying the clearest of waters, once it gets around to breeding in its usual profuse manner. Consequently, it is regarded as vermin by most South African fly-fishermen, which would probably stun the dedicated carp-catchers of the UK.

In African high-altitude cold waters its numbers remain low. It does not muddy the water, and often grows very large (possibly the largest carp in the world are in Africa in some of the high-altitude still waters).

The spread of carp throughout Africa is a relentless process, now quite unstoppable! They breed prolifically in warm water, often crowding out other more desirable species. Their feeding habits include dredging the bottom for molluscs, bloodworms and other life. They grow fast, and they grow very large on this diet. I have taken them on the fly up to 13,1 kg, but I am sure others have caught much bigger carp. It is generally believed that they grow to around 45 kg in the very large still waters.

Carp could never be described as being very responsive to flies, but nevertheless, they do most definitely go for them. They are especially worth fishing for just before the rainy season, which is normally just before their spawning period. At this time they can offer exceptional sport. During some years they are far more responsive than others, and nobody seems to know what triggers them off.

My diaries for 1970–1994 record 61 carp intentionally taken on the fly, and seven taken by accident while after other species. Thus I conclude that you really can take carp on the fly rod, on purpose – give it a try!

It is very important to get the fly to swim right past, and close to the carp's head. Flies which work include the Carp Fry, Walker's Killer, Viva Tadpole Lure, Mrs Simpson, and the Chorus Girl. I recommend an 0X tapered leader with a tippet of 4,5 kg. You will need a rod with plenty of butt power to stop big carp from getting into the reeds or lilies.

GRASS CARP

Many trout waters in Africa have been stocked with a small head of 'grass carp' *(Ctenopharyngodon idella)*. They were first introduced in

1967 with a shipment from Malaya. These Far East imports are wonderful weed clearers, and in high-altitude shallow impoundments they do their job rather well. They appear to be mostly vegetarian, and do not have the unsavoury habit of stirring up the bottom to muddy erstwhile clear water. They are known to take insects and other invertebrates as food.

Grass carp are often very active at dusk, and being rather large, can cause the most exciting surface disturbances. Many an inexperienced angler has seen the huge bow waves and boils in the water, and thought himself witnessing the biggest trout in the world. Fortunately, they are easily spotted, and always give themselves away by the sight of the large triangular dorsal fin.

The grass carp is a streamlined, muscle-packed, torpedo of a fish. It does not often take the fly intentionally, and is more often foul hooked – generally it gets off very quickly. However, fairly hooked ones with the fly in the scissor are taken every year in small numbers. A good one can exceed 15 kg, and this fish can really fight! It is very fast, taken to long runs, and very strong!

I know of no one intentionally fishing for them, but records indicate that the most successful flies are black or very dark, and almost always smaller than size 10. All grass carp should be returned with the greatest care – these fish are a real asset in the fisheries where they have been introduced.

MUDFISH (LABEOS)
Moggel (mud mullet)

Only in recent years has the moggel *(Labeo umbratus)* come to the attention of fly-fishermen. His range is southern Africa, and as a quarry for the fly-fisherman, he is almost in the realms of unexplored territory. But some anglers will tell you that this fish is the fastest thing alive in fresh water, and well worth pursuing. Ron Clay has taken more of these fishes on the fly rod than any one else I know, and he rates their fighting prowess as being higher even than the yellowfish – and that's saying something!

Moggel feed by dredging the bottom for microscopic algae and animal life ... hardly a

A magnificent carp of 7,8 kg taken by Nolan Owen-Johnstone on a Carp Fry fly.

lifestyle conducive to either fly-fishing or a reputation as a fighting fish, you might think, but they do take flies, and have also been reported many times taking small spinners. They are extremely common wherever they occur, and are often the commonest fish in the waters they inhabit. They are seldom caught, and even bait fishermen catch them in far smaller numbers than one might expect for such a common fish. Any bait angler will tell you that they can only be taken on the tiniest of baits, and that bites are very gentle affairs requiring considerable skill to strike positively.

The moggel is a very streamlined fish with a fin design more typical of high-speed saltwater fishes than of a mudfish. General body colour is silver. I am aware of a few fly rod taken specimens that weighed over 3 kg, with one of 3,8 kg which is the largest I have heard of – such a fish must have been absolute dynamite for the successful angler. Most of the fish I have seen have

A rare shot of a grass carp, fairly taken on a size 8 Muddler Minnow, at 11.30 pm, by Angelo Komis. (Photo: Angelo Komis)

153

Ron Clay with a moggel of 1,8 kg taken on a Black Lure.
(Photo: Malcolm Meintjes)

A good sized moggel from the Vaal River. Note the large 'V' shaped tail fin, which gives these streamlined fishes great speed.

been around 1,5 kg, which is a respectable size for a fish with so much energy.

The best time for fly-fishing for the moggel is in February and March. If you want to see something awe-inspiring at this time of the year (if the great spillway at Sterkfontein is running), then go there and have a look! Huge mud mullet congregate in the spillway lagoon, and they can be clearly seen trying to run up the raging torrent of the spillway. They are magnificent leapers, and repeatedly launch themselves metres into the air like super slim salmon ... a wonderful sight!

Moggel are adequately handled with an AFTM 7 or 8 fast tip-action rod. In still water, the most useful line is a super fast-sink type – nearly all your takes will be right on the bottom! However, in rivers, when you find moggel in rapids and at the tail end of rushing water, you will find an intermediate line very useful. Tippet size appears to be critical, and they are unlikely to be fooled by anything stronger than 2,5 kg. Ron Clay likes to use a 1,5 kg tippet and a tapered 3X leader.

Black flies work very well in slightly coloured water, but orange flies are very good when the water is ultra-clear. They are not worth fly-fishing for if the water is muddied. Moggel normally hit the fly hard, and go straight into a fast powerful run. The fight then settles into a number of high-speed runs. Once hooked they seldom get off, unless they manage to get into structure or weedbeds. Some of them are spectacular leapers, and fight like supercharged rainbow trout!

You may not hook many moggel if you decide to try your luck, and in fact most are taken by fly-fishermen intent on bottom-feeding yellowfish. However, I can assure you that the action will be startling once you hook one – it's certainly worth a try! They are most easily found around stream inlets in big still waters, and in pools and runs below rapids in rivers.

Other mudfish

Most species in this family have been taken with flies at one time or another. However, most are not worth pursuing with intent. Of those commonly taken in southern Africa, the Orange River mudfish is often reported by fly-fishermen, and the rednose mudfish is deliberately hunted by a small band of fly-fishermen. The other species, with the exception of those listed below, are seldom reported.

❑ Orange River mudfish (*Labeo capensis*). I would not recommend this as being worth while as a dedicated fly-fishing species. You might get one or two from time to time, but you are far more likely to strike a blank. I have taken two while casting flies for other species. One was a 2,1 kg specimen from Sterkfontein dam in South Africa, which took a size 2 tandem Black Lure meant for deep-water trout. I doubted at that time that anyone would have believed the capture of this fish without the testimony of Frank Hamilton, who happened to have witnessed the fight. However, just a few months later, Ron Clay took a similar-sized specimen, from the same water, on a Black Panacea. It may be that they like black-coloured flies? Both these fish were taken right on the bottom with lead-cored fly lines.

❏ Rednose mudfish *(Labeo rosae)*. This fish has considerable potential as a fly rod gamefish. It is strong, fast, and in shallow water often leaps spectacularly. It is also known as rednose labeo and red-lipped mudfish. In Africa, there are many species similar to this one, and many will fall for the same tactics as described below.

The rest of the list indicates some of these species regularly taken by fly-fishermen:

❏ Rednose mudsucker *(L. altivelis)*. Easily confused with *L. rosae*, above, but somewhat larger (up to 4 kg). Also known as manyame mudfish, luapula salmon, hunyani salmon, golden mudsucker or pumbu. Range is Lake Bangweulu, Zambezi River, Sabi River and in-between.

❏ Purple mudfish *(L. congoro)*. Also known as purple labeo or mumbu. Comes infrequently to the fly. Common in the Zambezi, and south to the Sabi River.

❏ *L. victorianus*. Common from Kenya southward, including Lake Victoria. Commonly taken on wet fly.

❏ A related species is the Lake Malawi salmon, or mpasa *(Barilius microlepis)*. Excellent sport on the fly, commonly reaching 2 kg. *B. microcephalus* from Lake Malawi is similar but smaller.

Fishing for the rednose mudfish

My experience with the rednose mudfish is limited to still waters in southern Africa, but the methodology given below will also work for other still-water mudfish. In streams, many mudfish congregate during spring in shallow water at the ends of pools and drop-offs. Fish for them in running water just as for the smallmouth yellowfish.

I have taken over 50 rednose muddies in still water on the fly, and every one of them was deliberately fished for with the fly rod! They have a first run which is unmatched by most other fish. They will make a dash for sanctuary in deep water, and it feels like nothing can stop them. Occasionally they jump, but that is the exception. They burn out fairly rapidly, but that first dash is when they often slip the hook. I have taken a very few by accident while fishing fairly deep for kurper with flies. However, that

An Orange River mudfish taken on a fly in the Vaal River by Angelo Komis. (Photo: courtesy Angelo Komis)

is not an approach recommended for results in still water. The method that does work for myself and many of my fishing friends is (quite surprisingly) with dry fly!

The best time is early spring (August to September in southern Africa), or just before the rainy season for other mudfish species in the more northerly countries. The rednose mudfish, sometimes in the company of smallscale yellowfish *(Barbus polylepis)*, will cruise the surface of still waters sipping down

Nice specimens of rednose mudfish (Labeo rosae) *taken on a size 16 dry Black Gnat at Loskop Dam, South Africa.*

small flies. At this time of the year, when the nights are still cold on high-altitude waters, these flies are usually a small black diptera. In the lower-altitude areas where it is warm, there are still lots of black diptera in early spring, as well as claret-coloured buzzers and the odd mayfly. The only time that the scenario is right is towards the ends of warm still afternoons, which are fairly infrequent in high-altitude waters such as Loskop Dam in South Africa (one of the best locations for fly-fishing for red-nose mudfish).

August in southern Africa is the windy season, but still afternoons (which are nearly always warm in Africa) nevertheless occur frequently enough in most years. The angler should get out in a boat, and cruise sheltered bays until he comes across the fishes rising. As September rolls in, the sport improves for a few weeks and then stops. We often spot some huge muddies while searching the bays in this way, and very often a large catfish presents itself as a bonus.

The correct outfit for the rednose mudfish is a fast taper rod (something around a ten foot AFTM 5 or lighter), with a tapered 5X leader and the finest point you dare to use (less than 1,5 kg). The best fly is undoubtedly a dry Black Gnat.

You will lose a few muddies in the reeds, but the fun is fantastic, as these mighty fish surge for sanctuary in their first dash for freedom. It is possible with muddies to strike very gently (the sting of the hook is then much reduced), thus avoiding to some extent the unbridled power of their first panic-stricken run. The fish are very sensitive and shy, and the angler must take great care not to make splashy casts.

Most of the fly rod caught muddies are of good size. We have had several over 2,5 kg, and some of these considerably better the official record size. We always return them ... they are not good eating, and anyway they deserve to go back after the fight they give!

BLUEGILL SUNFISH

The bluegill sunfish (Lepomis macrochirus) is an exotic import originally brought into Africa as a fodder fish for largemouth bass – an unfortu-nate mistake, as it turned out. The bluegills are now established in many waters in South Africa, and also in some waters in Namibia and Zimbabwe. The sad thing is that the bass do well enough using the local small tilapia as fodder fish ... they didn't need the bluegills anyway!

The bluegill sunfish is a prolific nest-building breeder with a real knack for devastating local fish populations and then becoming so over-populated that it stunts itself. Most agree that it is a menace, but is now so well established that it has become impossible to eradicate. In its natural homeland, it is kept down by a string of predators, among them the magnificent northern pike (Esox lucius), a fabulous sport-fish which grows to 25 kg. How I would love to see those in the cold waters of South Africa's magnificent Sterkfontein Dam.

Some fly-fishermen enjoy the bluegill sunfish and regard him as fair game. Bluegills never reach a great size, but they are frequently taken at 0,5 kg, and rarely even up to 1 kg. Most of the ones you catch will weigh less than 400 g. They are ravenous predators of small life forms, and will attack flies with gusto. The biggest specimen I have seen was taken by Barry Kent in KwaZulu-Natal using a Bath Plug Special. That one was 1,1 kg, a massive bluegill! Bluegills over 0,5 kg give a good account of themselves on light tackle. An AFTM 4 rod is about right for these little battlers. Bluegills are very tasty if cooked immediately after they are caught.

Bluegills will take any fly thrown at them, and often small flies (smaller than size 10) give the best results. If bluegills have a colour preference, then it is for black. They also respond exceptionally well to damselfly and dragonfly imitations.

In waters where other and larger predators exist, the bluegills will generally be found in the shallows around the edge of the dam, and especially in dense weedbeds. In waters where no large predators exist, the little ones still keep to the shallows, as the bigger ones are cannibalistic. Sizeable ones are often taken close to weed beds and along the edge of drop-offs.

If nothing else, an overstocked bluegill water is a great place to teach a youngster to fish by fly, or by any other means. Bluegill sunfish are always very keen to accommodate, and the young angler can have a lot of fun with these little, but relatively hard-fighting, sunfish.

PERCH

This fish was first imported into South Africa from the UK as long ago as 1896, but was unsuccessful. It was re-stocked in 1915, and again in 1926. It is typical of the British tradition to bring popular species of their local birds, fish and animals to add a kind of comfort in the then colonial surroundings. Birds such as chaffinches, goldfinches and greenfinches were also often released into the wild, often with mixed success. The tench and the carp were originally introduced into Africa in this way. The perch is renowned in Europe for the flavour of its flesh. As long ago as AD 350 Ausonius wrote:

To feast our boards, what sapid boneless flakes
Thy solid flesh supplies! Though river fed,
No daintier dish in ocean's pastures bred

The perch *(Perca fluviatilis)* can be found in several dams and natural lakes (vleis) in South Africa, in both the Cape and Gauteng. The biggest have been recorded from Paardevlei in the Cape, where several specimens over 2,5 kg have been taken. The best known location for perch is probably Florida Lake in Gauteng, South Africa.

The perch is a good sporting fish, and can be taken on flies with a fair chance of success. Once he gets to over 0,5 kg, he is a strong and dashing fighter, and very handsome with his dark stripes and scarlet fins. They fight reasonably well, and a big one will give you a merry dance as he charges around, constantly changing direction and all the while pulling hard.

Perch have spiny fins which they erect when in danger. These spines are not dangerous, and although they may prick a little if handled roughly, they will not do you any harm. Certainly, the spines on most kurper are a lot worse.

Perch are nearly always swimming in shoals, each member of which is a bandit in disguise.

A beautifully marked perch taken on a Booby fly by the author at Florida Lake, South Africa.

Like gangs of robbers, they hang around structure, terrorising the neighbourhood and feeding on anything that moves that will fit into their mouths. They will investigate anything resembling food, hence their predilection for artificial flies.

Perch love pilings and piers, sunken trees and rocks, but they are equally happy patrolling lily beds and the outskirts of dense weed. They are fairly sedentary as they get larger, but fish up to 2 kg will patrol a beat in shoals. Once you know where they are, they will usually oblige by being there the next time you visit. Perch have large, well-developed eyes, and are quite at home in the depths, but the waters they are known to inhabit in South Africa are all shallow. Those big eyes are sensitive to the bright highveld sun, and in Gauteng, South Africa, you can be sure that the perch will be close to the bottom during the day.

The one thing that will drag them up to the top is when they are hunting fry. The presence of large schools of fry will override all their inhibitions, and they will harry small fry even in the brightest light. Perch are great fish-eaters, and streamer flies that imitate small fish are the best patterns to use. The Vleikurper and the Gray Ghost are particularly good. Boobys also work well with perch, just as long as they are used properly (see the instruction in Chapter 11 for more information). Perch chase fry in straight lines. The usual indication is of fry leaping out of the water in a star-burst pattern, followed by a bow wave as the unfortunate chosen one is swiftly hunted down.

Some perch adopt a different lifestyle to those

The Cornish Jack reaches a good size, as shown here with this Lake Kariba specimen. (Photo: Irving Stevenson)

that hang-out around piles, concrete walls and other structures. These fishes form a kind of loose wolf pack which hunts on the move well out from the shore. If you catch one, you will probably catch several others, providing you get a feel for the direction the shoal is moving in, and then cast accordingly.

With all perch you must do your best not to lose one. If you do prick one, it will head for the horizon and all its buddies will follow as fast as they can! It follows, then, that you should keep them on a stringer (if you intend to eat them), or in a soft-mesh keepnet, or best of all in a live well, until the day's sport is over. Otherwise, if you return one, it's goodbye to the whole shoal.

The correct tackle is an AFTM 6 rod, ideally ten feet long. Perch are not fussy about leaders and any 0X tapered leader will do.

ALESTES

Alestes are shoaling fishes of the characin family (the same family as neon tetras and tiger-fish), with large eyes and large scales. In Africa there are several species of interest to the fly-fisherman. They readily take flies and can provide good sport, but most cannot be regarded as gamefish. Alestes swim on the surface in small shoals, and in the evening often jump a lot. They take flies very well at this time, and are good fun on a light outfit. Alestes are probably better known to anglers as bait for tiger-

fish, for which they are considered ideal. The following species are frequently pursued with the fly rod.

❑ The pinkfin *(Alestes grandisquamis* syn. *nurse)* is a fish of Lake Bangweulu, Lake Mweru, the Nile and the Congo River, and all over West Africa. It reaches a weight of 1 kg, but specimens of around 0,3 kg are most common. It is very keen on the fly and will take most flies offered to it. Best outfit is an AFTM 4 rod with a floating line and a small (size 12–16) dry DDD, Adams, or Greenwell's Glory.

❑ The lake salmon or silver alestes *(Alestes macrophthalmus)* inhabits Lake Bangweulu, Lake Mweru, Lake Tanganyika, and the Lua-pala River. This one grows in excess of 2 kg. The silver alestes is said to be very fond of silver flies, and the Fry Fly is an excellent pattern for this fish. Use an intermediate line.

❑ The imberi (or spot-tail) *(Brycinus imberi)* is found from the Pongola and the Limpopo rivers northward to Tanzania and the Congo river basin. It is the smallest of the Alestes to be commonly taken by fly-fishermen, reaching only 0,3 kg. It is most easily recognised by the blackish patch near the tail, and another smaller patch behind the gill covers. It rises well to dry Blue Dun and Grey Duster. It is a good fish to teach youngsters fly-fishing.

There are other smaller alestes which are commonly caught as bait for tigerfish, all of which will take the fly well.

MORMYRID FISHES

All the mormyrids are warm-water loving species and have northerly distributions which begin in Zimbabwe's northern waters.

The Cornish Jack *(Mormyrops anguilloides* syn. *deliciosus),* grows large, and can reach weights of 20 kg. Small ones feed largely on insects and shrimps; larger specimens prefer to feed on fishes such as tilapia, minnows and mudfish. The Cornish Jack is a strange-looking fish with a long broadish body, all propelled by a ridiculously small tail fin. As a consequence, it is not a formidable fighter. Nevertheless, because of its considerable weight it can give a great deal of fun to the fly-fisherman.

Perhaps its most notable feature is the rather mammal-like mouth equipped with rows of conical teeth. Like all fishes in its genus, it is covered in a gelatinous slime, almost like a skin, with a tint varying from yellow to purple. When dry, this 'slime skin' flakes off. The one-time Latin name of *deliciosus* refers to the supposedly excellent taste of its cooked flesh. Those who have tried it have almost without exception described it as awful. Apparently, it was named 'Cornish Jack' by the early settlers because of a superficial resemblance between this fish and the European pike, which is commonly called 'Jack' in England.

The mormyrid fishes are able to generate a weak electrical field, which is used as a kind of radar for hunting prey. It is undoubtedly a great asset when hunting in very deep or muddy water, where visibility is either poor or absent. Although the generated current is fairly powerful by fishy standards, it is not dangerous to man, and can only be felt as a very faint tingling sensation.

The habitat changes as the fish grows. Juveniles are denizens of the shallows and weedbeds, whereas the adults prefer deep, quiet water near drop-offs and in rock-bottomed pools. In large still waters they are commonly found where a river enters the lake or dam. Really top spots in rivers are slowly turning eddies with rocky bottoms, situated close to the main stream. Fly-fishing from a boat is the most rewarding method, since it is often difficult from the bank to get near to deep water in jungle-fringed rivers.

These fish are impossible on flies unless the water is very clear, and this restricts the fly-fisherman to the months just before the rainy season. In many ways, they are similar to carp in the techniques needed, but they are considerably better at taking the fly. Flies which are known to work are Mrs Simpson, Walker's Shrimp, Golden Shrimp, and the Grey and the Yellow Booby patterns. Large fish will sometimes be tempted with a size 1/0 Gray Ghost, or a size 2/0 Big Mamma Parmacheene, fished very slowly. All these flies should be fished with a lead-core line. The AFTM 9 outfit recommended for catfish and tigerfish will supply the

power you need. A 2 metre, 4,5 kg level leader of Maxima is adequate.

Work the pools carefully. You should aim to cover every foot of the water by casting slightly further to one side with each cast, until the whole pool is covered. The reason is that the fly has to pass quite close to the Cornish Jack before he will take it.

Western bottlenose (*Mormyrus lacerda*), also known as 'ndikusi', are occasionally taken on the fly in the Zambezi, Cunene, Okavango and Kafue river systems. These are relatively small fishes, reaching perhaps 2 kg. However, the eastern bottlenose (*Mormyrus longirostris*) gets much bigger, reaching 10 kg. This fish extends from the Zambezi north to Lake Tanganyika, and west to the Congo river system. A similar, but larger, fish in the upper Congo, *Mormyrus proboscirostris*, grows to 1,4 metres.

The bottlenoses seldom take a fly, but there are plenty of recorded occasions of quite large specimens being taken in this way. They are great shrimp and nymph eaters, and are also fond of small fishes. Fly-fish for the bottlenoses just as you would for the Cornish Jack: the secret is to thoroughly work your chosen pool in order to ensure that the fly passes very close to the bottlenose. The mormyrids all have similar habits, and all have the radar system described for the Cornish Jack.

KAFUE PIKE

The Kafue pike (*Hepsetus odoe*), or African pike, as it is also known, occurs in the Okavango, Cunene and upper Zambezi rivers, northwards through the Democratic Republic of the Congo and West Africa as far as the Senegal River. It is not present in the Great Lakes. This fish is a lover of papyrus-fringed and lilied clear-water pools. It is often found in quiet deep water and channels, but prefers fast water. Normally, it is not found in the company of tigerfish.

Charles Norman, the writer, reports that the finest specimens are found in the Linyati area. This pike is a good fighting fish, and the great shame is that they do not grow to a great size. Most caught are around the 1 kg mark, and a 2 kg fish would be a very good one anywhere. If you fancy a sport-fish which fights hard, can

A Kafue pike taken on a small spinner, all teeth and go! These fishes are great fighters on light fly tackle. (Photo: Malcolm Meintjes)

bite, and has the shape of a streamlined fury, then the African pike is it. The fish has a mottled brown-golden colour with beautiful emerald reflections. The scales are rough to the touch.

The Kafue pike is a multiple spawner, breeding several times in the course of the summer months. It constructs a floating mass of bubbles and foam within the shelter of marginal weeds, and the fertilised eggs are deposited therein. Both parents tend and guard the nest. The newly hatched fry wriggle through the foam and drop into the water.

The Kafue pike has a fearsome dental array, and they are extremely fierce predators! This fish will take anything alive that will fit its throat, and that includes fish of up to 40 per cent of its own body weight. Although the teeth do not interlock, they still demand plenty of respect. The teeth are back curving and very sharp on the back edge. They are also covered with an anti-coagulant mucus, which means that any bite you get will not stop bleeding for a long time, let alone heal.

The Kafue pike comes exceptionally well to flies, and once hooked, spends more time in aerial combat than any other fish in Africa. It is actually extremely easy to catch (some say too easy). Fish with an AFTM 6 fast taper outfit and a light leader, and the pike will give superb sport. A short (10 cm) steel trace is preferred, but it will generally stay on if you use thick nylon for the tippet. The Tigger series of flies, in smaller sizes than those used for tigerfish (try size 8), are good for the job.

CHAPTER 10

AFRICAN SALTWATER FLY-FISHING

Go thou to the sea, and cast an hook, and take up the fish that first cometh up.

St Matthew, XVll, 27

S altwater fly-fishing in Africa is probably the fastest growing branch of the sport. New adherents swell the ranks constantly. Once the bug bites there is no escape, and it is not hard to see why. Nothing can really match catching a kingfish or a garrick on the fly rod. The first time you see the line powering off the reel so fast that the handles are a blur, the first time you hear the ratchet scream as you have never heard a fly reel scream before, then ... *you are hooked!*

Saltwater fishing with a fly rod is, for many anglers, the pinnacle of sport-fishing achievement. It offers the opportunity to battle with the mightiest fishes that will ever come the way of the fly-fisherman. It is certainly true to say that if you can master creatures like big kingfish, barracuda, or sailfish with a fly rod, then you can probably master anything with fins! There can be little doubt that fly-fishing in the salt requires the highest level of fish-playing skill – perhaps not the finesse of freshwater fly-fishing, but certainly the power, the fury, the raw meanness, and the strength of the greatest fighting fishes can be found in saltwater fly-fishing.

Saltwater fly-fishing probably started in earnest in Africa, in the early 1970s, when a few pioneers discovered the amazing sport to be had in the northern KwaZulu-Natal estuaries. At about the same time, John Costello was exploring the potential of fly-fishing in the Transkei. A few articles appeared in the angling press, and the word was out. By 1980, there were saltwater fly-fishermen in action all along the coast. Today, the sport is extremely popular from the Cape to Kenya, and rapidly catching up with trout fly-fishing. Top surf venues for the visiting tourist are northern KwaZulu-Natal, the Mozambique islands and Kenya.

THE FLY ANGLER'S FISHES

One difference between saltwater and freshwater fly-fishing is that you nearly always know what fishes you are pursuing in freshwater, whereas in the salt there are many times when almost anything may turn up. Very often the saltwater fly-fisherman will narrow things down enough to know that he should be catching some kind of kingfish or queenfish, but he will not know which species; and he may well catch none of those, but instead end up with a few garfish. He may well be working on a strategy for grunter, only to end up with some kitefish and a kabeljou. Once in Madagascar, I caught three quite different species in 20 minutes: a queenfish, then a barracuda, and then a large blue boxfish – all fell to the same method and fly!

Strategies for saltwater fly-fishing are not as 'specific' as they are for freshwater. One method will work for many species of fish.

Kingfish

Kingfish often give away their presence by the scattering of small fishes across the surface which precedes their coming. I keep an eye open for this activity at all times. If I spot such

A very happy angler and a magnificent fly-caught kingfish. (Photo: courtesy Mark Yelland)

behaviour, I immediately cast as near to it as I can. I will often walk the dune tops looking for good gamefish locations. If I spot a deep sandy gulley, or perhaps just a slightly deeper area in the surf, or I find a reef within or just beyond casting distance, I will certainly give it a few casts. Deep water off shallow rocks (high rocks are not suitable for fly-fishing) can also be productive.

My introduction to the kingfishes was with the greenspotted (or brassy) kingfish (*Caranx papuensis*), and I suppose I have caught more of these than other species, through the years. They do not grow particularly large (a 3 kg specimen is a good one), but they fight well and are good sport on the fly rod. Distribution, as with most of the kingfish, is along all of the east coast of Africa, although the greenspotted is scarcer south of KwaZulu-Natal. The bluefin kingfish (*Caranx melampygus*) also occurs fairly frequently, and is about twice the size of the greenspotted. These two kingfish usually hunt in small shoals running just above the reefs and coming right into the surf edge. The bluefins

sometimes follow giant kingfish, picking up the smaller food fishes disturbed by the passing of their big cousins. Both of these small kingfish are excellent eating. Neither is fond of entering estuaries, and most are taken in the surf. Best places are near rock or reef structures.

The bigger species such as the giant kingfish (*Caranx ignobilis*) are much sought after, and specimens under 10 kg are taken regularly with the fly. Bigger than this they are a real handful and most escape. They are enormously strong and very fast, and will tax the skill of the best anglers. One can look forward to long blistering runs with the reel turning so fast that the handles become a spinning blur, quite capable of breaking an unwary finger. Giant kingfish are primarily fish predators, attracted to larger flies like the Lefty's Deceiver, whereas the smaller kingfish are commonly taken with small flies such as the Glass Minnow and the Clouser's Minnow. Giant kingfish regularly enter estuaries and tolerate almost fresh water. They hunt by sight and avoid turbid or cloudy water. Not so large, but large enough to reach

8–10 kg, is the yellowtail kingfish *(Caranx sem)*. This is a summer fish which seldom enters estuaries and has a distinct preference for clear water. It is most commonly found in small shoals patrolling drop-offs and the edges of reefs. Another superb fighting kingfish is the bigeye *(Caranx sexfasciatus)*, which hunts over reefs and is happiest near reef structure. This is a real die-hard fighter, which keeps going right to the end. Adults keep out of estuaries, and are lovers of clear clean water. They grow to almost 8 kg, although most are considerably smaller.

Closely related to the true kingfishes are the *Carangoides* kingfishes, which include the bludger *(Carangoides gymnostethus)*, a 10 kg plus fish which is fairly rare close inshore, but common over deep reefs. The ferdy (or blue) kingfish *(Carangoides ferdau)* is a lover of sandy beaches, but never enters estuaries, and takes a small fly well. They never grow really large and are commonly taken up to 3 kg. The yellowspotted kingfish *(Carangoides fulvoguttatus)* is scarcer than the others, and also a lover of deeper reefs. It grows to about 10 kg and is more often taken off boats than by the surf flyfisherman.

Queenfish

For ease of discussion, species such as pompano and leerfish are also included here. My first fly-caught African saltwater fish was a largemouth queenfish *(Scomberoides commersonnianus)*, referred to as just queenfish by most anglers, in the estuary mouth at St Lucia in South Africa. It was taken with a trout outfit and a Walker's Killer fly, and it weighed 7,2 kg. The capture of that fish was a story in itself, but it was sufficient to hook me on saltwater flyfishing for life, and endeared me to the fighting queenfish for all time. The largemouth queenfish frequently enters estuaries, but prefers the shoreline where it swims in small groups. It likes rock structure and reefs, but is often taken on sandy beaches. It is a fish of the summer months, and like the kingfish is best fished for at dawn and again at dusk. It comes well to small flies such as size 8 and 6 Glass Minnows and Clouser's. Small Lefty's Deceivers and

Blondes also work well. Maximum size is around 10 kg, but it is most frequently found at about 2 kg, and even these little ones give a good account of themselves.

The salad fish, or double dotted queenfish *(Scomberoides tol)* seldom gets big, but puts up a good fight on fly tackle. It forms shoals often with other species, and can be taken most easily on bonefish flies fished near the bottom. Both these queenfish are fishes of the Indian Ocean shoreline.

The garrick *(Lichia amia)*, or leervis, as it is called in Afrikaans, extends from KwaZulu-Natal right around the African Atlantic coastline, northward and into the Mediterranean. It is a favourite quarry of fly-fishermen, and inhabits the wave zone, usually at the backline of the surf. It is at home in turbid tumbling water, and also enters estuaries. A great fish predator, it comes well to larger flies such as Lefty's Deceiver, and to surface poppers. It is a threatened species in South Africa as a result of estuary pollution, and should never be killed unless necessary. Garrick grow big and are superb fighters on fly tackle.

The pompano (also known as southern pompano) *(Trachinotus africanus)* is a delicious eating fish from the South African and Mozambique coast, which also fights very well. It lives in the surf zone, and will also enter estuaries where it has a high tolerance for low salinity. It is a bottom feeder and should be fished for with

A small garrick or leervis (Lichia amia), *among the most popular quarry for saltwater fly-fishermen in southern Africa. They feed heavily on baitfish and are aggressive predators of the wave zone, reacting well to poppers and flies. They can grow very large and are magnificent adversaries.* (Photo: Ken Bateman)

163

ultra-fast sink fly lines and slow moving flies such as leaded Crazy Charly. It grows to about 12 kg. A small relative often taken on the fly is the largespotted pompano (*Trachinotus botla*) which grows to about 2 kg.

Milkfish

One of the finest fighting fishes in the world, the milkfish (*Chanos chanos*) is theoretically an ideal quarry for the fly-fisherman. The problem with this living torpedo is getting him to take the fly (or anything else for that matter). This is an Indian Ocean coastal fish which frequents bays and estuaries, and is able to live in completely fresh water. It is fond of estuarine mud flats and small inflowing freshwater streams, where it is often seen feeding – head down, with its tail protruding – on microscopic organisms and crustaceans in the bottom mud. It will take small flies. Trout flies such as small nymphs, Woolly Buggers, and tiny Mrs Simpsons (size 12 and 14) which should be retrieved right next to the fish, have often caused its downfall. It is a wary fish, and estuarine specimens need to be carefully stalked with sinking line and fine tackle (tippets of no more than 3,5 kg are recommended). Once struck it makes long breathtaking runs, taking a long time to tire. A heavy hand will soon get you broken off, and it needs to be played with considerable care and skill.

Springer

The springer (*Elops machnata*), also known as tenpounder and ladyfish, is a predator of the

A superb springer taken in an estuary. These fish are fantastic fighters, often going aerodynamic and producing fast and hard runs. (Photo: Irving Stevenson)

coastline, frequently penetrating estuaries. It is an evening feeder and hunts small fishes actively. Once hooked it often fights with fast runs and spectacular leaps, and is an excellent quarry for the fly rod. It is very popular with South African estuarine fly-fishermen. Most small fish and squid fly imitations work well, with a decided preference for white flies. It also takes a popper well. Should you spot the springer harrying small fishes, your chances of success are very high if you cast a small fish imitation into the mêlée. It is not particularly good eating, and is fished for more for its sporting prowess than anything else.

Mullet

These are wonderful sport on standard still-water trout outfits, such as a rod of AFTM 7 or 8 and a floating line. Small flies such as Zulu and Woolly Worms work well, tied to tippets of 3 kg. Several species occur on both coastlines, and all take flies. A mullet of 3–4 kg puts up an outstanding fight on light fly tackle. The best way is to hunt down the shoals by boat in estuaries, and then fly-fish from 30 or so metres away. They fight very well, making many fast runs and huge jumps before tiring. The striped mullet (*Lisa tricuspidens*) is the most sought after on the fly rod. The mullets are good eating, but have many fine bones to contend with.

Spotted grunter and kob

Spotted grunter (*Pomadasys commersonnii*) has only recently become of interest to fly-fishermen. Nowadays, it is a prime target for bottom fishing. It fights incredibly well on fly tackle, and the first rush is very powerful. Shrimp and crustacean imitators are the flies to use on a fairly fine (3,5 kg or less) tippet, Crazy Charlies and Snapping Shrimp, retrieved right on the bottom, being two favourites. Grunter can be spotted and fished for on mud flats, but the biggest specimens come from the surf around estuary mouths and from flowing deep muddy-bottomed holes in the estuary itself. Spotted grunter grow to around 9 kg and are excellent eating.

Occasionally, a kob (*Argyrosomus japonicus*), or kabeljou as he is also known, will pick up the fly meant for a grunter, and really surprise the fly-fisherman. I prefer to fish for these big bottom-feeding fishes with a lead core or tungsten core line and a large fish-imitating fly such as a white Lefty's Deceiver, size 3/0 or larger. A heavy tippet is advisable, not because of the fight (they fight poorly), but because of the need to lift an often very large fish from the bottom. Both kob and grunter have been taken at night on the fly.

Barracuda

A barracuda going at full speed on a fly rod is an experience never to be forgotten. Both great barracuda (*Sphyraena barracuda*), and seapike (*Sphyraena jello*), or pickhandle barracuda as they are also known, are extremely fast swimmers (after all, giant barracuda eat kingfish, and that would imply an awful lot of speed). The great barracuda prefers reefs, but is also taken from the shore and from estuaries. It becomes more common in the tropics, but is found as far south as KwaZulu-Natal in South Africa. It grows very large (to 37 kg), but is usually caught in sizes below 20 kg. A 10 kg specimen would be a very good catch on a fly rod. It has huge teeth, and the use of a wire trace would be wise. When landed it is dangerous if fingers or hands come close. Large flies work best, and it seems to have a colour preference for blue flies.

The sea pike is considerably smaller, but still reaches a good size of around 15 kg. It is wonderfully camouflaged and is very difficult to see. It occasionally occurs in large shoals. All of my shore-caught barracuda and pike have come from water near reefs. Sea pike are common in some estuaries (such as Kosi Bay in South Africa).

Garfish

The garfish (*Strongylura leiurus*) is amongst my favourite inshore targets for the lighter fly rod. On an AFTM 6 or 7 outfit, it fights spectacularly, leaping and tail walking, and changing direction at high speed. It is a common, highly predacious fish of estuaries, harbours and shallow water. The flesh has lots of green bones, but is good eating. It grows to 5 kg, but most are

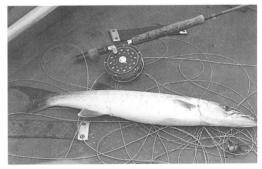

Sea pike (Sphyraena jello) *are commonly taken in estuaries. This one took a green and black popper and was one of several taken by Ken Bateman from a single shoal. Sea pike are noted for their effective camouflage and are almost impossible to see in the water.* (Photo: Ken Bateman)

considerably smaller. It takes Glass Minnows and similar flies very well if fished fast, just below the surface on a floating fly line.

Elf or shad

Elf (or shad in South Africa) (*Pomatomus saltatrix*) are among southern Africa's favourite gamefish. They are good fighters and are excellent on the table. However, in South Africa they are currently protected by a daily bag limit of four and a closed season from September to November inclusive. Shad have exceptionally sharp, flesh-tearing teeth, and the fly must be attached to a short wire trace. Flies need to be 'tough built' (i.e. glued at every stage of construction). Shad like to feed in shoals over sandy bottoms in clear water. They can grow to 14 kg, but most taken on fly rods are under 2 kg. Shad are distributed around both ocean shorelines of southern Africa.

TACKLE AND SKILLS FOR THE SALT

The fly-fisherman fishing the African surf and estuaries will find many species of fishes other than those described above, all of which will probably succumb to flies if fished for properly. One can never be really sure what fish will come along and take one's fly, but when you are fishing in the salt and you do get a take, you can be sure that whatever fish it is, you are in for a fight.

Saltwater fishes are hard, powerful, fast and determined: many have much more stamina

A bright red starfish. The African shoreline is fascinating in its diversity of life.

than tigerfish of similar size. To have any chance of success, your tackle needs to be in first-class order. Preparation must be complete, and everything thoroughly tested. Everything must be tip-top!

Saltwater fly-fishing demands reasonable competence in casting, and whether you fish estuary or surf, you will need to put out a minimum of 35 metres of line. If 15 metres is all you can manage, then get yourself booked into a casting clinic and learn the double haul technique. This casting method makes 35 metre casts easily attainable, and if you have a talent for casting you will very likely find yourself casting a great deal further. The important thing about casting clinics is to remember that regular practice after the clinic is essential. Practising every other day for six weeks will burn it into your mind, and then, like riding a bicycle, you will never forget it. In the meantime, if you confine yourself to estuaries, you may find eddies and eelgrass beds, piers, and the edge of mangroves, where you can still catch fishes with a short cast.

Saltwater fly-fishing can be a costly business.

Fig. 10.1: The hay-wire loop knot and the correct method of twisting it: 3,5 to 4 twists in the monowire are required before winding the wire around the main strand. It will break if this not done.

Not in terms of licenses, perhaps partially in terms of tackle, but mostly in terms of travel. It can cost plenty to get there! Obviously if you are lucky enough to live next to the big blue pond, then the problem is reduced. But if you want to sample the top fishing available in the Mozambique islands, Tanzania and Kenya, you may find yourself flying into locations inaccessible by any other route. Not that I ever met a really keen angler who cared that much about the cost of his sport! I have one friend who calculates that each trout he caught in 1993 cost him more than a week's food would have done. On the other hand, I have a really successful angling friend who catches them for less than they cost at the Hyper. But then, he spends his time looking for his fish in the water and not at the bottom of a glass.

Tackle strength – tippets and leaders

For most situations tackle need not be as strong as you might think, and a 6,5 kg tippet is sufficient for most species. If you are one of those intrepid souls with a yen for a blackfin shark on the long wand, then a thicker tippet will obviously be useful. However, while we are discussing these sharks in terms of estuary and surf, it is only fair to point out that you will either need to get hold of a stupid one that swims in circles, or you will need a boat to go after it. Furthermore, a long (extra long) wire trace will be needed to contend with abrasion by the skin which easily wears through nylon – and then there's those teeth! I once hooked a blackfin shark on (of all things) a size 2/0 Walker's Killer. It jumped all over the place for a couple of minutes and then headed straight out to sea. It broke my steel trace after pulling out 250 metres of line, during which time I was unable to turn it, slow it down, or indeed do anything with it at all. Anglers in the know who saw it leaping suggested afterwards that it was just a small one!

The great majority of the fishes you hook will be below 3,5 kg. These can mostly be handled with tippets of the same size, but the odd big fish is going to push you up to as much as 7 kg if you want to be reasonably sure of landing it. This seems high, but these fishes are immense-

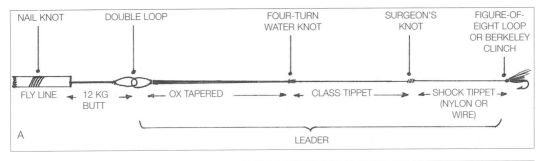

Fig. 10.2: Make-up of typical saltwater leaders: (A) leader make-up for IGFA records, etc; (B) a simple saltwater leader.

ly powerful, and a kingfish of only 5 kg that wants to reach a reef perhaps 50 metres away is actually unstoppable on a 3,5 kg tippet. Even a 7 kg tippet may have you heart-in-mouth before you turn him (if you do).

Elf (or shad) and other species with teeth make a wire tippet mandatory. Shad can shear nylon line, even of 25 kg size, with the greatest of ease. I am not too fond of mono wire for tippets, because the slightest kink or nick (perhaps from a rock) will cause it to break off, often during the cast. However, in its favour, mono wire is easy to attach to fly and leader using the hay-wire loop (see Figure 10.1). This wire knot must be tied correctly, and that means three or four 'X' turns before wrapping the wire. The surplus wire should be broken off by bending it up and down a few times. If you cut the surplus with wire cutters you will end up with a dangerous sharp edge. Another disadvantage of mono wire is its ability to tangle with the leader during the cast.

Braided wire is much safer, because it is almost immune from nicking. Plastic-coated braided wire has the in-built advantage of stronger knot strength, because you are able to weld the plastic together with a brief pass of a cigarette lighter once the knot is complete.

What counts against it is its habit of twisting permanently and forming unsightly fish-frightening spirals – and the unsightly mess of half stripped bits of plastic covering. You can use ordinary uncoated braided wire, which is fairly problem-free. Black wire is always preferable to bright wire.

Good knots for joining braided wire and nylon monofilament line are the Albright (best), the Grinner, and the surgeon's knot (see Chapter 2). Lubricate all your knots with saliva before pulling them up. Knots for saltwater fly-fishing must be pulled up neat and tight! Use pliers if necessary. If the knot is not tight, and if it gets jarred during a fight with a fish, the sudden pinching of the line will break the knot way below its correct breaking strength.

There are plenty of vacant saltwater fly rod records, and many existing records which could easily be broken by African fish. An important consideration is the incorporation of the 'class' tippet. This is the weakest part of the terminal rig, and the breaking strain used here determines whether your fish is eligible for a record or not. The International Game Fishing Association lays down rules which apply to record claims for saltwater game fishes caught on a fly rod. The rules are quite specific with reference to leaders. An extract from their regulations reads as follows:

Leaders must conform to generally accepted fly-fishing customs. A leader includes a 'class' tippet, and, optionally a shock tippet. A butt or tapered section between the fly line and the class tippet shall also be considered part of the leader, and there are no limits on its length, material, or strength.

A class tippet must be made of non-metallic material, and either attached directly to the fly or to the shock tippet, if one is used. The class tippet must be at least 15 inches long (measured inside connecting knots). With respect to knotless tapered leaders, the terminal 15 inches will also determine the tippet class. There is no maximum length limitation. The breaking strength determines the class of the tippet.

A shock tippet not to exceed 12 inches in length may be added to the class tippet and tied to the lure. It can be any type of material and there is no limit on its breaking strain. The shock tippet is measured from the eye of the hook to the single strand of class tippet and includes any knots used to connect the shock tippet to the class tippet. In the case of a tandem hook fly, the shock tippet shall be measured from the eye of the leading hook.

Some taper in the fly line will help the fly turn over, and, as a result, some like to build their end rig starting off with a length of 0X knotless tapered leader. The diameter of the class tippet can be measured with a micrometer, and, where the measurement is approximately the same on the tapered leader, this is the point at which the knot is tied. The excess tapered leader left after the knot has been tied is then cut off. I use a four-turn water knot (see Chapter 2) for this, which if tied and pulled up correctly is almost 100% strong. Some overseas authorities like to loop everything together, but this method has not caught on in Africa. The other end of the class tippet is then joined to the shock tippet, which might be wire or nylon. You should end up with a total length of 2,5 to 3 metres. In South Africa, many of the saltwater fly-fishermen prefer a much simpler approach. They tie a 2 metre length of 7 kg Maxima Chameleon to the fly line butt loop, and either tie the fly directly to the Maxima, or to a short (12 cm) wire tippet. The usual method of connecting the

leader to the fly line is by means of a butt loop of 12 kg line which is permanently attached to the fly line (see Chapter 2).

Shock leaders can be nylon or wire, and although I might use steel tippets for shad, I tend not to use a special shock leader unless fishing out at sea for fishes such as barracuda or sailfish. In the surf, the 2 metre straight length of 7 kg monofilament is usually adequate for my requirements, and the fly is tied on directly, using either a double clinch or tucked clinch knot (see Chapter 2). Out at sea, nylon shock tippets up to 50 kg are sometimes used. Such tippets should be previously made-up and stored on stretch racks to avoid coiling.

In the surf and in estuaries, you can expect far more takes with nylon than with wire, and unless something with teeth is definitely about, I stick to nylon.

Leaders for poppers in the salt

Popper fishing for garrick is a favoured method, and of course it works for other species too. Leader design in these big non-aerodynamic 'flies' is difficult and I battled with it for years. However, in *Tight Lines* magazine (November 1989), Robin Fick gave his leader design as follows:

Maxima as follows:	75 cm of 14–17 kg
then	20 cm of 12 kg
then	20 cm of steeply tapered leader line
and finally	75 cm of 5 kg

All in all a somewhat short and somewhat controversial leader, but it works!

Another which works is:

1,5 m	of 0X tapered leader
1 m	of 6 kg Maxima
0,5 m	of 5 kg Maxima.

My preference is for the latter, but only because of its longer length.

Rods

I would consider AFTM 8 a minimum rating for most saltwater fly-fishing, with AFTM 9 or 10

A river mouth in Africa. Note the formation of the sand banks as the river sweeps around: the edges of these can give good fishing at high tide. The structures on the left horizon are not Hi-tech, but simple wooden frames of unfinished huts.

being much more useful. However, as in all things, there are extremists, and you will find the odd person who has set out to prove he can do it all with an AFTM 3. Such extremists have my best wishes, but if you are serious about landing saltwater fishes on the fly, then for the sake of your own enjoyment let reason prevail. The same AFTM 9 rod recommended elsewhere in this book for tigerfish, catfish, and Nile perch will also serve well as a saltwater rod, providing the fittings are salt-proof. Out at sea, where you may find yourself in search of anything from small sailfish to tunny, a double-handled AFTM 11–13 outfit may be more useful, especially in terms of its capability to pump a big fish up to the surface from deep water.

The ideal rod is a dedicated saltwater stick with a reasonably fast tip speed, but more importantly with plenty of butt power. There are some excellent rods around which are able to punch big flies long distances and still have sufficient brute butt power to tame a big game-fish. The best are very expensive, and you are earnestly entreated to try the rod before you pay for it. You would also do well to take an experienced angler along with you to confirm the casting capability of your new rod.

Finishes on saltwater rods must all be saltwater proofed. Ideal rings are single leg types with hard silicone carbide centres. My preference is for a tungsten tip ring. The handle must be cork, and for saltwater use an extension butt is a must. On some of the deep-sea rods a double cork handle is incorporated into the design, and for fishes that are in the habit of diving deep (such as tunny) this is a very useful feature. You do not need this feature for estuary or surf.

With most of the really tough 'deep' sea saltwater fly rods, casting ability has been sacrificed for sheer lifting power (tarpon rods are typical of these types). Such rods are of no use for distance casting in surf and estuary, and the beginner must ensure that he does not buy one of these simply because it says it is a saltwater fly rod!

Fly reels for the salt

Ordinary trout fly reels are not suitable for saltwater use. They are not strong enough for the task, they are not corrosion proofed, and they do not have suitable braking and control to handle big, fast fish. A saltwater fly reel must have an exposed rim for control of a running fish, and a good smooth disc braking system. You need a large fly reel, with plenty of capacity to carry hundreds of metres of backing, together with the large-sized fly line necessary to throw the big flies used. The drum should be balanced, and the whole reel ruggedly built from saltwater-proofed materials. The centre bearing pin should be considerably more substantial than a trout reel – it will have to handle great strain, and may very often become burning hot as a result of the high-speed runs of the gamefishes.

It is very important to keep your reel properly lubricated, and to wash it after every day's use. My preference for lubricating the spindle is a silicone grease. With reels that are used in harsh conditions such as salt, sand and rocks, it is important to take care, when putting the reel down, that mud and sand do not enter the reel. It is a very good rule never to put a reel down on sand! If dirt or sand does enter the reel by mistake, switch to another reel until such time as you can clean the dirty one out with fresh water. Most saltwater anglers use reel pouches to protect their reels when not in use, and you are strongly advised to do the same. These pouches can be placed over the reel while it is still on the rod.

The simplest way to pre-set the disc drag mechanism on a salt water fly reel is to set it so that it commences slipping just below the test curve of your rod (see Figure 10.3). Do not attempt to change the clutch setting during a fight with a powerful game fish. Pre-set it, then leave well alone.

If you are right-handed, your reel should be set for left-hand wind (you need the best hand for the rod). This means you will almost certainly have to change the disc brake mechanism over (most leave the factory set for right-hand wind ... great if you're left-handed!). Do this carefully, following the instructions which come with the new reel – it can sometimes be a trifle complicated (a good tackle shop will do it for you, but give them a day or two to get it done). The modern reels are designed to apply

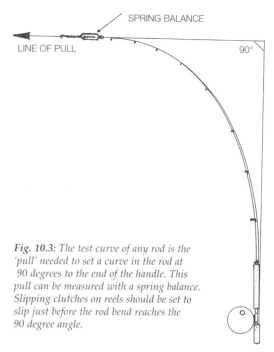

Fig. 10.3: *The test curve of any rod is the 'pull' needed to set a curve in the rod at 90 degrees to the end of the handle. This pull can be measured with a spring balance. Slipping clutches on reels should be set to slip just before the rod bend reaches the 90 degree angle.*

the brake against the running fish, and to wind freely when the angler winds in – this is why you need to change it over!

Having said all this about clutch/brake mechanisms, I am obliged to point out that in South Africa, the best centre-pin reel anglers in the world (the KwaZulu-Natal Scarborough reel surf anglers) regularly land massive fishes without the aid of a brake or check mechanism. It's all done by skilful 'palming' of the reel. Indeed, there are a few saltwater fly-fishermen in Africa who, having seen this, have applied it to their fly-fishing. They take the smallest Scarboroughs (the quality products have unbelievable free-running qualities), drill out the reel seat and the back support for improved lightness, and then use these for fly-fishing. I have seen the odd one fitted with a clutch mechanism made from teflon discs, and I have to admit it worked splendidly. Personally, I will stick to my System Two for now, and await the day when someone gives me a Billy Pate or a Fin-Nor before I change.

A final word on reels. No matter if you have the best saltwater fly reels in the world, always clean them after a day's fishing. Even if you are on a fishing holiday and are fishing every day, reels must be cleaned on a daily basis. It's not enough to give the rod and reel a swirl in the swimming pool – by washing, I mean swirl the reel in a bucket of clean freshwater, strip it and run it under the tap, re-rinse, and then re-assemble to dry. Once dry, re-oil the spindle.

Saltwater fly lines

Purchasing a 'saltwater taper' might be a mistake if your activities are likely to be confined to surf and estuary. These specially tapered salt-water lines are really designed to cast the very large flies often indicated as the correct patterns for deepsea fly-fishing.

Out there, the usual method is to attract game-fish using a hookless 'teaser' lure. The big fly is then cast (usually a short distance), to seduce the fired-up gamefish. In Africa, it is much more common to operate from a ski-boat, hunting down frenzied feeding packs of predatory fish. Having found them, the tactic is, once again, a short cast with a big fly. The saltwater taper is perfectly designed for this job. However, if there is only a small fly on the line, the tip of the fly line taper drops very rapidly during the cast, and markedly shortens distance. False casting is also more difficult. Such a line will work for surf and estuary, but not as well as an ordinary 'weight forward' taper would.

Most accomplished surf and estuary fly-fish-ermen carry a collection of lines from 'floating' right through to lead core sinking.

❏ For 'popper' work, a floating line is a must and my preference for this task is a Bass Bug taper line. Bass Bug lines are designed to turn over bulky, lightweight, non-aerodynamic flies.

❏ For general work in shallow water, my personal preference is for an intermediate line, and the transparent Monocore line (also known as 'slime lines') by Scientific Anglers is a top product. It becomes almost invisible in the water.

❏ For fishing into deep water such as you might find along the edge of a reef, I like to use either tungsten dust or a lead core line. Incidentally, all my surf and estuary lines are made up as shooting heads. The lead core can also be very useful at times in a running surf where the angler needs to fish right on the bottom.

❏ For those areas where one needs to handle deeper, but not excessively deep water, I find a

A pensive Mark Yelland, master angler and fly-fishing safari guide, watches net fishermen working the surf.

type IV Cortland is adequate. These thin high-density lines are also very useful if casting into an onshore wind.

As a matter of course, I wash all my fly lines after a visit to the sea, rub them down with a thin film of line conditioner, and store them in the dark. Some of my lines are 20 years old, and still good as a result of this care.

If you can afford it, the ideal is perhaps to have a reel for every line. But saltwater reels are extremely expensive, and for most of us this is quite impractical. A 'quick-change line system' is the answer, and the system which I use was developed by Irving Stevenson. Irving runs a fishing camp on Inhaca Island off Mozambique which specialises in deepsea fly-fishing for tro-phy gamefish. He knows the problems, and a workable practical solution to line changing is a must for him in his professional life:

❏ The first thing is to tie a loop in the braided backing line (using a figure-of-eight loop knot) of around 175 mm in length. This loop will be used to join the backing to the reel end of the shooting line (of the ready made-up shooting heads). Each head is pre-assembled complete with its shooting line. At the end of each shoot-ing line, tie another smaller loop which will be used to join it to the backing line.

❏ Each complete shooting head fly line is stored on a plastic hoop of approximately 15 cm diameter (see photograph on page 173). The line is generally stored with the leader already knotted on. The shooting line loop is passed over the backing loop, and then the plastic reel

The author puts out a long cast into the gathering dusk at St Lucia. This is often a good time to fish, especially on a rising tide. (Photo: Ryan Steele)

is passed through the backing loop, thus forming a double loop knot. The complete shooting line can then be wound off of the hoop – there's no need to re-thread the line through the rod rings, it's all done outside the rod! When you have finished with the line, wind it back on the hoop and un-loop it. All simple and easy!

The knot which joins the shooting line (the flattened monofil or whatever you use) to the shooting head (the fly line), is critical. A nail knot is not suitable here, since the great power of the saltwater gamefish can be sufficient to strip the nylon coating of the fly line, resulting in a lost line. The answer is to strip off the nylon coating yourself, and form a loop with the fly line's braided interior. Nail polish remover or acetone will soften and remove the nylon. Join the loop with a soft glue such as Pattex, and before the glue dries firmly whip the join with a strong terylene fly-tying silk. Finish off with a final layer of glue. Do not use Superglue, since it will become brittle and eventually cause the fly line to snap off. You can clinch the shooting head loop you have just made to the shooting line with a standard tucked clinch or a double

clinch knot, or you can tie another loop in the shooting line and then double loop knot (see Chapter 2) the shooting head to shooting line.

A nail knot (see Chapter 2 for nail knot and for butt loop) is a suitable knot for the leader end of the fly line. It should be tied properly with the leader line going through the centre of the fly line. Form a short 10 cm butt loop here to which leaders can be attached, then you won't have to re-knot into the fly line itself every time you change the leader. A nail knot in this position for saltwater fly-fishing provides an inbuilt 'weak' spot which protects you from possible loss of the fly line.

TIDES AND TIDAL EFFECTS

In freshwater, everything happens directly or indirectly as a result of the weather. In estuaries an additional great force comes into play, and this is the power of the ever-changing tides. All things in the estuary and in the surf are affected by the tides, and the angler needs sufficient knowledge to be able to predict what kind of tide to expect, and also what time to expect it! Tides can affect the angler's catch quite markedly.

John Costello putting in a long cast from the rocks into deep water. John is a very accomplished saltwater fly-fisherman, and was largely responsible for energising the growth of the movement in the 1970s. (Photo: Louis van der Westhuizen)

Tides are caused by the gravitational pull of the sun and the moon, in conjunction with the rotation of the earth. Every day the moon (which is the principal worker in the coming and going of the tides) rises 50 minutes or so (depending on where you are) later than the previous day. The tides follow suit, and you can be sure from day to day that the tides will occur 50 minutes later than they did on the previous day. The other important thing to remember is that the complete cycle of 'low to high to low' tide takes roughly twelve hours.

Most of us have to take our fishing when we can, and if you live far from the coast and are limited by time, then you may have no choice regarding the tide you can fish. When you arrive, the tide is running, and nothing can be done about it. You will have to deduce as much as you can from the state of the tide, and also from talking to other anglers. Once you have the times of high or low tide, you can quickly calculate the time of the 'bottom' or 'top' of the tide, and write up your own tide table. Having done this, you can use your precious fishing hours to best effect.

The next question we want answered is 'What

kind of tide can we expect?' This is simply deduced by observing the state of the moon. On cloudy days this might be difficult, but fortunately in Africa most places have a high percentage of clear sky. You can usually find the moon in daylight if you look for it. The full moon and the new moon alternate every 14 days, and at these extreme phases of the moon you can expect the greatest tides – these are

The plastic hoops used for fast line changeover are shown here together with leader monofilament and preferred wire. A fly reel like the Hardy Salmon can be used in the salt, but it must be washed in fresh water at every opportunity. The System Two, although designed for the salt, needs the same treatment.

known as 'spring' tides. By greatest, I mean that during these tides the difference between the low tide mark and the high tide mark is furthest apart. The power of the tide decreases after a spring tide for seven days until the middle of the cycle (remember, it's a 14 day cycle from spring tide to spring tide). At the middle of the cycle the tide will be at its smallest difference between low tide and high tide. This is known as a 'neap' tide. At the time of the equinoxes (September and March for southern Africa) the spring tides become even greater, and these are the biggest tides of the year.

If you have access to a tide table, you can work out tide times for further up the coast. As you move northward up the coast the tides become later and later. For example, the tide in Maputo (Mozambique) is approximately 70 minutes later than the same tide in Cape Town. There is another effect that you must consider with regard to estuaries, and that is the 'delay' effect. The delay varies depending upon the structure of the estuary (narrow mouthed or wide mouthed, deep or shallow). The tide may be as much as an hour or two later just a kilometre or two inland of the estuary mouth.

Which tides are best for fishing? The answer is highly debatable, but most active sea fishermen will tell you that the incoming tide is the best for fishing, and the best time of all is at the top of the tide. Almost all will tell you that a spring tide, and a couple of days each side of it, is the very best of all, neap tides conversely being the worst. Also, since storms seem to be so often linked to a full moon spring tide, many feel that the catch on such a tide will be better. Divers support this theory, and say that there are more fishes about during a full moon.

The English are great believers in the washing action of the tide itself causing the difference in quality of fishing from tide to tide. In other words, an incoming strong spring tide disturbs lots of food off the bottom because of its strength, and this brings the fishes on the feed much more readily than a weak or retreating tide would.

SALTWATER FLY-FISHING STRATEGIES
The estuary

The estuary is the place where the river meets the sea, where the freshwater of the rain and spring-fed river mixes and mingles with the water of the mighty oceans. The environment in such places is constantly changing, and characteristically marked by enormous gradients. Food production in such places is on a par with tropical jungles, so estuaries are potentially rich feeding areas for those fishes able to exploit them.

Estuaries are subject to massive, and sometimes sudden changes in temperature, salinity, turbidity, dissolved oxygen content and the flow and direction of the current, in response to tidal influences. Not too many fishes can handle this, but those that can are able to use a resource not available to other fishes. Thus it is not unreasonable to expect fast growth rates in estuarine fishes, and for subsequent predation upon the smaller species and other food forms by gamefishes either entering from the ocean or already in the estuary.

Most of the fishes in estuaries spawn at sea, re-entering the estuaries either in a juvenile stage or later as adults. Some species spend their entire lives in the estuary and never go to sea. Those which spawn at sea often travel great distances to return to the estuary, even in some cases in their 'larval' form ... the flathead mullet (*Mugil cephalus*) is an example of this.

In spite of the often small size of estuaries, compared with some inland waters, the size of the fishes in estuaries (fishes which are readily

The tidal Ntafufu River in the Eastern Cape. High tide will bring the water, and the fish, right into the roots of the mangroves on the far side. Good sport can be had searching the roots with a fly.

Sunset at the mouth, where the river meets the sea. Louis van der Westhuizen casts over a spot where the waters mix, and where gamefishes often hunt for fry. (Photo: courtesy Louis van der Westhuizen)

available to the fly-fisherman), is often very impressive ... not only this; but weight for weight, there is little in freshwater that can match the fighting performance of the fishes of the salt.

Some estuaries are subject to being sanded in for long periods, and are often closed either until the rainy season or until the great equinoctial spring tides open up the sand bars which prevent the running of the tides. Such blocked estuaries do not offer as good fishing as the permanently open ones. However, the fishing can become excellent as soon as the estuary mouth opens. Fishes which normally mature sexually so as to re-enter the sea for breeding seem able to hold back until the estuary opens. They do not normally perform any kind of forced breeding while waiting, and will, in fact, reabsorb their gonads if unable to reach the sea during the breeding season.

Most fishes which use estuaries for spawning seem to do so in late winter and spring. Such fishes normally breed in close proximity to the coast. On the other hand, fishes such as the permanently resident estuarine roundherring (an important fodder fish), will move right up the estuary to ensure that the young fry are not washed out to sea on the tides. As these fry grow in strength, they drift back down the

Kabeljou (Argyrosomus japonicus), *commonly known as kob, must be fished for right on the bottom. They are known to exceed 70 kg in weight. This one was caught by Ken Bateman on a 'static' Yellow and Red Tarpon fly.* (Photo: Ken Bateman)

175

river, and eventually settle nearer to the sea. Some gobies and silversides are also important food fishes which live and breed permanently in estuaries.

Wading in saltwater

Some of the wadeable estuaries in Africa, and especially those with lagoons behind the river mouth, have crocodiles and hippopotami. Common sense should tell you not to wade in such places, but very often regulations will enforce it.

Where you are able to wade, it is best to proceed with a shuffle rather than by lifting your feet. By shuffling, you will frighten off, or push away, sea urchins, stonefish, stingrays and other nasties. You should always wear some kind of shoes. Many diving shops will sell you a pair of diver's shoes. These are generally ankle height and zip up at the side. They are soft, comfortable and extremely practical. Some fly-fishermen wear running shoes ('tackies' as the South Africans call them, 'trainers' in the UK) for wading, but I find these tend to quickly fill up with sand and become very uncomfortable.

Jellyfish can be a hazard for the wader at certain times of the year. It is amazing how difficult they are to see, and the small bluebottles which are so common in the Indian Ocean definitely need to be seen! Very often a careful look at the edge of the surf will reveal the presence of washed-up ones. The gas bag on the top of the jellyfish often dries in the sun, and is then fairly easy to spot. These jellyfish can give an extremely painful and irritating sting. Wading in jeans is one way of beating them, but when you come to remove the jeans, the stinging filaments which adhere to them can still sting you, so be careful. The standard treatment is monosodium glutamate; another is a product called 'Stingose'.

Finding fishes in estuaries

It is perhaps easiest to find estuary fishes from a boat, but many fly-fishermen enjoy good results from the bank. There are two major ways to find your fish: by deductive reasoning or by sight.

Finding estuary fishes by sight

Fortunately for the African estuary fisherman, the water generally clears and becomes transparent as the tide gets into full swing. Armed with a pair of polarised sunglasses it is amazing how much 'fish sign' can be seen.

Tiny indentations, ripples, and little rises spread over an area will give away the position of a shoal of plankton-eating fry – you soon get used to spotting this. Small mullet often jump, and when they don't, they very often cause little bow waves as they swim just below the surface. Over shallow water, if you can wade slowly without sudden movement, you may even see your quarry – it may be no more than one or several just discernable grey shadows, but it will be fishes. Sometimes, you will see a telltale 'V' in the surface current as large fishes feed head-down in the shallows. The big aggressive hunters can be seen bow waving as they chase fry. Sometimes several bow waves are seen at once. These big hunters come and go quickly, and you must be ready to cast your fly accurately into their predicted path.

With a boat, it is often possible to drift right into the food fish shoals, and on occasion shoals of mullet will hang around a slowly drifting boat for no apparent reason. Look through these shoals, deeper into the water, perhaps a metre or more down, and you may be rewarded with the sight of the wraithlike shadows of big garrick and kingfish. They harry the shoals, picking on the weakest and slowest, and will readily respond to the correct imitative fly fished at the right depth. These great fishes also come and go quickly, and yet again you must be ready to fish to them on the instant.

If your luck is really in, you may see a shoal of gamefishes herding and slashing at a shoal of small fishes. Such sights are often accompanied by plenty of splashing. A cast into this mêlée is almost a guarantee of a fish.

Finding estuary fishes by reasoning

For the highly mobile shore angler, fishes are to be found in many places, especially around river mouths, where it is often easy to cast into eddies, and in riffles downstream of a sand bar. Sand bars and gravel bars are often good hold-

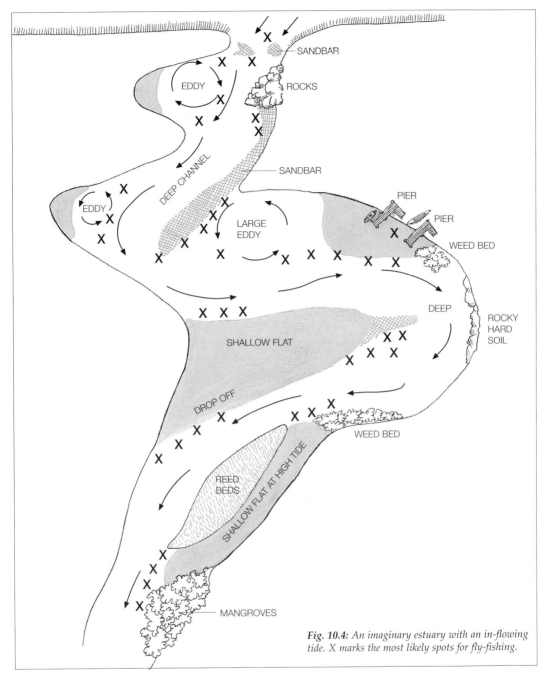

Fig. 10.4: An imaginary estuary with an in-flowing tide. X marks the most likely spots for fly-fishing.

ing areas. Deep gravelly runs are favoured by fast-moving fishes working upstream, and some of the bottom dwellers will actively hunt up and down such runs. Eddies produce well, especially along the intermix where the mainstream and the eddy meet. Most sport-fishes move fast, hunting by sight. Thus they prefer clear water, and will often avoid muddy water when they have the choice.

Fodder fishes will be where there is plenty of their own food, providing that they can also feel a little secure. Food and security are the prime considerations of tiny fishes. If they are really hungry, they might be tempted to forego security, but this is highly unlikely, considering the typical rich food sources of the average estuary.

Figure 10.4 shows the sort of areas where you might expect to find fishes. If you look at this imaginary estuary you will immediately notice that fishes are to be found only in certain spots. In many ways, the estuary fly-fisherman is in a similar position to the fly-fisherman working a stream for trout. He must also learn to read his water. He needs to know a little about the likes and dislikes of his quarry, and from this information deduce where his quarry is. Nearly always, this means learning about the behaviour of the food forms (fry, crustacea, etc), and knowing what they are looking for. Understanding how the big fish's food behaves is the fastest way to find the big fish. Hot spots are basically where food accumulates – where it initially attracts the fodder fishes, and where these in turn attract the gamefishes.

Some of the fodder fishes will be plankton eaters, and they will be found where plankton accumulates. Such a place might be where the main current meets a whirling current of a large slow eddy. The bigger the eddy, the more food it is likely to collect. In fact if you notice a scum on the surface this will often be a smear of tiny living creatures – the plankton.

Larger fodder fishes such as mullet are more likely to feed out in the open, depending a great deal on speed and agility for escape. Intermediate-sized fry will hover at the edge of the shallows as near to the main current as they dare, always instantly ready to dash back to safety. Try to cast from as far away as you can into such spots, because you may otherwise frighten the fry yourself.

Other spots where fry may be found include the edges of weed and reed beds. These are especially good if the edge is next to a drop-off. Garrick are particularly familiar with this, and will grab any fry (including your fly) silly enough to leave the refuge of eel-grass or other vegetation. Fry also swim over rocky areas which the big fishes cannot get into. Sandy areas around rocks are often homes to small gobies and can be exploited with Muddler Minnows.

Gamefishes will always patrol a sharp drop-off from a shallow flat, or from an area rich in structure such as tide-sunken mangroves. The fry work the shallow bank for plankton, and if, in their enthusiasm, they drift over the edge of the drop-off, they are snapped up by patrolling predators.

Other good places are the holes on the downstream side of gravel or sand bars. Any kind of depression will entrap food, and the small fishes will be there feeding on it. Grunter will also feed in such holes. Kob visit places like this to dine on small fry, and you can often find a good specimen here. Such depressions are easily found with an echo sounder, but can also be spotted at low tide as disturbances in the flow pattern of the tide. If you find these, take a couple of shore bearings and then fish these holes when the tide is running in, or topping out. The holes move about a lot – they come and go constantly, so don't expect them to be there a couple of months later.

Piers and pilings offer an illusion of security to all sorts of creatures. Everybody knows it, and big fishes often visit such spots for a quick meal. You need to be very quiet, no knocking or banging on the timbers when fishing from jetties, so as not to frighten off the food forms (often banded glassies and prawns).

Finally, the deep in-flowing channels right at the mouth of the estuary will often have a traffic of gamefishes passing through. Although such fishes may not be seriously feeding, they will take anything coming by that looks easy. This situation represents one of the few when the angler using bright-coloured flies is likely to have better luck than the imitative fly-fisherman. A good fly in this situation is Clouser's Deep Minnow, finished in the colours of the Micky Finn. Some tremendous battles can be fought out here, the fast current being mostly on the fish's side.

All estuaries are subject to seasonal visitation: at certain times there will be high populations of fish, and few at others. The coming and going of some species can be predicted within a week or two. The grunter run in August at St Lucia in South Africa is one of the best known of these.

Cut-away banks often indicate deep water close in, and are always worth a good search with the fly.

Many of the food fishes which the big gamefishes feed on are very structure orientated.
(A) Tree stumps, piers and mangroves are all excellent spots for searching. Many big fishes will move through such struc-
ture in the course of the day. (B) The swirling current indicates rock structure under the water: often a good holding spot
for fry and always worth a cast. (C) This bay produced excellent shad when fished with a steel trace and a Natal Halfbeak
fly. The fish were at the edge of the eddy and the fast water. (D) Estuarine roundherring will often shoal in quiet estuary
backwaters like this, and the bigger fishes will come in looking for them.

'Catch and release' is very much alive among saltwater fly-fishermen. Here Ken Bateman has tagged a springer prior to releasing it alive. Valuable information on populations, breeding and movements is obtained from the 'tag and release' programme. This one took a white Lefty's Deceiver. (Photo: Ken Bateman)

Finding fishes in the surf

There are certain things to look for in the surf which can improve your chances. Traditionally, the most exciting find is the sight of small fishes jumping, with predators slashing into the shoal and creating masses of disturbance in the surface. A fly cast into this activity will nearly always result in a strike! These fry fishes may be anything from 3 cm to 20 cm long. Sometimes, they might be quite large, at half a kilogram. The ideal size of fry for the fly-fisherman to take advantage of is the small ones up to 10 cm. You can easily miss this activity, especially if the shoal of fry is small. Thus it is important as a surf fly-fisherman to continuously look around. Monitor the surf and the sea all the time, and never stop doing it!

Terns and small gulls, like the grey-headed, also feed on small fishes. The sight of a flock of these birds wheeling over the sea often signifies the presence of a shoal of small fry. If the birds are constantly diving into the sea, you will know they are feeding on the little fishes. There are nearly always some gamefishes near these shoals, and a cast in the direction of the birds is often rewarding.

Sometimes if you are standing on the edge of rock pools, reefs, or rocky promontories when the sea is clear, you may even see fishes. A cast made straight at them might spook them; but if you cast further out and retrieve so that the fly swims past quite closely, you will often get a strike.

Places to fish in the surf

One could be excused for standing in the surf looking out to sea and thinking 'Where in all this ocean can I find a fish ... it's so vast!' The shoreline, too, seems to go on for ever. But in fact there are definitely preferred spots where chances are better, and we shall look at some of these. The best places are where the fishes are ... sounds a bit trite, but is oh so true!

Fishes show preferences for certain shore types, either because food is to be found there, or because of topographical considerations which force them to come close. Promontories are in this latter category. Wherever a spit of sand, rock, or land thrusts out into the sea, fishes moving along the shore have to eventually come up to it. They are then forced to swim close to the point – and the angler waiting there – to continue their journey. The best promontories are where the point is shallow, but the sea on either side is relatively deep. Fan cast around in order to cover the whole area. If there are rock structures and reefs in the immediate area, it makes the point even more desirable from an angler's point of view.

Bays are often good, especially deepish bays which are subject to heavy surf. Shores which have been cut away by wave activity are also worth casting from, especially if the cut-away plunges steeply into the water, creating a kind of gulley.

Rocks are always good places to explore, and they always give best results where they face the deepest water. The working of the currents through rock gulleys can also form excellent spots as a result of the current bringing plenty of food items to these areas. The little fishes come for the small food items, and the gamefishes in turn come for them. Do be careful on rocks not to get trapped by the incoming tide, and also be careful not to get washed off into the sea. Better results will generally be achieved by casting parallel with the waves, especially from rocks which jut out into the sea, providing access to deep water.

Very shallow surf is not often worth fishing with the fly rod, especially if, in spite of being shallow, a strong tide is running. It can even be dangerous trying to stand in such water. At least a metre of water is needed for best results, and it always pays to look for surf dropping rapidly to this depth.

Off some of the coasts and islands of Africa there are vast flats fronted by coral reefs. Benguera Island is one of the best of such places. Bonefish have often been seen on these flats along with other gamefishes. The flats are perhaps a maximum of a metre deep, and are generally less. Such places can be hunted with a flat-bottomed boat or they can be waded. Whatever method you adopt, the secret is to move slowly and quietly. You are looking for any kind of action, and such action may first be perceived some way off. The trick then is to stalk up to the fish without being spotted, before putting out a long cast and presenting some kind of bonefish fly to the quarry.

FLIES AND IMITATION FOR SALTWATER

No saltwater pattern actually imitates any kind of fly. Imitative insect fly-fishing (with the exception of the occasional hatch in an estuary) would be doomed to a hard future in the salt. Most saltwater flies are either brightly coloured, aggression-generating bunches of fly-tying material, or they imitate small fishes, shrimps and other crustaceans.

Saltwater fishes are opportunist feeders, attacking almost anything that looks like a meal. However, I have known many occasions when they are quite fussy about what fly they will take. On such occasions they will very often go for an imitative pattern (and they may well be choosy about which pattern). At other times, they will seem to react only to suitable colour presentations. Very often they will ignore super bright, over-flashy or fluorescent patterns, but will freely take a dull pattern.

It would seem that saltwater fishes can be almost as fussy as trout. The truth is that there is a real case for imitative fishing in the salt: those who deliberately set out to imitate the creatures of the surf and the estuaries undoubtedly improve their results markedly. Saltwater fly-fishing, once a 'chuck and chance it' affair, has finally come to maturity. Imitative fly-fishing is in!

John Costello of Port St Johns in the Eastern

Garfish are very often taken by the saltwater fly-fisherman. This one, taken by Ken Bateman, put up a spectacular aerobatic display. It took a white sandal foam popper. The hat is not obligatory, but the basket is! (Photo: courtesy Ken Bateman)

Cape was perhaps the first angling writer to bring the facts of African imitative fly-fishing in saltwater to the fore. In an article in the South African *Fly Fishing* magazine, John put forward his ideas on imitative fly-fishing and the proper depths at which such imitations should be fished. It was an eye opener for many surf fly-fishers, and lifted the lid off the little-known fact that imitative fishing pays! Other anglers, including the author, had also been experimenting in this field, and it was fascinating to see how all these people were reaching the same conclusions independently of one another's findings.

Undoubtedly, if you take the trouble, either by spooning your catch or by water observation, to assess what the fishes are feeding on, and then deliberately imitate such food forms, your results must improve. Spooning a saltwater fish is no different to spooning a trout (see Chapter 11). Examining stomach contents will teach you a great deal about the gamefishes' foods.

Wherever the subject of food fish (fry) is raised, I have attempted to give some idea of which fly best represents that bait fish. I would especially refer you to the section of Chapter 12 relating to the food fishes of the surf and estuaries. There is also a table at the end of that same chapter which provides information on the commoner fishes and crustacean food forms, and the appropriate flies and methods. The saltwater fly patterns described in Chapter 13 include a note on the creature being imitated, if they are known to be imitative.

In the surf and in estuaries, the food forms most commonly needing imitating are small fishes, crabs, prawns, shrimps, other crustaceans, sea lice, molluscs, worms, and so on. When emulating these, first try to match the living food form's movement and its colours. When choosing or tying saltwater fly patterns, particularly take care to simulate any small spots of obvious colour which may occur. Such 'key colours' are often the trigger for the feeding fish. A good example of key colour is the red spot on the tip of the beak of the tiny half-beaks which sometimes sport in the surf. Another 'key' in almost all saltwater flies is the eyes ... these should never be left out of the dressing!

Easy non-imitative approach

If you are a raw beginner to fly-fishing the estuaries and surf, and not yet familiar with the various food forms, the following simplistic approach should help. Try flies which are green and white, blue and white, or pink and white. These colours cover over 90 per cent of the colours in the commoner food forms. Having chosen your fly, try it at different depths. Fish the eddies, the edge of fast runs and the gulleys at the mouth of the river.

CHAPTER 11

THE FISH'S LARDER – THE INSECTS

Toast:

'One final cast for luck, and the really last throw in honour of a fair lady ...
If they don't rise to that, then they are no gentlemen!'

Anon.

A diagrammatic approach to fly-fishing might be to think of it as centring around imitative fly-fishing, with dry fly-fishing extending off to the left, and lure fly-fishing off to the right. Think of it as a spectrum of skills from which you can draw the optimum method to fit the prevailing conditions. Under this approach, it would be reasonable to expect that it is important to build your angling strengths at the core (imitative fly-fishing), and then to extend your skills from this base. For example, perhaps you are currently strong in lure fly-fishing, but lacking in other skills. A study of imitative fly-fishing would bear quick results! Almost certainly, you will markedly improve your successes with such an approach.

At the core of this philosophy is the imitation of African water creatures. This chapter is about simple entomology, and Chapter 12 is about food fishes and other life forms – effectively an overview of the fish's larder. Both these chapters provide some ideas of what to look for, and what to do when you find it.

THE AFRICAN FLY-FISHERMAN'S HATCH

In European and American literature the 'hatch' (the emergence of insects) is generally identified with trout fishing. In Africa, it may also be identified with fly-fishing for other species such as yellowfish, kurper, and so on.

The 'hatch' is traditionally part and parcel of imitative dry fly-fishing. The insects hatch from a nymphal form (through a process known as ecdysis) and numbers – perhaps thousands – emerge onto the surface of the water prior to their first flight.

Many African fly-fishermen, but certainly not all, tend to apply a broader view to this process than their counterparts in other parts of the world, and they will often refer to underwater creatures which may be particularly plentiful at a specific time as a 'hatch'. They are obviously incorrect referring to an abundance of non-hatching creatures as a hatch, but they do so, and they have been doing so for the last hundred years! Perhaps reading this book may convert a few of these anglers, but in the meantime, 'overseas visitors beware'! Such a fly-fisherman might include dragonfly nymphs, caddis, tadpoles, or whatever he has noticed as a prevalent food form in his definition of 'hatch'. The angling visitor to Africa, or the beginner, would do well to ask any angler who says he is fishing to a hatch, 'What kind of hatch is it?' He may find that what he really needs is not a dry fly but a large wet Walker's Killer or other suitable dragonfly nymph imitator.

Matching the hatch

The surface 'hatch' may last for days, hours, or even only minutes. But the experienced angler also knows that the longer these hatches last, especially heavy hatches, the greater is the

Not all insects are worth imitating. Fish seldom eat pond-skaters, which detect an approach quite easily and are capable of prodigious leaps to escape. These hyaenas of the surface will eat any sick or dying insect they find.

chance that the fishes will start feeding exclusively on the hatching creature. In other words, the fishes become preoccupied with a particular food form, usually to the exclusion of all else. The fly-fisherman who ties on the correct fly can usually be sure of some good fishing. This process of selecting an imitation of the hatching insect is known as 'matching the hatch'. The angler who can do this both theoretically and in practice can markedly improve the chances of success.

A keen sense of observation can be a real asset in determining just what is appearing on the surface. Rises might occur because of hatching sedges or buzzers, or mayflies (which are considerably scarcer in African waters than in Europe and the UK), or because of quantities of floating snails, or maybe windborne land insects such as ants or termites. What is important to know, is that without the usual mayfly

Ryan Steele collecting insects in an African high-country stream.

emergences that other continents have, knowledge of the other insect groups becomes very significant to the African fly-fisherman. Knowledge of the habits of water creatures can lead the angler to the correct choice of fly, when there is perhaps no evidence at all of insect emergence.

Choice of method

Fishes spend more time feeding on submerged food than they do at the surface. The flexible African fly angler might decide, based on the prevailing conditions, to use any of the methods in the skills spectrum. If the trout are rising to floating adult flies, the best choice will most likely be a dry fly. On the other hand, if the trout are chasing fry, the angler will almost certainly switch to a lure fly.

The angler may well find the water seemingly dead, with no evidence of food form activity. In such conditions, a strip retrieved attractor lure fly may be the correct initial approach. Perhaps it is a hot day and the marginal sedge plants have large numbers of blue damselflies roosting there. In such a situation, the angler may well decide to go sub-surface nymphing. The choice of strategies and tactics are endless.

Let us look at this in more depth. Obviously, artificial flies imitate all kinds of things, but most of the living originals fall into well-defined groups. It is these groups, and the different stages of their development, that you need to know about. It is not necessary to get down to knowing each individual species of insect (unless of course you want to): knowledge of the group is quite sufficient. In fact, there is little literature available on identification of specific insects related to angling in African waters. You can find out a great deal about similar insect groups from other parts of the world (European and American literature is a particularly rich source of information), but accurate African information is difficult to come by. The best way to learn is to acquire a basic understanding, such as follows in this chapter. Keep a diary of visits to the waterside, and log brief descriptions of insects against date, emergence time, and weather conditions. It will not be long before you start to build a very useful natural history of the insects in your favourite waters.

Spooning: the autopsy

Knowing what is inside your first trout of the day can make the difference between a poor day and an excellent one. Just what has he been eating? What is on the fish's menu today? Perhaps the fishes are totally preoccupied with a particular food form? These are the kinds of questions often answered by the very important technique of spooning your catch.

You need a marrow spoon and a small dish (ideally a white one). Today it is easy to acquire marrow spoons, or the modern equivalents. Some are conveniently built into the handle of a priest.

First kill the fish. You cannot perform this operation on a live fish! Insert the spoon right way up down the throat and into the stomach, then give it one full turn. The spoon will now be filled (providing there are some stomach contents, sometimes there are none). Put a little water in the dish, push the contents of the spoon into the dish, and then tease them out. You will find several insects and other food forms in various states of digestion, but there is nearly always sufficient good material to be able to make a positive identification. The photographs in this chapter will give a good idea of what to expect and will also form an aid to identification. Once you have identified the most prevalent food form, you can tie on a suitable imitation, and then work out a strategy.

Spooning. The spoon is inserted well down into the stomach, twisted a full turn once, and then withdrawn. The contents are dropped into a small container of water and teased out for examination.

When identifying the food forms, allow for the effect of stomach acids on the coloration. For example, normally black coloured tadpoles are bleached white very quickly, and small fry also loose all their colour. Insects seem better able to withstand the effect of the acids, and they retain their colours much better.

MAYFLIES (EPHEMEROPTERA)

Mayflies have an interesting life cycle which starts with the egg, progresses to an aquatic nymphal stage, and then to a sub-adult non-reproductive winged stage known as the dun, which in turn further develops into a final winged mating adult stage known as the spinner.

Adult mayflies are easily recognisable as small up-winged flies of various colours, usually with two or three long fine tails. From a fly-angler's point of view the Ephemeroptera (or ephemerids, as this order of insects are often called by fly-fishermen) are probably the best known group of angler's insects. World-wide, there is probably more written on these insects, in relation to their importance as models for imitation by the fly-tier, than on any other insect group; in Africa, however, almost nothing has been published for the fly angler. In the South African Cape, some of the common mayflies have vernacular names, but most African mayflies do not have common names, and they are not easily identified. Consequently, in this chapter, the mayflies are simply referred to by their hatching dun (sub-adult) colour types ... not very scientific, but it offers a workable method of identification. Typically, a mayfly may be referred to as a 'slatey winged olive body type', or 'mottled brownish winged sepia body type', and so on.

Small numbers of mayflies exist in all clean African waters wherever fly-fishermen ply their trade. In Africa, it is very unusual to experience the huge hatches which are the norm in the temperate countries. However, such hatches as do occur are certainly significant, and fishes will often ignore everything else to get at them. As the mayflies float downstream, wings cocked like miniature yachts, and the grey shadows of fishes rise from the depths to sip

A typical small stream, high-country dark mayfly dun (Leptophlebia) from South Africa.

A

E

C

them from the surface ... the fly-fisherman's heart leaps in anticipation.

Trout respond to mayflies with total preoccupation once a good hatch starts. This means that imitations of mayflies are very important, and the angler must be properly prepared for the sport to come. Mayfly hatches are generally more common on running water than on dams, but it would be a foolhardy still-water fly-fisherman who did not carry some imitations of these flies and their nymphs.

Most African mayflies are small (although I have seen hatches of large sulphur-winged species on the Mooi and Sabie rivers in South Africa). They tend to be a phenomenon of late winter, spring, and summer in most of the high-altitude waters. They hatch at other times, but much more sparsely. An autumn hatch period is also common on many waters. The density of hatches in summer is usually highest in the afternoon and evening, whereas the winter hatches are often mid- to late-morning events. In South African high-country still waters, it is a common occurrence for a sizeable hatch to occur in the depths of winter, often within hours of a hard frost being burnt off by the morning sun. Most African mayfly species are imitated by size 12, 14, 16, and 18 dry flies.

Trout and yellowfish will often rise selectively to mayflies and their nymphs, even if they are a minority hatch among other insects. Chances are, then, that even in a mixed hatch of sedges and mayflies, fishes will ignore the sedges and become preoccupied with the mayflies.

The mayfly nymphs – an overview

The keen trout angler who regularly performs stomach examinations of his catches will often find the various mayfly nymph types turning up, both streamside and by still water. The guide to the various mayfly families given below includes an indication of the preferred fly-fishing method for each type. The simple outline drawings of nymphs emphasise the recognition points of the various families. Once

Spoonings

(a) *Typical mixed spooning: the dots are daphnia.*
(b) *A semi-digested frog removed from a Blyde River rainbow.* (Photo: Malcolm Meintjes)
(c) *Dragonfly nymph with an imitation next to it. Note the multitude of daphnia.* (Photo: Malcolm Meintjes)
(d) *Typical terrestrials: grasshopper and assorted beetles, with two buzzer pupae.* (Photo: Malcolm Meintjes)
(e) *Bloodworms, larval form of the buzzer.* (Photo: Malcolm Meintjes)
(f) *Mayfly nymphs. This fish was preoccupied with feeding on them, since no other food forms are evident.*
(Photo: Malcolm Meintjes)
(g) *An unusual preoccupation with the predatory larvae of the great water beetle (Dytiscus); note the artificial fly shown for comparison.* (Photo: Malcolm Meintjes)
(h) *Snails, all from the trout on the right.* (Photo: Malcolm Meintjes)
(i) *Autopsy during a termite fall. The fly was found inside the trout, and obviously had not been there long.*

you have established the mayfly nymph type on which the trout are feeding, you can then go ahead and fish with a preferred imitation and method based on the habits and movements of that nymph. In general, the nymphs take on the colours of surrounding vegetation. If you net a few (use an aquarium net), it is often possible to tell how close the nymphs are to hatching by examining the wing cases, which darken as hatching time approaches.

The burrowing and clinging nymph types cannot easily be movement imitated until such time as they move to the surface to hatch. Even then, the clinging types very often crawl up reed and sedge stems. However, in nature, these small creatures are subject to the whims of the stream, and they often lose their grip and get washed down in the current. Trout are waiting for this, and they nab the drifting mayfly nymphs avidly. Often, a dead drift with a floating line will imitate these washed away crawlers very well.

The easy mayfly nymphs to imitate are the bottom dwellers which crawl or swim (some are very active swimmers). The crawlers can be movement imitated with a very slow 'figure-of-eight' retrieve, and the swimmers can be imitated with a slow strip retrieve consisting of small ten centimetre pulls.

The most useful time to imitate mayfly nymphs is when they come up to hatch. They swim for the surface, and are very vulnerable at this time. Trout (and other fish), frogs, and numerous insect predators will often feed heavily on the nymphs during the early stages of a

A 'parachute' tying of a Tups Indispensable floats high on the water, busily imitating mayfly duns. The white tuft on top has been added by the tier to improve visibility.

hatch. If you are not sure whether the trout are feeding on nymphs or duns, just watch for bubbles rising immediately after the rise. Bubbles mean that the fish took from the surface and is feeding on duns rather than nymphs; no bubbles means you can stick to your nymph imitations – he's still eating nymphs!

The best method for nymphing to the mayfly nymph-eating trout on still water is to use a floating line and a sink and draw retrieve. In still water the figure-of-eight retrieve is my favourite, but you can often do better by simply allowing a sink-tip line to drift around in a cross-wise wind. In this way, a weighted nymph can perform very much like a live nymph crawling along the bottom.

Emerging mayflies

The point at which the mayfly emerges is often underrated by most fly-fisherman. Emergence is an important stage in the life cycle, and one which can be exploited with good effect. Presentation for emerging insects should be with a floating line just as for a dry fly, although an occasional twitch often livens things up. However, flies must float in the surface film and not on it. Flies to try are the Mayfly Emerger and the Emerging Nymph. A poorly proofed hackled dry fly will also float in the surface film, rather than on it.

The dun (sub-imago or sub-adult)

When the mayfly nymphs are ready to hatch into the dun form, they swim to the surface, often making several attempts before hatching through the surface film. Once the nymph reaches the surface film, the nymphal skin splits, and viewed from the surface the mayfly appears to pop out of nowhere. The wings dry very quickly, enabling the mayfly dun to rapidly become airborne. This speed is an essential aid to survival, with so many hungry fishes waiting for a quick meal. Imitations of the emerging mayfly can often be successful, especially in the early stages of the hatch.

The hatched mayfly dun is not yet a full adult, and still has to go through this 'dun' stage before final adulthood. The dun is very important to the trout as a food item, and consequently is perhaps the most important winged stage of development. It is quite possible, though unusual, that the trout may become so preoccupied with the nymph stage that they ignore the prolifically hatching duns. But generally speaking, the duns are what they want, and this is a magical time for the dry fly-fisherman. Lots of other creatures also feed on the duns, including birds and dragonflies.

Swallows seem to have foreknowledge of an impending hatch of duns, and will often queue up on fence wires and telephone wires waiting for the start. Almost as the first dun hatches, the birds are whirling above the surface catching the mayflies. Another situation which is often a warning of an impending hatch is a sudden calm after a period of wind. Yet another is if the sun comes out after a period (two days or more) of grey cloudy weather, when the duns will almost certainly hatch, even in a stiff breeze. In still air, it is also not unusual in African countries to encounter hatches just after dawn, especially on high-altitude still water.

The newly hatched duns head for anything taller than the surrounding vegetation. As most fly-fishermen know, this can include the angler's face, ears and clothing. Once landed, perched on a stem or leaf or whatever, they moult for the final time and emerge as a spinner or imago.

The spinner (imago or full adult)

The final metamorphosis to full adulthood can take several minutes, or hours, depending on the species. Once the dun has settled, it splits the outer skin, transforms into the spinner, and flies off. The fragile dun shucks are left behind.

The duns are exquisitely delicate creatures, but the spinners are crystal-winged shining insects of even greater beauty. The males have bigger eyes than the females, but are otherwise similar. The spinners have a typical undulating flight, and often a group of them will be found undulating up and down in the afternoon sun. The spinners usually mate quickly, and the females then return to the water to lay their eggs. Some species lay on aquatic vegetation, even crawling down the stems and under the water, and are largely ignored by the trout.

Spent spinners of the 'Red Border-wing' mayfly (family Baetidae).

Others dip their abdomens in the water while fluttering above the surface, and lay their eggs from this position – these are the ones that the trout usually go for.

Some of these spinners may get stuck in the surface film, or simply die right there when egg laying is complete. These so-called 'spent spinners' are taken avidly by the trout. Trout will rise selectively at times to the spinners, even while a hatch of duns takes place. This behaviour illustrates how important it is to observe the water closely in order to determine precisely what the trout are rising to. Most of the spent spinners are well imitated by just two or three imitations – the Sherry Spinner is a particularly good all-round one for Africa. Perhaps better known in Africa, and very popular, are the Holsloot Spinner and Robin Fick's Mayfly Spinner.

Fishing to imitate spent spinners can vary from the intensely exciting to utter frustration. The fishes appear to be more than usually size conscious when it comes to mayfly spinners. Fly size choice (and this can mean going down to size 20 at times) can thus make a big difference! Very often it is essential that the fly is actually in the surface film and not on top of the water. The Carabou Spider fly is very useful for handling this situation.

The mayfly families – a closer view

There are several families of mayflies, whose nymphs may differ considerably both in lifestyle and in appearance, and whose two adult forms may differ in habits from species to species. These are important stream-side factors when choosing a correct imitation – the more you know, the better off you are! In Africa, the seven main families of interest to the fly-fisherman are:

❏ Leptophlebiidae
❏ Baetidae
❏ Caenidae
❏ Ephemerellidae
❏ Trichorythidae
❏ Heptogeniidae
❏ Oligoneuriidae.

The Baetidae and the Leptophlebiidae are the most important of the larger species; the Caenidae and the Trichorythidae (collectively known by the common name of 'angler's curse' among African fly-fishermen) are the most abundant of the smaller ones. (There are additional African mayfly families restricted to warmer tropical waters where trout cannot survive, which are not described here.)

Leptophlebiidae

The Leptophlebia mayflies have free-swimming nymphs, not particularly agile, and often prefer slow or still water. However, at higher altitudes, they are commonly found in the quieter parts of fast-flowing streams, where they can be extremely abundant in the shallows, under plants, stones and rocks. Most of the adults are dark-coloured flies with dark brown or reddish coloured bodies, often with heavily mottled dark wings. The nymphs are in the size range 6–15 mm. There are some 40 known species in southern Africa alone. The 'September brown' mayfly (*Adenophlebia peringueyella*), with a wingspread of about 30 mm, is perhaps the best known African member of this family. Overseas, a typical member of this family is the 'claret dun'.

The Leptophlebia nymphs are often dark brown, or deep golden coloured, or a mixture of both, and some are a charcoal grey. The various

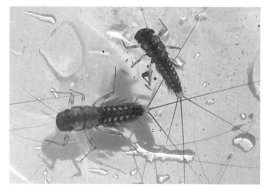

Leptophlebia mayfly nymphs from a South African Highveld stream.

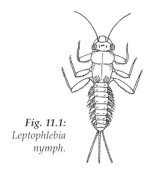

Fig. 11.1:
Leptophlebia nymph.

Pheasant Tail dressings, the Leptophlebia Nymph and the Charcoal Nymph are good imitations.

The Leptophlebia nymph's gills (seen alongside the abdomen) are mobile and capable of generating a current of water across them, a useful adaptation for life in slow-moving or still water.

Baetidae

The Baetidae mayfly nymphs are adapted very well to cool, clear, flowing water conditions. They are smallish, usually 4–10 mm long. The Baetidae nymphs are commonly found clinging to rocks, weeds and large gravel particles.

Some 60-odd African Baetidae species are known. Some of these are large, and prey on the smaller species and on other nymphs. They are all fast, active, darting swimmers, and their fringed tails are an evolved adaptation for swimming. Some African still-water species are also known, a commonly occurring olive coloured form being particularly important.

The Baetidae nymphs of the stream and river species are mostly coloured in greens from very

The beautiful shining wings of a high-country baetid spinner.

Caenis or angler's curse. The one on the right has discarded its dun skin and has become a spinner; the other is still a dun and has not yet emerged from the dun skin.

Fig. 11.2:
Baetidae nymph.

pale olive to dark olive; a few are dark brown, and some are sandy coloured. The PVC Nymph and the Sawyer's Olive Pheasant Tail are good imitators for the green types. That splendid fly the Gold-ribbed Hare's Ear (especially the black-wingcased American variation, is excellent for the sandy coloured ones. Some of the adults are noted for their slatey coloured wings. The common South African two-winged mayfly, the 'red border-wing' (*Cloeon lacunosum*), which is about 10 mm long including tails, is perhaps the best known of the African Baetidae. Overseas, mayflies such as the 'iron-blue', and the 'olive duns' are all members of this family.

The odd small jerk interspersed in the retrieve will imitate the darting motion of the nymphs.

Caenidae

The Caenidae are popularly known amongst anglers as the 'angler's curse'. These little mayflies often hatch in countless thousands, spiralling above the banks in smoky columns consisting of vast numbers of insects. The adults of all the species are small. Because they hatch in such huge quantities they present the fly-fisherman with problems typical of these miniature mayflies. Firstly, they are tiny and relatively difficult to imitate well. Secondly, because of their small size they demand ultra-fine tippets; and, finally, because there are so many of them on the water during a hatch, the trout can literally cruise around with his mouth open taking in as many as he wants – nothing is likely to convince him that your imitation is special!

The caenis nymphs are as small as 2–4 mm in length. They are of the burrowing type, and spend their lives just under the surface of the bottom silt. This silt adheres to their bodies and forms an excellent camouflage. Generally speaking, these insects prefer slow-flowing and still water, but there are a few stream species. The nymph ties are useless if they are any bigger than a size 18. However, if you use a 3X short shank 14 hook, a heavier but correct size (and more useful) nymph can be tied. Of the nymphal dressings available, a dark brown rendering of Dick Walker's 'Nymph of Feather Fibre' is the most useful option.

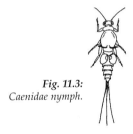

Fig. 11.3:
Caenidae nymph.

These caenis nymphs are very commonly found in the stomach autopsies of still-water trout. The imitation nymph should be fished deep and very slowly. The Baby Doll fly can be used to take advantage of the key colour, white, found in the caenis nymphs.

Ephemerellidae

The Ephemerellidae mayflies belong to the swiftly flowing streams of the southern and eastern Cape in South Africa. The six species are known only from this area. The adults are three tailed and rather small (6–10 mm).

These mayflies have the somewhat unfortunate (for them) characteristic of hatching very slowly, and the dun takes some time to escape from the floating nymphal case. For trout this makes them a prime target, and a pretty easy one at that.

The Ephemerellidae nymphs are crawlers, and they live among dense weeds and stones. Most are dark brown in colour. The adults tend toward dark coloured wings. The Pheasant Tail Nymph is a good imitation for these Ephemerellidae nymphs, and there are two useful methods for fishing it:

❏ When the nymphs are hatching, fish your imitation just under the surface. De-grease the last few inches of the leader for the best effect, and use a floating line.

❏ Trout wait for these rather weak nymphs to be dislodged by the swift currents from their tenuous holds, and are used to picking up loose ones. Fishing across and down with a sinking line can be very successful.

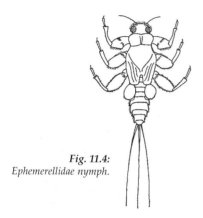

Fig. 11.4:
Ephemerellidae nymph.

Fig. 11.5:
Tricorythidae
nymph.

Upstream roll casting into good-looking lies, and then allowing the fly to dead drift down, is another very useful method. In Europe the 'blue-winged olive' is typical of this family.

Tricorythidae

Trycorythidae are smallish mayflies found commonly in fast-flowing streams. They are not relevant to European fly-fishing, but similar species have carved a name for themselves in American fly-fishing. Most African fly-fishermen, if asked, would group the adults along with the Caenidae and treat them in the same way.

The nymphs are usually small, but individual species give a size spectrum of 5–9 mm. The adults are generally referred to as 'trichos', and they are clear-winged with bodies which are often sooty coloured. There are in excess of 20 species, nearly all of which have small brown-coloured nymphs. The nymphs are solidly built, slow-moving clamberers, and can be found clinging to the underside of stones in swift currents. Trout are quite used to picking up dislodged ones in the fast currents.

The best method is to fish a size 16 Pheasant Tail Nymph (or a Hot Spot) on a fast-sinking line. Cast upstream and dead drift back.

Heptageniidae

The Heptageniidae are stream insects commonly found in Africa. The adults are 9–12 mm long with two tails. Adult body colours are generally yellowish to brownish, with wings tinted yellow. The adult males have very large eyes, which is an adaptation to a nocturnal existence.

The nymphs are very flat, often with large heads and large eyes. They vary from 9 to 13 mm long. They are agile crawlers but poor swimmers, and they spend their time clinging to rocks and weeds. Some Heptageniidae nymphs are especially adapted to an existence

Fig. 11.6:
Heptageniidae
nymph.

spent clinging to long trailing weeds that swing in the current. In Africa, the nymphs hatch in the dark, and the adults are not normally part of the daytime fly-fishing scene. As such, it is the nymphs which are of main interest to the fly-fisherman. Trout are especially fond of picking up detached and free-swimming examples of these nymphs. The nymphal colours vary from yellowish to brown.

A weighted Gold-ribbed Hare's Ear is the correct fly to use. The best method is upstream casting next to dense flowing weedbeds, and then dead drifting back.

The European 'yellow may dun' and the 'dark dun' are typical of this group.

Oligoneuridae

The Oligoneuridae are an African family and are not represented elsewhere. Many of the species are confined to tropical and sub-tropical waters, but others are stream dwellers on the high mountain escarpments. In areas where trout are traditionally stocked, these nymphs can be common. They are particularly well known on the South African Drakensberg escarpment.

The adults are mostly milky white and large (10–20 mm). In some areas, they are locally thought of as real 'mayflies' (like the big European ones), but this is a different family.

They are unique in that the dun moults into an imago during flight, so that the adults never alight, but fly until spent. Mating takes place during flight.

Nymphs are large (up to 22 mm), and usually brown in colour. The nymphal forelegs have large brush structures which are used for filter feeding. They are normally found in fast-flowing waters. The imitation which is most useful is the White-gloved Howdy. This should be fished on a sinking line, downstream and across with a very slow retrieve designed to emulate the movement of a bottom crawler. Dead drifting is also a good method.

SEDGES (TRICHOPTERA)

The life cycle of the sedges (caddis or tent-winged flies) consists of the aquatic egg, larva, and pupa stages, followed by the winged adult. The adult sedges can hatch at any time of day, but the intensity normally increases as the day passes. The very small ones are often the first to hatch during the morning. Sedges often hatch prolifically during the evening, offering the fly-fisherman excellent opportunities to dry fly as well as to fish imitations of the other life stages.

The sedge larva

This is the little creature known to school children everywhere as the 'caddis'. The caddis is so well known because of his habit of constructing a little case, made of all kinds of bottom detritus, to protect his body.

The name 'caddis' is derived from the pedlars of old who were inclined to sew to their clothes samples of the materials they sold. One material in particular was called 'caddice' and the pedlar adorned with many bits of caddice was known as the 'caddis man'. The caddis larva,

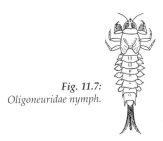

Fig. 11.7:
Oligoneuridae nymph.

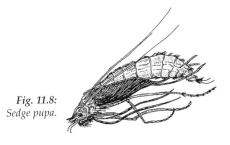

Fig. 11.8:
Sedge pupa.

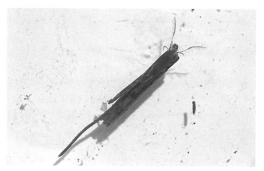

Cased caddis larva: this species is from still water and builds its case from shreds of reed stems.

Caseless caddis larvae of the family Rhyacophiliodea.

supposedly performing the same trick, was hence known as the 'caddis grub'.

Some types of caddis larvae are caseless and free swimming; others build only protective webs. These two types are so common in Africa that they are also well worth imitating. The caddis types that do build a 'house' get added protection and camouflage, and also sufficient weight to help the insect maintain its position in a current. The fast-water types tend to build heavier shelters than those in still water (it is obviously not important to have heavy ballast in still water).

Almost every genus builds a larval house which is characteristic of that genus. The cases vary from 3 to 15 mm long. One genus might use bits of small snail shells to build the case, another might use twigs, and yet another will use sand from the bottom. When the time comes to transform into the pupal stage, the caddis larva seals up the end of his case with silk, often simultaneously attaching the case to a bottom structure with this same silk.

The caddis larvae receive somewhat less attention from fly-fishermen than they should. This is surprising when you consider just how common these little creatures are in Africa, and that trout will feed on them avidly at times.

In 1968, the UK fly-tier and master angler Steve Stephens tied up some imitations of the heavy caddis types for me. They were made quite simply by mixing sharp sand and quick-set epoxy glue, and spreading this around the hook shank in a body shape. The head was black varnished silk, and the legs were imitated by a few fibres of black hen hackle ... the fly was

called the 'Sandy Sedge'. A slow figure-of-eight retrieve is required for caddis larvae imitations, and it needs to be interspersed with tiny sharp jerks for best results. All caddis larvae imitations must be fished right on the bottom.

The 'Caddis Stick' series of flies are perhaps the very best imitations of all; the Hot Spots are another group of great sedge larva-imitating flies.

In the immature stages of sedge flies, there is always a small spot of colour – usually green or amber – in the thoracic region. The trout get used to finding the colour spot, by which they easily identify the caddis as a food form. The consequence can be a preoccupied feeding pattern, and thus it is important that a similar key colour spot is included in your imitation. In Africa, that is most likely to be green during the colder months and amber in the warmer months. Nevertheless, species with either colour do coexist, and the angler is well advised to carry both dressings in all seasons.

The caddis pupa

When the time arrives for the larva to have completed its metamorphosis within the caddis case (usually about two weeks), the pupa breaks free of the case and either swims as quickly as it can towards the surface, or crawls along the bottom towards the bankside. Once at the surface, the adult sedge fly hatches, and then makes off as fast as it can across the surface. This pupal migration normally occurs en masse, resulting in heavy preoccupied feeding by the trout.

The method for the types which are hatching

at the bank is to use a fast-sink line and a very slow steady retrieve. If the hatch is on the surface, the method is to use a floating line and to retrieve with a slow 'sink and draw'.

The pupa is perhaps the most useful stage for the fly-fisherman to imitate. Good flies for pupae imitation include the Invicta, Pearl Pushkin, and Walker's Nymph.

The adult sedge

The adults are characteristically recognised by the tent-like shape of the wings, and the often exceedingly long antennae. They come in several shades of tan, grey, cream, and brown, often heavily mottled. They vary in size from big ones of about size 8 to little ones which would find a size 18 much bigger than they are. The names 'sedge' and 'longhorns' are in common usage to describe these insects. Overseas, more so than in Africa, the adults are often referred to as caddis flies. The name 'longhorns' in fact describes a few of the species which have extra-long antennae.

The adults hatch all through the year, with smaller ones being the norm in the colder months. The big species appear in summer, when traditionally the hatches are during the late afternoon and evening.

There are several good imitations of the adults such as the Soldier Palmer Pink, DDD, Walker's Red Sedge, Wickham's Fancy, G and H Sedge, and the Troutbeck Beetle. The Bi-visibles are also effective.

The hatching adult sedge

The fishes often become preoccupied with the pupae, but occasionally when larger sedges are hatching they will switch their attentions to the adults. The big sedges with wings buzzing furiously are very attractive to trout. In a good hatch they will be seen skidding all over the surface, and the trout will be making slashing attacks with big splashy rises. The sedges will hatch even in a fairly stiff ripple, and a very buoyant artificial is a must. All this lends itself to a very exciting form of dry fly-fishing. Use a well-greased imitation such as a DDD or a G and H Sedge. Just this once, a greased leader is admissible (which is not the case in ordinary

Cased caddis larva: this species from the family Limnephiloidea builds a case from sand particles, and is found in fast-flowing water where the weight of the sand helps keep it on the bottom.

Adult sedge. (Photo: Joe Joannou)

dry fly-fishing). Cast as far as you can, and retrieve in long pulls sufficiently fast to ensure that the fly tips-up onto its hackles, and appears to skip across the tops of the wavelets. Takes are usually very positive.

The ovipositing adult sedge

These can be conveniently split into two types, the diving sedge and the better-known type which lays its eggs by sticking its abdomen in the water.

The diving sedge

The diving sedge is one of nature's marvels. The female returning to the water literally dives from flight straight through the surface film and into the water. She then paddles furiously with her legs and propels herself to the bottom. Once there, she chooses a suitable site and lays her eggs. In many cases, she is able to return to the surface again.

As the female sedge enters the water, her body is encapsulated in a shining bubble of air. This bubble is so bright that it is often nearly impossible to discern the sedge within. The bubble provides her with oxygen. This type of breathing is known as plastron breathing, and the bubble always stays the same size, because the oxygen is continuously replaced with carbon dioxide. Hence, the sedge returns to the surface carrying the same size bubble as the one she entered with.

Some authorities have rightly considered that the sedge within its bubble is distinctive enough to justify an imitation. Gary LaFonteine's 'Diving Caddis' is a good one, as is Robin Fick's 'White Death'. Antron fibre in such fly dressings is an effective trap for air, thus simulating the bubble.

The surface-laying sedge

The surface-laying sedge females return to the water fluttering across the surface. They haphazardly stop here and there to dip their abdomens in the water and release their eggs. A fair proportion of these sedges end up spent and struggling in the surface film. This is the time to cast out a well-proofed DDD and simply leave it there. The cruising trout suck these imitations down in total innocence. There is nothing wrong with standing at the ready and casting to every rising trout, but sometimes it's nice to relax and to just enjoy the waterside until that big one glides up under your fly, engulfs it and then explodes into fury as you drive the hook home! An occasional twitch of the rod tip to simulate the struggling insect will often bring a slashing rise from a watching but unsure fish. This is heart-stopping stuff – you are never sure just when the take will come!

BUZZERS (CHIRONIMIDAE)

The Chironimidae are a large group of non-biting midges belonging to the order of flat-winged flies known as Diptera. Their life cycle has three aquatic forms, egg, larva and pupa, and a single free-flying adult form. In the UK and America the adults are generally referred to as midges and the pupae as buzzers, but in Africa almost everybody calls both the pupae and the adults buzzers. In spite of the attempts of several authors to convert the African fly-

fishermen to the correct terminology, they have failed ... 'buzzers' it is!

Buzzers exist in all kinds of waters, but are most prevalent in still water. However, that is not to say that they do not occur in running water, because they most certainly do! Hatches of adult buzzers occur on most days in spring, summer, and autumn. Many of the species hatch only in the dark, but there are many others that hatch throughout the daylight hours. On occasion, the hatches are tremendously heavy, and trout and other fishes become totally preoccupied with them. Chironimids are at times the most important insects for the still-water fly-fisherman in Africa.

The adult buzzers and their pupae come in a range of sizes from diminutive size 22 to large size 8. The larger ones are commonly represented in Africa by the large pale olive buzzer and by the very common claret buzzer. The other extreme is occupied by tiny black buzzers. In between are a bewildering variety of colours including golden, olive, black, sepia, green, red and orange.

The chironimid larva

The adult females lay their eggs in a jelly-like mass which quickly sinks to the bottom. These then hatch into the larvae. The larval form is the common bloodworm. These thin bottom-dwelling 'worms', which vary considerably in size, most commonly red in colour, and less commonly brown, cream, yellow or green. The red coloration is due to the presence of haemoglobin. Because of the oxygen-retaining capability of haemoglobin, bloodworms are able to survive in waters with low oxygen levels. Consequently, they can survive in the bottom ooze of still waters at great depths. Adult buzzers are often seen hatching over water of depths in excess of 50 metres, such as you might commonly find in Africa's great lakes and the larger water impoundments.

Some bloodworms are free swimming, some species build mud tubes, and others are found in heavy populations among silkweed, where they are generally thought to be feeding. The bloodworm achieves locomotion by a lashing of the tail which results in a kind of figure-of-eight movement. This movement is impossible to copy, and thus most anglers use a very slow fig-ure-of-eight retrieve when retrieving their bloodworm imitations.

Bloodworms are a staple diet of the trout and other fishes including carp, moggel, and yel-lowfish, and thus they are well worth imitating. Very often, when there is no surface activity, the trout are browsing heavily on bloodworms at the bottom.

Trout are not built to filter the bottom ooze as carp can, but rather crop their food from the bottom. If you spoon your first fish, and find a mass of bloodworms, twigs, and other detritus, you will know that a bloodworm imitation is very likely to be successful.

Patterns to try include the Red Larva, Digger's Red, and the Red Booby. In fact, almost any red fly fished right on the bottom with a very slow retrieve is likely to work.

Buzzer pupae

The pupae of the Chironimidae are the best known, and their imitations the most fished of all the life stages. Pupal development, from larva to adult, is very rapid, and may be com-pleted in as little as one and a half to three days.

Just prior to final emergence, i.e. before the pupae swim for the surface, they will emerge from their burrows and sway rhythmically at the bottom.

You will need to fish a correctly coloured pupal imitation (the types with foam breathing tubes like the Claret Buzzer dressing would be correct) using a sinking line right on the bot-tom. Fish it extremely slowly if you are to take advantage of this activity.

The British are rather fond of using a floating line and a long leader of 6–8 metres for the bot-tom swaying pupa method. The figure-of-eight retrieve should take at least ten minutes for 30 metres, and the floss breathing tube pupae imi-tations are the ones they use (they sink faster). You must be sure the fly has sunk right to the bottom before retrieving, which can be some-what time consuming, but nevertheless very effective.

Prior to final emergence, the pupae may undergo further colour changes. When condi-

An adult buzzer on a window pane. Very often the hatch-ing buzzers are drawn to lights, and can easily be found and recognised the next morning, on the windows and around the outside lights, at the fishing lodge or farm house.

tions are right, they leave their burrows and swim slowly to the surface. Recent discoveries suggest that the pupa only makes one journey to the surface, and not several as previously believed. One can assume that they do not spend very much time swimming about at mid-water – this explains why some anglers fail to catch trout with buzzer artificials. You must fish either right on the bottom (if that's where the trout are), or right at the surface. Also, the pupae hatch only when they reach the surface film, and not during the journey up as some anglers believe.

Buzzers are very much subject to the whims of nature when it comes to hatching. They are very prone to changes in surface tension, and this can affect their hatch time. Usually, they complete ecdysis within seconds, but under some conditions they are forced to hang sus-pended in the surface film by the physics of the situation for long periods (even hours). The fly-fisherman needs to understand this situation,

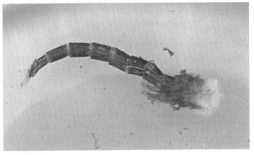

The chironimid pupa, popularly known as the 'buzzer', is a very important food for many species of fish.

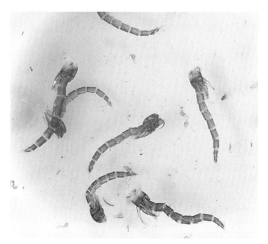

Buzzer pupae shucks are often found accumulating at the edge of the downwind shore. They indicate recent or even current buzzer activity. Should you find them in numbers then try the artificial with confidence.

because even though the trout may be feeding avidly on the trapped pupae, there may be no sign of the adult buzzers flying. This in turn may lead the angler to misread the situation, and hence choose the incorrect imitation. If you assess the situation correctly, you may well have a limit bag quite quickly. However, tie on a sedge imitation in a buzzer hatch, and you may catch nothing!

Fortunately for the fly-fisherman, the surface-trapped buzzer is given away by a characteristic trout rise form known as head and tailing. The fish's back appears to roll out of the water in a quiet splash-free rise, almost like silent porpoising, and very specific to this situation. The common factors which seem to bring on head and tailing are hot, calm evenings, foggy mornings, and days on which either a plankton or algae scum can be seen on the water. In spite of this predilection, trout can and do 'head and tail' at any time, and can do so even in the condition of a stiffish breeze with a fair ripple running.

Pupa behaviour in the surface, prior to hatching, follows a laid down pattern, which is not too difficult to simulate. There are three types of behaviour:

❏ the pupa stays in a head up and tail down pose, virtually without movement;

❏ it swims horizontally just under the surface in 10 cm dashes;

❏ it dives downwards intermittently for short distances.

For the first type, buzzer pupa imitations have been developed which have buoyant plastazote foam breathing tubes built into the head of the pattern (the Claret Buzzer is an example). The other two types both use a fluorescent white rayon floss imitation breathing tube.

Greased leaders should not be used for surface buzzer fishing because of the easily visible surface distortion caused by the grease.

Large hatches can often take place right at the boundary of calm and rippled water on breezy warm days. To fish this situation, get round to a lee shore, with the wind behind you, then cast as far as you can with a floating line. Far more buzzers hatch over depths of two metres or more than over shallows. The best Chironimidae pupa fishing times are at dusk and at dawn, and no serious fly-fisherman would miss these magic hours.

The standard method is to use a floating line, with a three metre non-greased 3X or finer leader. Retrieve in steady but slow pulls of 10–20 cm. Sometimes a shallow 'sink and draw' retrieve can be more effective. This covers both the horizontal swimming pupae and the shallow diving pupae.

For the buzzer types which hang suspended in the surface film (the size 10 olive, size 8 claret, and the size 10 orange types are in this group), a different method is recommended. Use a floating fly line, and tie on a well-greased G and H Sedge as a point fly at the tippet, so that it will act as a float (a 'take' indicator). Set up a dropper only 5–10 cm from the point fly (if your local regulations allow it, a further dropper can be added ... in South Africa a two fly limit applies).

Use a foam breathing tube buzzer imitation on the dropper, and do not grease the leader, tippet or dropper. Cast out and either let it lie with an occasional twitch, or retrieve as slowly as you possibly can. At the slightest take, the sedge will dive under, and a gentle flick strike should connect every time. Sometimes, as a bonus, they take the sedge as well!

For stream work, I prefer the Suspender

Buzzer, which I tie directly to the point without any droppers. Buzzers only hatch in the quieter water in streams, so use this method in deep slow runs and pools. The Suspender Buzzer can also be used effectively in still water on a floating line, by allowing a cross breeze to drift it around. Mend the line occasionally to ensure a good drift. This is a very good method with light tackle in very clear water. The Suspender Buzzer can also be deadly on days with no surface activity, if fished at the bottom with a short 25 cm leader (no tippet) on a fast-sink line and with a figure-of-eight retrieve.

For all this buzzer pupa work, I prefer AFTM 6 outfits, but I know of several anglers who conduct these usually sensitive methods quite successfully with AFTM 9 rigs.

Adult buzzers

The adults appear to pop out of nowhere as they hatch from the pupal shucks, and they waste no time in getting airborne. They fly rapidly over the water with their legs just touching the surface, often going a bit haywire and whirling around before making another straight dash. The pupae are much easier prey than the adults and thus trout tend to ignore the adults. Nevertheless, the buzzers hatch so often throughout the year in Africa, that there are times when trout do take the adults. There are not many dressings that beat Richard Walker's Adult Buzzer imitation. You may need them from size 10 right down to 20.

Use a floating line and allow the Adult Buzzer fly to drift with the breeze, or just float where it is. My personal preference is to cast to cruising fishes by predicting the direction they are moving in (from the rises) and then casting slightly ahead. Another successful method is to simulate the natural skating fly by quickly skimming the imitation across the water. Pause occasionally to make up for the whirling motion of the natural fly as it simply spins right where it is.

The adults are always worth observing closely. This gives you the chance to assess the correct colour pattern for both your pupal and adult imitation. Sometimes the trout are very specific about what they will take, and this is usually because there is a spot of some key

colour in the natural pupa or adult. In many pupae there is a spot of haemoglobin in the abdomen, and trout may be homing in on this. A good way to learn is to catch pupae and adults whenever the chance presents itself (normally you'll be much too busy trying to catch trout ... but make the time if you can). If you are unable to determine the correct colour, try either a claret or a black buzzer of size 12.

Another way of assessing colour type is to examine the dross either washed-up or at the edge of the shore, on the downwind side of the dam or lake. You should find plenty of pupal shucks (nearly always lots of claret ones in African waters), and a few dead unhatched ones as well, plus all sorts of other creatures. You will have a fair idea of both the hatch of the evening before (which gives you the chance to be ready for the coming evening), and also what is probably hatching at a lower, but ongoing, level during the day. You won't always be right, but often enough you will be.

PHANTOM MIDGES (CHAOBORIDAE)

The phantom midge (also known as the plumed gnat) is an insect which is often ignored by fly-fishermen ... most don't even know it exists! The phantom midges are in fact very common insects in Africa. The adults are missed by most fly-fishermen because they hatch in the dark. They look very much like small, pale, ghostly greenish-white chironimids (midges).

The life cycle consists of egg, larva, pupa and adult. The thin larva is 10–12 mm long, and virtually transparent except for a couple of dark red spots, one at each end of the body. They look like eyes, but are believed to be some kind of stabilising mechanism. The antennae are adapted for seizing prey. The pupae (approximately 8 mm long) are similar to buzzer pupae but without the breathing spiracles.

Often in January, and through February and March in southern Africa, one catches trout absolutely stuffed with the glassy larvae and

Fig. 11.9: The phantom midge larva.

The daddy-long-legs, or crane fly, is a frequent snack for a trout. These very common semi-aquatic and terrestrial insects are found in a range of many species, most of which are similar in colour and easily copied with one or two fly patterns.

the pupae of the phantom midge. In spoonings, they show up as glassy worms, with sepia 'eye' spots, often with an overall greenish hue.

I have caught many trout which have fed on these larvae. When you first spoon them they look rather like a lot of small seeds, but what you see is the red spots (turned sepia by stomach acids) among the transparent bodies. These red spots are the key colour for the feeding trout, and your imitation must have this spot of colour if it is to work. The spoonings very often have quite a few daphnia mixed with the phantom larvae.

Good flies are the Barney Google for the imitation of the larva, and the Silver Phantom or a Grey Buzzer for imitation of the pupae. These should be small flies, in common with the naturals. The recommended method is a floating line with a greased leader with the very slowest of movement for the retrieve.

CRANE FLIES (TIPULIDAE)

The adults of the many species of daddy-long-legs vary a great deal in size and colour, but even so they are very similar in cursory overview, and thus most of the fly-fisherman's needs can be served by one pattern. The life cycle is egg, larva, pupa (all of which may be aquatic or terrestrial, depending on species), and the winged adult.

Daddy-long-legs adults are weak flyers, readily falling onto the water surface in the lightest

of breezes, and even on calm days. When 'daddies' are about, trout find them irresistible, and will feed on them with gusto.

'Daddy fishing' is a form of dry fly-fishing that is really worth while, and there are times when this can be the best method available to you. Dick Walker was probably the first person to notice that daddy-long-legs tied with the legs trailing backwards are much more effective than those with legs haphazardly all around. However, he believed his most important discovery was that the fly is most effective when motionless. The fly should be well siliconed before use, cast out on a floating line and fished statically. The leader should not be greased.

Recently, I have been having great success fishing the daddy-long-legs on a slow sinker in the waves at the downwind side of a dam on very windy but sunny days. It makes a lot of sense, since the waterlogged natural flies should be fairly common in the detritus downwind of the dam. I also have a friend who catches well using this fly on a super-fast sinking line right on the bottom, using a figure-of-eight retrieve ... that doesn't make so much sense, but there you are!

FLY MISCELLANY – DIPTERA

We have already looked in some detail at some of the Diptera, namely the chironimids, the crane flies, and the phantom midges. However, the Diptera are a huge order of insects, with several other insects that are of interest to the fly-fisherman. The Diptera are characterised by a single pair of membranous wings.

Given below are some of the better-known water-related Diptera, other than the main ones covered elsewhere in this chapter. These insects can usually be imitated well by the Black Gnat in both its dry and wet forms, and also by the Adult Buzzer. Where aquatic larval forms are relevant, the Beams' Woolly Worm is a useful pattern.

Blackflies (Simuliidae)

The blackflies are biting flies found throughout Africa, and are common both in the tropics and in high altitude streams. Some of the tropical ones carry a parasitic worm which causes river blindness, a disease which is so bad that the World Health Organisation is involved in intensive research to combat the fly. In West Africa, Sudan, Angola, Zambia, Democratic Republic of the Congo, Tanzania and Malawi, the disease is a problem in the warmer areas.

In mountainous areas where the blackflies are frequently met by anglers, they are renowned for their persistent biting, but these at least do not carry human-related diseases (although they can still be a problem for stock-related disease). They are common on most streams in the Cape and the high KwaZulu-Natal rivers. The blackfly larvae are aquatic, often forming colonies on the exposed surfaces of rocks in swift water.

Snipe flies (Athericidae)
These too are biting flies which are associated with aquatic habitat. The larvae are predacious and kill by injecting poison into their prey. The adults become interesting to the trout when, after egg-laying, they fall onto the water, often in large quantities. They are small insects, and a size 16 or 18 Black Gnat is a good imitation.

Net-winged or mountain midges (Blephariceridae)
These are insects occurring in unpolluted swift mountain streams. They resemble small crane-flies (daddy-long-legs) and are about the size of a mosquito. The larvae are aquatic and vegetarian. The larval and pupal stages are able to adhere to rock surfaces in the swiftest water. They are found only in southern Africa. The Adult Buzzer is a reasonable dry imitation, as is the Tricho.

Hover flies (Syrphidae)
The adult insects are known as drone or hover flies and are occasionally around in large numbers. At such times, if they fall onto the water, trout often get interested in them. The well known rat-tailed maggot is the larva of the one of the Syrphidae. It likes to grow up in foul or biologically polluted water, and is thus seldom found where trout are.

The adults are usually banded, with yellow on

Diptera come in many shapes and forms and are important to all insect-eating fishes. Many of these are terrestrial, and this Diptera feeding on a flower at the edge of the water would interest any fish that found it.

a black or blue background (rather bee-like). You will not often need to imitate these; nevertheless, should the opportunity occur, the Jindabyne fly should be fished dry with an occasional twitch.

DRAGONFLIES AND DAMSELFLIES (ODONATA)
In Africa this order of insects is vitally important to the fly-fisherman, no matter what inland sport-fishes he pursues. Even the mighty tiger-fish will take dragonfly nymph flies, and at the other end of the scale, trout, yellowfish, bass, catfish, kurper and others will all avidly take Odonata imitations. The nymphs exist in vast quantities in all African waters, far more than is commonly believed.

The order contains some of the most striking insects. They are often beautifully coloured, and exhibit amazing powers of flight. Their large well-developed eyes place them among the most keen-sighted of all insects.

The African Odonata includes some 1 000 species, divided into two sub-orders: the Anisoptera (dragonflies) and the Zygoptera (damselflies). We will deal with these sub-orders separately, but let us first overview the main differences between them:

The adults – sub-order characteristics
The dragonfly and damselfly adults are easily distinguishable. The damsels are slender-bodied, and usually settle with their wings either

upright or folded over their body. The dragonflies are generally thick-bodied and settle with their wings at right angles to the body. Most dragonflies are considerably larger than damselflies, and are fast, nimble, and actively predacious. In fact, the dragonflies often prey on the smaller, slower damselflies. The damselfly's eyes are situated on the side of the head, whereas the dragonfly's eyes join together at the top of the head.

The nymphs – sub-order characteristics

The damselfly nymphs are slender insects, generally not larger than 25 mm. The body terminates with three feathery gills which look just like tails. The dragonfly nymphs are thick-bodied, with very conspicuous eyes. They grow up to 75 mm long and are very active. Both types crawl fairly rapidly, and the dragonfly nymphs also use a very effective rectal propulsion system to jet themselves forward rapidly if needed. Damselfly nymphs are normally metamorphosed within a single season. Dragonflies can take as much as three years for full development, although most complete their cycle much more rapidly.

Top: A rendering in blue bucktail of a damselfly male; Bottom: The living insect. For many fly-tiers the fishing is secondary and the flies come first.

Life cycles

The life cycle consists of egg, nymph and adult. The newly hatched nymphs are predacious from the minute they hatch. They are fierce, relentless hunters and will eat anything they can overcome. They grow by moulting their skins, which become tight as they grow, each new skin providing a new growth period known as an instar. The big dragonfly nymphs can go through as many as 12 instars.

The damselfly nymphs swim for the shallows and the banks in the hot days of summer and hatch there. The dragonflies prefer to hatch at night, and they will crawl up a convenient reed stem or a rock where their skin splits and the adult emerges, dries its wings, and flies off.

Damselflies

The adults

Adult damselflies are not usually of much interest to the trout, but occasionally they will show curiosity in the bright blue males (espe-

A typical, olive-bodied adult female damselfly.

202

cially those which have fallen and are struggling in the water surface). Then the fly-tier can bring out his blue lurex or blue bucktail-bodied creations, and actually use flies which were previously reserved for demonstrating one's uncanny creativity to anyone who would look ('ooh and ah' fly-tying).

However, the olive-bodied adult females are often found in spoonings. These are the females which return to the water to lay their eggs. Some of these crawl down reed stems and go right under the water to lay. Any trout spotting these will take them. Reed-fringed bays would be a good place to find such trout. The truth is that imitating adult damselflies is mostly time wasted, time which could be very fruitfully applied to the nymphs.

The damselfly nymphs

The damselfly nymphs have focused the attention of fly-tiers since trout came to Africa, but in recent years some really fine imitations have become available. These have resulted from the realisation that damselfly nymphs are a very important part of the trout's diet. My personal favourite is the Red Eyed Damsel; others include the Jalan, Cliff Henry's Demoiselle Nymph, the Wiggle Nymph, and Hugh Huntley's Damsel Fly.

The nymphs occur in a wide range of colours. However, whereas dragonfly nymphs are most likely to adopt the colours of surrounding vegetation, the damselfly nymphs are more likely to have their own specific coloration. In Africa, they most commonly occur in olive, followed by browns, bright green, black, grey, and yellow. Olive imitations are excellent in most African trout countries, and generally they are all you will need. In Mpumalanga in South Africa, yellow nymphs are common and an imitation for these can be very productive. In the entire Cape and KwaZulu-Natal, brown imitations can be very useful on some days.

Damselfly nymphs hatch during the daylight hours and there is a definite preference for very hot sunny days. At such times, a migration from the deep water towards the sides often takes place. Sometimes the damselfly nymphs crawl along the bottom toward the shore, but

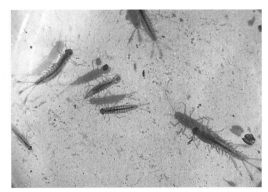

Damselfly nymphs, and in the centre a single Dytiscus beetle nymph.

very often they swim shoreward by lashing their tails. The tail-lashing nymphs like to swim just a few inches below the surface, where they create quite a disturbance and are easily picked up by cruising trout. Trout can become preoccupied with damselfly nymphs during these migrations. This state of affairs is given away by surface swirls (caused by trout tails just below the surface), and by occasional splashy rises. It is simple enough to imitate the nymphs' movement at this time, by using an intermediate or a floating line and retrieving in fairly slow strips about a foot below the surface.

Once the nymphs reach the sides, they crawl up vegetation to hatch. So, on a hot sunny day when the flash of blue damselflies is all about you, and the trout appear to be slashing at near-surface nymphs (maybe even jumping occasionally), you will know what to do!

Dragonflies
Dragonfly nymphs

Nearly all of the dragonfly nymphs are large enough to form a full meal package in one for a hungry trout. The nymphs prey on small aquatic nymphs, other insects, small fishes and crustaceans. They will often gather in shallow water weedbeds in order to feed on the fry hiding there. The dragonfly nymph's major enemies are large fishes, but they also eaten by large water beetle larvae and water scorpions.

The dragonfly nymphs walk with a sluggish crawl when waiting for their prey, or they don't move at all. However, they have a turbo-speed mechanism which they use to pounce on prey, or to escape from danger. This is their rectal propulsion system, which they operate by expelling water through the rectum at high speed. In this way they can take quite fast leaps forward over a few centimetres. Trout are very much attuned to this sudden dash. Often they cruise the edge of weedbeds, hoping to disturb the nymphs, which give themselves away by suddenly jetting forward as the trout frighten them. Fortunately for fly-fisherman, this sudden jet forward is easily imitated by interspersing sudden fast strips into the retrieve.

The colour of the nymphs is generally cryptic,

and their excellent camouflage hides them well. Consequently, a weed-dwelling nymph is likely to be green in summer, but the same nymph in the same weedbed in autumn will probably be brown to match the dying weed. The bottom-dwelling nymphs will always be dark brown or sepia; they will always match the bottom. It is for the above reasons that the green Hamill's Killer is such a good fly around weedbeds in summer, but less effective in the same area in winter. The Mrs Simpson is an excellent fly in winter because it emulates the brown nymphs prevalent at that time. Excellent local patterns

A large deep olive-coloured aeshnid nymph from a clear stream.

The husk of a hatched dragonfly. Most of the larger dragonflies hatch at night, but many Corduliidae hatch at dusk and early morning.

The author with his 5,7 kg cock rainbow trout from Trout Hideaway in South Africa. This fish had 13 large olive aeshnid dragonfly nymphs in it, and a large mass of trout eggs. (Photo: Ryan Steele)

Primeval dragon? This imitation tied by Murray Peddar looks almost as if it climbed out of a Jurassic swamp 200 million years ago. The wonderful natural effect of the body is achieved with Antron wools. Dragonflies have remained unchanged for millennia, and were on the planet long before the first trout.

to try include the Wolf's Woolly Worm, the Don's Dragon, the Green Mamba, and Terry Ruane's Dragon. The Booby flies are absolutely deadly for dragonfly nymphing trout, but they must be fished correctly as instructed under the detail on these flies.

Adult dragonflies

Sometimes trout will jump to take adult female dragonflies intent on egg laying, and fairly often the olive-bodied adult females are found in trout spoonings. Nevertheless, the occurrence is seldom worth pursuing. The trout will also take the spent and dying dragonflies which are caught in the surface film during their death throes. These are rare events, though, and effectively there is little point in imitating the adults.

There are four main African families of the dragonflies which are different enough to be worth the fly-fisherman's while to know a little about. The important African dragonfly families are described below.

Aeshnidae

The adults have long flight periods, seldom resting, unless it is very hot. This family includes the huge emperor dragonflies. Many of them have long slender abdomens, and most are large to very large.

The nymphs, some of them up to 75 mm long, have elongated bodies, with a mask which is long and flat. These nymphs can take three to four seasons to metamorphose. Coloration varies from shades of green, through deep olive, to brown. They are very active, using rectal propulsion frequently. They are not particularly secretive, and are often taken by trout

A Libellulidae dragonfly female, possibly of the genus Leucorrhinia, drying its wings on a reed stem.

A Libellulidae dragonfly nymph.

which quickly spot these nymphs if they leave their cover. A good retrieve to simulate the nymph is 10–15 cm jerks right on the bottom.

Libellulidae

The Libellulidae are the largest African dragonfly family. They are small to large-sized species, with abdomens which can be short, broad, or slender. The hind wing is often very broad. Their bodies are usually powdery coloured and not metallic. The adults usually rest on twigs and branches with their wings held forwards.

The nymphs have robust shortish bodies often

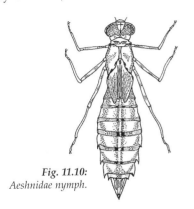

Fig. 11.10: Aeshnidae nymph.

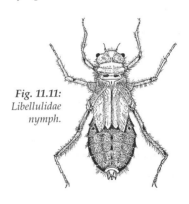

Fig. 11.11: Libellulidae nymph.

covered with fine short hairs. They hide in the bottom detritus among vegetation, and ambush their prey from hiding. They like rocky, gravelly and pebbly surroundings. They use their rectal propulsion like a jet system to overtake their prey as it swims past. Their coloration is always the same as their surroundings, so imitations need to take cognisance of the bottom, and vegetation coloration. Use a slow figure-of-eight retrieve, right on the bottom, with an occasional 10–15 cm strip.

Gomphidae

The adults generally rest flat on the ground, sunning themselves in hot areas with wings held horizontally and open. Adults are mostly green or yellow, marked with black or brown.

The nymphs are variable in body shape, but most have oval-shaped flat bodies. They have smaller eyes (which in this sub-order are also not joined) than the other sub-orders of nymphs. Most Gomphidae nymphs are sandy

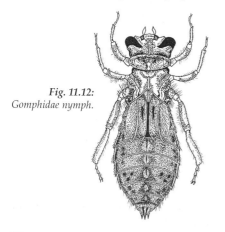

Fig. 11.12: Gomphidae nymph.

A beautiful Gomphidae golden dragonfly: several similar species are found commonly in Africa.

coloured and mottled. They like gravel, sand, and loose particle substrate. They grow to 40 mm and can take three years to mature. The retrieve is the same as for the Libellulidae.

Corduliidae

These are African insects with only a few small species in southern Africa. They tend to fly along a particular beat, often far from water. In tropical countries, they are medium to large insects with long, slender abdomens. Bodies are often reddish-brown to black with yellow markings.

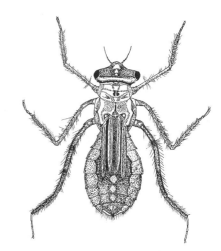

Fig. 11.13: Corduliidae nymph.

The nymphs are typified by short and broad bodies with long slender legs. They clamber among vegetation actively hunting their prey. Imitations should be fished around weedbeds at medium to deep depths with a slow retrieve.

In Australia and New Zealand a great deal of effort is expended in imitating the pre-hatch stage as the mature nymphs head for the shore in the late hours before dusk. It is a very successful approach handled by fishing 'just subsurface' imitations on a floating line. Most of these are Corduliidae imitations. Such an approach works very well in African waters and is thoroughly recommended.

STONEFLIES (PLECOPTERA)

No great importance has ever been attached to the stoneflies by any African fly-fishing author that I have read. Still-water fly-fishermen never give them a thought, and most streamside anglers ignore them. Nevertheless, trout eat these insects wherever they occur, and the dark-ish stonefly nymphs frequently appear in spoonings, especially in the high areas of southern Africa.

The adult stoneflies are mostly nocturnal and short-lived, which is why they are seldom seen by anglers. The nymphs need swift-flowing and well oxygenated water – in other words, most trout streams!

There are relatively few stonefly species in Africa and only two families. The family Perlidae are found from the Cape to Ethiopia. The Perlidae nymphs reach 25 mm length, and are voracious predators, feeding on other small nymphs. Most of these stonefly adults are greenish brown with silvery wings which are folded fan-wise along the body. They are scarce in the Western Cape, and become more common as you go northwards. Some of the species can tolerate warmer waters.

The Nemouridae are found only in southern Africa, mostly in the clear cold mountain streams of the Cape provinces, with a few scattered species on the Mpumalanga escarpments. These small stoneflies (5–8 mm) can be differentiated from the Perlidae by the way they furl their wings around their abdomen at rest. Nymphs of the Nemouridae feed only on vegetable matter. The adults are often seen early in the day, or on dull and drizzly, or misty days. One of the species, *Desmonemoura pulchella,* has brown and yellow banded wings.

Stonefly nymphs are most easily found by turning over rocks in the stream. The adults hide during the day (although one species is

Creative fly-tying: a lifelike rendering of an American Yellow Stonefly, dressed by Murray Peddar.

A stonefly nymph from a Highveld stream in South Africa.

Fig. 11.14: Stonefly nymph.

diurnal). Adults fly very poorly, but are able to run very fast. They always look rather waspish at first glance, and certainly don't look good running up one's arm. There are some beautiful stonefly nymph imitations on the African market, exquisitely tied to tempt the angler, and every last one of them imitates an American stonefly, which will never appear in the flesh on an African stream. Of the flies that do imitate African stonefly nymphs, most useful are the Montana Nymph, Ted's Stonefly Nymph, Little Redwing, and the Charcoal Nymph. The natural stonefly nymphs live among rocks and pebbles at the edge of the stream, and also on the stream bed. Upstream nymphing is the recommended method.

ANTS (HYMENOPTERA) AND TERMITES (ISOPTERA)

These wholly terrestrial creatures are normally of no interest to any fish species. A couple of flying ants, or termites, falling on the water are going to do nothing to excite them into a feeding frenzy. The imitations are certainly not worth fishing dry on a 'chuck and chance' basis. However, it is quite a different story on late afternoons and evenings in summer and autumn just before a storm, or just after a heavy rainfall. At such times, these insects emerge in their thousands. All it takes is a slight breeze to blow them over the water, and the surface will erupt into action as the feeding fishes gorge themselves on this easy meal.

The ants or termites, trapped by surface tension, struggle in the surface film. They send out 'dinner's ready' signals as they vibrate their wings, and it's not long before the fishes start to rise to them. In this situation, especially if a light breeze continues to drive the insects onto the water, the fishes will quickly become totally preoccupied with them. At such times, the man

Flying ants trapped in the surface. Trout rise avidly to these ants, but become very discriminating as time passes.

with the right imitation can have some very good sport. However, the sport is generally short-lived. The trout quickly find themselves in a food soup, and all they need to do is cruise around with their mouths open and engulf the ants or termites at will. When food is that easy, it's not long before they ignore even the best of imitations. Nevertheless, for a good half hour, the angler can often have some really good fun before the fishes start to be discriminating.

In Africa there are a lot more species of ants than in Europe. However, the whole spectrum of these creatures can be copied by three dressings, which should be either black, brown, or reddish to imitate most of the types.

The termites can be copied by one pattern – I like Barry Kent's Termite. The ant imitations can be proofed, cast out and just left to float, but the Termite fly needs to be twitched constantly to simulate the struggles of the natural in the surface.

BEETLES (COLEOPTERA)

Some say the beetles must be God's favourites, because there are more different species of them than any other creature on earth (some 350 000 species have been described worldwide). Certainly, in Africa, there are enormous quantities of beetles of all shapes, colours and sizes. A great many of these live in or near water, and trout and other fishes know all about them. Beetles are very commonly found in spoonings, perhaps more so in river fishes than still-water ones, but still commonly in both environments.

Terrestrial beetles

Trout will cruise the edge of the ripple on the lee shore of a dam, sipping down any of many species of beetles and other insects. River trout (and other fishes), on a breezy day, will rise to surface-entrapped beetles as they drift by. Some fishes are content to lie under a favourite bush sucking in beetles all day long, at least until a hatch of mayflies or sedges commences. Effectively, the beetles are far more important to fishes, when there is no hatch occurring, than is often realised.

Because of the many species of these insects available to the fishes (in Africa a fish could rise to 20 different beetles), there are no specific patterns for handling them. Fortunately, though, there are some very good general patterns available! Perhaps the best of all is the Coch-y-Bonddu.

Beetles seldom sink, because of air trapped in the elytra (wing cases), and are nearly always taken at the surface. Dry fly-fishing should be the best answer – although, in still water, fishing just under the surface with an intermediate line can also produce magical results.

The lure fly-fisherman can often do well using a dark fly with a little iridescence in it. A small black lure fly such as a Black Panacea in size 8 or 10, jazzed-up with a little Flashabou in the wing, or Barry Kent's Bathplug Special can be just the right medicine. Among the more nymphy patterns, the Black and Peacock Spider tied with a short stiff cock hackle in place of the usual long soft hen hackle is a very good one. This and the Coch-y-Bonddu fished just in the surface on a floating line (don't oil the fly in any way), with a slow steady retrieve, can be exceptionally deadly.

In the high country grassland throughout Africa, there is a small (4 mm) shiny pale brown beetle which swarms every summer, often in vast numbers. I don't know its vernacular name, but most fly-fisherman refer to it as the 'little brown grass beetle'. On breezy days these are blown onto the water in large enough numbers for trout to become virtually preoccupied with them. This is a time when a size 14 or 16 Coch-y-Bonddu on a floating line is supreme.

Water beetles

As well as the terrestrial beetles covered above, there are also diving water beetles of various types, some of which are fierce predators, even taking small fishes among their prey. The order Caraboidea includes the aquatic beetles of the families Dytiscidae (the diving beetles), and Gyrinidae (the whirligig beetles).

Dytiscus beetles

The great diving beetles include species which reach a considerable size, are extremely unpleasant, and which have larvae so ferocious that they will even feed freely on dragonfly

Beetles such as this one perched on a waterside sedge plant often fly or are blown onto the water. Most fish will eat beetles, and they are found in at least 50 per cent of stream fish spoonings.

A little brown grass beetle, well imitated by the Coch-y-Bonddu fly, which can be deadly if fished in a lee shore ripple when these beetles are out.

nymphs. These larvae need to return to the surface from time to time because, like the adults, they are air breathers. The larvae are armed with a pair of hollow jaws, through which they inject poison into their prey. Once the victim dies, they then inject digestive juices into the

Fig. 11.15: *The great diving or water beetle.*

209

victim, and the dissolved tissues are sucked back into the larva, leaving an empty shell of the victim behind. Frightening creatures indeed! They pupate in the mud at the side of the dam.

The Dytiscus larvae are imitated well by most of the lighter-coloured dragonfly nymph imitations, Leslie's Lure being a good one. Flies up to size 4 long shank (some grow to a length of 10 cm) are quite in order for imitating these sometimes large larvae. They do not have a rectal propulsion system, and are best imitated by a figure-of-eight retrieve.

The adults are imitated best of all by the Black Phantom, which covers most of the species. However, some of the adults are sandy coloured, and some are black with orange patterning which varies from species to species. There are no imitations for these! Why not? you may ask. And there are very good reasons. For a start, the adults are seldom found in spoonings, and usually there is perhaps only one when they are found ... this is because of the Dytiscus beetle's excellent defense systems.

Firstly, these beetles are extremely slippery and, if you try to pick one up, it will shoot from the fingers like a wet fruit pip. Secondly, the frightened beetle has a sharp spine on the underside which may well pierce the fingers of the unwary. Thirdly, this creature exudes a white fluid which has a disgusting odour, and which has a temporary stunning and toxic effect on fishes and frogs (their main predators). Finally, as if that was not enough, they also emit an explosive ammonia-smelling fluid from two anal glands. Obviously, this beetle and its larva are prime prospects for a monster movie! Certainly, the adult is not worth imitating unless your trout are particularly stupid or suicidally inclined. The larva can be seen on page 187 (spooning number G), and on page 203, (damselfly nymphs).

One of the smaller Dytiscus beetles turns up fairly regularly in spoonings, and this is the exception to the rule. It is not as unpleasant as the other members of the family, and the trout and yellowfish find it palatable. This is the one for which the Black Phantom in size 8 is a good imitation.

Whirligig beetles
These delightful little beetles are part of the wonder of a river. The incessant gyrations of these glittering creatures have often kept me spellbound for half an hour next to a quiet pool. I have never seen a trout take one, and have found them rarely in spoonings.

BACKSWIMMERS (NOTONECTIDAE)
These little chaps are often confused with the Corixidae, but are in fact quite different. The backswimmers are highly predacious hunters, which spend their lives upside-down right under the water surface. Their feet are sensitised to every surface movement, and they will grab anything edible that comes their way. They can cause a wound to a human which is similar to a wasp sting in terms of experienced pain, so leave well alone! They kill by injecting a protein-splitting enzyme into their prey, and then suck out the body contents. They are cannibalistic when food is in short supply.

Their backs are keel-shaped and often silver in colour. The underside (which is what you see when you look down on them in the water), is often brown or black. Some have a spot of orange. The eyes are very pronounced. Barry Kent's African Beetle is probably the best imitation of the orange and black one. The others are imitated by the various corixid patterns. Backswimmers carry air around with them and will often dive, especially if frightened.

Trout feed on these insects, particularly in late autumn and winter when the backswimmers are around in large numbers. I have found trout

Backswimmers. Trout will sometimes feed heavily on these insects, and they are well worth imitating.

stuffed with these insects – presumably they are immune to the backswimmer's bite.

LESSER WATER BOATMEN (CORIXIDAE)

These hemipterids (bugs) are fully aquatic creatures, and they are exceptionally common in all the shallow waters of Africa. They are easily recognised by the characteristic darting swim to the surface in order to trap a bubble of air for breathing. The air bubble is trapped under the body, giving a silvery sheen to the abdomen. Unlike the backswimmers, corixids swim right way up. These bugs are important to the fly-fisherman, and especially to the still-water fly-fisherman.

There are lots of different species of Corixidae in African waters, most of which are fairly similar in appearance. They are either tan, brown, or olive coloured. They can be adequately covered by three or four different imitations. In general, they are creatures of shallow water, and tend to avoid the deep open water of the large dams.

Not so long ago, corixids were always tied weighted, and fished 'sink and draw', which is still a good method. They were most successful when fished around weedbeds and next to stands of rushes and reeds. Nowadays, there are alternatives at hand, and the floating corixid imitation is a particularly good one. The pattern, the Plastazote Corixid, is fished on a sinking line. When pulled in, the fly submerges, and as the pull ceases the fly rises up in a most realistic manner – effectively the opposite of 'sink and draw'.

For most of the African fishing year, the dressings with brown backs and white bellies are adequate, but as winter approaches, small olive-coloured corixids appear. They are very important to the winter fly-fisherman. These small olive corixids abound until spring arrives, and then they are replaced by the usual summer brown-coloured types. Winter trout are often stuffed to the gills with the little olive corixids, even on the coldest of days.

Good imitations of the olive corixid are the Green Duster, the Olive Corixid, and the Olive Chomper.

The little olive corixids are always in shallow

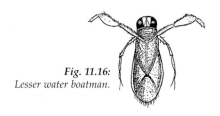

Fig. 11.16:
Lesser water boatman.

water, and as a result they are often rendered torpid by the usual high-altitude winter temperature drop which occurs overnight. In the morning, the trout take advantage of the comatose corixids, and eat as many as they can before the sun warms the little creatures back into activity.

MOTHS (LEPIDOPTERA)

Next to fishing, my greatest interest is in butterflies, an interest which is closely followed by a love of the other insects. Fishes are not as interested in adult butterflies as I am, but as a naturalist, I find a great deal of pleasure in watching these beautiful creatures which are often so much a part of the waterside scene.

What many fishes do like is the night sister to the butterflies – the moths! Yellowfish, landlocked salmon and brown trout in particular are exceptionally fond of moths. The group which receive most attention from the fishes are the very common 'swift moths', which are generally buffy or white, with a 25–40 mm wing-span.

The moths are most prolific on thundery evenings and warm damp nights. They begin to fly about half an hour before dusk, and it is usually during the last moments of light that the imitations are at their best. Many a huge 'brownie' has fallen to the patient angler who waited for dusk to dangle a moth imitation over a mighty trout's lair. These are often brownies almost uncatchable by other means.

The moths flutter about, and some fall into the water where they are trapped. The moth continues to try and beat his wings, and in doing so sends out vibrations that mean 'dinner' to any nearby fish. Any cruising brown trout or yellowfish that senses a moth will take it ... this applies to running or still water. The best imitation is Dick Walker's Chicken. The Soldier Palmer Pink is another good one.

This moth has just landed on the water, and his wings are not yet trapped in the surface film. Most fish will take moths: they represent a good meal for a fish!

Grasshoppers are favoured food items of most gamefish. This one has been blown onto the surface of a clear water trout dam, and is unlikely to reach the other side without getting eaten.

The larval form of both butterflies and moths are the various caterpillars which are commonly found along banks and in overhanging trees and vegetation. Should these fall into the water, then all fishes will take them. There will never be a preoccupied feeding session on caterpillars, since they are an erratic food source. Imitations exist (a dry Olive Woolly Worm is one), but caterpillars are not generally worth imitating unless it is a very breezy day and plenty are being knocked out of the vegetation by the buffeting of the wind.

GRASSHOPPERS AND LOCUSTS (ORTHOPTERA)

I can remember a good many occasions when trout and yellowfish were caught that were packed with grasshoppers. I remember a trout that Steve Barrow caught in Lesotho that was stuffed so tight with black crickets, they were falling out of its mouth as it was netted. These examples typify the importance of terrestrials in African fly-fishing. In all these cases, the fishes were taken from streams and rivers. When it comes to still-water fishes, the amount of naturally eaten grasshoppers is very much less. Even so, still-water fishes like them!

Africa has an enormous number of grasshoppers per acre when compared with the northern and temperate countries of the world. In some high-country places, clouds of grasshoppers erupt from the grass with every step you take. The grasshoppers, just like butterflies, are solar powered – they need sunlight to be really active. They will only be hopping and flying once the sun has been up for an hour or two. There are some truly beautiful wing colours in African grasshoppers – reds, clarets, oranges, blues, and clear winged types. However, most settle on the water with wings closed, so this rainbow of colours is unimportant.

Their body colours are important, and these vary from soft tans to browns, through olives and bright greens. The locusts are often very brightly coloured, but remember that many of the really bright ones are poisonous, and the fishes will ignore these. The green grasshoppers are creatures of the summer, but many of the more sombre coloured ones fly throughout the African year.

Obviously, all your hopper fishing is going to be with dry flies on a floating line. In still water you will find that you need a ripple running before you get results. In my experience, grasshopper imitations fished on a flat calm will not get many takes. The entrapped grasshoppers twitch and move a lot, and a retrieve (rather than letting them lie) certainly generates more strikes. In fact, in rippled still water, I find a retrieve which is just fast enough to generate a small wake works the best.

On running water this retrieve is not necessary, and a few twitches will bring the desired result. The stream angler should aim to swim the hopper down under overhanging grasses and other sedgy vegetation, since this is where

Some African locusts and grasshoppers are exquisitely coloured. This one (a pyrgomorphid), sporting a stunning bright green and black coloration, would be a good model for the Viva Fly.

Fig. 11.17: *The larval form of the Cape alderfly, commonly known as the 'toebiter'.*

most hoppers fall in (though the flying ones can fall in anywhere). Whenever possible, try to use polarised sun glasses, and spot your trout before casting; then cast so as to drift your imitation right over him. Sometimes it is very pleasant to sit at the end of a long run, and just watch for the odd rise which you can respond to by flicking out your grasshopper fly.

There are several patterns to choose from, including Joe's Hopper, Muddler Minnow, the DDD, and the Dark Ferrash. The Muddler can be improved by the addition of a pair of side kickers of goose primary fibres. All these flies should be well proofed before use. I have had most success using the Muddlers in sizes 8 to 12. If you find a trout feeding on crickets, try a proofed Black Muddler Minnow.

On those really breezy hot days on still water, fish the lee shore on a floating line, casting well into the ripple, and retrieve with longish pulls and twitches ... there are summer days when this can beat every other method!

ALDERFLIES (MEGALOPTERA)

The alderflies or toebiters are found in Africa, but very few species are present. The family Sialidae has only one species in the Cape, and the family Corydalidae has seven species from the mountainous regions of the Cape and KwaZulu-Natal. The common Cape alderfly (*Taeniochauliodes ochraceopennis*) is one of the largest, with a wingspan of 60–80 mm. The larva is carnivorous and has powerful jaws,

capable of biting fiercely if handled – hence the name 'toebiter'. The larva can be up to 40 mm long. It pupates out of the water, usually in moss. Thus it is only the larva which is of interest to the trout. Here is a big meal all in one go, so who can blame them ?

Ed Herbst's Toebiter is the best imitation, followed by big ties of Beams' Woolly Worm in long shank size 4 to 10. Wolf's Woolly Worm and other dragonfly nymph imitations also work. Figure-of eight and dead drift retrieves work. Use a sinking line.

ROOT GRUBS

Not a particularly scientific heading for these creatures, but since they include larvae across several orders and families, the title is apt. Referred to here, are any white grubs which live in grass and other vegetation roots.

Much of Africa is subject to seasonal rainfall, e.g. in Gauteng in South Africa the winter is very dry and the summer very wet. Kenya also has clearly defined wet and dry seasons. This means that in most areas where there are fly-fishing opportunities, there are major changes in water level during the course of the year. This is why lakes with lily pads are so hard to find (for example in Gauteng); the fluctuating water level kills them!

The spin-off for the angler from this constant water level change is that grasses and other vegetation are able to establish themselves during the retreat of the water's edge. Insects lay their eggs on this vegetation, and, as a result, small white grubs of various kinds get established in the roots.

When the wet season comes along and the water levels are restored to their normal high, the grubs are flushed out of the roots. These grubs form an easily exploited food source for trout and other fishes which cruise the shallow

Fully aquatic cranefly larva. These are really of interest to the trout when banksides are freshly flooded. (Photo: Don Lort)

edges. Imitation of these grubs at such times can be a deadly method for the fly-fisherman. Similarly, the flooding of freshly built dams, where trout were introduced as the filling began, can offer fantastic opportunities to fishermen imitating these grubs. Most of the grubs are the larvae of craneflies (daddy-long-legs), beetles, and moths.

When the trout are feeding on the root grubs, such opportunities are given away by the rising of trout close in, or their tails are seen breaking surface as they root about in a head-down attitude. A good fly to exploit this situation is the Ivory Nymph. The Walker's Yellow Nymph is a second choice. Fish with a floating line, a short leader, and a slow retrieve.

AFRICAN DRY FLY IN PERSPECTIVE

Insects, according to American research, exist on the bottom of normal lakes and streams at the rate of 25–50 kg per hectare. A fair proportion of this may be ephemerids (mayflies). This amount of eternally replenishing protein is adequate to comfortably support plenty of trout or other species. Logically, nearly all of their required protein intake is freely available in this bounteous larder. It stands to reason, then, that trout will feed largely under the water, rather than at the surface.

One might then argue that dry fly-fishing is a total waste of time unless a hatch is actually in progress. In actuality this is not the case. However, the dry fly enthusiast is probably reduced to fishing during only 15 per cent of the fish's total feeding activity. There is no doubt that the potentially most successful fishing (which is the fishing available over the longest percentage of available time), is going to be with a wet fly. Be that as it may, dry fly-fishing is perhaps the second most fun a person can have standing up.

A wand of a rod, a light line, the heart-stopping take of a lusty trout, and wispy clouds of busy ephemerid duns flittering above the water, make for a magical kind of enjoyment hard to equal anywhere.

SUMMARISED TABLE OF IMITATIVE FRESHWATER (SMALL FOOD FORM) FLY-FISHING

Group name	Life stage	Suggested imitations	Colours of common naturals	Size	Recommended method
Order EPHEMEROP-TERA Mayflies					
Family **Leptophlebiidae**	Nymph	Leptophlebia Nymph	brown and chestnut	12 to 16	slow and deep
		Charcoal Nymph	grey, magenta spot		as above
		PTN	sepia and brown		as above
		Mallard and Claret	sepia and claret		as above
	Dun	March Brown	wing mottled brown, body dark brown	12 or 14	dry
		Highveld Dun	wing slatey, body dark olive	12 or 14	dry
		Brown Bivisible	wing and body brown	12 or 14	dry
	Spinner	Adams	wing speckled grey, body dark grey	12 to 16	dry
		Sherry Spinner	wing glassy, body olive to ginger brown	12 to 16	dry
		Claret Spinner	wing glassy, body claret to chestnut	12 to 16	dry
Family **Baetidae**	Nymph *(streams)*	Olive PTN	dark olive	14 to 18	darting retrieve near weed and fast runs
		GRHE	sandy, darker wing case	14 to 18	as above
	Nymph *(still water)*	PVC Nymph	olive to pale olive	12 or 14	weedbeds, reeds, slow and deep, or on bottom
	Dun *(all waters)*	Olive Dun	wing slatey to green, body olive to olive brown	14 to 20	dry
		Blue Dun	wing slatey, body grey	14 to 20	dry
		Machadodorp	as Blue Dun	12 to 16	wet, mid-water slow
		Mooi Moth	wing clear, body white to grey	12 to 16	dry
		Greenwell's Glory	wing yellow to ginger, body light olive	12 to 18	dry
	Spinner	Sherry Spinner	wing glassy, body brown to olive brown	14 to 20	dry
		Red Spinner	wing pale ginger, body brown	14 to 20	dry
		Lunn's Particular	wing glassy, body grey	14 to 20	dry
Family **Caenidae**	Nymph	Nymph of Feather Fibre (brown)	dark to pale brown sometimes white spot	16 to 20	a) slow and deep b) during hatch fish at surface
		Baby Doll (white)	brown, clear white spot	12 or 14	as above
	Dun	Last Hope	pale cream to white	16 to 24	dry
		Blue Dun	grey	16 to 24	dry
	Spinner	Tricho Spinner	wing glassy, body grey	18 to 26	dry

Group name	Life stage	Suggested imitations	Colours of common naturals	Size	Recommended method
Family **Ephemerellidae**	Nymph	PTN	chestnut to sepia	14 to 18	dead drift, or across and down over stoney bottoms and between weed beds with sinking line
		GRHE (with blue dun thorax)	body dark sand, wing case dark slate	14	as above
	Dun	Orange Quill	wing grey, body orange	14 to 18	dry
		Blue Winged Olive	wing grey, body olive to grey/olive	14 to 18	dry
		Hendrickson	wing grey, body grey/brown	14 to 18	dry
	Spinner	Sherry Spinner	wing glassy, body sherry	14 to 18	dry
		Sherry Spinner & Sac	as above, egg sac green to orange	14 to 18	dry
Family **Tricorythidae**	Nymph	Charcoal Nymph	grey to charcoal	16 to 24	slow fig-of-8 at bottom
	Dun	Blue Dun	wing white to grey, body dark grey	18 to 28	dry
	Spinner	Tricho Spinner	wing glassy, body sooty	18 to 28	dry
Family **Heptageniidae**	Nymph	GRHE	yellowish pale brown	12 or 14	weighted nymph dead drift on floating line
	Dun Spinner *(night)*	Yellow Bi-visible	whitish yellow	12 or 14	dry (late dusk)
Family **Oligoneuridae**	Nymph	White Gloved Howdy	brown to claret	8 to 12	sinking line down and across, very slow retrieve
	Dun	Yellow Bi-visible	cream	10 to 14	dry
		Light Cahill	wing yellowish, body grey/yellow	10	dry
		Ginger Bi-visible	wing whitish, body pale brown	10 or 12	dry
	Spinner	Sherry Spinner	wing glassy, body sherry	10 to 14	dry
Order **TRICHOPTERA** Sedges (caddis)					
Superfamily **Hydropsychoidea (Net makers)**	Larva	Ivory Nymph	body cream, head black	8 to 16	right on bottom, dead drift
		Walker's Yellow Nymph	body yellow, thorax brown	12	as above

Group name	Life stage	Suggested imitations	Colours of common naturals	Size	Recommended method
Hydropsychoidea (cont)		Walker's Green Nymph	body bright green, thorax brown	10	right on bottom, dead drift
	Pupa	Invicta	tan to brown	8 to 16	near surface, slow retrieve
	Adult	Soldier Palmer Pink Whickham's Goddard & Henry's Sedge (rusty under)	all rust brown and rust, wing mottled grey, body brown/grey	8 12 or 14 10	dry dry dry
Superfamily **Rhyacophiliodea** (Free living forms, found in running water only)	Larva	Steve's Caddis Hot Spot, Green Longhorns	bright green, also olive, orange thorax soft green, head and body brown head and thorax brown, body green or orange	10 to 14 16 12 to 18	fig-of-8 on bottom as above as above
	Pupa	Olive Pearl Pushkin Invicta Walker's Nymph Yellow	body and thorax olive, wing dark green, head grey brown head and thorax brown, body yellow	12 to 18 14 to 18 14	sub-surface fig-of-8 as above as above
	Adult (emerging, or surface egg layer)	Wickham's Henryville Special Henryville (all grey version)	ginger wing slately, body green wing grey or mottled, body blue dun	14 14 to 18 16	dry dry dry
	Adult (diving egg layer)	Pearl Pushkin (thorax weighted version)	silver under water	12	floating line, sink and draw
(Purse case makers micro caddis)	Adult	Troutbeck Beetle Adams Grey Duster	brown grey mottled grey	20 20 or 22 20	dry dry dry
Superfamily **Limnephiloidea** (Tube case makers)	Larva (caddis worms)	Sandy Sedge Caddis Stick Hot Spot	head black, legs black, body granules sand gravel, etc. head black or cream or orange, body olive or brown head brown, thorax green or orange, body brown	10 to 18 Is 12-14 10 to 16	fig-of-8 on bottom, or dead drift deep with Hi-D line as above as above
	Pupa	Pearl Pushkin Hot Spot	body olive-grey, wing case green, thorax grey body brown, thorax orange or green	12 to 16 10 to 16	sub-surface, slow on floater, or sink and draw on inter-mediate line as above

Group name	Life stage	Suggested imitations	Colours of common naturals	Size	Recommended method
Limnephiloidea (cont)	Adult *(emerger, surface egg layer: still water)*	Walker's Sedge	mixed ginger and browns	10 to 12	dry with fast retrieve on floating line
		Goddard & Henry's Sedge (green bodied version)	body green, wing grey or mottled	8 to 12	as above
		DDD	grey mottled brown	12 or 14	dry, static
		Soldier Palmer Pink	light ginger	8 to 14	dry, static
	Adult *(emerger, surface egg layer: running water)*	Henryville Special	wing mottled, body olive or brown	12 to 16	dry
		Whickam's	all ginger/brown	12 to 14	dry
		DDD	grey/mottled brown	14	dry
	Adult *(diving egg layer)*	Fick's White Death	all silver	8 to 12	floating line, sink and draw
		Diving Caddis	all silver	8 to 12	as above
Order DIPTERA Family **Chironomidae Buzzers, Non-biting Midges**	Larva *(blood-worm)*	Digger's Red	scarlet	10 to 16	weighted fly on a floating line, very slow retrieve in deep water, use a tungsten core line
		Red Larva	scarlet	10 to 16	as above
		Red Booby	scarlet	10	25 cm leader, lead-core line, fish static
		Green Larva	green	10 to 14	floating line, allow to sink, very slow retrieve
		San Juan Worm	scarlet	12	static on bottom
	Pupa *(buzzer)* a. *Bottom swaying, still water*	Suspender Buzzer	body claret, thorax sepia	12	Hi-D line, 25 cm leader, fig-of-8 retrieve
		Claret Buzzer	all claret	8 2Xss	floating line, long leader, very slow retrieve
		Large Olive Buzzer	body pale olive, thorax grey	8 2Xss	as above
	b. *Horizon-tal swimmer*	Red Buzzer	body silver sheen over scarlet, thorax brown	12	floating line, short 2 m leader, very slow retrieve
		Ribbed Sepia Buzzer	body dark brown, clear segmentation, red spot at thorax-body joint	12	as above
	c. *Head up, hanging*	Claret Buzzer	all claret, bright white breathers	8 2Xss	floating line, 3 to 4 m leader, Goddard & Henry's Sedge indicator, exceptionally slow retrieve

Group name	Life stage	Suggested imitations	Colours of common naturals	Size	Recommended method
Chironomidae (cont)		Small Olive Buzzer	all pale green with silver sheen	12 to 16	as above
	d. *Hanging, running water*	Orange Silver Buzzer	body bright orange, segmentation silver	10 to 14	floating, dead drift at dusk
	e. *Surface undulating diver, still water*	Yellow Olive Buzzer	body shiny yellow, thorax pale grey, red spot at tail	10 to 14	floating line, slow sink and draw
		Black Buzzer	all black	14 to 20	as above
		Green Buzzer	all green body, shiny	10 to 14	as above
	Adult	Dick Walker's Adult Buzzer	wing clear, several different body colours	10 to 20	dry, static with occasional twitch
Order ODONATA					
Sub-order **Zygoptera Damselflies**	Nymph	Red-eyed Damsel: Olive, Brown, or Yellow	all olive most common then browns, yellow, grey, and black	ls 8 or 10	floating line, long slow strips, swimming 0,3 m down
		Wiggle Nymph	as above	12 or 14	as above
		Hugh Huntley's Damsel Fly	olive or brown	ls 10 or 12	floating line and long leader, fished fig-of-8 on bottom
		Jalan	yellow	ls 8 or 10	slow sinker, fastish strip near top
	Adult female	Drab Damsel	dark bistre, wing pale blue dun along body	ls 12	floating line, slow sink and draw, near weed beds and reeds
	Adult male	Blue Damsel	brilliant blue, wing pale blue dun held along body	ls 10	dry, static occasional twitch
Sub-order **Anisoptera Dragonflies** Superfamily **Aeshnoidea** Family **Aeshnidea**	Nymph (winter)	Mrs Simpson	browns	ls 2 to 10	fast sink, slow strip with accelerations
	Nymph (all year)	Walker's Killer	sepia to dark browns	ls 2 to 12	as above
		Viva Booby	black to dark olive	10	25 cm leader, lead-core, fastish strips with 15 second pauses
	Nymph (summer)	Hamill's Killer	various shades of green and olive	4 to 10	floating or slow sink, slow strip interspersed fig-of-8, with occasional fast strips
		Terry Ruane's Dragon	mottled green/brown	ls 2 to 10	as above
		Wolf's Woolly Worm	olives	8 or 10	as above

Group name	Life stage	Suggested imitations	Colours of common naturals	Size	Recommended method
Family **Gomphidae**	Nymph	Don's Dragon	mottled sandy, dark grey, mottled browns, mottled greys	8 or 10	around base of weedbeds, gravel, sandy bottoms, fig-of-8 on sinking line, occasional fast strip
		Mrs Simpson	as above	8 or 10	as above
Superfamily **Libelluloidea** Family **Corduliidae**	Nymph	Corduliid Fly (Australian)	greys, grey mottles on white, pale olives, sandy, mottled bistre	4 to 10	at dusk or dull days, floating line slow strip retrieve just sub-surface
		Hamill's Killer	pale olives	4 to 10	over and around weedbeds, sinking line, fig-of-8 with odd 25 cm dashes
		Lord's Killer	sandy	4 to 10	as above
Family **Libellulidae**	Nymph	Don's Dragon	mottled browns, olive, grey, sandy	8 to 12	fast sinker, fig-of-8 with odd spurts, colour to suit bottom, pre-weighted hook and dressing upside down
		Walker's Killer	dark browns	8 to 12	as above
		Terry Ruane's Dragon	mottled browns and olives	8 to 12	as above
	Adult	Not normally imitated			
Order DIPTERA Family **Chaoboridae** **Phantom midges**	Larva	Barney Google	translucent	12 to 16	floating line, leader grease to within 20 cm of fly, extremely slow retrieve
	Pupa	Silver Phantom	grey and semi-translucent	12 to 16	as above
	Adult (dusk)	Grey Buzzer	as above, 2 sepia spots	14 or 16	floating line, short leader, just sub-surface shallow sink and draw
Family **Tipulidae** **Crane flies** **(Daddy-long-legs)**	Larva	Ivory Nymph	white	ls 8	freshly flooded bank sides, floating line, fig-of-8

Group name	Life stage	Suggested imitations	Colours of common naturals	Size	Recommended method
Tipulidae (cont)	Adult	Dick Walker's Daddy	bronzy, browns, greys	8 to 12	dry, static
	Drowned adult	Dick Walker's Daddy	as above	8 to 12	downwind shore, sinking line, static or very slow fig-of-8
Family Simuliidae Blackflies	Adult	Black Gnat	black	16	dry
Family Athericidae Snipe flies	Adult	Black Gnat Snipe and Purple	black black	16 or 18 16	dry across and down sub-surface
Family Blephariceridae Mountain midges (Net-winged midges)	Adult	Adult Buzzer	black	14 to 18	dry
Family Syrphidae Hover flies	Adult	Jindabyne Dronefly	striped yellow on black as above	10 10	dry dry
Order PLECOPTERA Stoneflies Family Perlidae	Nymph	Olive Montana Nymph (weighted)	olive	10 to 14	floating line, fly near bottom, dead drifted back
Family Nemouridae	Nymph	Ted's Stonefly Montana (green thorax)	chestnut black and green	14 14	floating line, fly near bottom, dead drifted back as above
	Adult (night)	Little Redwing Charcoal Nymph	tan and brown mottled dark grey	16 14	as above as above
Order HYMENOPTERA Ants	Adult, black	Black Ant Whoulston's Ant	black black	12 to 16 12 or 14	dry, occasional twitch as above
	Adult, brown	Brown Ant	brown	10	as above
	Adult, red	Red Ant	Vienna red	16	as above

Group name	Life stage	Suggested imitations	Colours of common naturals	Size	Recommended method
Order ISOPTERA Termites	Adult	DDD	wing clear to pale blue dun, body tan	8	dry, frequent twitches
		Kent's Termite	wing clear, body brown	8	as above
Order COLEOPTERA Beetles	Adult (terres-trial)	Coch-y-Bonddu	brown to reddish	16	a. high summer streams, floating line, dry b. still water, floating line, just sub-surface in lee shore ripple edge, very slow retrieve
		DDD	browns	10 to 14	dry
		Black and Peacock Spider (with cock hackle)	black	8 to 16	intermediate line, very slow just sub-surface
	Adult (diving)	Black Phantom	black	6 or 8	sinking line, sink and draw retrieve around weeds
	Larva (diving)	Leslie's Lure	tan	2	slow sinking line, fig-of-8 retrieve
		Terry Ruane's Dragon (tan)	tan	1/0 to 4	as above
Order NOTONECTIDA Backswimmers	Adult	Kent's African Beetle	black and orange	12 to 16	shallows, intermedi-ate line, and sink and draw retrieve in winter
		Silver Corixid	browns and tans	12 or 14	all year, slow sinking line, sink and draw around weed beds and reeds
Order CORIXIDA Lesser water boatmen	Adult	Silver Corixid	browns	10 or 12	sink and draw, on a sinking line around structure and weeds
		Plastazote Corixid	browns	10	float and draw, using leader with length as depth, and super fast sink line

Group name	Life stage	Suggested imitations	Colours of common naturals	Size	Recommended method
CORIXIDA (cont)		Olive Corixid	olive	18	floating line, slow sink and draw in shallows, in winter
		Green Duster	green/olive	18	as above
		Green Chomper	as above	18	as above
Order LEPIDOPTERA					
Moths	Adult	Chicken	cream to white	6 to 12	dry
		Soldier Palmer Pink	ginger to brown	8	dry
	Larva *(caterpillar)*	Olive Woolly Worm	olive	ls 8 to 12	dry
		Green Larva	green	10	intermediate line, fig-of-8 retrieve
Order ORTHOPTERA Grasshoppers and Locusts	Adult	Muddler Minnow	browns and tans	4 to 10	dry, wake retrieve in still water
		Joe's Hopper	browns, yellows	8	dry
		Dark Ferrash	dark brown, sepia	8 or 10	dry
		DDD	fawn	8 to 12	dry
		Green Muddler	greens	8	dry
Order MEGALOPTERA Alderflies	Larva *(toebiter)*	Herbst's Toebiter	brown	6 to 10	sinking line across and down, or dead drift
	Larva *(other spp)*	Beams' Peacock Woolly Worm	black	ls 8 or 10	as above
	Adult	Alder	black	8	dry
Class HIRUDINAE Leeches	Adult	Thom Green's Leech	black, or brown, or olive, or green, or grey, or red, or yellow	2 to 8	deep and very slow
		Black Lure	black	2/0 to 8	as above
Class GASTROPODA Snails	Adult *(lake bed)*	Black and Peacock Spider	black, dark olive	12 to 16	sinking line, bottom, very slow fig-of-8 retrieve
	Adult *(surface)*	Cliff Henry's Floating Snail	olive	10	floating line, greased leader, extremely slow retrieve

Group name	Life stage	Suggested imitations	Colours of common naturals	Size	Recommended method
GASTROPODA (cont)		Fuzzy Wuzzy Orange	olive, but orange from below in transmitted light	8 to 12	floating line, slow troll retrieve
		Dullstroom Orange	as above	8	strip retrieve at surface with floating line, warm summer evenings
		Red Setter	as above	10	as above
Class CRUSTACEA Order CLADOCERA Daphnia (Water fleas)	Daphnia bloom	Dullstroom Orange	orange	10	strip retrieve between 1 and 2 m down, slow sink line
		Red Setter	orange	10	as above
		Hot Spot, Orange	orange	12	slow retrieve 1 to 2 m depth on floating line
		Hot Spot, Green	green	12	as above
		Orange Puppy	orange	8	fast strip, slow sink line, just under surface on bright days

Abbreviations:

DDD	Duckworth's Dargle Delight
GRHE	Gold-ribbed Hare's Ear
PTN	Pheasant Tail Nymph
fig-of-8	figure-of-eight retrieve
ls	long shank
ss	short shank
2Xss	two-times extra short shank

CHAPTER 12

THE FISH'S LARDER – CRUSTACEA, FISH AND OTHERS

All things bright and beautiful
All creatures great and small.

Cecil Frances Alexander, 1848

Having studied the insects (and their relationship to fly fishing) in the previous chapter we will now investigate equally important food forms from other phyla of the animal kingdom.

LEECHES (HIRUDINAE)

The leeches are an important year-round food item for freshwater bass, but are apparently of interest to trout only during spring and autumn. I cannot remember ever spooning a trout and finding it full of leeches, with the exception of a 2,4 kg rainbow caught at Sterkfontein Dam in the South African Free State during early September. That one was full of black leeches, and the fly, a size 2 Black Lure, was taken fiercely while fished along the bottom.

African leeches come in several shades and sizes. Black, brown, green, grey, mottled olive, and red are the commonest colours. Heys Hope dam, near Piet Retief in South Africa, has some yellow ones. As you go north in Africa, the leeches become more common, and in Kenya there are large populations of blackish leeches. The most commonly found type in southern Africa is a dark brown species which could be anything from a size 2/0 long shank to a size 8 long shank. Good patterns are Thom Green's Leech, and the Black Lure. Leech imitations should always be fished deep and slow.

SNAILS (GASTROPODA)

Anyone who has, on picking-up a freshly caught trout, felt the grinding of the snails inside the fish, will know how important these little fellows are to the trout. Trout and other fish species avidly eat freshwater snails. It is interesting that some trout live on an almost exclusive diet of snails, whereas others from the same area do not. The trout may pick the snails off the water weeds, but mostly they take them from the bottom.

On some hot days, and also in the early African winter when the vegetation decays, the snails migrate to the surface. They then proceed to crawl about under, but actually attached to, the surface of the water. While in the process of rising from the bottom, the snails are exceedingly easy for the trout to grab. At this time they are traditionally copied by the Black and Peacock Spider, and the trout are relatively simple to catch. This same fly is the correct pattern for bottom snail-feeding trout as well. The correct retrieve is a very slow figure-of-eight. Dam walls and weedbeds are good areas to fish the bottom snails. However, in some of the deeper lakes, fishes will feed on snails at 50 metres and deeper. Sterkfontein Dam in the Free State is a good example of such a water.

The surface migration of the snails is believed to be related to slight drops in the dissolved

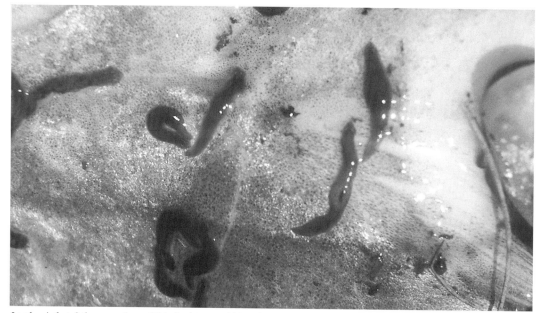

Leeches infested the operculum of this dead trout within minutes of placing it in the water. Leeches are very common in Africa, and the larger ones are a useful food source for fishes.

oxygen content of the water. In fact, this theory goes along well with the appearance of surface snails concurrent with increasing water temperature in summer (which results in lower dissolved oxygen) and the decay of aquatic vegetation in autumn and winter (which has the same effect).

Once the snail makes it to the surface, it hangs

Snails are a very important item in the fish's diet. Some trout feed exclusively on them.

by its foot in the surface film, and locomotes around by using its foot in the normal way. At this time, the trout (already interested in the rising snails) begin to get preoccupied with the snails at the surface. The angler sees only a good rise in progress, which soon spreads all over the water. His normal reaction to such a rise is to start throwing imitations of flies about, eventually ending in total frustration as he tries every fly in the box, to no effect. The rise gets busier and busier, and the angler gets more and more frustrated, eventually going home puzzled and fishless.

Your first priority, then, if you find yourself fishing to a rise in which the trout are determined to ignore all your best efforts, is to establish just what is going on. Sometimes the situation is clouded by the simultaneous hatch of sedges or other flies, all of which will be ignored if the snails are up. Normally, the snail migration takes place on still days, but hopefully there will be a slight breeze and then you can go downwind and check the water – the floating snails will be readily apparent. Failing any kind of breeze, you will have to wade out and very carefully examine the surface. The floating snails are not easy to see when spread out, and

This floating snail is locomoting around under the surface itself. Only the right imitation will work when the snails are 'up' like this.

The giant red water mite is easily imitated with a turn of red wool on a tiny hook, but trout seldom eat them.

you will need to be diligent in your observations.

Perhaps the most useful imitation is Cliff Henry's Floating Snail. Taff Price, in his book *Stillwater Flies*, suggests a Deer Hair Snail. Another fly that occasionally works, and then only really at dusk, is the orange-bodied Fuzzy Wuzzy. A modified Black and Peacock Spider with plastazote underneath the herl body is a possibility, but the balance must be right. The secret of success with surface snail imitations is to get them working under or just in the surface film and not on top of it. There exists a great deal of scope here for someone to design an effective fly – if you succeed you will probably go down in the annals of fly-fishing for ever.

For some reason that no one I know has ever been able to explain, there are times (when the snails are up), when the lure fly-fisherman can score with a 'just sub-surface' retrieved orange lure fly. This may have something to do with the fact that surface snails, when viewed from underneath in strong light, have a definite orange tinge. The two flies which I know work are the Whisky Fly and the Red Setter. In both cases, contrary to expectations, a fast retrieve does the trick. Perhaps the combination of key colour and a fast retrieve (which gives no time for critical examination), causes an instinctive strike by the fish ... who knows?

WORMS (LUMBRICULIDAE)

The trout fly-fisherman, according to legend, is supposed to abhor the very sound of the word 'worm'. Herein lie tales of all the major cheats over the centuries ... 'He fishes with *what*?'

Worms are supposed to be the downfall of any trout, respectful or otherwise, and no trout in his right mind can turn his back on the dreadful temptation of the 'worm'. The higher class wormer even came to the point of calling them 'garden hackles' in the hope that it didn't sound quite so appalling. Sun-dried worms on the banks of a fly-fishing establishment would bring on almost fatal apoplexy in any purist unlucky enough to find them. So, why is the dreadful worm here in this holy of holies – a fly-fishing book?

Well, for a start, the bass anglers love imitating worms, and they have even gone so far as to invent flies that imitate worms. Brave stuff this, but, let's face it, effective stuff too! In my experience, the truth of the matter does not justify the strength of anti-worm feeling. On many occasions, on those waters where both the fly-fisherman and the wormer rub shoulders (and there are plenty such in Africa), the fly-fisherman usually catches the most fishes. So, dare I say it, perhaps the deadly fly is too easy, and the living worm the method needing the real skill?

Most worm imitations in trout fly-fishing are in fact imitations of bloodworms, the San Juan Worm in larger sizes being perhaps the only exception that comes close to a garden crawler. In bass circles there are some excellent worm-imitating flies such as the Water Pup and the Giant Shimmy Leech.

Worms, being slow-moving creatures, should have their artificials fished in the same way. A nice slow figure-of-eight retrieve with occasional accelerating twitches is very effective here. The bites are most likely to be gentle affairs, and very often no more than two light taps are felt. The strike needs to be quick in response to these taps.

CLASS CRUSTACEA

There are a great many creatures among the crustacea which are fed upon by fishes. Their importance may seem highest among the food sources enjoyed by estuary and saltwater fishes, but they are very important to freshwater fishes as well. In African freshwaters crabs are common, as are shrimps, isopods and daphnia. The variety of these creatures is much greater in saltwater, where there are many more species and a greater variety of forms.

Water fleas (daphnia)

I would not suggest a size 28, or smaller, intricately tied fly, using the flue of a Dodo feather, or the wool from the right testicle of a fero-

Fig. 12.1: An enlarged representation of a daphnia. In reality most species are not much bigger than a pinhead.

cious Cape Buffalo. In fact, to attempt to tie an imitation of a daphnia would be the deepest kind of foolery. However, there is no doubt that not only are daphnia extremely common in African waters, they are also a very important part of the diet of freshwater fishes everywhere. Trout are very often caught absolutely full of daphnia. Daphnia are easily recognised in spoonings, especially if examined with a hand lens. They look like small brown translucent seeds.

Essentially, for trout to feed on daphnia, the daphnia must be present in clouds – what the angler refers to as a 'daphnia bloom'. The daphnia live in colonies and 'herd' in living masses of brown-orange colour, which can be very dense in optimal conditions. The trout has to do little more than cruise through the cloud to sieve out a sizeable meal. When the 'blooms' are of sufficient density to be of interest to the trout, they will usually be found somewhere downwind in clear water over depths of one metre or more.

The 'bloom' moves up and down in response to changing light intensity. What is really happening is that the daphnia are following the movement of their food, which is algae (mostly single-celled plant forms). These are moving in response to the light. It is not so much that the algae are freely mobile, but rather that their buoyancy changes as the light causes more oxygen to be released from within them.

The presence of these 'blooms' is a good thing for anglers because, surprisingly, we can capitalise on the presence of the daphnia and on the fact that the trout are eating them. Trout are not difficult to catch when feeding on daphnia, and I am confident of a good day's fishing if, when I spoon the first trout of the day, I find the little creatures there.

The method depends upon appealing to a combination of the aggressiveness of the fishes and their preoccupation with a food item which exhibits a key colour. In this case, the key colour is that of the daphnia themselves – usually orange or brownish-orange, but sometimes pink, and occasionally green. The theory is that the key colour (the colour of our fly), being indicative of food, will arouse interest; and that the sight of a small fish (the shape and movement of our fly) feeding competitively on daphnia, will arouse aggression. Together the two stimuli will result in the trout attacking and ingesting the fly. Of course, the theory may be so much hogwash, but since it works ... who cares?

The depth at which you fish your imitation is very important. On bright days it will not be very far down, whereas on dull days the daphnia will be deeper – maybe two or more metres down. If you find a green floating algae scum in a favourite bay or downwind shore, you could also try fishing just under the scum ... sometimes the daphnia are there, and the fishes are just below them!

Good flies are the Dullstroom Orange, the Whisky Fly, Parson's Glory, and the Orange Puppy. When the daphnia are green, try the various black and green dressings, such as the Viva, and also the Snot Tadpole Lure.

As a direct imitation, the Barney Google, which has two eyes which are good copies of real daphnia (the fishes apparently ignore the rest of the fly), works rather well. The Orange Hot Spot nymph is another good one. Something that often works very well indeed is to combine the two types, perhaps a Whisky Fly on the point, and an Orange Hot Spot on the dropper.

Fishing lures through daphnia blooms is an interesting example of the lure fly-fisherman doing some real imitative work. In Europe, some of the lure fly-fishermen have gone overboard with fluorescent pink Tadpole Lures and equally horrific creations. I have not found them very good here.

Crabs and prawns (Decapoda)
River crabs

River crabs belong to the genus *Potamon*. They grow to a maximum carapace size of around 60 mm, and are found very commonly in all African still and running waters.

River crabs are scavengers of animal matter, but anything they can overpower is fair game. They are (to the chagrin of most fly-fishermen) very fond of attacking and cutting fast-sink fly lines. Static fly-fishing in Africa is thus a rather

Freshwater crabs can be imitated with flies. It is especially worth while imitating the soft skinned crabs known as 'peelers'.

An estuarine crab photographed at St Lucia. (Photo: Geoff Taylor)

expensive sport, and can easily cost you a fly line a day! It does not pay to leave a line just lying on a river or lake bed in Africa.

River crabs are well able to defend themselves from most small creatures with their powerful pincers, but they are nevertheless preyed upon by many water creatures, including fish. African otters feed on them extensively, much more than they do on fish.

Crabs can walk in any direction, but when disturbed, they almost always scuttle sideways in typical crab fashion. This sideways movement is very important in the retrieves and design of crab imitations.

The *Potamon* crabs differ from saltwater crabs in that they have no larval stage: the young are exact miniatures of the parents. River crabs grow by progressively moulting the hard outer layer of the body. When this exoskeleton is new it is very soft. These soft crabs are known by anglers as 'peelers'. All freshwater fishes will feed avidly on soft peeler crabs. In fact, some really big trout and yellowfish feed almost

Living snapper shrimp.

Dead snapper shrimp.

All estuarine fish love snapper shrimps, although very few good imitations exist. The living colour varies from dark blue to mottled olive green. Fish will certainly pick up sick ones. These (although in black and white) still show the colour change of dead ones, which is always white and yellowy-orange, not pink!

exclusively on a diet of dragonfly nymphs and freshwater crabs. The favoured crab is one of approximately 25 mm across – the softer the better. Catfish and largemouth bass are also keen crab eaters.

There were no true crab imitations for the African fly-fishermen until fairly recently, with the advent of a modification to the Walker's Killer fly which turned it into a crab imitation. The Walker's Killer Crab is a fair imitation and it works, but a great deal of scope exists here for the keen fly-tier to invent a really good imitation (and I don't mean these rock-hard plastic crab flies that are being foisted onto the saltwater angler by several fly-fishing shops). Peeler crabs are much lighter in colour than hardened crabs, and I am sure this colour difference is very important – the fishes would easily spot the peelers by this colour, which is best described as a greyish bistre. One could pre-bleach the partridge feather in the Walker's Killer pattern ... that might come near to the colour, as also would hen pheasant breast feathers. You could also try tying in the first layer of feathers using a pale fluorescent grey, and then overlay this with feathers dyed to the correct colour.

Estuary crabs

These are very similar to the freshwater crabs above, but they do have a larval stage. They also tend to come in a wider colour range, and grow much bigger. Most estuary crabs are dark olive to olive brown, but the peelers are greyish

and slightly darker than their freshwater cousins. As in freshwater, the peeler size most popular with the fishes is about 25 mm across the carapace. The Walker's Killer Crab variation in its original partridge shoulder feather colour is right for saltwater. Many saltwater crabs have a touch of blue in them, and an underbody of fluorescent blue helps the salty versions to be more effective. Many of the 'Killer' fly types also make passable crab imitations when the dressing is swivelled through 90 degrees, as in the Walker's Killer Crab.

I like to fish these imitations (freshwater and salt) with a super fast-sinking line. The effective retrieve is slow pulls with frequent stops.

Freshwater shrimps and small crustaceans

I remember, some years back, when we used to spend a lot of time in summer pursuing blue kurper with bait fishing tackle in Hartebeespoort Dam in South Africa, that a favourite bait was a freshwater shrimp. We would catch these with small nets, by pushing the nets up against stands of reeds and other vegetation. The shrimps were very common and we caught plenty of them. I wonder why it is, then, that most of the fly-fishermen in Africa seldom give freshwater crustaceans a second thought. In many waters, the little crustaceans are abundant and the fishes love them! In KwaZulu-Natal, the *Caradina* shrimp is found in rivers at altitudes of up to 1 400 metres and is often preyed upon by fish. In addition to the shrimps of the Decapoda order, there are also small crustaceans that belong to the Amphipoda (*Gammarus pulex*, the shrimp of European fly-fishing literature, is an amphipod).

Most of these small crustaceans are easily copied by a single imitation: all that is required is to choose the correct size. You can try the Golden Shrimp, Olive Shrimp, Sparkle Shrimp, and the Chomper. Sizes between 10 and 14 should cover most types. A slow, even retrieve with an occasional 10 cm jerk is correct.

Saltwater shrimps and prawns

Prawns of all shapes and sizes abound in African estuaries and in the salt, and they are very important as a food source to many fishes. There are many different prawns around the African coastlines: cracker shrimps, mud prawns, sand prawns, river prawns, and all the edible (restaurant) prawns are all well known to anglers. Bait anglers use them extensively, and the saltwater fly-fisherman imitates them with many of his flies.

Many saltwater fly-fishermen fail to realise that imitative fly-fishing is as important in the sea as it is in freshwater. There is a great tendency in saltwater flies to simply imitate colour. (This has nothing to do with the pink flies which are unashamedly sold as imitators of prawn colour. The fact is that one never comes across a freshly boiled prawn moving along the sea bed. The colour pink is attractive to saltwater fishes in the same way that trout like orange, but it has little to do with prawns.) The natural prawn colours are greens, olives, dull blues and browns. When a prawn or shrimp changes his exoskeleton he often turns yellow or orange, and these are consequently good colours for prawn imitation. On some corals and other structures, one comes across brilliant scarlet shrimps and also brightly striped ones. However, these types often have symbiotic cleansing relationships with fishes, which very often will not eat them.

The approach which believes that colour is everything is at least a good start. Really good prawn imitations, however, usually try to imitate the prominent eyes of the originals. They also often make an attempt to imitate shape, and, most importantly, they are able to imitate

the movement of the original if retrieved properly. The bonefish flies are examples of this, and they are nearly all very good flies.

For best results with prawn imitations, knowledge of their haunts is certainly an asset. Fish over the right kind of mud and sand flats, around piers and rocks or on the edges of reefs, and the results should be worth the effort. Prawns and shrimps either walk very slowly, or, like their big cousins the lobsters, they swim backwards with a flick of their tail – this is a quick movement, and since it is related to a fear reaction by the prawn (which fishes are tuned into), this is the movement to copy! One should fish on the bottom, and use a jerky retrieve consisting of pulls of 25 cm or more.

There are some imitations offered in shops which look as though they could swim off the display board, they are so realistically tied. I don't like these, and I do not find them particularly effective. The fishes appear to know they are not real, whereas they are never so sure of the fur and feather flies. Good flies include the various bonefish flies, Golden Shrimp, Irish Blonde (in small sizes), and Salty Bead Eye. Flies for saltwater shrimp and prawn imitation are best in sizes from 2 to 6.

SQUID

Squid, along with octopus, represent the epitome of development among the invertebrates. Squid have a primitive communication system which takes advantage of their ability to control the colour of any part of their skin by means of chromatophores. Small squid sometimes venture into the shallow surf, and even into the mouths of estuaries. They are a favourite source

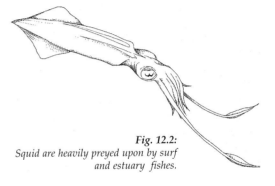

Fig. 12.2:
Squid are heavily preyed upon by surf and estuary fishes.

of food with many of the gamefishes, and thus imitations of them are essential at times. From the fly-tier's point of view, their main features are their tentacles, large eye, and streamlined shape. Another very important aspect of any squid fly design project is that when they are scared or in a hurry, they swim backwards very rapidly using a jet propulsion system. The normal forward motion is rather slow. This backward swimming (which to a gamefish is a fear response), is important to copy in the imitation. Consequently, the fly needs to be tied with the squid's eyes at the bend of the hook and not at the hook eye: it follows that the tentacles will also be at the same end (the bend).

There are some very simply tied imitations available, in which thick chenille is simply worked around the hook, tapering fatter toward the hook bend. A Pantone pen is then used to mark the eyes. These imitations work, but as a rule not too well. However, the Calamari Fly is a good one to try, and certainly a closer imitation is achieved with this dressing. The retrieve needs to be rather fast strips with occasional slowish pulls. The important thing is to correctly assess the depth at which the squid are swimming, and to use a suitable sinking line for correct depth retrieval.

FISHES
Freshwater fishes and fry
All African freshwaters contain good stocks of small fishes, all of which are of interest to any larger predatory fish. Fishes burn up their energy reserves at quite a rate when hunting, and any hunting fish has to get more energy from the prey he catches than he uses in catching it, otherwise he will eventually starve! A small fish may involve a predatory fish in a long chase with no certainty of success. Effectively, this means that a predatory fish will probably limit his hunting to weak, sick, or injured fishes, and is less likely to chase a fish in good health. There are some imitations designed specifically to emulate an injured fish: the Foam Fly is one.

Perhaps the best known example of fishes chasing healthy fry occurs when big brown trout herd the fry at the back-end of the season. They herd them towards a suitable shallow (but

A small straightfin barb (Barbus paludinosus) *from the Bronkhorstspruit area in South Africa. Fishes feed readily on such fry.*

not too shallow) spot by swimming around them, and then they attack. They do this by swimming through the shoal of fry with mouths open, and tails beating furiously, hoping to either swallow or damage a few. Fry that are injured are then immediately engulfed as the trout turns. The surface erupts and the disturbance can be heard metres away. Casting into this mêlée with a Polystickle will usually produce an instant take!

Smaller trout are not successful fry eaters, and few fry turn up in spoonings. Big trout eat a lot more small fishes, but even then nowhere near as commonly as they eat insects, snails and crustaceans. Brown trout are certainly more predatory on fishes than are rainbows. Big brown trout are traditionally hunted with large lure flies. The preferred method is a lead-core line, right on the bottom, using a fast strip retrieve.

The rationale behind lure fly-fishing, then, is simply one of presenting the trout (or other fish species) with a fry imitation which looks remarkably easy to catch. The key word here is 'easy'. One thing about the fly-fisherman's retrieve is that it is never so good that it exactly simulates the movement of the original, and this is one time when we can actually capitalise on our deficiencies. The trick, then, is to retrieve the lure fly so that it moves like a sick or injured fry, or an easy-to-catch fish. In the latter case, this is a knife-edge situation: if the retrieve is too natural, or too artificially simple (even too strange), the predatory fishes won't bother to chase the fly. Experience is the best teacher, and some anglers such as Louis van der Westhuizen have got this down to a fine art. One of the simplest ways to add spice to a fry retrieve is to stop occasionally, perhaps for just a second or two.

One of the opportunities presented by this kind of lure fly-fishing is the chance to cover an enormous amount of water during the course of a day's fishing. The angler who stays in one spot all day, continually casting at the same piece of water and hoping that a fish comes past does himself no favours. We call this short-sighted approach the 'heron syndrome'. The good angler, on the other hand, approaches his lure fly-fishing in a logical way. The fishes are not spread out like holes in a sponge. They move according to prevailing environmental conditions, and in response to the whereabouts of their food.

When you arrive at the water, try to establish what the weather pattern has been for the last day or two, then spend some time applying the methodology in Chapter 3. Isolate the area most likely to have fishes in it, pick a spot, and then commence fan casting around. After a few casts take a few steps sideways, and again search the area by fan casting around. Keep this up, and eventually you will have very thoroughly covered the entire hot area.

Lure fly-fishing should always have an aim in view. The master aim might be to find the fishes using an attractor lure fly; and then, having located them, to start fishing imitations to them. Maybe you want to test if high-contrast patterns will get the fishes to make aggressive strikes; or, if it's brownies you are after, you may wish to appeal to their territorial instincts. Whatever the reasons, and there could be any number of choices, think out a strategy and then work it through. If you have not already been strategising your fishing, you will achieve immediate improvements in your results.

There are many fly imitations of small fishes available to the angler. Many of these are specific imitations designed to copy a certain family or species of fish. The fly-fisherman needs to know what copies what, and should always attempt to fish the correct fly to copy the indigenous fishes in his water.

Imitative fry flies
Catlet imitation
Small catlets abound in many African streams. Favourite imitative patterns include the Catlet Muddler, which is specifically designed to represent the small catfish and catlets. These little fishes like stony bottoms, dam walls, and anywhere rocky or gravelly; they also have a strong preference for clear water. They move either very slowly or in short sharp dashes which must be simulated in the retrieve. The Catlet Muddler is deadly if used correctly!

Kurper and other cichlid imitations
Small kurper swim in short, fairly fast dashes, with long periods of almost immobility, or very slow movement. If small kurper are surprised in open water, then they will swim rapidly in long gliding dashes heading for the shore. A long-haul strip retrieve with five-second pauses is effective in imitating this movement. A few of the good flies are the Vleikurper (top choice), Gray Ghost, Church Window (Lady Purple), Grey Booby, Yelland's Kurper Fly, Vleikurper Polystickle.

Small yellowfish and mudfish imitation
These fishes are silvery or golden, with darker backs, and they can be found at home in all streams and many still waters. There are a great many species, but most can be copied by standard imitations. They vary in size from very small (nymph size), up to large fishes when fully grown.

Good flies include the Polystickle, Carp Fry, Frog Nobblers, Anhinga and Gold, and others. The various strip retrieves all work with these flies. However, there is no doubt that for still water the troll retrieves (see Chapter 5) are the most effective of all for minnow imitations.

Small trout imitation
In many African waters the trout are self-sustaining, and no stocking takes place (the streams of Lesotho and Malawi are prime examples of this).

The fishes breed well in certain streams and dams in some areas, and trout fry are common in such waters.

All trout are cannibalistic and the Baby Rainbow Trout and the Little Brown Trout are good imitative flies. Retrieves should be fast and smooth, with occasional pauses.

Attractor lure flies for fry eaters

There are a great many attractor lure flies available, some of which are very good flies. The best combine the attributes of an attractor pattern with imitative properties, imitating large nymphs, tadpoles and fishes. Imitative strip retrieves are the right way to go. Examples are the Viva Tadpole and the other Tadpole Lures, Puppies, Dog Nobblers, and Frog Nobblers.

Aggression-generating lure flies

Some of the attractor lures go one step further, and, through the correct application of colour and contrast, they become aggression generators. These include the Micky Finn, Dullstroom Orange, Yellow Panacea, Tanager, Mike's Secret, and lots more. They are normally fished with fast strip retrieves on slow-sinking or floating lines.

Silhouette lure flies

Finally, there are the various silhouette fry-imitating lure flies, which show up well against the sky when seen from underneath by the fishes. These are excellent flies at dusk and dawn, and include the Black Lure, Black Panacea, Black Marabou, and others. A floating line and a slow strip retrieve is the best method for these flies.

With all these lure flies one should never forget that they are primarily fish and fry imitators, and should always be fished as such!

Very tiny fry

The imitation of very small fry presents its own problems, in that the habits and size of the fry are in many respects similar to nymphs. These tiny fishes like to hide under weeds, and they stick very closely to shallow areas where they

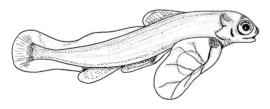

Fig. 12.3: *Typical appearance of a freshly hatched fry (this is a brown trout alevin). The yolk sac underneath is usually a distinctive orange colour. Most fry will be silvery with a dark brown or green back.*

feel safe. The best fishing spots, if you intend to imitate tiny fry, are weedy shallows, edging up to a sudden drop off. The predatory fishes naturally cruise this kind of feature, and the sudden appearance of an easy-to-catch fry will prove irresistible.

The movement of very tiny fry differs from their larger brethren, and it is important to realise that a strip retrieve is a waste of time. Little fishes operate in jerky, direction changing movements of about 5–8 cm. Your retrieve must aim to simulate this rather than the much longer glides of larger fry, which are imitated by various strip retrieves. The retrieve with which I have had good results is a series of accelerating 10 cm pulls with frequent pauses and direction changes achieved by laying the rod over from right to left and back again.

Good flies are the Iven's Green and Brown Nymph, the Porringe, Peter Ross, and finally the Steele's Taddy for situations where silhouette fishing is needed. These flies should all be tied size 12 to 14 for this task.

Estuarine and saltwater fishes and fry

There are a great many small fishes inhabiting estuaries around the coasts of Africa, and even more of them in the surf. It is only in very recent years that anyone has bothered to look at these small fishes from an imitative point of view. The imitation of these small fry is in fact very important, and the angler who uses deliberate imitations will always outfish the one using garish monstrosities.

In estuaries, it is also very useful to have a working knowledge of the fry fish's habits and preferences. Such knowledge can help you to locate the gamefishes themselves (which feed on the fry), and also to better understand the correct retrieves which imitate these small fishes. It is very obvious that a good representation of an estuarine roundherring, cast into the areas where these small fishes easily find the plankton that they feed on, and retrieved slowly so as to correctly imitate its natural movement, is going to perform better than a fluorescent pink lure which is 'chuck and chanced' all over the estuary and strip retrieved any old way.

Many of the small estuarine fishes are season-

The fast water of the estuary mouth is a pathway for the gamefishes from the sea. Look for channels and deep runs, and fish with a lead-core or tungsten dust fly line.

al, some migratory. All the fly-fisherman needs to do is to keep a diary of the spoonings of captured gamefishes, and it won't be long before you build up a complete picture of what is going on. The other important aspect is to observe the behaviour of the small fishes relative to the changing tide.

For example, the St Lucia estuary in South Africa is a world-famous angling location offering some excellent fishing. However, the various fish species come and go at fixed times throughout the year. During the Christmas season, the deep estuaries are alive with small moonies (or kitefish), but at other times they are quite hard to find, and no longer worth imitating. In June, the same swims may well be full of small sea perch (also known as river bream or perch). You may well find an absence of grunter in the estuary during July, and trying to catch them with shrimp imitations could be pointless; but by August it's a different story ... the grunter are back! All estuaries have these seasonal movements, and very often different estuaries have different fish behavioural patterns, which is why keeping records can be so important.

The importance of key colours in estuarine and saltwater fry imitations is just as great as in freshwater fly patterns. The gamefishes might well get preoccupied, feeding on a shoal of halfbeaks. It won't be long before they get a fixation on the red spot on the halfbeak's beak ... so make sure your imitation has that. The silver lateral flash on the estuarine roundherring is another example. Most importantly, all good saltwater flies must have eyes, the bigger the better.

Below, we will look at some of the commoner estuarine fodder fishes. There are many additional species, both in the estuaries and in the surf. However, if you acquire imitations of the ten species below, they will also serve to imitate almost all of the other species you may come across. Estuarine fry fishes are easy to imitate with flies, and anyone who ties their own flies will have little difficulty inventing dressings for the specific fish species from their favourite estuary. Given below are some imitative suggestions and some retrieve strategies.

Estuarine roundherring (*Gilchristella aestuarius*)
This is a common small fish, growing to a maximum of 7 cm, but more likely around 5 cm. It is translucent, with a bright silver lateral stripe. The eye is silver with a black pupil. The back is

235

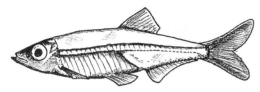

Fig. 12.4: Estuarine roundherring.

normally green. Similar fishes are found from Mozambique and further north with brown backs.

The estuarine roundherring ranges from the Breede River in South Africa north to Kenya. It shoals in estuaries, and filter-feeds during the day on estuarine plankton. It is a very important food item for fishes and birds. The entire life of this small fish is spent inside the estuary: it never ventures out to sea.

The Mono Fly, and the Green and the Chartreuse Glass Minnows are excellent imitations. Also useful is the Irish Blonde, and Clouser's Deep Minnow.

The estuarine roundherring is a fairly sedentary fish unless frightened. A floating line and a slow retrieve with occasional accelerations is the method for fishing over shallows. However, the gamefishes usually feed on odd ones which have left the shoal and perhaps strayed over deeper water. Immediately on becoming aware of the gamefish, the little prey fish will head for safety at top speed. Retrieves over deeper water are best done in the fast troll style, accelerating the strips from time to time, and using a sinking line.

Spotted halfbeak (Hemiramphus far)
There are also halfbeaks from the genus *Hyporhamphus* which can be grouped here from a fly-fishing perspective; so can young garfish.

The spotted halfbeak is an elongated, slender fish, with a long, needle-like lower jaw. It can grow to 50 cm, but it (and other smaller related

species) is commonly found in shoals of 6 cm (or smaller) fishes. The beak is black with a red-orange tip. The body is silver to white below, and green above. The tail has a brilliant blue appearance underwater, but appears yellowish to dusky out of water (fly-tiers note well). The flanks sometimes show 4 to 9 large dusky spots.

The halfbeak is a common shallow-water shoaling fish. It can jump well, and often gives its location away by skipping across the surface – something it always does when pursued or frightened. It is a plankton feeder.

Distribution is from the South African Cape all the way up the eastern coast of Africa and across to the Far East.

The favourite imitation of many African fly-fishermen is Tom Lentz's Needlefish; the Natal Halfbeak is probably even better. If you see the halfbeaks jumping, you will probably get best results by fishing with a floating line and using a fast strip retrieve. These imitations are useful 'search' patterns when you don't know what's about. Fish these flies on a sinking line, and use a fast strip retrieve.

Cape moony (Monodactylus falciformis)
The Cape moony (also known as moonfish or kitefish by anglers) is a silver, round, compressed-bodied fish with a large prominent eye. Young fishes display vertical striping which is less obvious as they get bigger. Fins are black to greyish with a pearlescent sheen on the anal and dorsal fins. They grow to 20 cm, but are commonly found around 5–7 cm in estuaries. There is a similar common species, *M. argenteus* (the Natal moony) which can be regarded as the same from a fly-fishing point of view.

The moonfish shoals in large numbers, usually closely packed, and is totally tolerant of fresh water. It prefers to shoal around structure

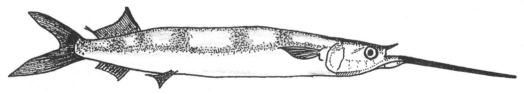

Fig. 12.5: Spotted halfbeak.

Fig. 12.6: Slimey.

This moony took a Pink Shrimp fly that was actually intended for something that might normally eat him. Moonies often shoal in fast tidal water, either hugging the bottom or rising to midwater in pursuit of food. (Photo: Ken Bateman)

(piers, reefs, etc.), and can be found feeding at any depth (most often right on the bottom).

The two species are found from the Cape right up to Kenya. They are basically plankton feeders when small, but are quite able to attack and break down quite large fish and crustacean remains if necessary.

The Moonfly tied with the back weighted and the hook inverted is the best imitation.

Slimey (*Leiognathus equulus*)

The slimey (also known as soapy) is a deep-bodied, compressed fish, not as round as the

Mark Yelland is a professional fly-fishing guide working out of Johannesburg into most African fishing resorts. Here on Margaruque Island in Mozambique, Mark is about to return a fly-caught green-spot kingfish. Mark is very much a follower of the 'catch and release' philosophy, and believes it to be just as important in the sea as inland.

moony, but tending that way. It has a prominent yellowish eye with a black pupil. The body is silver, with fins which have a distinctive yellowish tinge, and occasional vertical dusky bars. From above, the back is blackish, going brown towards the dusky tail fin.

Slimeys are found all up the eastern African coast, extending right across to Malaya. They are commonly found in lagoons and estuaries, and out to sea (even in deep water), throughout the year. The young fishes like estuaries and mangrove-lined waters. Here, in late summer, they shoal in large numbers of 7 cm individuals, feeding on the plankton. They grow to about 20 cm maximum, and for these larger specimens food is prawns, crabs and marine worms.

The Integration Blonde is usually considered the best fly for imitating slimeys, but the dark-backed Lefty's Deceivers are just as good. White versions of the Lefty's Deceiver with peacock herl backs are most useful. I like a slow-sinking line and a slow strip retrieve for fishing these flies. However, slimeys often browse on crustaceans on the bottom and, to imitate these, nothing is better than a jerky retrieve, using a lead-core line.

Mullets (*Mugil* species)

There are several mullet species, but from a fly-imitating point of view they can be regarded as one species. The fly-fisherman not only imitates the very young mullet in order to catch the gamefish, but also hunts down the mullet themselves as a sport-fish in their own right. Indeed, larger mullet are great fighters on fine fly-fishing tackle!

Mullet are cylindrical, bullet-shaped fishes with pointed snouts. They are silvery bodied, with dusky, or grey, or bluish (in the case of the longarm mullet) backs. Some of the mullets are magnificent jumpers, able to easily clear two

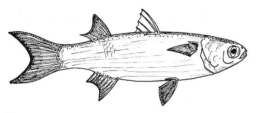

Fig. 12.7: Mullet.

metres. Fins are generally dusky. Some of the species are longitudinally striped. The eye is small, but distinctive.

The fly-fisherman should be interested in imitating the very small specimens which commonly inhabit estuaries and river mouths. They are a favoured food for most of the larger game-fishes – garrick and kingfish find them almost irresistible! Some mullet are found around the Atlantic coast (*Liza richardsoni*, the southern mullet); others are spread all up the eastern African coast. *Valamugil cunnesius*, the longarm mullet, is of great interest to the fly fisherman, because it is common in east-coast lagoons, and moves into estuaries when quite small (4–5 cm). This, and several other species, has a distinctive yellow splash (an important key colour) on the gill covers.

Lefty's Deceiver tied in colours to imitate the mullets (don't forget the yellow cheeks) is my favourite. I like a grey bucktail back over white Fishair. Use a floating line and a fairly fast troll retrieve.

Cape silverside (*Atherina breviceps*)

Because of their close similarity, we will consider the Cape silverside and the hardyhead silverside (*Atherinomorus lacunosus*) as the same from the point of view of the fly-fisherman. There are also other less frequently met silverside species, which can be covered by the same imitations. Silversides are small fishes (usually 7–9 cm) with a broad head, which makes them

look rather like small mullet. The body is silver with a pale green back. Live specimens have an iridescent blue stripe along the flanks. Fins are dusky, and the eye is large. Underwater these fishes appear partially translucent.

The silversides are widely distributed from the Cape to the Red Sea. These little fishes are found close inshore and in estuaries. They form large shoals during the day which split up at night to feed on near-surface plankton. The Irish Blondes and Glass Minnows imitate these fishes quite well. A blue Surf Candy is also good, but the best of all is the Blue Silverside. Strip retrieving on a medium-sink line around reefs and estuarine structure is the way to go.

Gobies (*Psammogobius knysnaensis*)

There are many small goby species all up the eastern African coast. In some places they are the commonest fishes. They are small (many around 7–10 cm) with elongated bodies and flattened, broad and bluntly rounded heads. They are carnivorous and predatory.

Colouring is often cryptic olives or browns, and many are impossible to see unless they move. The eyes are large and situated toward the top of the head. They usually hide among rocks and weeds, but some inhabit open sandy areas where they cover themselves in sand and ambush passing prey. Gamefishes will take them if they see them move, and they are of interest to bottom-loving big fishes such as kob. They are largely ignored by most fly-fishermen. However, as you go north up the coast of Africa, they become more and more common, and thus more important as food for gamefish.

A large (size 3/0) edition of the Catlet Muddler tied on a stainless steel hook is the best pattern for anything feeding on gobies. The Muddler Minnow is also pretty good. These

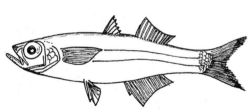

Fig. 12.8: Cape silverside.

Fig. 12.9: Sand goby.

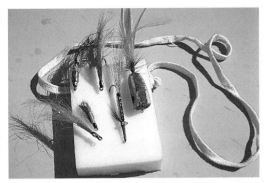

The answer to carrying saltwater flies when wading flats and when surf or estuary fly-fishing is to carry spare flies on a block of plastazote suspended around the neck with a bootlace.

imitations should be fished right on the bottom, slowly, with a figure-of-eight retrieve interspersed with an occasional dash. Big Mrs Simpsons and Walker's Killers also work.

Glassnose (*Thryssa vitrirostris*)

These small anchovies are slightly elongated, with a compressed body. The nose is blunt, with the eyes well forward. They are silver bodied with a bluish dorsal surface. The belly is white and the fins are dusky yellowish. The inside of the glassnose's mouth is bright orange. *Thryssa setirostris* is more tropically distributed and similar enough to be imitated by the same flies. These small fishes are usually 7–15 cm long. They are found all up the eastern African coast.

The glassnoses are lovers of calm bays and estuaries, and often shoal in huge numbers. They prefer the midwater zone, where they feed on plankton and other small fishes, including the fry of the estuarine roundherring. Gamefishes find them very attractive, and a good imitation is often a winner – especially in winter and spring when these fishes are very common.

The Argentine Blonde, blue Clouser's Minnows, and blue and white Lefty's Deceivers are all good imitations. They are all improved by the addition of a tuft of fluorescent orange at the throat with additional tufts of yellow as cheeks. A jerky strip retrieve on a medium sinker is a good method.

Glassies (*Ambassis* spp.)

Both the banded and the slender glassy are very common in estuaries. The slender glassy (*Ambassis natalensis*) is the commoner around the southern African estuaries, with the roles reversing and the banded glassy (*A. productus*) becoming commoner as you go north up the coast of Africa. These small fishes (5–10 cm) are almost transparent, with the internal structures often clearly seen. The general colour is a silver with a dusky yellow tint and with a very distinct silver pearlescent lateral band. The eye is largish and silvery yellow with a black pupil.

They spend long periods hanging motionless in midwater, where their translucency often makes them hard to see. They feed on planktonic crustacea and anything else of animal origin they can find. They are often found around jetties and wharves.

The 'transparency' of these small fishes makes for one of those situations where tying the body of the fly using tin-coloured tinsel rather than silver really pays off. The tin colour appears almost translucent under water. Mylar tubing is now readily available in tin colour. Apart from the bright silver stripes on fishes like the estuarine roundherring (best rendered in silver), the tin-coloured Mylar is many times better from a point of view of realistic colour on all surf and estuary flies.

Good flies are the African Tangler, the Integration Blonde, the Mono Fly, and small

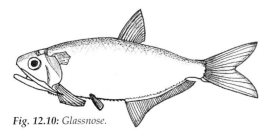

Fig. 12.10: *Glassnose.*

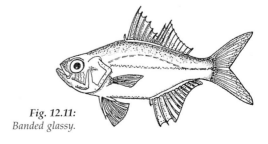

Fig. 12.11: *Banded glassy.*

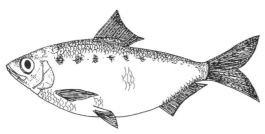

Fig. 12.12: Razorbelly.

Lefty's Deceivers. Fish them with a floating line with fairly fast strips, but with long pauses in between (10–20 seconds).

Razorbelly (*Hilsa kelee*)

This is a very compressed small fish with a deep V-shaped belly. The back is dark blue-green and the sides bright silver, with no apparent lateral line. It has a large distinctive eye with a small black spot behind the gill covers.

The razorbelly (also known as kelee shad) is a coastal water species which swims in large shoals. These shoals occasionally enter estuaries throughout the year, but purposefully enter them from September to February for spawning and subsequent growth of the fry. Razorbellies are plankton eaters.

The large gamefishes are very fond of razorbellies. Some fly-fishermen like to use largish (size 4/0) Lefty's Deceivers and Platinum Blondes to imitate these small fishes. However, when tying them, it pays to use only sparse material on the back of the fly because the back is very thin in the actual fish. These flies are improved by the addition of silver Krystal Flash on the sides, and a definite attempt should be made to incorporate a large eye. They are slow movers when feeding, and a slow hand-over-hand troll retrieve with a floating line gives best results.

Pursemouths

These small silvery fishes occur in shallow warm seas, and are often found in brackish estuarine waters. There are many species, and only two of the commonest are mentioned here. They are also known as 'majorras'. Pursemouths have an interesting tube-like mouth which they extend to dredge the bottom for small amphipods, worms and other food. Pursemouths feed only in daylight.

Pursemouths love shallow water, and occur in small shoals from KwaZulu-Natal northward. The threadfin pursemouth (*Gerres filamentosus*) is perhaps the best known in this group. The back is bluish-green, and the deep body is silver. Bluish blotches (sometimes very pale) can be seen in vertical bars on the body. The dorsal fin has a distinctive second filamentous spine. Fins are dusky.

There is no specific imitation of the threadfin pursemouth at present (a challenge for the fly-tier), but the Argentine Blonde comes fairly close. Another good one to try is the African Tangler, suitably modified by marking vertical pale blue stripes on the wing with a fluorescent Pantone pen. All green materials in the African Tangler should be changed to pale cobalt, and a sparse overwing of blue bucktail added.

The smallscale pursemouth (*Gerres acinaces*) is the next most important member of the purse-mouth family. It is rather fussy about its environment and is most likely to be found only in very clear estuarine systems (such as Kosi Bay), where it is present all year round. It is mostly a silver-grey colour with dusky fins. There are faint brown bands along the body, and a distinctive bright blue edge to the lower edge of the tail.

This is yet another common estuary fish with no specific imitative fly available. However, the Integrated Blonde has long been regarded as the closest pattern available. The brown body bands are so faint as to be hardly worth bothering about. However, the blue edge to the caudal

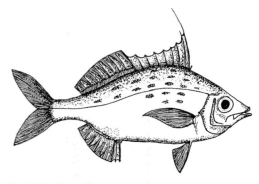

Fig. 12.13: Threadfin pursemouth.

fin is a key colour flash, and as such must be imitated. A few strands of fluorescent blue bucktail under the tail work well. A body made of tin-coloured Mylar tubing is also a great improvement.

When fishing to imitate any pursemouths, remember to fish right on the bottom. A lead core fly line and a slow retrieve with occasional dashes work well.

FROGS AND TADPOLES (AMPHIBIA)

Adult frogs are, surprisingly, found occasionally in trout autopsies. I have never found a platanna in a trout, and the frogs I do find are always of the *Rana* type. Also of interest is that the fish has always been from a river (never still water). It is probably not worth while setting out to capture a trout with a frog (they do not take them very often), but it is certainly worth trying for a bass or largemouth yellowfish with a frog imitation. The ideal fly is the 'Frog'. Of much greater importance to the inland fly-fisherman is the tadpole stage of froggy development. Trout and most other fishes love to eat tadpoles!

Tadpoles come in a bewildering variety of sizes and colour types in Africa. There are the small black *Rana* tadpoles, which are probably the most important, but there are also a lot of other types. The tadpoles vary in size up to whopping 80 mm creatures. Colours vary from black through mottled browns and greens to pale sepia and even almost translucent. There are even a few which flash a silver side (looking rather like small fishes) as they dash off to hide.

Tadpoles become important in the fish's diet around November south of the equator (March further north), and continue to be so for the next five months, right through to autumn. By then, most have metamorphosed and left the water to start their adult existence. When spooned, the tadpoles appear white as a result of bleaching with stomach acids, a process which is fairly rapid. The inexperienced angler may mistake these bleached tadpoles for fry at first sight.

Good imitations for the small black tadpoles are Steele's Taddy and Kent's Marabou Tadpole. For the very large tadpoles, the Olive

Tadpoles exist in enormous numbers in African waters. They come in sizes from 5 mm to 60 mm and many differing colours. All predatory fish take them, and their imitation is important.

A giant tadpole, nearly 8 cm long. These are frequently encountered in early spring at high altitudes in southern Africa. A tandem-tied Olive Marabou Muddler is the usual imitation.

Marabou Muddler is a good fly. Tadpole imitations should be fished around weedbeds in shallowish water (say 1–1,5 metres deep). A good method is to set up a 'chase rig' with the Taddy on the dropper about 10 cm back from say a Walker's Killer on the point. Retrieves are slow strips with occasional accelerations in the larger-sized patterns.

MISCELLANEOUS FOOD FORMS

Fishes eat many things which have not been covered in the text above, but they tend to be things out of the ordinary, and hardly worth the effort of imitating. Cigarette stubs are an example most of us have heard of ... yes – I have seen it often! Nevertheless, it will take a lot before I am tempted to tie an imitation of a dog-end.

Bass in particular eat just about anything that moves. They are in fact very fond of small

Fig. 12.14: Swimming mouse.

snakes. These are catered for in the plastic lure industry, but not by flies. I have caught one trout that had a small snake in it, but that is all! What I have found in trout from time to time is small mice. If trout spot a mouse crossing a stream, they would appear not to miss the chance. Perhaps Murray's Mouse, which is intended for bass, may prove to be a good trout fly? Once again, it is river trout that eat the mice: it would seem that river trout are much more voracious than their still-water brethren.

Finally, I have on two occasions caught river trout with lizards in them. In both cases the lizards were the type with the blue tummies. I am sure that yellowfish also take lizards. Bass will take lizards, frogs, small snakes and small birds.

COMMON ESTUARY FOOD FORMS – IMITATION AND METHOD FOR FLY-FISHING

Table 12.1 Small fry

When	Common name of fry copied	Scientific name of fry	Some imitative flies in order of preference	Size	Method (based on habits)	Where
All year	Estuarine round-herring (resident in estuaries) *Note:* Also occurs in South Africa – freshwater at Groenvlei (Wilderness) and Lake Sibaya	*Gilchristella aestuarius*	Glass Minnow African Tangler Mono Fly Clouser's Deep Minnow Irish Blonde	2 1/0 1/0 1 1	Mid-water slow 'troll' retrieve	All estuaries East
All year	Halfbeaks	*Hemiramphus* sp. *Hyporhamphus* sp.	Natal Halfbeak Tom Lentz's Needlefish Skipping poopers	1/0 1/0 2/0	Surface fast retrieve	East coast
All year	Gars	*Strongylura leiurus*	Tom Lentz's Needlefish Lefty's Deceiver in Green	5/0 5/0	All depths (a) 'Holding shoal' retrieve (b) Fast jerky retrieve	All
Spring and summer	Young mullet	*Liza* spp. *Mugil* spp.	Lefty's Deceiver Platinum Blonde Clouser's Deep Minnow	2/0 3/0 2/0	Surface and just sub-surface, slow retrieve	All coasts
Winter/ spring	Glassnose	*Liza* spp. *vitrirostris*	Argentine Blonde Blue Clouser's Minnow Lefty's Deceiver *In muddy water:* Honey Blonde	2, 1 2 2, 4 2	Midwater slow troll retrieve	East coast
All year	Moonfish (kitefish)	*Monodactylus falciformis*	Moonfly	2/0	Middle to bottom Holding retrieve	East coast

When	Common name of fry copied	Scientific name of fry	Some imitative flies in order of preference	Size	Method (based on habits)	Where
Winter	Slimeys (soapies)	*Leiognathus equulus* and *Gazza minuta*	Integration Blonde Moonfly Lefty's Deceiver	2, 1/0 2/0 2/0	(a) Bottom lead core figure-of-8 retrieve (b) Midwater slow	Eastern Cape northward
All year	Silversides	*Atherinomorus lacunosus* *Atherina breviceps*	Blue Silverside Irish Blonde Chartreuse Clouser's Deep Minnow Grey Clouser's Deep Minnow Glass Minnow *At dusk:* Black Lure	1, 2 2 1 1 2 2	Surface slow or strip fishy retrieve (dusk to dark)	Eastern Cape northward
Late spring Summer	Slender glassy	*Ambassis natalensis*	African Tangler Mono Fly Integration Blonde	1, 2 1 2	Surface or midwater figure-of-8 retrieve	East coast of southern Africa
All year	Banded glassy	*Ambassis productus*	Mono Fly Integration Blonde	1 2	Midwater figure-of-8 retrieve	East coast
All year	Pursemouths	(a) *Gerres filamentosus* (b) *G. acinaces*	(a) Argentine Blonde (b) Integration Blonde	1/0 1/0	Bottom slow troll retrieve occasional jerk	East coast
Winter	Razorbelly (kelee shad)	*Hilsa kelee*	Lefty's Deceiver White Platinum Blonde	2 1	Midwater troll retrieve	Eastern Cape north to Red Sea
All year	Gobies	*Psammogobius* sp.	Muddler Minnow Boobys	1 2	Bottom short dashes Booby retrieve	Estuaries

Table 12.2 Crustacea/Insects

When	Common name	Scientific name	Flies in order of preference	Size	Method	Where
All year	Shrimps and prawns	Various	Crazy Charly Snapping Shrimp Pink Shrimp *Note:* Size 12 for Grunter Boobys	6, 4 6,4 6 4	Bottom slow retrieve occasional twitch Booby retrieve	All coasts
All year	Crabs	Various	Walker's Killer Crab Mrs Simpson	2/0 2/0	Bottom long slow pulls with 20 seconds rest between	All coasts

When	Common name	Scientific name	Flies in order of preference	Size	Method	Where
All year	Peeler crab Note: Probably the most popular food of large fishes in estuaries	Various	Moonfly tied at 90° on back weighted hook Walker's Killer Crab	4/0 2/0-	Bottom long slow pulls with 20 seconds rest between	All coasts
All year	Insects	Various	*Dry fly* Greenwell's Glory Soldier Palmer Pink *Wet fly* Greenwell's Glory	12 10 10	Leave at rest on surface Just sub-surface figure-of-8 retrieve	All coasts

CHAPTER 13

WINNING FLY PATTERNS

'...I know a Trout taken with a Flie of your own tying will please you better than twenty with one of mine.'

Charles Cotton. *The Complete Angler Part II*, 1676

This chapter lists those flies considered to be the most useful for Africa. Many are African designs, while some are overseas patterns which may or may not have been changed locally. Compiling such a chapter is not easy and the flies listed here have, of necessity, been selected quite ruthlessly. I have some 600 fly patterns listed for Africa of which about 300 have been designed on this continent. All these hundreds of flies work, but not consistently enough to have been included in this chapter. The flies listed here are all top performing patterns and offer the beginner a short

cut to sifting through the hundreds of available patterns. For the expert there are detailed dressings with notes on variations and on substitutions of rare materials. Details on how to use the flies – the correct retrieves and fly lines – are given; and the original purpose of the fly is indicated.

All the flies listed in this chapter are illustrated on the colour plates. However, throughout this book a wide choice of flies is given to support techniques discussed or to imitate specific food forms. Many of these flies are not covered in this chapter, but most are illustrated on the

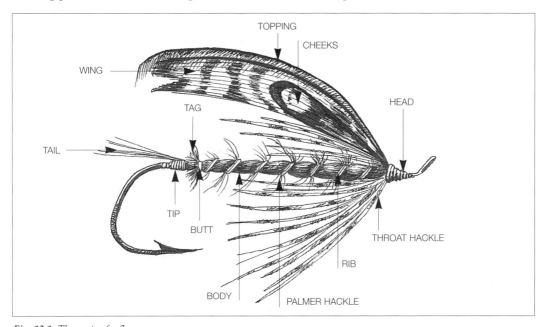

Fig. 13.1: The parts of a fly.

Examples of fly tying materials. The collecting of these can become a hobby in its own right.

colour plates and one can check the correctness of purchased patterns, or even attempt to tie them from the plates.

The design of new flies can only be successfully accomplished if it is based on a basic knowledge of appropriate food forms, the sens-

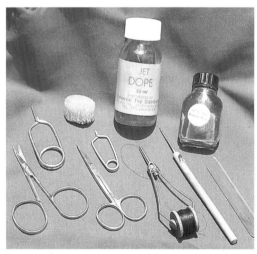

Basic fly-tying equipment. Back, left to right: hard wax, cellulose varnish, liquid wax. Centre: hackle pliers. Front: scissors (2), bobbin holder with silk, needle, sharpening stone.

es of the fish, and a thorough appreciation of available fly dressing materials. All this can be learnt, and many accomplished anglers design flies which are superb fish catchers. Many designs never come to light, but now and then someone like Lionel Walker comes along and gives us a fly which is used to good effect at some time or another by every fly-fisherman in Africa. Yours may just be the next one!

Regretfully, there is not enough space in this book to give instructions or a comprehensive background to fly tying. Nevertheless, such knowledge is easily acquired and perhaps no better source exists than the books by John Veniard. A good beginner's course is a first class way to get going. Fly tying is not a difficult skill to acquire, and anyone can do it!

ADAMS

Plate 8   TROUT

An excellent dry fly for running water. Designed to imitate sedges, it is often used to imitate mayflies in Africa.

Hook: 14, 16, up-eye.
Silk: White.
Tail: Grizzle and brown hackle fibres tied short.
Body: Dubbed muskrat.
Hackle: Medium-brown and grizzly cock mixed.
Wings: Grizzle hackle points tied spent for sedge, up for mayflies.

ADOLF

Plate 4   TROUT, YELLOWFISH

This is a superb general pattern invented by the late Don Lort of Johannesburg.

Hook: 10 to 12, round bend, down-eye.
Silk: Black.
Tail: Tuft of hot orange rayon floss, as long as the hook bend is wide.
Butt: Red silk.
Body: Dubbed black seal's fur, ribbed with thickish oval silver tinsel (optionally, the body may be pre-leaded).
Hackle: Hot orange hen, length as body.

This fly should be fished deep in still water, just

off the bottom, and may be retrieved in slow pulls as in a nymph retrieve, or alternatively may be strip retrieved to imitate a small fish. A particularly good fly in winter or cold conditions. Casting upstream and dead drifting is the method for rivers.

AFRICAN TANGLER

Plate 3 SALTWATER

This fly is named in honour of Charles Norman's wonderful book *African Angler*, but particularly to honour Charles himself who has done so much for our sport in Africa.

This fly imitates the estuarine roundherring, an important food fish in African estuaries. It also a useful imitator of the Cape silverside and the slender glassy.

Hook: Sizes 4 to 3/0, stainless straight eye. Favourite size is 1/0.
Tail: Twenty strands of lime Krystal Flash. Before tying in, paint the individual fibre tips black with a Pantone pen. Fibre length as hook.
Body: Under the body, tie in and glue a 10 mm length of pipe cleaner. While the glue is wet, slide over a length of silver Mylar tubing, flatten this side to side, and tie down at the ends. Front end, use fluorescent red thread; back end, use black thread.
Wing: White 'Fishair', or white polar bear hair. Tie the wing with approximately 30 fibres of sufficient length for them to cover the tail as well. From a sheet of thickish, bright silver Mylar, cut two cheeks at the base of the wing on either side.
Head: Head of white silk, built up large with eyes painted on, and Pantoned green on top.

Use an intermediate fly line in estuaries; cast across eddies, backwaters and slow-moving scummed water. The retrieve should be slowish long pulls with frequent rests.

ANT, BLACK

Plate 8 TROUT, YELLOWFISH

A dry fly. Ant hatches in Africa are usually much more dense than European ones, and there are many more species of ants, some of which are quite large.

Hook: Size 14 or 16, up-eye.
Body: Waxed black tying silk shaped as an ant body, and varnished with 'Cellire' (a black varnish).
Hackle: Black cock.
Wing: Pale blue dun cock hackle tips, sloping backwards.

Versions of this fly in dark red (size 14) and in brown (size 10) are useful in Africa. Ant imitations should be fished in the surface film (not on it), and twitched occasionally for best results.

BEAMS' WOOLLY WORM

Plate 4 TROUT, YELLOWFISH

All the versions of this fly are very good, some very good indeed! The Peacock version is exceptional, and the green-butted modern modification is a star performer. The orange version comes into its own in coloured water; the brown works very well in ultra-clear water. This range of flies was designed by the late John Beams and is among the best general imitator patterns.

Peacock Woolly Worm

Hook: Size 8 to 12, down-eye, bronze round bend.
Tail: Fibres taken from one half of a black cock hackle.
Body: Green peacock herl wound over black silk while the silk is tacky. Taper slightly. Tie the butt with one turn of hot orange chenille. The tendency today is to tie the butt from one turn of fluorescent red wool. The body hackle is tied in a sparse open-wound palmer using a black cock hackle. There should be no more than two and a half turns, certainly never more than three. Tied from the tail all the way to the head. Rib the body with oval or round silver tinsel.

Orange Beams' Woolly Worm

In this variation, the body is dubbed orange seal's fur with palmered body hackle and tail of natural ginger cock hackle.

Brown Beams' Woolly Worm

This one has a body dubbed with brown seal's fur, and with a ginger palmered body hackle.

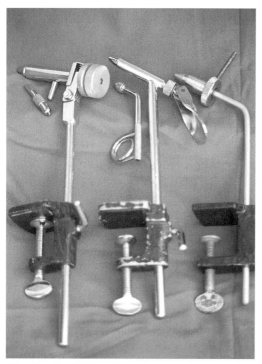

Fly-tying vices by Veniard, purchased in 1962 and still doing an excellent job. Note the pin vice insert for midge tying and the hand-held vice for bankside tying.

Green Butt Beams' Peacock Woolly Worm

A recent modified version of the Peacock Woolly Worm, using a fluorescent signal green Antron butt in place of the usual red.

All the Beams' Woolly Worms are best fished slow and deep.

BLACK AND PEACOCK SPIDER

Plate 6   TROUT

A snail imitation.

Hook: Size 10 to 14, down-eye. Although not standard, the fly is very usefully tied on a 2X short shank hook.
Body: Bronze Peacock herl, tied ball shape.
Hackle: Large soft black hen (i.e. long-fibred). Many commercial dressings use cock hackle, which is incorrect, and nowhere near as effective as hen hackle.

Fish this fly in still water extremely slowly on a floating line with well-sunk leader. Typically, a 25 metre retrieve should take at least ten min-

utes. In rivers allow this fly to tumble down the current using a slow sinking fly line and a dead drift.

BLACK GNAT

Plate 6   TROUT, YELLOWFISH, MUDFISH

A dry fly. A very useful imitation of many small dipterids.

Hook: Size 14 to 18, up-eye.
Tail: Three wisps of stiff black cock hackle.
Body: Brown turkey tail feather herl.
Wing: Pale starling.
Hackle: Black cock.

The Black Gnat is also popular tied as a traditional wet fly.

BLACK PHANTOM

Plate 5   YELLOWFISH, TROUT, BASS

A general imitator of diving beetles and dragonfly nymphs.

Hook: Size 8 to 12, round bend, bronze.
Silk: Black.
Tail: Squirrel tail dyed black.
Body: Black chenille.
Wings: Twelve dyed black partridge hackles, laid in three sets of two on each side (four feathers in three overlapping sets, twelve in all).

Most commercial ties have only six feathers (sometimes even fewer), and they do not work as well as the properly tied pattern. The original New Zealand pattern called for six pairs of 'pukeko' feathers. Veniard suggested dark purple dyed heron as a substitute.
Note: Examples of this fly with jungle cock cheeks are known.

The fly should be fished upstream with a slow sinking line. The retrieve is a slow steady pull with occasional fast 10 cm pulls. It is an exceptionally good fly for yellowfish and smallmouth bass.

BLONDE

Plates 2 and 3   SALTWATER

These are possibly the most popular flies for fishing estuaries and surf around Africa.

The generic Blonde dressing

Hook: Size 4 to 5/0 Cadmium plate standard length. Stainless steel hooks are, of course, quite acceptable.
Tail: Approximately twice the shank length of bucktail, tied in at the bend of the hook.
Body: Silver tinsel.
Wing: Sufficient length of bucktail to reach the end of the tail fibres from the head, tied in just behind the hook eye. Wing should be set at 45 degrees.
Head: Clear varnished-over built-up tying silk. Paint on eyes as big as possible.

Strawberry Blonde: Tail of orange, wing of red.
Platinum Blonde: All white.
Honey Blonde: All yellow.
Black Blonde: All black.
Pink Blonde: All pink.
Integration Blonde: Tail of white, wing of black.
Argentine Blonde: Tail of white, wing of medium blue.
Irish Blonde: Tail of white, wing of green.
Violet Blonde: All violet.
Red-head Blonde: All hot orange.
Note: Use a tying silk of the same colour as the tail.

Using the Blondes

Attractors
Strawberry Blonde: Shallow water.
Honey Blonde: Murky water.
Black Blond: Silhouette fly for dusk and dawn fishing.
Violet Blonde: Deep clear water.
Red-head Blonde: Clear water over dark bottom.

These attractor Blondes should be fished with a fast troll retrieve.

Imitators
Platinum Blonde: All small estuary fish.
Integration Blonde: Indian Ocean estuary fry.
Argentine Blonde: General imitator.
Pink Blonde: Considered a shrimp and prawn imitator.
Irish Blonde: Possibly the best all-rounder for Africa.

PJ Jacobs, editor of the The Complete Fly Fisherman magazine, published in South Africa, returns a small queenfish to the surf. (Photo: courtesy PJ Jacobs)

Retrieves should be designed to match the natural movement of the food forms (refer to Chapter 12).

BLUE DUN

Plate 8   TROUT
A dry fly which imitates many grey and slatey coloured mayfly duns and small midges.

Hook: Size 14 to 18, up-eye.
Tails: Fibres from dyed medium blue dun cock hackle.
Body: Mole fur spun on lightly waxed yellow silk.
Hackle: Dyed medium blue dun cock.
Wings: Starling.

Many commercial patterns use black silk, and this is not correct. The use of yellow silk produces an olive colour when oiled for floating, which is essential to the effectiveness of this fly.

BLUE SILVERSIDES

Plate 2   SALTWATER
This saltwater fly is an imitation of the Cape silverside. These fishes have rather largish heads and an iridescent blue bar along the side, which is only visible in fresh silversides straight from the water (it quickly fades after death).

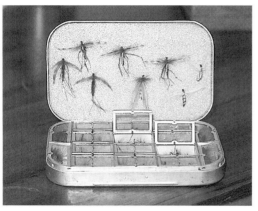

A silmalloy dry fly box by Wheatley. It is important that dry flies are not crushed. The little sprung lid compartments make it easy to organise and find flies.

Hook: Size 2 or 4, long shank, stainless steel.
Silk: Black.
Tail: Natural black squirrel tail fibres.
Body: Blue fluorescent 'multi-yarn' in three layers, each layer reversing direction.

Ribbed in open turns of blue Lurex, and then overlaid with touching turns of clear 'V'-rib.
Shoulder: One turn of fluorescent scarlet wool.
Wing: 4–6 strands of pale green Krystal Flash, with a sparse wing of chartreuse bucktail over.
Throat: White Fishair fibres.
Eyes: Chrome-plated large 'lead-eyes' tied under the hook, pupil painted black.
Head: Spun pale-coloured deer hair, clipped to shape.

Fish with a medium sinking line, and a strip (fish-imitating) retrieve, occasionally interspersed with pauses.

BOOBY

Plates 3 and 5   TROUT, BASS, SALT

The Booby is a generic pattern originally developed in the UK. It is extremely deadly since it imitates many larger food forms. The following patterns are well proven in African waters:

Yellow Booby

Floats: White plastazote.
Body: Canary yellow Antron, ribbed silver oval tinsel.
Tail: Fluorescent yellow marabou with a few strands of pearlescent Flashabou.

This one works well on cold days and after sudden temperature drops. It is also very good in very clear deep water when a good ripple is running on top.

Viva Booby

Floats: White plastazote.
Body: Black wool, ribbed silver oval tinsel.
Tail: Fluorescent signal green Antron tuft, under black marabou.

The Viva Booby is probably the most useful all-round Booby pattern. A deadly fly.

Egg Booby

Floats Orange polyethylene foam.
Body: Fluorescent salmon-pink suede chenille.
Tail: Hot orange marabou.

A fly designed by the author for the depths of winter in African high country, when big

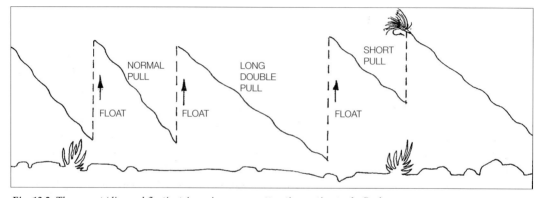

Fig. 13.2: The correct 'dive and float' retrieve gives a very attractive motion to the Booby.

Boobys with floats made from plastazote foam are much more durable.

spawning trout come onto the gravel beds. A great fly for trophy fish.

Orange Booby

Floats: White plastazote.
Body: Hot orange Antron ribbed with gold oval tinsel.
Tail: Three bunches of marabou. Top third scarlet, middle third fluorescent yellow, and bottom third scarlet.

A fly for windy summer days in normal clarity dams.

Red Booby

Floats: Crimson polyethylene foam.
Body: Crimson rayon floss ribbed fluorescent scarlet floss.
Tail: Scarlet marabou.

This fly was designed especially to catch trout feeding on bottom bloodworms. It should be fished static.

Retrieve all Boobys (except the Red Booby) by stripping a fairly fast pull of between half and one third of a metre. After each pull, count (from ten to fifteen depending on the float size). Rest while counting, and then make another strip. This strip-rest-strip-rest method allows the fly to rise up in the water between pulls, resulting in a wonderfully attractive undulating motion of the fly.

For all Booby flies, the most radical, but important, thing to remember is the length of

the leader. This must always be less than one metre, but, for best results, it should be no more than 25 cm.

BUZZER, ADULT
Plate 8   TROUT
A dry fly which imitates adult non-biting midges (buzzers).

Hook: Size should be chosen to match adults, usually in the size range 8 to 18. Dick Walker (its inventor) favoured a down-eye hook for this fly.
Silk: Pre-waxed to match the adult.
Body: Dyed feather fibre to match the adult – the following are popular: black, sepia, dark olive, light olive, orange, red, green. Some of the types, especially the black and the sepia, benefit from an extra turn of crimson-dyed feather fibre at the wing root. The thorax should be thickened by turning an extra feather fibre at this point. The black and the sepia bodies will need a white rib of stripped white cock hackle stalk.
Hackle: Cock hackle as body colour.
Wings: Two short white cock hackle points, lying back.

BUZZERS
Plate 7   TROUT, YELLOWFISH
These flies are imitations of Chironimidae (non-biting midge) pupae and are very useful in African high-altitude still waters.

Claret Buzzer
This fly was designed by Steve Stephens, and is probably the most useful African buzzer imitation of all time.

Hook: For best results, the '2X extra short-shank' bronze Mustads are preferable. A sedge hook is acceptable, or, at a pinch, an ordinary length round-bend.
Sizes: 8 to 12 in sedge style (the size 8 is useful in ordinary round-bend), sizes 4 to 8 in extra short-shank. A size 6 extra short-shank will meet most requirements.
Breathing tubes: Rear – use very short fluorescent white rayon floss. Forward – tie in two

Table 13.1 Buzzer colours

Buzzer	Hook size	Rear tubes	Forward tubes	Body colour	Lifestyle
Large Pale Olive	8	Floss	Floss	Olive brown floss, 2 turns red fluorescent floss at tail end, all overwound PVC	Diving
Small Pale Olive	12	Plastazote	Plastazote	Dark olive floss overwound PVC	Suspended
Orange Silver	10	Plastazote	Plastazote	Orange floss overwound open turns silver Lurex then PVC over	Suspended
Yellow Olive	10	Floss	Floss	Gold open wound Lurex, thin overlay olive gold floss; 2 turns red fluorescent floss at tail end, all overwound PVC	Diving
Small Black	14	Floss	Floss	Black silk varnished twice	Diving
Red	12	Floss	Plastazote	Scarlet floss overwound open turns sliver Lurex, then PVC	Horizontal swimming
Green	10	Floss	Floss	Emerald floss overwound PVC	Diving
Ribbed Sepia	8, 10	Floss	Plastazote	Black floss overwound open turns of fine flat silver Lurex; 2 turns red fluorescent floss behind thorax, then PVC over	Horizontal swimming

slim short pieces of white plastazote, each side of the head.

Body: Single layer of black silk varnished. While still tacky, wind open turns of red Lurex over. When dry, overwind a single thin layer of claret rayon floss. Overwind the floss with a single layer of thin clear PVC. Lay it 'turn next to turn' to simulate segmentation (a good technique to apply to many other nymphs). The body must be slim. *Note:* The body tie should extend to half-way round the hook bend.

Thorax: Dubbed mole's fur on waxed silk. Dark grey chenille is an acceptable substitute.

When you have tied your first Claret Buzzer, drop it into a glass of water and see how the 'glow-through' effect becomes apparent.

Table 13.1 lists the most commonly occurring colours and their tyings. It is a good idea to have a complete collection at hand, to suit most of the buzzer hatches you may come across.

Three types of Buzzer pupae swimming actions are apparent in the live creatures.

Imitations are needed to cover these. The swimming action of the artificial is controlled to some extent by the designs of the breathing tubes. In the imitations, plastazote gives a 'top up' in the surface type; floss breathing tubes are more suitable to swimming types.

CADDIS STICK

Plate 6   TROUT

All Caddis Stick flies should be weighted by tying a tightly rolled thin sliver of wine bottle lead foil along the back of the hook, prior to putting on the dressing. This will also cause the fly to swim with the hook point up. As a result, it is less inclined to hang up. These flies imitate the sedge larva in its case as it moves about the bottom.

Hook: Size 8 or 10, down-eye. In South Africa, a long shank 12 is popular.

Silk: Black.

Tail: Tuft of fluorescent signal-green Antron.

Body: Slimly dubbed dark olive seal's fur, ribbed fine copper wire.

Hackle: One turn of black cock hackle, fibres as long as body, tied sloping back.
Head: Varnished black.

Fish the Caddis Sticks deep on a long leader with a fine tippet (3X to 5X), on a floating line. Retrieve in short jerks with an occasional long slow pull. Allow the fly to sink well down before retrieving. It is important that the fly is fished right on the bottom.

CARP FRY

Plate 7	TROUT, BASS, YELLOWFISH, KURPER, CARP

A wet lure fly imitation of small carp fry.

Hook: Size 6 to 10, long shank, straight eye, bronze.
Silk: Black.
Body: Coppery-orange rayon floss ribbed with silver wire. The body should taper gently. The shoulder is two turns of red fluorescent wool.
Hackle: False throat hackle of hot orange cock.
Wing: Grey squirrel tail. Optionally, jungle cock cheeks can be added.

Retrieve on a slow-sink line in jerky 10 cm pulls with occasional long fast pulls. It also performs well if retrieved very slowly on a floating line, i.e. 10 minutes for a 25 metre retrieve.

CHARCOAL NYMPH

Plate 6	TROUT

One of the author's flies for general imitation of dark mayfly nymphs.

Hook: Size 10 or 12, down-eye, round-bend.
Silk: Black.
Tails: Black cock hackle fibres.
Body: Charcoal Antron wool wound to a slight taper, and ribbed with fine copper wire. At the thorax end of the body, wind in three turns of magenta fluorescent DRF floss.
Thorax: Black seal's fur, well picked out.
Wing case: Fibres from the tail feathers of a black cock.
Head: Black silk varnished with clear Cellire.

Use a floating line, allow the nymph to sink,

Fantastic fly tying by Murray Peddar. This rendering of the Charcoal Nymph is considerably more realistic than the standard version, but is also more difficult to tie. It is unlikely to ever appear in packets in shops, but the home tier can make himself as many as he wants.

Big brown trout often cruise the shallows at dusk seeking surface-bound moths.

and fish it deep (it helps to weight it to achieve this). Retrieve very slowly.

CHICKEN

Plate 8	TROUT, SALMON, BASS

A dry fly, originally called the Ghost Swift Moth. It works well on both running and still water.

Hook: Size 8, long-shank, down-eye.
Silk: White.
Body: Cream ostrich herl tied fat. Palmer the body with a stiff fibre cream cock hackle.
Hackle: One cream and one pale ginger hackle behind.
Wing: Large bunch of swan secondary fibres tied flat. (Goose primary fibres will also do as a substitute.)

This fly can be retrieved along the surface at a fair pace to cause a fish-attracting wake, or just left to lie. A great dusk fly for brown trout, landlocked salmon and bass.

CLOUSER'S DEEP MINNOW

Plate 3   SALTWATER

A modern saltwater fly which is already rated by many as the greatest saltwater fly ever invented. Its success is based on the sparse dressing used.

Hook: Size 1 or 2, stainless Mustad 34007 or pre-sharpened cadmium plated.
Silk: Black, or white.
Body: None.
Eyes: Bath chain chrome eyes tied 5 mm back from hook eye.
Wing: Tied in two parts. First, use a maximum of 20 strands of white bucktail. Lay these over the eyes, and continue the tying-down to 5 mm behind the eyes. Second, turn the hook over in the vice, and (in front of the chain eyes only) tie in 15 strands of pearlescent 'Krystal Flash' (or a colour to suit the bucktail wing) as if it were a throat hackle (in this case an upside-down wing). Turn the hook back to the normal upright position, and again tying only in front of the chain eyes; tie in a top wing of 15–20 strands of bucktail. Colour choice here is either chartreuse (try fluorescent chartreuse bucktail

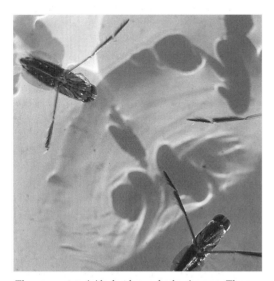

These are not corixids, but brown backswimmers. These are easily simulated with upside-down ties of the Silver Corixid.

... it's deadly), rust-brown, or grey. Varnish the head. I have found a blue version to be quite useful for reef fishing. The yellow and red (as the Micky Finn) version is very good in dirty water conditions.

A weighted version of Clouser's Deep Minnow is also given, and is equally good as the above – more so in some applications. The weight is provided by 'lead-eyes'. The lead eyes cause the fly to swim upside-down, and consequently it must also be dressed upside-down, i.e. with the wing under the hook. There is no throat hackle in this version.

Retrieval of this fly should be a strip retrieve – vary the speed.

COCH-Y-BONDDU

Plate 8   TROUT

A very famous fly which has withstood the test of time all around the world.

Hook: Size 12 or 14, up-eye.
Tag: Flat gold tinsel (modern dressings often use gold wire).
Body: Two or three strands of twisted coppery peacock herl.
Hackle: Coch-y-Bonddu cock hackle.

Dry or wet fly. Fish the wet fly version on still water in the lee shore at the edge of the ripple, especially when the grass beetles are about. Use a floating line and a slow retrieve. The dry fly is a great terrestrial insect imitator.

CORIXID, SILVER

Plate 6   TROUT

Imitations of lesser water boatmen are very useful in African fly fishing.

Hook: Size 12 or 14, down-eye.
Silk: Brown.
Tag: Silver Lurex.
Body: Tie the body of white floss. Lay silver/white pre-wetted Raffine along the underside of the body. Tie it in stretched and while still wet.
Wing case: Use thick dyed brown fibres from the primary feather of the goose. Leave one

fibre sticking out on each side. Tie these two fibres down at the head so that they point back and up, to simulate the paddles.
Head: Varnish the insecty head.

Corixid imitations work best if fished 'sink and draw'.

CORIXID, OLIVE

Plate 6   TROUT

This is one of the author's patterns designed to imitate the small winter season olive corixids. It is most effective in the early morning in winter.

Hook: Size 14, down-eye (on which the fly is tied as if size 18).
Silk: Olive.
Body: Olive ostrich herl with a body-length wing case of olive-dyed swan primary fibres. Goose is the correct substitute, although a poor one.
Paddles: Olive-dyed swan primary, one fibre the length of the body on either side.

Fish this fly slowly 'sink and draw' style, close in, using a floating line. Cast along the bank where trout are feeding on the comatose corixids.

DADDY-LONG-LEGS

Plate 7   TROUT

Take particular care to dress this dry fly with all the legs trailing backwards.

Hook: Size 10, long-shank round-bend, down-eye.
Silk: Brown.
Body: Swan secondary (or goose primary) fibre dyed a muddy cork colour, tied in, twisted ropewise and wound over a whipped and varnished hook shank. Varnish should be tacky.
Legs: Cock pheasant centre tail fibres, each knotted twice and tied trailing back.
Hackle: Ginger cree, or ginger cock hackle. Long in fibre.
Wings: Cree or cuckoo, cock hackle points tied sloping back.

A useful substitute for the body is brown ostrich herl. Alternatively, try four fibres from a natural peacock primary. A version with a dark

Daddy-long-legs.

grey body and a dark blue dun hackle is also useful in Africa.

This fly should be well proofed with floatant, and allowed to dry properly. Cast out and simply leave it to lie without movement.

DAHLBERG DIVER

Plate 1   BASS, SALT

The diving collar behind the head is the action maker, and this should be carefully trimmed to the correct shape.

Hook: Stinger bug hook, sizes 8 through 5/0. Sizes 2 and 4 are most useful for bass, and size 1/0 for estuary. For estuary work a medium wire cadmium-plated hook is preferred. Heavy stainless steel hooks spoil the action. A weed guard is useful for bassing, but not necessary for the salt.
Silk: Black.
Tail: Tied one third forward from the hook bend as follows: Inside, a substantial bunch of turkey marabou mixed with a few strands of matching Krystal Flash. On each outer flank, a pair of selected well-marked grizzle spade hackles, tied bright side outwards.

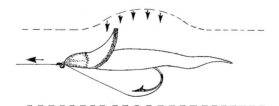

Fig. 13.3: *The Dahlberg Diver. The deer hair collar forces the water upward as the fly moves forward through the water. This in turn pushes the fly down in the water thus causing it to dive.*

Head: The head is spun deer hair (natural or dyed). A common error is to make the collar too thin. The 'deerhair spinning' should always be glued to the shank 'as you go' in this pattern. Simply put one spot of fresh varnish on the hook shank immediately prior to each spinning. The head, tied in this way, will stand a lot of punishment from casting, and from fish.

The colour patterns most popularly used are:

Head	Tail
(a) Natural deer hair	White marabou, natural grizzle, silver flash.
(b) Yellow deer hair	As above but yellow dyed marabou, and yellow dyed grizzle, pearl flash.
(c) Black deer hair	Black marabou, natural grizzle, silver flash

Use a floating line and a tippet of around 4 kg. The rod should always be held low with this fly to ensure proper diving action. The best retrieve is to twitch it back. Also use occasional long pulls with rests in between. The fly returns to the surface during these 'rests', and it is during this upward movement that it is most often taken. Now and then, between the usual retrieve action, let it rest motionless on the surface for a minute or so.

DAMSEL, RED-EYED

Plate 6   TROUT, YELLOWFISH, BASS

This fly is possibly the best of many damselfly nymph imitations originating in KwaZulu-Natal.

Hook: Size 8 to 16, long-shank nymph hook or standard round bend (size 12 is most useful).
Silk: I use black, but it is not important.
Tail: Marabou fluff to match body colour (ends of body strands).
Body: Olive-green or brown, or primrose yellow marabou.
Eyes: Red Tuff chenille.

Flashabou or Krystal Flash is often added to body and/or tail by commercial tiers.

Once the eyes are tied on, lead wire should be wrapped behind the eyes and over the thorax area. The marabou body wrap is done by first tying the points in at the tail, and then wrapping the marabou fibres around the silk to form a 'body' rope. The silk can also be 'dubbed' with marabou strands for the thorax and head wind. The best effect for legs and tail flash is by using Krystal Flash of matching colour, i.e. copper with brown, dark green with olive, and yellow with primrose.

Fish this fly near the bottom and around weedbeds. I use a floating line and let the leaded fly sink. The retrieve is slow pulls with occasional fast 10 cm strip-ins. A killing pattern!

DIGGER'S RED

Plate 4   TROUT

A South African wet fly bloodworm imitation by Malcolm Meintjes.

Hook: Size 8 to 12, long shank.
Tail: Red marabou.
Body: Streamlined body of brown dubbing mixed with fluorescent red yarn.
Rib: Pearl flashabou.
Head: Scarlet seal's fur.

Needs to be fished very slowly right on the bottom for best results.

DON'S DRAGON

Plate 7   TROUT, BASS

A useful imitator of smaller dragonfly nymphs.

Hook: Size 4 to 12 (depending on the species), down-eye.
Silk: Black.
Tail: A few fibres of Krystal Flash, not more than 3 mm long.
Body: Do the legs and the eyes first! The body shape of the original nymph is achieved by winding the dubbed silk over a ready-laid-down shape using either wool or lead wire. The pre-laid body is then overwound with the dubbing mixture.
Eyes: Use a figure-of-eight binding to tie in a short piece of suede (tuff) chenille across the hook (at right angles and on top) where the eyes should be.
Legs: Then, at the waist, tie in a few fibres of Krystal Flash, also at right angles to, and on top of, the hook – this will simulate the legs.

When the dubbing has been wound on, the eyes cut back to within 2 mm of the head, and the legs trimmed to 4 mm length, then the fly is complete.

Don Lort, this fly's inventor, was a master of using the coffee grinder to blend dubbings. All his dragons were in fact a mixture of colours, since he quite rightly believed that all insects were not accurately represented by a single colour. The resulting blends were either grey (his favourite), olive, or sepia brown. He incorporated five per cent of fluorescent wool, and usually blended four or five different colours to achieve the required result. He used drab browns, greys and greens with just a touch of bright blue and orange. The correct Krystal Flash was yellow for green nymphs, olive for grey nymphs, and 'root beer' for brown nymphs.

These nymphs were mostly tied at size 10. He would fish them right on the bottom using a Hi-D line and retrieving in very slow pulls.

DUCKWORTH'S DARGLE DELIGHT

Plate 8 TROUT, BASS, YELLOWFISH
This dry fly is better known by its abbreviated name, the 'DDD'. It was originally designed to imitate beetles.

Hook: Originally size 12 to 14 dry fly. Now often seen in 6 to 12, down-eye.
Silk: Danville's black or brown.
Tail: Bunch of deer hair (the original patterns used klipspringer hair for tail and body).
Body: Deer hair spun and trimmed to shape, tapering back.
Hackle: Brown cock.

Some commercial tiers incorporate Flashabou ... a mistake in my opinion. Dr Tom Sutcliffe invented this fly and he advocates an untidy tie for best results.

This fly floats well in all conditions and is a good general buggy imitation. The best all-round size is a 12. Cast out and twitch occasionally. There is no need to ever grease the leader with this fly ... a great advantage. A superb dry fly! I know of many anglers who achieve great results fishing this fly on a fast sinking line near the bottom in running water where it is most likely taken as a drowned terrestrial or as a snail.

EMERGING NYMPH

Plate 4 TROUT
An old South African pattern from the 1950s.

Hook: Size 12 to 8, down-eye.
Tail: Three fibres of cock pheasant centre tail.
Body: Bronze peacock herl, ribbed flat gold tinsel.
Wing: Cock coch-y-bonddu hackle fibres, bunched and standing up vertically.
Wing cases: Magpie tail slips sheen side outermost, tied around the wing roots and over the thorax (substitute black bantam tail).
Thorax: Bronze peacock.
Throat hackle: Brown partridge tied spent.
Hackle: Hen cinnamon and black, tied sparse.

This fly should be fished on a floating line just in or slightly below the surface film.

CLIFF HENRY'S FLOATING SNAIL

Plate 6 TROUT
Hook: Size 12 or 14, down-eye, wide-gape bronze (or better is a 'Stinger' style hook as used in bass poppers).
Silk: Black.
Body: Split cork, shaped almost as a flat-bottomed pear, is epoxied to the hook with the flat end of the cork to the eye. I like to paint the cork grey-olive prior to tying in the herls. The durability is improved if the herl is also glued down as you go. Cover the cork by winding stripped peacock herl almost to the flattened top. The last two turns are bronze peacock herl.
Note: Ideally the flat end of the cork should float on the surface with the body hanging below. Judicious use of lead wire (very little) as a tag can achieve this result.

Cast out with a floating line, and retrieve exceedingly slowly (half hour each cast).

FUZZY WUZZY

Plate 4 TROUT
A lure fly from New Zealand which works well as an attractor pattern.

Hook: Size 2 to 10 Limerick (size 8 for Africa). *Note:* Any long shank hook will do if you cannot find the Limerick.
Silk: Black.
Tail: Black dyed squirrel.
Body: Chenille, either black, red, yellow, green, or orange. Orange is the usual tie for Africa.
Hackle: Both the hackles are black hen, one tied at the head, the other half way down the body. Use long-fibred hen hackles.

For dusk fishing, retrieve on a floating line with very slow pulls. At other times scratch the bottom with a fast-sink line and medium to slow pulls.

GIANT SHIMMY LEECH

Plate 1   BASS

This all-black lure fly is so realistic that at first sight it looks as though it might bite the fish, rather than the other way around. This is a fly rodder's substitute for the ubiquitous bass worm.

A key feature with this lure fly is the large eyes. Many tie in some lead foil along the back of the hook; it then swims upside-down, and hangs up far less.

Tied on a stainless hook, the Great Shimmy Leech is a great estuary fly.

Hook: Size 1/0 through 5/0 Salmon Iron. Preferred size is 2/0. The hook should be weed guarded.
Silk: Black.
Tail: Rabbit fur zonker strip, i.e. a cut strip of skin (with the black fur on) approximately 3 mm wide and 9–10 cm long. This is tied in at the top of the hook bend in such a way as to leave sufficient zonker strip protruding forward for the finishing tie-in at the head, which is done last.
Body: This is somewhat unconventional, but tied in a manner of interest to any fly designer. Start at the tail end, and tie on each side of the hook an equal bunch of black turkey marabou. Move forward along the hook shank and repeat this operation (i.e. tie in two more marabou bunches each time). Four lots of these tyings will be ample to bring you within 10–12 mm of the

hook eye. The body thus formed will fluff out nicely. Each of the tyings of marabou should be covered at the root with black chenille. This builds a substantial and very mobile body.
Head: Bring the previously tied in zonker strip tightly over the back, and tie in on top of the head. Wind tying silk over this head, leaving 4–5 mm of black body chenille still exposed behind the head. To each side of the chenille part of the head, epoxy a large plastic moving-pupil doll's eye.

A very slow figure-of-eight retrieve using a fast-sink line and a relatively short 1,5 metre leader is the correct method for bottom-dwelling bass. In estuaries, switch to a lead-core line and a three metre leader, and change to a medium-pace retrieve. Most bites will be felt as two soft taps which must be struck immediately.

GLASS MINNOW

Plate 3   SALTWATER

For some fly-fishermen it is hard to believe that some of the smaller saltwater flies are the really deadly ones. This fly is an example of the truth of this theory.

Hook: Size 6, or 8, straight eye, stainless steel, long shank.
Silk: Green.
Tail: None.
Body: None.
Wing: Bright green buckTail: over a few strands of pale green Krystal Flash, over white bucktail. *Note:* The dressing should be sparse. Pre-glue the bucktail fibre butts prior to tying in whilst still wet or tacky.
Head: Green silk varnished with lime-green cellulose varnish. A thin collar of red floss is tied behind the head. Eyes are painted black pupil on yellow.

Chartreuse Glass Minnow

Hook: Size 4 to 8, straight eye, stainless steel longshank.
Silk: Green.
Tail: None.
Body: None.

Wing: Fluorescent chartreuse bucktail, over a few strands of chartreuse Krystal Flash, over white bucktail. The fly works just as well tied with Fishair. Ideally, the top wing layer should stand up at an angle of 30 degrees or more for best action.

Head: Wind fluorescent signal green floss over the head silk and varnish clear. A thin collar of fluorescent scarlet rayon floss is tied behind the head. Eyes are dark green pupils on yellow.

The Chartreuse Glass Minnow is a truly superb surf fly!

Brown Glass Minnow

Hook: Size 4, straight eye, stainless steel, long-shank.

Silk: Brown.

Tail: None.

Body: None.

Wing: Brown bucktail over pale purple Krystal Flash, over white bucktail.

Head: Brown silk varnished clear with a thin fluorescent red rayon floss collar. Eyes are black pupils on pale violet.

Best results are achieved using sinking or fast-sinking lines, and a fast strip retrieve. This is an excellent fly for the Kenyan, Tanzanian and north Mozambique surf.

GODDARD AND HENRY'S SEDGE

Plate 8   TROUT, BASS

This is a very good dry fly, especially in the evenings when larger sedges hatch in profusion. It is more usually known as the G and H Sedge.

The pattern can be varied to suit the differing colours of the many sedge species, by changing the hackle and the colour of the underbody dubbing fur.

Hook: Size 8 or 10, fine wire, down-eye.

Silk: Green.

Body: Spun deer hair. This is then trimmed and clipped to a sedge wing shape – this shape is important, and usually badly rendered in commercial ties; it should be a slim tapering tent shape.

Underbody: A typical version would use dark green seal's fur. Another useful version is made-up from a mixture of amber and rust seal's fur. Dub the fur on to tying silk previously tied in at the tail end of the body. Stretch the dubbed silk under the body and tie-in at the head.

Hackle: Two rusty dun cock hackles with stripped stems. Tie them in so that the stem ends are left protruding to form the antennae. Wind-in three turns of hackle, tie-off and varnish the head.

More colour versions for use in Africa are pale dun hackle and ginger underbody, and ginger hackle and chestnut underbody.

GOLD-RIBBED HARE'S EAR

Plate 6   TROUT

One of the best mayfly nymph imitating flies ever designed. It is a pattern with its roots in antiquity. The version given here is the American pattern, the one which is most effective in Africa.

Hook: Size 12, long shank, bronze. Versions tied on short-shank hooks are useful in African streams.

Silk: Yellow.

Tail: Black cock hackle fibres.

Body and thorax: Fur from a hare's mask dubbed on yellow silk. The body is ribbed with fine gold wire. Pick out the thorax with a dubbing needle. For weighted versions a flat gold tinsel rib is preferred.

Wing case: Black cock hackle fibres.

Head: Black varnish.

This nymph can be usefully tied with a brass bead head for use in streams. Ensure the bead is made of brass and not gold-plated plastic (the latter provides no weighting advantage).

Fish the GRHE on either a floating or slow-sinking line. My preference is for the floater, which gives me better control. In still water, use a slow retrieve of short 2,5–5 cm sharp pulls with three or four seconds' rest between each pull.

In running water, trout will take it just below the surface during a rise. If no rise is obvious try casting upstream with a slow-sinking line.

GREEN CRAZY CHARLEY

Plate 3   SALTWATER

An imitative saltwater pattern which is effective in both surf and estuary.

Hook: Size 6 or 8 stainless steel.
Silk: Green.
Tail: Optional: 8 short strands of chartreuse Krystal Flash.
Body: Fluorescent lime green rayon floss, overwound with tight turns of pale green 7 kg monofilament or Swannundaze ('V' rib).
Wing: Tied under the fly 'bonefish style' at an angle to cover the hook point. Chartreuse bucktail (fluorescent chartreuse is favoured by some). I like to add, equidistant along the wing, three wide black stripes using a black waterproof Pantone pen.

Add optional lead eyes on top of the hook, and this fly becomes the Green Deep Water Charley, painted yellow with black pupils. This an exceptionally good fly fished deep and slow and imitates shrimp and especially prawns very well indeed.

GREENWELL'S GLORY

Plate 8   TROUT

A dry or wet fly. The best known dry fly in the world!

GEM Skues wingless variation

Hook: Size 14, up-eye.
Tail: Whisks of greenish-yellow olive cock.
Body: Well waxed yellow silk, rib of fine gold wire.
Hackle: Furnace cock, with medium blue dun behind.

In southern Africa, smaller flies in sizes 16, 18, and 20 are very useful. I prefer these tiny flies without a rib.

GREY DUSTER

Plate 8   TROUT

A dry fly and a superb general imitator of surface insects.

Hook: Size 12 or 14, up-eye.

Silk: Brown.
Body: Dubbed light rabbit fur, lightly blended with blue dun rabbit underfur.
Hackle: Badger cock well marked with a black centre and white (not cream) list.
Tail whisks: Badger cock hackle.

Tied on a size 20 hook, this fly becomes a very useful caenis imitation.

HAMILL'S KILLER

Plate 5   TROUT, BASS, BARBEL,
                                              SALTWATER

Hamill's Killer is one of the best New Zealand 'killer' patterns.

Hook: Size 12 to 1/0, long shank. The most useful size is 8.
Tail Black squirrel tail.
Body: Scarlet chenille.
Wing: This fly has a full 'killer' wing of the Walker's Killer type, but uses fewer feathers. For this fly use six feathers on each side, three pairs of two, with each of the three pairs overlapping (twelve in all). You have a choice of either olive-green dyed 'grey partridge' hackles, or olive-green dyed mallard breast feathers. My preference is for the former. It is very important to get the correct shade, some commercial ties are done in too bright or too dark a green, some even in an atrocious turquoise. You need a soft, almost pale medium olive-green.

It imitates summer dragonfly nymphs and the most useful method is to use a slow or medium sinking line, and to retrieve in 25 cm slow pulls, accelerating each pull as you go. A very good fly indeed.

HENRYVILLE SPECIAL

Plate 8   TROUT, BASS, YELLOWFISH

A superb dry fly imitation for smaller sedges.

Hook: Sizes 12–20, Mustad d.e. 94840.
Body: Green floss.
Hackle: Grizzle cock trimmed on top (grade AAA).
Underwing: Wood-duck fibres (sparse).
Overwing: Matched slips of slate duck quill.

They must be tied flat over the back and tent-like.

Throat: Optional dark-ginger cock.

HIGHVELD DUN
Plate 8   TROUT

One of the author's patterns devised to imitate the slatey and brown-winged duns with olive-brown bodies that hatch so commonly on still and running water. The fly normally hatches in the early morning, up to 10.30 or so.

Hook: Size 12 or 14, up-eye.
Silk: Green.
Tail: Dark honey cock hackle fibres.
Body: Olive polyfur dubbing blended 50/50 with chestnut polyfur.
Hackle: Dyed iron blue dun cock.
Wings: 'Wonderwing' style from the spade hackles of a dark speckled hen (in this method, the fibres are stroked back on the feather and bonded with cellulose glue. The tip and stem fibres are removed, leaving only the required wing.) Tie in vertically and split 45 degrees. Some tiers prefer slips from a natural mallard primary, since this is more in keeping with traditional dry fly styles.

HOT SPOT NYMPH
Plate 6   TROUT

This fly is a deadly modification of the Pheasant Tail Nymph. It is a good mayfly and sedge pupae imitator and will also perform well in 'daphnia bloom' conditions.

Hook: Size 12, 14 or 16, down-eye.
Silk: Black.
Tail: Dark natural 'red cock' hackle fibres.
Body: Three fibres twisted together of rich bronzy-red centre cock pheasant tail feather. Ribbing of fine gold wire.
Thorax: First, tie in at the thick end of the just made body, 12 or so fibres (from the same cock pheasant feather) which will later be used to form the wing case. Then wind a ball shape of fine lead wire as a base for the thorax, apply varnish, and while still tacky, wind over one layer of fluorescent orange, or fluorescent lime green, or fluorescent red wool. Bring the wing

case feathers over the top, and tie in at the head allowing the ends to be tied under as a throat hackle imitating the legs.

The lead weighting, if done in this way, gives the fly the correct attitude in the water.

Retrieve with a slow figure-of-eight on a floating line.

INVICTA
Plate 6   TROUT, BASS, YELLOWFISH

A very fine fly for use in sedge hatches where it imitates both the pupa and emerger.

Hook: Size 12 or 14, down-eye.
Tail: Golden pheasant crest feather.
Body: Seal's fur dyed amberish-yellow, ribbed gold twist.
Body hackle: Palmered red game cock.
Wings: Hen pheasant tail feather slips.
Hackle: Red cock with a few turns of a blue jay's feather. The 'blue' of the shoulder hackle (the jay feather), must be bright sky blue. Commercial patterns in Africa almost always have a deep blue dyed guinea fowl hackle, which is incorrect and spoils the fly.

In the UK, they fish this fly 'loch style' tied on as the dropper. It is used to work the wave tops. I have tried this at Sterkfontein Dam in South Africa with excellent results. The usual method is to fish this fly on a floating line, just sub-surface, in slow pulls.

JALAN
Plate 4   TROUT

This excellent wet fly is the invention of Dr Alan Bowmaker of KwaZulu-Natal and imitates damselfly nymphs.

Hook: Size 12–8, longshank, straight eye.
Silk: Black.
Tail: Small dyed yellow feather slip from a mallard primary.
Butt: Gold Lurex.
Body: Dubbed amber seal's fur, well picked out, and wound over an underbody of gold Lurex.
Hackle: Short fibred black cock.
Head: Insecty, varnished black.

The Jalan is most successfully fished on a sinking line in running water, where it can usefully be dead drifted close to rocks and other lies. In still water it is very effective fished on a floating line with a slow and steady retrieve. At times a leaded version can be very killing if fished right on the bottom.

KENT'S AFRICAN BEETLE

Plate 6   TROUT

A backswimmer imitation designed for cold conditions.

Hook: Size 14, down-eye.
Silk: Black.
Tail: Two very short (2 mm) black cock hackle points.
Body: Back two thirds of black wool, front third of hot orange floss. On the underside of the body, form the back (don't forget that this bug swims upside-down) by stretching wet silver Raffine from tail-end to head. It is important to wet and stretch the Raffine as you tie it in.
Head: Formed from black silk, with two tiny red glass beads for eyes, tied on each side of the head, so that they are visible (just) from underneath. These eyes are optional. The eyes were a later modification to the fly. They probably help, but even if they don't, they give it a bit of character!

Backswimmers always swim just under the surface, unless frightened, in which case they dive quite quickly. Consequently, you should use a floating line, and fish these flies very shallow. The retrieve needs to be steady pulls of 20 cm or so.

KENYA BUG

Plate 7   TROUT

The wet fly is much loved in Africa and is a good general nymph pattern.

Hook: Size 12 to 6, down-eye.
Tail: Black cock hackle fibres (also known with blue dyed guinea fowl feather fibres).
Body: Black wool ribbed silver tinsel.
Hackle: Large soft black cock hackle.
Head: Black.

In still water, the fly is best fished deep and very slow, with occasional sharp pulls. Dead drifting works well on streams, but anglers also report good results fishing down and across. An excellent African traditional pattern.

LEFTY'S DECEIVER

Plate 7   SALTWATER

These flies are superb fish imitators offering great potential for designs to copy most saltwater fry. The choice of colours is left to the tier. A common mistake with the Lefty's Deceiver is to over-dress it.

Hook: Cadmium plated or stainless steel, size 2/0 upwards (for estuary use you would be unlikely to exceed size 5/0, although the originals are tied up to 14 inches long for deep-sea work).
Tail: None.
Body: Tinsel (Mylar foil is recommended by the originator, but try Fingering Floss – it is both easier and more durable).
Wing: Six to twelve saddle hackles tied at the rear along the top of the hook shank. Mix in a few strands of pearlescent Flashabou, or suitably coloured Krystal Flash. The feathers should not splay. Do not be tempted to skimp on feathers.
Hackles: Polar bear, or calf tail, or bucktail, tied all around the hook and sloping backwards over the body and rear wing. Recent versions of the Lefty's Deceiver have a beard (or throat hackle) of red Flashabou, red Krystal Flash, or squirrel tail. Some tiers add cheeks to match or complement the tail feathers.
Head: Tying silk varnished with clear polyurethane. Head colour is usually red or white with suitable eye painted on. Small dumbbell-shaped lead eyes can be incorporated to get the fly down fast.
Colours: An all-white version with silver tinsel body is most popular. This same fly is also a fine imitation of the razorbelly, which is a winter-dwelling fry in estuaries. Also given is a version using yellow saddle hackles for the wing, a red bucktail hackle, and a gold tinsel body. An all-green version is favoured for imitating small garfish.

Some versions of Lefty's Deceiver and a Jansen's Halfbeak.

The originator's own favourite used white feathers on the inside and olive-dyed grizzle saddle hackles on the outside. This was further flanked with a couple of olive-dyed grizzle breast feathers over the bucktail. A topping of peacock herl finished it off.

LEPTOPHLEBIA NYMPH

Plate 6   TROUT

These imitations of high country mayflies are very useful in all African trout streams and offer a broad spectrum of interest to trout.

Hook: Size 12 to 14, down-eye.
Silk: Brown.
Tail: Golden brown (deep ginger) hen hackle fibres spread apart by tying silk. The naturals have tails which are widely spread.
Body: Mixed dark brown and ginger seal's fur (or Antron) well picked-out to represent gills. A dash of fluorescent orange in the seal's fur mixture improves it somewhat. Rib with fine gold wire.
Thorax: The original calls for black seal's fur, but sepia is nearer to African specimens. You

can usefully use a mixture of 20 per cent claret and 80 per cent dark chestnut for best results.
Legs: Two turns of dark brown hen hackle.

Fish the imitations slowly just off the bottom for best results.

MAYFLY EMERGER

Plate 8   TROUT

This little dry fly is the work of Robin Fick of South Africa and copies the nymph at the time of emergence.

Hook: Size 10 to 18 Mustad 94840.
Silk: Colour as fly body.
Tail: Hackle fibres to match body colour, split into two by a ball of dubbing.
Body: Ultra-translucent dubbing in greys or browns, ribbed fine gold wire.
Thorax: As body.
Wings: White polywing material tied in a hoop over the thorax.
Legs: Four turns of cock hackle, trimmed underneath to form an inverted 'V'.

Cast the fly in the path of rising trout, and let it rest. Do not attempt a retrieve! A slight twitch can be usefully applied from time to time.

MICKY FINN

Plate 4   TROUT, BASS, TIGERS, SALT

One of the best contrast attractor flies ever designed. A good fly after sudden temperature drops.

Hook: Size 8 or 10, down-eye.
Silk: Black.
Tail: None.
Body: Medium flat silver tinsel with narrow silver oval tinsel for ribbing.
Wing: A very small bunch of yellow bucktail over which is a very small bunch of red bucktail, with a bunch of yellow bucktail (equal in size to the first two bunches together) over this.
Cheeks: Optionally, Jungle Cock.

This is a fly you fish fast. Use a fast strip retrieve with metre-long pulls. Choose the line to suit the circumstances. In winter, you will probably need to fish right on the bottom, in which case a super fast-sinking Kevlar cored fly line is ideal. On bright summer days, you may still need to get down, but an ordinary fast-sink line will now be adequate. On dull overcast days, my preference is for a slow sink line.

MONTANA NYMPH

Plate 6 TROUT, BASS, YELLOWFISH

These nymphs combine imitator and attractor concepts and can be very useful in difficult conditions. An American fly.

Hook: Size 8 to 12, long shank (most popular is 12).
Silk: Black.
Tail: Two black cock hackle tips.
Body: Black chenille (there is no rib).
Thorax: Lay down lead wire to form a thorax, glue it and while tacky, wind over one layer of yellow or fluorescent green chenille. Wind the hackle of black cock through the thorax, approximately two turns only.
Wing-case: Black chenille pulled over the top.
Head: Varnish black.

A very effective method for the weighted Montana Nymph is to fish it on a floating line over deep water with a long leader. Alternate the retrieve from occasional figure-of-eight retrieving to accelerating 10–20 cm pulls with pauses of a few seconds in between.

MOONFLY

Plate 2 SALTWATER

Kitefish (also known as moonies) are imitated by this fly. Small moonies are preyed upon by many predators, some very large! The fly is quite complex in the tying, but well worth the effort of knocking up a few. The retrieve should be designed to let the fly hover in the current for 20 or 30 seconds before giving it a fairly fast half-metre haul.

Hook: Size 2/0 or 4/0, cadmium plated down-eye.
Silk: White.
Tail: White Fishair, marked black with a waterproof felt pen, on the top and lower edges.

Body: White fluorescent silk over lead wire.
Upper and lower wing: Long fibres (length to edge of hook bend) of white Fishair tipped black with a waterproof pen. Tie these wings in before attempting to tie the side wings. The angle of tie-in for the upper and lower wings is 45 degrees.
Side wings: For those familiar with freshwater flies this process is similar to building the wing of the Walker's Killer. Here we use six feathers (three on each side). The innermost is a fluorescent white hen hackle, the outer two are both stem-stripped white goose cosettes. Use a black waterproof felt-tip to mark the outer feathers lightly with 5–6 vertical stripes. An easier feather to work with is from the flank of the silver pheasant.
Eye: The eye, of 6–7 mm diameter, is painted onto a mallard grey breast feather. It helps to first paint the eye feather with a coat of varnish, and to allow this to dry before painting on the eye, which has a yellow background and a black pupil. If your artistry is up to it, a fine outer ring of black is very realistic. The completed eye feather is then tied in as a cheek, flat against the side wing, one on each side.
Head: Tied as small as possible.

MRS SIMPSON

Plate 5 TROUT, BASS, BARBEL, YELLOWFISH, SALT

The Mrs Simpson is undoubtedly one of the best flies in the world. In Africa it is generally regarded as a top dragonfly nymph imitator, but it also imitates small fish well.

Preferred sizes for various applications are as follows:

Trout: 6, 8, 10
Bass: 2, 4, 6
Yellowfish: 2, 4, 6
Barbel: 2/0
Saltwater: 4/0, 2/0, 1

Note: Sizes 2 and larger are best tied on salmon irons for freshwater, and stainless hooks for saltwater.

Hook: In the larger sizes 4/0 to 1, use low-water salmon irons (Partridge make good ones) or stainless steel Mustads. For the smaller sizes

2 to 10, use long-shanks.

Silk: Black.

Tail: Black dyed squirrel tail.

Body: Green, yellow, or red chenille. In our African waters we use only the red version. I believe fluorescent red wool makes the best body for local conditions.

Wing: Tied alongside the fly in three groups on each side overlapping one another. Tie in six triples of 'blue' rump feathers of the cock ringneck pheasant (18 feathers in all). Pre-strip the feather stems prior to tying in.

Head: Black varnish.

There are commercial versions of this fly on the market tied with cock pheasant centre-tail feathers, which is patently wrong. They should be avoided.

Mike Salomon's fly which took the one-time Southern Transvaal rainbow trout record was a Mrs Simpson with the head varnished gold.

Lady Purple (Church Window)
Plate 4

A locally developed African version of the Mrs Simpson known as the Lady Purple, or as the Church Window, is commonly offered in shops. It uses cock pheasant 'church window' feathers for the wing. These feathers are found further up the back of the pheasant.

Hook: Size 2 to 10, Limerick bronze.

Silk: Black.

Tail: Black cock hackle fibres.

Body: Green, yellow or red chenille. Red is by far the most popular.

Wing: Three leashes (triples) of cock pheasant back feathers tied alongside the body.

The Mrs Simpson itself is properly retrieved in imitation of a dragonfly nymph, i.e. on the bottom in slow but accelerating pulls of 10 cm or so. However, you can also strip retrieve it quite fast when the trout seem to take it as a small fish. It's a great September barbel fly when stripped in fairly slowly. Tie up your Mrs Simpsons with weed guards for bass, and throw them right into the structure – you need an 0X point for that job.

MUDDLER MINNOW

TROUT, BASS, Estuaries

This is a world-famous fly with a great reputation for big fish. However, in Africa, the Catlet Muddler is a better fly for general use. Nevertheless, many still favour the original Muddler Minnow because it is a great grasshopper imitation. For estuary work it is a better fly than the Catlet Muddler (no catlets in the salt).

Hook: Size 1 to 12, long shank, down or straight eye.

Silk: Black.

Tail: Small section of 'oak turkey' wing quill slip, slightly longer than the hook gape.

Body: Flat gold tinsel. Note that sufficient bare hook (approx. 6 mm) must be left to allow for the spinning of the head.

Wing: Bunch of grey squirrel tail hair, sided by fairly large sections of mottled oak turkey wing feather slips, almost as long as the squirrel hair, tied in at an upward angle of 30 degrees.

Original Muddler Minnow.

Catlet Muddler, illustrating the modifications made to the standard muddler to meet African requirements when imitating small stream catlets.

Note: Impala hair is recommended for the larger sizes (an African modification).

Head: Natural deer body hair is spun onto the bare hook and then clipped short at the front and tapering back. Many commercial Muddler Minnows are produced with a ball shape head. Some of the fibres that are sloping back must be left unclipped.

Muddlers are usually retrieved to imitate small fishes, and the standard fishing method is a slow-sink line and a strip retrieve with occasional short jerks. Strip retrieving with a floating line over shallows also works well, and is quite exciting as the bow wave of a pursuing trout follows the fly. Finally, one can imitate grasshoppers by greasing the muddler and casting it out on a floating line. Twitches and short pulls is the correct retrieve.

MUDDLER, CATLET

TROUT, BARBEL, BASS

Many African streams and still waters are populated with small catfish known locally as catlets. This fly, one of the author's modifications, imitates catlets.

Hook: Size 6 or 8 gold down-eye, long shank, round bend. (If you can't find these, use a bronze hook.)
Tail: Natural squirrel tail fibres.
Body: Gold fingering floss with a shoulder of three turns of red fluorescent wool.
Head: Spun deer hair clipped flat to a catfish head shape, leaving sufficient fibres on the side to form largish pectoral fins.
Wing: Natural squirrel tail fibres tied low.

The Catlet Muddler is most effective fished on fast-sink lines with fastish pulls of 10 cm or so. Occasionally, it is very effective fished with a figure-of-eight retrieve along the bottom. A very succesful pattern!

NATAL HALFBEAK

Plate 2　　　　　　　　　　　SALTWATER
The tying of this fly is a little unconventional, so it is described in some detail. Start at the tail and work forward. The proportions of head and body are important. It was designed by the author in the 1970s to imitate the small halfbeaks in the KwaZulu-Natal surf, but works well on all African coasts.

Hook: Size 2 to 2/0, 3X long shank, stainless, straight-eyed. A forged hook is preferred, but do ensure that this long hook is strong and does not easily bend in the shank.
Tail: Tied in three layers, to same length as the hook shank. Undertail 12 strands of white bucktail, with 10 strands of fluorescent yellow bucktail over, finally 12 strands of blue bucktail over all. Finish off with 5 or 6 strands of green Krystal Flash on top.
Body: Lay down underbody of any darkish wool, gluing each layer as you go. Wrap the wool with a single layer of close-wound fine embossed silver tinsel (DMC d'argent à broder, M1-fine 5 gr (10) is an ideal tinsel and is obtainable from most haberdasheries). Varnish this and while still wet slide over pearlescent Mylar tubing. Flatten this slightly and vertically before the varnish dries. Use a green waterproof Pantone pen and paint the back. If the fly is for surf use, mark three green spots on each side to simulate the species found there.
Throat: Deep bright blue cock hackle.
Head: Use green tying silk and wrap the remainder of the hook shank for the head and beak, tapering gently toward the hook eye. Tie in chain eyes 3 mm forward of the head and body join. At the hook eye tie in 3 mm of fluorescent red silk – this is a key hot spot and should not be omitted. Paint pupils green, and then varnish the complete beak and head.

The Natal Halfbeak works well in clear conditions. The retrieve should be in short fast jerks with an occasional long gliding pull in between. There are times when it is very effective fished just an inch or two under the surface on a floating line.

PEARL PUSHKIN

Plate 6　　　　　　　　　　　　TROUT
Named after a much-loved Persian cat of devious cunning who thought himself inviolate. Like the cat in the definition of a ball race, this

cat is also very fast when approached with scissors. Joking apart, this wet fly is a very useful sedge pupa imitation.

Hook: Size 10 to 14, Yorkshire Sedge style.
Silk: Black.
Body: Lay down a single layer of tying silk. Overwind one layer of either fluorescent lime green or orange rayon floss. Overwind three strands together of pearl Flashabou. Ensure a complete coverage, but do not wind excessively. The result must be a thin body.
Thorax: Dubbed pale olive-green, or (in the orange body version) cream Antron fibres. Take two or three turns of the dubbed silk around the thorax. Stroke the fibres downwards to form a small beard under the hook.
Note: As a general guide, the thorax is about half the size of a normal ephemerid nymphal thorax tie.
Wing case: Approximately ten fibres of oak turkey tail.
Note: Although this is not actually copying real wing cases, it is tied in the same way as the GRHE wing case.
Wings: These are pupal wing cases. They look good, but are not essential. On either side of the thorax sloping back, tie in the points of two small bottle-green neck feathers of the ringneck pheasant, length 6–8 mm.
Hackle: Tie a throat hackle of half a dozen grey partridge hackle fibres for the small sizes. Use Cree cock hackle fibres dyed olive for larger sizes.

Fish the Pearl Pushkin during a sedge hatch on a short 2,5 metre leader of not more than a 4X point. I find this great fun on an AFTM 5 outfit with a floating line. Retrieve is a slow 'sink and draw'.

PHEASANT TAIL NYMPH

Plate 6   TROUT
An important imitation of many mayfly nymphs and sedge pupae.

Hook: Size 12 or 14, down-eye, bronze round bend.
Silk: Black.

Tail: Small bunch of dark natural red cock hackle fibres.
Body: Three fibres of rich bronzy-red from the cock pheasant centre-tail.
Thorax: Tie in the wing case fibres (approximately 12 fibres) as for the body. Wind a ball-shaped thorax, with the ends of the centre-tail fibres used to wind the body. Bring the wing case over the completed thorax, and tie in.
Head: Varnished black.

In general, I find a sink tip line right for these nymphs when fishing from the shore. However, if flies are hatching, I switch to a floating line. The retrieve should be slow, with occasional twitches. An excellent stream pattern for dead drifting.

PORRINGE

Plate 6   TROUT
The Porringe's claim to fame is that it is a small general attractor pattern, which is useful when trout are feeding on unknown small beasties. Designed by the author in 1974.

Hook: Size 12 or 14, down-eye.
Silk: Black.
Body: First half (head end) is fluorescent orange rayon floss silk, the second half is fluorescent white rayon floss silk (both about four layers). Overwind the whole body with two or three layers of cloudy PVC
Wing: Half the length of the body and rather sparse, from the fibres of a hot orange cock hackle.
Head: Built up large with silk, and varnished black.

Most usefully fished on a floater, allowing the fly to first sink to the bottom, and then retrieving slowly with figure-of-eight bunching and occasional twitches. Imitates tiny fry, insects and other small creatures. A good 'searching' pattern.

RAB

Plate 8   TROUT, BASS
This dry fly was designed by Tony Biggs, a well-known fly-fisherman of the Cape. The

267

Red Arsed Bastard (RAB) is an effective fly which has built a solid reputation for taking fish. It is designed to sit well up on the surface rather like a thistledown, and as such, one should not overdo the dressing. It has gathered a few modifications in its wanderings, and there are at least three common variations in the dressing.

Hook: Size 12 to 16 fine wire down-eye, e.g. Mustad 94840.
Silk: Bright red. A layer of silk should be wound on the shank before commencing the pattern.
Tail: Three alternatives: a bunch of white hackle fibres, or ginger cock hackle fibres, or a mix of equal parts of white and red/brown cock hackle fibres. In all cases it should be tied thin.
Butt: Red silk (this has been left out in some literature).
Body: The body is tied on the last half of the shank (the forward half will be covered with the hackles). Originally, this called for a mixture of two cock pheasant centre-tail fibres, two fibres from the primary of the Egyptian goose, and six golden pheasant crest fibres. This was all twisted together with the tying silk to form a 'rope' which was wound to the halfway position along the shank (up to the rear hackle).

Following this, it was suggested that six pheasant tail fibres alone would do the job just as well as the complex mixture above. This option seems to come with a white rear hackle and forward hackle of guinea fowl feather. Sometimes known as the 'Brown RAB'. The versions you see around today nearly all have just peacock herl for the body.
Legs: Whatever body you tie, the important thing is to splay out the ends of the fibres at the 'end' of the body tie, i.e. at the centre of the hook shank.
Hackles: The dressing in Jack Blackman's *Flies and Fly-fishing in South Africa* called for a first hackle of ginger and a second hackle of white (this is the same dressing that calls for the peacock body and the white tail). An article in the British angling press called for a first hackle of red and a second of ginger, this one also suggested dubbing some pure Antron onto the

tying silk which tied down the hackles. Finally, the pattern given in *SA Flyfishing* magazine called for a first hackle of ginger, and a second hackle of red (the correct version).
Head: Red silk tied prominently.

Amid all these options, I favour the version given by Jack Blackman, which works better for me than the others and is particularly easy to see in poor light.

RED SETTER

Plate 7   TROUT, YELLOWFISH, BASS
I give here the popular African version, which differs from the New Zealand original.

Hook: Size 6 to 10, down-eye.
Silk: Black.
Tail: Natural red cock hackle fibres.
Body: Orange chenille in two sections with a white cock hackle between the two.
Hackle: Long-fibred white cock.
Head: Black varnish.

Fish this fly deep and slow for best results. This is a very popular still water fly.

ROYAL COACHMAN

Plate 8   TROUT
A wet or dry fly. The wet fly is also known tied up as a streamer.

Hook: Size 10 to 14, up-eye.
Tail: Golden pheasant tippet fibres.
Body: Divided into thirds. Two outer thirds of bronze peacock herl, and the centre of scarlet floss silk.
Hackle: Natural light 'red cock'.
Wings: Slips from a white duck wing quill.

The dry fly is a high visibility attractor which will often bring fish up in 'no rise' situations.

SHERRY SPINNER

Plate 8   TROUT
A dry fly which is a good general imitator of many mayfly spinners.

Hook: Size 14, up-eye.

Tail: Pale honey dun cock hackle.

Body: Mix up amber coloured dubbing, consisting of orange seal fur, light orange seal fur, green seal fur and a touch of hare poll. Blend the mixture. Dub it, and then rib with fine gold wire.

Wings: Many dressings show no wings. However, most call for pale blue dun hackle tips tied flat.

Hackle: Pale honey dun, ideally with darkish centre.

Seal's fur dyed a sherry colour does become available, but it appears not to be as effective as the dubbing mix. Commercial ties are usually done with polyfur on the body. A modern version, called the PVC Sherry Spinner, uses gold-coloured floss on the body with thin PVC wound over.

SNAPPING SHRIMP

Plate 3   SALTWATER

A bonefish style fly, excellent in very clear water.

Hook: Size 4 or 6, stainless.

Silk: Black.

Tail: Hot orange tag of Antron.

Body: Neutral-coloured Antron.

Wing: Under the hook, bonefish fly style, dark brown teased out Antron, or Fishair.

Head: Varnished black with eye painted on.

The correct method over shallow water is to use a floating or intermediate fly line, and a retrieve designed to emulate frightened prawns. Ideally, short fastish dashes represented by jerks, with slow, long pulls in between.

SOLDIER PALMER PINK

                                      TROUT

A first class dry fly for general use on both flat and rippled surfaces.

Hook: Size 8, up-eye.

Tail: Ginger cock hackle fibres.

Body: Start off with a body of ginger ostrich herl. Palmer a natural 'red cock' hackle along the body. Use a long-fibred feather for this.

Soldier Palmer Pink. Note how the hackle fibre points work with the surface tension of the water to make the fly float.

When the palmer hackle is complete, tie in a body rib of fluorescent pink floss. Now, with sharp scissors, clip the hackle to size (approximately 1,5 cm diameter). This artificially stiff hackle floats very well when proofed. The hackle stems should be left protruding at the front to simulate antennae.

Often works well with a fastish retrieve, when sedges are buzzing across the surface. Also very good if allowed to float with no retrieve. This fly has taken some very big trout, bass and yellowfish over the years ... a top dry fly pattern.

SUSPENDER BUZZER

Plate 6   TROUT

This fly imitates non-biting midge pupae and has built-in buoyancy.

Hook: Size 10 to 16, round bend bronze.

Silk: Black.

Breathing tubes: White fluorescent floss at tail only.

Body: Black seal's fur or black silk only.

Rib: Silver wire.

Wing case: Orange slips of goose shoulder feather.

Thorax: Peacock herl.

Head: Expanded polystyrene bead wrapped in neutral 'Pantihose' nylon mesh, and tied in. Use a non-cellulose based varnish, otherwise the polystyrene bead will dissolve.

This dressing can be rendered in any colour to suit the hatching buzzers. The most useful versions after the black above are: light olive, claret, orange, red and dark brown. The modern tendency is to replace the polystyrene bead with a piece of shaped plastazote, which is much more durable and also inert to cellulose fly varnish.

It should be fished almost static on the surface with a floating line, or retrieved very slowly on a neutral density line. Use a longish leader. Do not grease the leader. The most useful retrieve is a very slow figure-of-eight. It can also be deadly fished on the bottom with a super fast sinking line, a short 25 cm leader and a figure-of-eight retrieve.

TADDY, STEELE'S

Plate 6 TROUT

This is one of the easiest flies to tie, once you get used to doing something a little different. The Taddy must be tied correctly if it is going to work as well as it should, and sadly most commercially tied 'Steele's Taddys' are tied incorrectly. Most are too large, often too long, and almost always never finished with the properly varnished head. I know, I designed it! It imitates small black *Rana* tadpoles and is also an excellent 'silhouette' imitation of many insects.

When tying the Steele's Taddy, aim for a slim but rounded head. Don't be tempted to use too much material.

Hook: Size 12, originally straight-eye, but down-eye will do.
Silk: Black.
Body and head: Black-dyed squirrel tail hair, tied 'reverse' and cut-off square with bend of hook (no longer than the bend!) On completion, varnish head with three coats of clear varnish.

Commence by winding silk on the first third (not more) of the hook shank from the eye towards the bend, and then stop winding. Varnish silk, and (while tacky) lay a small bunch of black squirrel tail fibres evenly around the shank, all pointing forward. Wind the silk forward and evenly, over the hair towards the eye. Varnish this, then wind it back over itself. You now have a rough paintbrush effect! Pull all the hair backwards (evenly around the

hook), and secure loosely with three turns of silk at the spot where the head ends and the tail starts. You may need to push the hair slightly forward to round-up the head a bit. Tighten the silk, and whip finish in four turns, then as per dressing above.

Use a fast-sinking line and retrieve in medium to slow longish pulls. When fishing the 'silhouette' approach during the evening rise, use a floating line, and retrieve slowly in a series of tiny twitches. On those days when trout are seen actively pursuing tadpoles, use an intermediate line, cast into the area of activity, and retrieve slowly in short twitches.

TADPOLE LURE

Plate 4 ALL FISH

Tadpole lures hail from Europe and were developed for giant freshwater reservoirs. They are all deadly flies, and because of the simplicity of their dressings are ideal for the beginner in fly tying. The dressings given below are African versions of this fly.

Viva Tadpole Lure

Hook: Size 8 or 10, pre-weighted along the back.
Silk: Black.
Tail: Black marabou with an undertail tuft of fluorescent signal green Antron. Versions of this fly with no marabou in the tail and just the green tuft are also known.
Body: Black chenille, ribbed oval silver tinsel
Collar: One turn of fluorescent signal green wool behind the head.
Head: Varnished black.

This is a fantastic fly, extremely deadly in all waters and most conditions. Let it sink right to the bottom and strip it back with a troll retrieve on a fast sinking line. It also works well when the daphnia bloom is green as opposed to the more normal orange.

Cyril's Choice

This Tadpole Lure was designed for Cyril Ramaphosa by Steve Barrow and has proved very successful. It is a winter fly.

Hook: Size 8, long shank, pre-weighted along the back.
Silk: Black.
Tail: Fluorescent lime-green marabou.
Body: Front half is black chenille, rear half is yellow chenille.
Collar: None.
Head: Varnished black.

Retrieve in long, but slowish strips along dam walls and through gullies and stream beds. A good cold water fly.

Snot Tadpole Lure

Hook: Size 8 or 10, long shank pre-weighted along the back.
Silk: Black.
Tail: Fluorescent lime-green marabou.
Body: Fluorescent lime-green chenille.
Collar: None.
Head: Varnished black.

This one has caught so many trout that it cannot easily be ignored. Its name arose from a group decision after it was the only fly that caught fishes on a typical cold winter's day at Swartwater Dam in South Africa. One of the lads thought its colour deserved the name, and some other wag declared 'it's s'not a bad fly' ... ugh! Anyway, it stuck.

I don't know why; but on cold days with a leaden sky and a ripple on the water; this Snot Tadpole Lure fly is sometimes quite deadly. Fish it fast, just under the ripple on an intermediate line.

TANAGER

Plate 4   TROUT

An old very deadly pre-war pattern from Kenya, at one time also known as the 'Budgie'.

Hook: Size 10–8, down-eye.
Tail: Fibres of blue feather from the vulturine guinea fowl.
Body: Yellow floss.
Wing: Tips of two yellow tanager feathers, back to back inside, with blue vulturine guinea fowl outside.

Use dyed yellow hen hackles as a substitute for the 'tanager' (a South American bird). 'Vulturine guinea fowl' is now very scarce in most fly tying circles, although relatively easy to find as road casualties in Kenya; perhaps an excuse for a Kenyan pen pal? Fortunately, the spade hackles from a jungle cock make a passable substitute, especially if dyed bright cobalt blue.

Fish with a fairly fast retrieve near the bottom.

TERRY RUANE'S DRAGON

Plate 4   TROUT, BASS

A South African dragonfly nymph imitator with a big fish reputation.

Hook: Size 4 to 10, 2X long shank.
Silk: 6/0 olive or brown.
Body: Either olive green, or brown, or mottled green and brown Danville bug chenille. The body can be pre-shaped to advantage using bits of pipe cleaner along the sides. It should in any event be tied fat.
Head: Note that the tie-off is behind the head in this fly.
Eyes: Take a 10 mm length of weed-eater green cutting nylon. Melt it flat at each end, and tie it on top of the head using a figure-of-eight binding. The chenille is then over-wrapped, both in front and behind the eyes, to form the head. The realism of the eyes is quite stunning; they almost look alive.
Hackle: Shortish fibre natural 'red cock' hackle tied underneath as a throat hackle.

This fly should be fished deep in slow pulls with intermittent fast short pulls of 10 cm or so.

THE 'TIGGER' SERIES

Plate 2   TIGERFISH

These flies were invented by the author in 1970 and have since become very popular all over Africa, wherever fly-fishermen seek out tigerfish.

Hook: Initially, I tied the Tiggers on salmon irons, but found that they were not strong enough (some of them snapped). Eventually, I settled on bronze flat-forged Mustad 9262. These are quite short in the shank, which is advantageous for striking. The Mustad stainless hooks used for the salt are also strong enough. Spend time ensuring a really sharp point on your hooks prior to tying the fly. Sizes 2, 4, and 6 are most useful. Larger hooks are quite difficult to drive into the hard mouth of the tigerfish.

Silk: Black Perivale bird silk, or equivalent very strong fine braided terylene.

Tail: None.

Body: Lay down a single wrap of silk along the hook shank, varnish with polyurethane varnish. While tacky, poke the nylon-covered braided trace wire through the eye of the hook and lay it along the back of the hook with 25 mm extending at the rear. Wrap the shank and wire to the bend with silk. Bend the protruding wire forward over the hook, and wrap forward with silk; trim the wire 4 mm from the eye. Wind the silk back to the bend and varnish it again.

Note: It helps to nibble the nylon-covered wire for better grip. You have now completed a very strong hook to wire.

Tie in the soft braided copper wire with ten turns of silk at the butt end. Wind the silk forward to the eye and varnish. Wind the copper wire in tight turns to the head. Wrap the head area with silk to build-up a firm platform for tying on the wing.

Varnish the copper body. When all the polyurethane varnish dries the body is very strong. Make a few bodies, and then let them dry before mounting the wings.

Wing: Bucktail of no more than 50 mm length. Intersperse Flashabou if you wish, but it won't last very long. Sparsely tied wings are most effective. Glue the wing root prior to tying in. Fishair can also be used for the wing. If the wing gets chewed off, it is a simple matter to replace it thus ensuring a long life for these flies.

Head: Build up large, and varnish black.

The table below lists proven colour dressings which we know definitely work. You can of course try your own colour combinations to your heart's content.

Tigger colour	Tigger name	When to use
Black	Zulu	Evening
Red over yellow	Micky Finn	After cold snap
Red over white	Parmachene	All times, deep
Green over yellow	Vleikurper	All times, shallow
Orange	Whisky	All times, overcast
Black over violet	Chris's	Clear, very deep

Note: Because of the slight tendency of the wire leader to kink after a few casts, some authorities today prefer to leave the wire out of the dressing, and make up a separate 10 cm wire leader. The problem of kinking arises because of poor casting, and accomplished casters do not suffer from this problem.

Cast out, and allow the fly to sink to the required depth, then strip retrieve the fly back. There is no doubt that the troll retrieve is the most effective method. The strike should be firm. If you lay the rod over and strike hard and sideways, your chances of driving the hook into the scissor will be markedly improved.

VLEIKURPER

Plate 4   TROUT, BASS, SALTWATER

Fifteen years ago, Barry Kent (RSA) and I invented a Vleikurper fly which, to say the least, was complex in tying, and possessed of difficult exotic components. Nevertheless, it did catch fish, but not particularly well. Later, still dissatisfied with this solution, I experimented with bucktail versions of this dressing, and after much trial and error, came up with the pattern given below. The Vleikurper was first published in Taff Price's *Fly Patterns, an International Guide*.

Hook: Size 4 to 8, long shank, gold, down-eye.

Silk: Black.

Body: Olive-gold rayon floss tied to end above the point of the hook, with the remainder of the shank showing. Final forward quarter of the body fluorescent red wool. Rib with gold wire.

Wing: Dark green bucktail over a few fibres of yellow-green bucktail. A thin topping of a few fibres of bright scarlet bucktail goes over the green. The wing must be tied sparse.

Cheeks: Triangularly cut small pieces of copper Lurex, tied in tight at the base of the wing with points to rear.

Hackle: Throat hackle of yellow bucktail.

Head: Tied large like a small fish, and varnished black. Paint eyes of black pupils on pale green.

The retrieve should be fastish with fish-like dashes and darts. Occasionally, stop completely for 5–10 seconds. Incidentally, it is a grand trolling fly, pulled slowly behind a rowing boat.

WALKER'S KILLER

Plate 5   TROUT, BASS, ALL SPORT-FISH

Undoubtedly the most popular wet fly in Africa. The designer was Lionel Walker (RSA), whose stated aim was to produce a fly that looked like a nymph, that appeared to be a good mouthful, was durable, would maintain its shape, had a good entry into the water, would swim upright, and would take big fish. The Walker's Killer succeeded in every one of these aims, to the point where today it out-sells every other fly made in Africa.

The origin of the Walker's Killer cannot entirely be traced to Lionel Walker. It is virtually identical to at least two New Zealand flies, namely the 'Lord's Killer', and the 'Killwell's Number One'. Mr Walker had strong affiliations with New Zealand, and thus this is no surprise. The only real difference is in the wing feathers, the design and structure being otherwise identical. Nevertheless, the tiny change was enough to give birth to Africa's best-loved fly, and Lionel Walker will always be thanked for that!

Hook: Size 2 to 14.

Silk: Black.

Tail: Black cock hackle fibres.

Body: Red chenille (often offered in shops with green or yellow).

Wings: Eighteen tips of English striped partridge hackles, tied in three layers of three feathers each, on each side of the body.

Note: The feather groups are tied at the tail end of the body, at the middle of the body, and finally just behind the head, all overlapping one another.

Kenyan variations

Pombe King

This is a Walker's Killer tied with lead along the back. The samples I have seen all had eyes painted (black pupil on yellow) on the head.

Pombe Queen

This Kenyan variation of the Walker's Killer is also weighted to swim upside-down by adding weight to the back of the hook shank. This fly differs from the Pombe King in the way that the 18 feathers are laid alongside the hook. In the Pombe Queen the feathers are separated in the same way as the Mrs Simpson, i.e. they are not tied on top of one another, but each set of three is moved along the shank so that they overlap; the result is a longer fly.

The recommended retrieve by Lionel Walker was to fish deep with a fairly fast jerky action aided by movement of the rod tip. The Walker's Killer and the Pombes fish very well when retrieved slowly and deep, with little 10 cm dashes to simulate the rectal propulsion of dragonfly nymphs. They will even catch with a strip retrieve (when presumably they simulate small fish).

WALKER'S KILLER CRAB

                     ALL

This modification arose as a result of Mike Salomon noting the similarity of the Walker's Killer to some crabs.

First: Prepare the hook by weighting it along the back with lead wire so that it swims upside-down and thus becomes comparatively weedless.

Second: Tie the normal pattern at 90 degrees to normal, in other words, flat on the hook. You can strengthen this wet 'flatness' of the feather webbing by using woodcock third covert feathers as the first feather layer instead of the usual partridge feather. The rest of the feathers remain partridge, the modification being merely mechanical.

Third: Add legs to one side only. Most easily tied from bucktail and whipped at strategic spots to imitate leg joints. The whole leg assembly should be attached to the centre top of the

Fig. 13.4: Walker's Killer Crab.

hook prior to tying the wing feathers. In fact the legs appear to be spurious ... they look good, but they do little.

You can get closer to the colour of a peeler crab by using the blue and striped feather from the vulturine guinea fowl, or alternatively, try a cobalt-dyed jungle cock saddle feather.

Crabs do a sideways scuttle along the bottom, but, apart from the furiously moving legs, the movement is in fact a smooth one. Very often the crab will stop for a few seconds and then be off again. Simulate this movement with steady pulls and frequent rests, and you are into a killing pattern!

WALKER'S NYMPH

Plate 6   TROUT

Lionel Walker designed these flies as general nymph imitators. They are all excellent patterns.

Hook: Size 6 to 12.
Silk: Black.
Tail: Bunch of black cock hackle fibres for the Red and the Green versions, and ginger cock for the Yellow version.
Body: Yellow, or scarlet, or green, chenille.
Hackle: Black cock, or ginger in the Yellow version.
Wing case: Two small pairs of striped partridge (over one another), tied in on each side of the body, leaving one quarter of the body showing at the tail end.

Use a floating line over shallow water (approx. one metre) in winter, and retrieve with a figure-of-eight. Expect hard takes. In winter, when sedges and mayflies are hatching in the morning after a ground frost, this method can be quite deadly.

In summer, fish the Walker's Nymph deep and slow, once again using the figure-of-eight retrieve.

WHISKY FLY

Plate 5   TROUT, BASS

An out-and-out lure fly designed to annoy trout into attacking. A real killer!

Albert Whillock's original pattern

Hook: Size 6 or 8, long shank.
Silk: Black.
Tail: Red feather fibre.
Body: Gold tinsel (you will often find gold fingering floss on local factory-tied flies). Some commercial patterns have incorrect orange floss bodies.
Wing: Four hot orange dyed cock hackles. A popular modification uses hot orange marabou.
Hackle: Tied as a throat hackle, hot orange cock.
Head: Varnished black.

The Whisky Fly is an English pattern and, as you might imagine, has been modified extensively in Africa. Perhaps best known and most effective is the resulting southern African form of the Whisky known as the 'Dullstroom Orange'.

The Dullstroom Orange

Plate 4

Hook: Size 4, 6 or 8, long shank.
Silk: Black.
Tail: None.
Body: First third red fluorescent wool, the rest is gold fingering floss.
Wing: Hot orange bucktail.
Hackle: Tied as a throat hackle, black cock.
Head: Varnished black.

The proper retrieve for Whisky Fly and Dullstroom Orange is a fast strip (or even a troll retrieve for those who go in for that kind of thing). I have found it to be very effective in situations where there is deep water and plenty of surrounding weedbeds.

WOOLLY BUGGER

Plates 4 and 7   TROUT, BASS

The dressing for the standard Black Woolly Bugger is given below. A version of this Black Woolly Bugger in which the body has been substituted with peacock herl is considered deadly. A variation of the Woolly Bugger with a fluorescent signal green butt (known as the Woolly Vugger in South Africa) is very effective. A very popular modification of the peacock bodied version uses a gold bead head and two or three strands of blue Lurex in the tail (a top stream fly in slightly coloured water).

Don Lort had a version of his own, which was all yellow (including the body hackle) excepting the body itself, which was tied from black marabou ... this was indeed a deadly fly for largemouth bass.

Steve Barrow favours an all olive green version which he fishes deep and slow with excellent results.

The standard dressing for the Black Woolly Bugger is as follows:

Hook: Size 2 to 8 (or even larger for bass), long shank.
Silk: Black.
Tail: Bunch of black marabou.
Body: Black marabou, palmered with a long-fibred black cock hackle, and ribbed with oval silver tinsel. The body is wound from marabou fibres tied in and twisted around the tying silk to form a rope prior to winding.

I prefer to weight my Woolly Buggers with lead along the top of the shank, causing them to swim upside-down. Favourite method is to fish them slowly with an ultra fast-sink Kevlar cored fly line, a braided fast-sink leader, and a tippet of 3 kg. For rainbow trout in dams, I use the same rig, but change the retrieve up to a fast jerky strip-in.

YELLAND'S KURPER FLY

Plate 3   BARBEL

This lure fly is by Mark Yelland and has been designed especially for barbel.

Hook: Size 2/0 Salmon Iron.
Silk: Black.
Body: White Antron wool.
Wing: Pale blue Krystal Flash mixed with olive Krystal Flash.
Hackle: Three turns white cock spade hackle.
Head: Varnished black.

Use a floating or a sink-tip line in the shallow bays of still waters. Retrieve with a slowish but jerky strip retrieve. Attempt to pass the fly as close as possible to visible barbel.

YELLOWFISH FLY

Plate 6   YELLOWFISH

This fly was designed by Theo van Niekerk of Gauteng especially for yellowfish. It is also commonly known as the 'TVN' fly.

Hook: Size 6 to 10, longshank (plenty of commercial versions appear on standard shanks).
Silk: Hot orange.
Tail: Orange deer hair or cock hackle fibres.
Wing: None.
Body: Should end opposite the hook barb. Leave approximately 5 mm of bare hook for the head. Well waxed black floss or embroidery silk, open ribbed with gold thread. Pre-weighting the body with one wrap of wine bottle foil will help get the fly well down in fast water.
Head: Spin a deer hair head and trim it slim and tight. Hold back the spun hair and finish with a head of tying silk. Clear varnish to finish.

First identify good spots in the river by observation, then fish upstream by roll casting into hot spots as you go. If you spot a fish, then cast just beyond and to one side of him. Most times, if the cast is clean (not splashy), the fish will take the fly confidently.

GLOSSARY

AFTM or AFTMA: American Fishing Tackle Manufacturers Association, the body which defines fly line weighting standards as applied to the first 30 feet of any fly line.

Aggression generator: A fly which by application of colour, contrast and body shape causes the fish to attack it in an attempt to drive it away from his territory.

Attractor fly: A fly which is designed to attract fish as a result of colour pattern, rather than a fly which imitates a living food form.

Backing line: Sometimes referred to as 'spool filler'. This is the line wound onto the reel as a backing behind the fly line itself. It fills the spool so that the wound-on fly line reaches the correct level on the spool. It also acts as emergency line in the event of a big fish taking out all of the fly line. Usually made of non-stretch braided terylene.

Blank: An unfinished rod before eye rings, handle and fittings are added.

Braided leader: A tapered line between fly line and tippet which has been braided, rather than the usual tapered monofilament nylon.

Butt loop: A short length of nylon terminating in a loop (attached to the tip end of the fly line) to which the leader is attached.

Buzzer: Non-biting midge adult.

Chase rig: A terminal rig in which one fly (the larger one, on the point), appears to be chasing a smaller fly (on the dropper) approximately 10 cm away.

Class tippet: A length of nylon monofilament line in the leader rig which is in conformity with IGFA regulations in the event that a landed fish is to be claimed for a world record. The class tippet is submitted along with the claim to IGFA, and its measured strength defines the line class within which the record is claimed.

Classical casting: A style of fly casting originating in Victorian times which is severely limited by traditions embedded in its techniques.

Dampening: The ability of a rod to dampen (counteract) spurious vibrations.

Dapping: A method of fly-fishing using a line of floss, which is easily buoyed up by the wind, allowing a fly to be dibbled across the surface.

Dead drifting: Drifting a nymph or other fly at the same speed as the current so that the fly appears to be 'dead in the water'.

Dibbling: To fish by allowing the bait to bob and dip on the surface (*see* dapping).

Double haul casting: A modern method of casting which by the application of hauls on the line increases line speed, thus providing more distance as a result of more power.

Dropper: An additional fly (or flies) tied to a short length of line at the knots used to join leader to tippet, or at the leader taper step-downs.

Dry fly: A fly which floats.

Dubbing: A process used in fly tying to wind short fur fibres or other material onto the fly body.

Dun: The sub-imago form of a mayfly; the form which hatches from the nymph into the intermediate winged dun stage prior to final shuck change into the fully adult form known as a spinner.

Echo sounder: An electronic depth measuring device.

Emerger: The hatching insect in the act of leaving the nymphal shuck at the surface, but not yet air-borne or capable of flight.

End rig: The line set-up at the end of the fly line, usually consisting of a fastening method for leader to fly line (such as a butt loop and a double loop knot), and also the leader itself, the tippet, and fly or flies.

Floatant: A chemical used to ensure flotation of the fly on the water surface; either a spray or a solution into which the fly is dipped.

Flying hook: Some saltwater flies carry an additional hook which trails at the very end of the fly, usually just covered by the wing or tail. Usually used for fish which are 'coming short' (tapping the fly but not taking it).

Fry: Properly refers to very small fish which have only recently hatched from the ova stage, and which are usually still carrying a yolk sac. Fly-fishermen commonly refer to any very small fish as fry, up to a length of 50 mm.

Gamefish: A fish which is traditionally hunted using sporting methods such as fly or lure fishing, as opposed to bait fishing. The term also implies a fighting fish with higher than average speed and power.

Hackle: Feather from a chicken's neck.

Head and tailing: A rise form similar to porpoising, where the back of the fish is seen to roll out of the water.

Herl: Usually individual strands (fibres) from large feathers such as peacock or ostrich. These are wound around the hook shank to form a body on the fly.

Imago: Adult form of the insect life cycle.

Keel hook: A hook designed to move the centre of gravity of the fly in such a way that it swims upside-down. The shank is usually in the shape of a keel, hence the name.

Larva: The stage an insect goes through after the egg stage. Most fly-fishermen incorrectly distinguish larva as a legless crawling or wriggling life stage.

Leader: The usually tapered line between the fly line itself and the tippet. The thick end is always tied to the fly line, and the thin end to the tippet.

Line mending: The process of keeping in touch with the leader and fly by ensuring there is no slack line in the fly line itself.

Lure fly: A fly which does not necessarily set out to imitate anything in particular (although many imitate small fish and larger insect nymphal forms). Usually tied on a long shank hook and fished with a strip retrieve. Attractor flies and aggression generating flies fall into this group.

Monofilament: Single-strand line, such as in most nylons and in steel monowire.

Mud cline: A condition occurring on downwind mud-bottomed shores in strong wind conditions, where clear water and muddy water meet at a clearly defined boundary usually close to shore. The clear water extends under the muddy water where fish wait for food.

Nymph: A water-dwelling, legged, mobile, feeding, intermediate life stage which usually (but not always) turns into a semi-static pupal stage prior to the hatching of the adult insect.

Palmer: A palmered fly is one which has a cock hackle feather wound along the full length of the body.

Parr: A young first-year trout or any salmonid which still carries parr marks along the body (usually thumb print size, dark coloured marks).

pH: A standard logarithmic scale for measuring acidity and alkalinity.

Plug: A fish-imitating device usually made from plastic or wood and mounted with several hooks, used as a lure to catch fish.

Popper: A largish to large surface fly designed to pop and gurgle when drawn forward suddenly across the surface.

Priest: A slim, blunt, weighted instrument used to kill fish humanely.

Pupa: The final aquatic life stage of an insect before it hatches into the adult; a case within which the winged adult form metamorphoses. Often, but not always, a fairly static life form which after internal transformation swims to the surface to hatch.

Scissor hold: A term for a hook hold where the hook is embedded in the scissor (where the jaws meet); a very firm hold which is unlikely to allow the loss of a fish.

Shock tippet: Usually a term reserved for multiplier or fixed spool reel fishing. It properly refers to the extra strength length of nylon which absorbs the shock of casting. In fly-fishing it is used to denote a thicker piece of nylon in the end rig, usually placed there to survive the attack of sharp toothed fish.

Side kickers: The legs of a grasshopper.

Sinker: A sinking fly line.

Spinner: A device with a spinning blade of bright metallic material, usually with a treble hook, which sends out attractive vibrations as it is drawn through the water. Used to catch gamefishes.

Spoon: Fly-fishermen use a long slim spoon (marrow spoon) to remove the contents of a fish's stomach in order to examine them, and hence determine what the fish has been eating.

Stockie: A term which refers to freshly stocked trout, both rainbows and browns.

Sub-imago: A pre-adult insect stage prior to the final adult stage (imago). In mayflies this is the winged 'dun' stage of the life cycle.

Sweet casting: A modern system of fly casting which uses the maximum potential of the fisherman to cast well and accurately, in an easy, relaxed manner.

Thermocline: A condition occurring in deep vast waters in Africa (it can occur in any waters in colder climates), where the water forms a distinct boundary layer at depth as a result of the specific gravity of water changing at 4 °C.

Tippet: The final length of fine nylon or wire between the fly and the leader.

Trolling line: A heavy lead-cored nylon-covered line used to tow bait or lures at depth.

Weed guard: A strand of monofilament tied into the fly to protect the hook from hang-ups.

Wet fly: A fly that sinks.

Wind knot: A knot which usually occurs as a result of incorrect wrist control during the cast. The knot manifests in the tippet or leader, usually substantially reducing the breaking strain of the line. A major cause of lost fish.

Zonker strip: A long, thin strip of rabbit fur.

APPENDIX 1

SIMPLE CONVERSIONS

Angling is one of those sports which is practised world-wide, and is also steeped in tradition. Consequently, some of the literature contains metric units of measurement, some only imperial, and very often there is a mixture of the two. Many fishermen consider the only 'proper' units for fishing to be pounds and ounces, and feet and inches. Personally, I cannot deny that the weight of a fish in pounds hits my eardrums with much more excitement than it does in kilograms (the numbers are bigger!). Since both units appear in this book – sometimes for historical reasons, often purely aesthetic, and let's face it, often because it sounds good – a conversion table may prove useful.

Linear measure	Weight measure
millimetre = 0,039 inches	gram = 0,035 ounces
centimetre = 0,394 inches	kilogram = 2,2 pounds
metre = 39,4 inches	
	ounce = 28,57 grams
inch = 2,54 centimetres	pound = 0,455 kilograms
foot = 0,305 metres	
yard = 0,914 metres	gram = 15,5 grains
	pound = 7 000 grains

Appendix 2

LIST OF GAMEFISHES COMMONLY PURSUED BY FLY-FISHERMEN

FRESHWATER

Common angler's name	Alternative name	Scientific name
Brown trout	Brownie, Spotty	*Salmo trutta*
Rainbow trout	Rainbow, Flasher	*Oncorhynchus mykiss* (syn: *Salmo gairdneri*)
Brook trout	Brook charr	*Salvelinus fontinalis*
Landlocked salmon		*Salmo salar*
Tigerfish	Tiger, Kibebe, Lokel, Tsage, Manda, Binga	*Hydrocynus vittatus*
Goliath tigerfish		*Hydrocynus goliath*
Smallmouth yellowfish	Yellow	*Barbus aeneus* (syn: *holubi*)
Largemouth yellowfish		*Barbus kimberleyensis*
Natal yellowfish	Scaley	*Barbus natalensis*
Smallscale yellowfish		*Barbus polylepis*
Largescale yellowfish	Linyonga	*Barbus marequensis*
Codrington's yellowfish	Zambezi yellow, Upper Zambezi yellowfish	*Barbus codringtoni*
Pifu		*Barbus trachypterus*
Nkumbwa	Malawi Yellowfish	*Barbus johnstonii*
Rhino fish	Matonzi	*Barbus mariae*
Whitefish	Witvis, Witte-vis	*Barbus andrewi*
Clanwilliam yellowfish		*Barbus capensis*
Athi River barbus	Kasimba	*Barbus tanensis*
Rippon Falls yellowfish	Kasinja	*Barbus radcliffi*
Barbel	Sharptooth catfish, Catfish, Barber, Ndombi, Maramba, Armont	*Clarias gariepinuss* (Similar are *C. ngamensis, C. lamotti, C senegalensis*, etc.)
Vundu	Sampa	*Heterobranchus longifilis*
Blue kurper	Mozambique tilapia, Mgwaya, Bream, Kurper	*Oreochromis mossambicus*

Common angler's name	Alternative name	Scientific name
Three-spot bream	Threespot tilapia, Kafue bream, Njinji	*Oreochromis andersonii*
Nembwe	Olive bream, Tsungwa, Yellow-bellied bream, Sengwa	*Serranochromis robustus*
Thinfaced bream	Thinface largemouth, Thinface tilapia, Mushuna, Lisamba	*Serranochromis angusticeps*
Green happy	Green bream, Seao	*Sargochromis codringtonii*
Pink happy	Pink bream	*Sargochromis giardi*
Yellow-belly		*Boulengochromis microlepis*
Black kurper	Tilapia, Black tilapia, Ngege	*Oreochromis nigra*
Bulti	Ihere, Rogene, Logokpa	*Tilapia nilotica*
Vleikurper	Banded tilapia, Banded bream	*Tilapia sparrmanii*
Redbreast kurper	Mbufu, Mbanje, Mbungu	*Tilapia rendalli* (syn: *melanopleura*)
Largemouth bass	Black bass, Bucket-mouth, Largemouth	*Micropterus salmoides*
Smallmouth bass		*Micropterus dolomieu*
Spotted bass		*Micropterus punctulatus*
Florida bass		*Micropterus salmoides floridianus*
Nile perch	Aigle, Haffash, Kisangulu, Dzo	*Lates niloticus* (Similar are *L. albertianus*, *L. macropthalmus*)
Sangala	Lake Tanganyika Nile perch	*Lates microlepis* (also *L. mariae*, *L. augustifrons*)
Common carp	Mirror carp, King carp	*Cyprinus carpio*
Grass carp		*Ctenopharyngodon idella*
Mud mullet	Moggel	*Labeo umbratus*
Orange River mudfish		*Labeo capensis*
Rednose mudfish	Rednose labeo, Red-lipped mudfish	*Labeo rosae*
Red-nose mudsucker	Golden mudsucker, Manyame labeo, Manyame mudfish, Luapula salmon, Pumbu, Hunyani salmon, Mumbu	*Labeo altivelis*
Purple mudfish	Purple labeo, Purple mudsucker, Mumbu, Congoro, Seela	*Labeo congoro*
Kuruka	Chibule	*Labeo horie*
Ningu	Lake Victoria mudfish	*Labeo victorianus*
Nile Mudfish	Lebiso	*Labeo niloticus*
Lake Malawi Salmon	Mpasa, Lake Nyassa salmon	*Barilius microlepis*
Bluegill sunfish	Bluegill	*Lepomis macrochirus*

Common angler's name	Alternative name	Scientific name
Perch	European bass	*Perca fluviatilis*
Kafue Pike	Pike, African pike, Mulomezi, Nyeru	*Hepsetus odoe*
Pinkfin Alestes	Pinkfin, Mutula	*Alestes grandisquamis* (syn: *nurse*)
Lake salmon	Silver Alestes, Manse	*Alestes macropthalmus*
Spot tail	Imberi, Mbela	*Brycinus imberi*
Doorbela	Ngara	*Alestes baremose*
Cornish Jack	Zambenenje, Elephant snout	*Mormyrops anguilloides* (syn: *deliciosus*)
Western bottlenose	Ndikusi	*Mormyrus lacerda*
Eastern bottlenose	Hotama, Fukarusesha	*Mormyrus longirostris*
Congo bottlenose		*Mormyrus proboscirostris*

SALTWATER FISHES

Most saltwater fishes may be taken with the fly at some time. This listing merely nominates the most popular quarry of the fly-fisherman. The numbers refer to *Smiths' Sea Fishes*.

Common angler's name		Alternative name	Scientific name
Greenspotted kingfish	210.20	Brassy kingfish	*Caranx papuensis*
Bluefin kingfish	210.19	Bluefin Jack	*Caranx melampygus*
Giant kingfish	210.17	Jack, Karambisi	*Caranx ignobilis*
Yellowtail kingfish	210.21	Blacktip kingfish	*Caranx sem*
Bigeye kingfish	210.22	Dusky Jack	*Caranx sexfasciatus*
Bludger	210.12		*Carangoides gymnostethus*
Ferdy kingfish	210.10	Blue kingfish, Ferdau's cavalla	*Carangoides ferdau*
Yellowspotted kingfish	210.11		*Carangoides fulvoguttatus*
Largemouth queenfish	210.38	Queenfish, Talang queenfish, Spotted leatherskin	*Scomberoides commersonnianus*
Doubledotted queenfish	210.40	Saladfish, Needle-scaled queenfish	*Scomberoides tol*
Garrick	210.33	Leervis	*Lichia amia*
Pompano	210.47	Southern pompano	*Trachinotus africanus*
Largespot pompano	210.50	Moonfish, Wave Trevally	*Trachinotus botla*
Milkfish	58.1	Dandang, Salmon herring	*Chanos chanos*
Springer	36.2	Tenpounder, Ladyfish	*Elops machnata*
Oxeye tarpon	37.1	Indo-Pacific tarpon	*Megalops cyprinoides*
Atlantic tarpon	N/A	Tarpon	*Megalops atlanticus*
Bonefish	38.1		*Albula vulpes*
Southern mullet	222.7	Harder	*Liza richardsoni*

Striped mullet	222.8	Striped harder	*Liza tricuspidens*
Flathead mullet	222.10	Grey mullet, Bull-nosed mullet	*Mugil cephalus*
Spotted grunter	179.10	Small-spotted grunt, Javelin fish	*Pomadasys commersonnii*
Kob	199.1	Giant kob, Kabeljou, Salmon, Salmon bass	*Argyrosomus japonicus*
Great barracuda	224.3	Barracuda	*Sphyraena barracuda*
Pickhandle barracuda	224.7	Sea pike	*Sphyraena jello*
King mackerel	249.12	Sierra, Spanish mackerel, Couta	*Scomberomorus commerson*
Garfish	113.3	Yellowfin needlefish, Needlefish	*Strongylura leiura*

BIBLIOGRAPHY

The following list contains both reference ('how-to') books, and fishing adventure/story books which, through 'real life adventures', contain valuable information. It would be an enormous task to present here all the books written on fly-fishing, and in fact I could not do it. What is given here is a list of books I have read which appear relevant. Many of the really good reference works are now out of print, and have become very expensive. There is a modern craze to collect such books, which pushes up their value, and they become hard to find. Nevertheless, the keen fly-fishing bookworm can often find such treasures by searching second-hand bookshops, a pursuit which offers a great deal of pleasure in its own right. *Note:* the most important works are in **bold** print.

Barnard, K H, **South African Shore-life**, Maskew Miller Ltd, Cape Town, 1954.

Bates, J D, **Streamer Fly Tying and Fishing**, Stackpole Books, USA, 1950.

Bates, V, *Sporting Tactics for Course Fish*, Herbert Jenkins, London, 1962.

Bennion, B, **The Angler in South Africa**, Hortors, South Africa, 1923.

Bergman, R, **Freshwater Bass**, A.E. Knopf, New York, 1969.

Biden, C L, *Sea Angling Fishes of the Cape*, Oxford University Press, London, 1930.

Blackman, Jack, *Flies and Flyfishing in South Africa*, Accucut, Durban, 1985.

Bowmaker, A P, Jackson P, & Jubb, R A, *Biogeography and Ecology of Southern Africa, Freshwater Fishes*, The Hague, 1978

Branch, Margo & George, **The Living Shores of Southern Africa**, Struik, Cape Town, 1981.

Brill, W G, *Tight Line Tips for Anglers*, Automatic Printing Press, South Africa, 1966.

Brooks, J, *Complete Book of Fly Fishing*, Outdoor Life, USA, 1972.

Buckland, J, **Trout and Salmon Flies Pocket Guide**, Mitchell Beazley, UK, 1986.

Bucknall, G, *Fly Tying for Beginners*, Benn, UK, 1974.
– *Fly Fishing Tactics on Still Water*, Muller, UK, 1966.
– *Reservoir Trout Fishing*, Pelham, UK, 1968.

Calver, Jim, *Bank Fishing for Reservoir Trout*, A & C Black, UK, 1979.

Carl Forbes, D, *Catch a Big Fish*, Newnes, London, 1967.

Church, Bob, **Bob Church's Guide to Trout Flies**, Crowood Press, UK, 1987.
– **Bob Church's Guide to New Fly Patterns**, Crowood Press, UK, 1993

Church, Bob, & Jardine, Charles, **Stillwater Trout Tactics**, Crowood Press, UK, 1989.

Clegg, John, *The Observer's Book of Pond Life*, Frederick Warne & Co, UK, 1956.

Clegg, Thomas, *Hair and Fur in Fly Dressing*, Booklet by Veniards.

Cockwill, Peter, **Big Trout Fishing**, Hamlyn, UK, 1987.

Colyer, David, **Fly Dressing**, Vols 1 and 2, David and Charles, London, 1975, 1981.

Copley, Hugh, **The Game Fishes of Africa**,

Witherby Ltd, London, 1952.

Crass, Bob, *Freshwater Fishes of Natal,* Shuter and Shooter, Pietermaritzburg, 1964.

– *Trout in South Africa*, Macmillan, Johannesburg, 1986.

– 'Trout fishing in Natal', *Daily News*, South Africa, 1971.

Curtis, Brian, *The Life Story of the Fish*, Jonathan Cape, London, 1949.

Ferris, G, *Fly Fishing in New Zealand*, Heinemann, New Zealand, 1972.

Fick, Robin, *A Simple Guide to the Aquatic Life of the Still Waters of Natal and My Imitations Thereof*, Fly Fishers Association, South Africa, 1994.

Flick, Art, *Master Fly Tying Guide*, Crown, USA, 1972.

– *New Streamside Guide*, Crown, USA, 1969.

Fogg, Rodger, *Stillwater Dry Fly Fishing*, A & C Black, London, 1985.

Frazer, Gordon, *Mastering the Nymph*, Blandford Press, UK, 1987.

Frost, W E & Brown, M E, *The Trout*, New Naturalist Monogram No 21, Collins, UK, 1957.

Fulsher, K, *Thunder Creek*, Freshet Press, USA, 1973.

Goddard, J & Clarke, B, *The Trout and the Fly*, Winchester Press, UK, 1980.

Goddard, John, *Trout Fly Recognition*, A & C Black, London, 1966.

– *Trout Flies of Still Water*, A & C Black, UK and USA, 1969.

Halford, F M, *The Dry-Fly Man's Handbook*, UK, 1913.

Harder, J, *Index of Orvis Fly Patterns, Vols 1 and 2*, Orvis Co Inc, USA, 1978 and later years.

Harris, J, *An Angler's Entomology*, New Naturalist Series, Collins, UK, 1952.

Harrison, A C, *et al., Freshwater Fish and Fishing in Africa*, Nelson, South Africa, 1963.

Hey, S A, *The Rapture of the River*, A A Balkema, Cape Town, 1957.

Hill, L, & Marshall, G, *Stalking Trout*, Seto Publishing, New Zealand, 1985.

Hilliard, Helen, *A Trout Rod in Natal*, CNA, South Africa, 1955.

Hintz, O S, *Fisherman's Paradise, Tales of Taupo Rainbows*, Max Reinhardt, New Zealand, 1975.

Horne, Charles, *Big-Game Fishing in South Africa*, Howard Timmins, Cape Town, nd.

– *Saltwater Fishing in Southern Africa*, Howard Timmins, Cape Town, 1961.

– *Fisherman's Eldorado*, Howard Timmins, Cape Town, 1955.

House of Hardy, *The Hardy Book of Flies*, Hardy, UK, nd.

– *To Cast a Trout Fly*, Hardy, UK, nd.

I G F A, *World Record Game Fishes* (published annually), Fort Lauderdale, USA.

Imms, A D, *Insect Natural History*, New Naturalist series, Collins, UK, 1947.

Impey, A, *Angling in Rhodesia*, Howard Timmins, Cape Town, 1959.

– *Angling in Southern Africa*, CNA, South Africa, 1961.

– *Bass Fishing in Southern Africa*, M D Collins, Rhodesia, 1966.

Ivens, T C, *Stillwater Fly Fishing*, Deutsch, UK, 1952.

Jones, L, *et al., Anglers Atlas*, several small guides to South African coastal fishing.

Joubert, Flip, *The Great Sea Angling Manual*, Perskor, South Africa, 1980.

– *The Great Freshwater Angling Manual*, Perskor, South Africa, 1988.

Jubb, R A, *Freshwater Fishes of South Africa*, Balkema, Cape Town, 1967.

Kingfisher, *A Trout Fisher in South Africa*, Flowers, South Africa, 1922.

– *Trout Flies*, Cranton, UK, 1938.

Kite, Oliver, *Nymph Fishing in Practice*, Jenkins, UK, 1963.

Koller, Larry, *The Treasury of Angling*, Hamlyn, UK, 1966.

Kreh, Lefty, *Fly Fishing in Salt Water*, Crown, USA, 1974.

– *Salt Water Fly Patterns*, Maral Inc., USA, 1988.

La Fontein, G, *Caddisflies*, Winchester Press, USA, 1981.

Lawrie, W H, *International Trout Flies*, Frederick Muller, London, 1969.

Leonard, J Edson, *Flies*, JLB, USA, 1950.

Leuver, P, *Fur and Feather*, Kangaroo Press, Australia, 1991.

Lewis, Stanley, *African Angling*, Stewart Printing Co., South Africa, 1948.

Lindsley, E, *Insect Photography for the Amateur*, Amateur Entomological Society, UK, 1976.

Livingstone, A D, *Tying Bugs and Flies for Bass*, J B Lippincott Co., USA, 1977.

McClane, A J, *Standard Fishing Encyclopedia and International Angling Guide*, Holt, Rinehart, and Winston, USA, 1965.

McDonald, John, *Quill Gordon*, Alfred Knopf, USA, 1972.

Macam, T T & Worthington, E B, *Life in Lakes and Rivers*, New Naturalist series, Collins, UK, 1951.

Macnae, W, & Kalk, M, *Natural History of Inhaca Island, Mocambique*, Wits University Press, Johannesburg, 1958.

Marinaro, V C, *A Modern Dry Fly Code*, Crown, USA, 1950.

– *In the Ring of the Rise*, NLB, USA, 1976.

Martin, Roland, *One Hundred and One Bass Catching Secrets*, Winchester Press, USA, 1980.

Meintjes, M, *Trout on the Veld*, Meintjes, South Africa, 1983.

– *Trout Trails of the Transvaal*, Classic Trout Promotions, South Africa, 1986.

– *Suggestive Fly Fisher*, Classic Trout Promotions, South Africa, 1987.

– *Trout Trails Revisited*, Classic Trout Promotions, South Africa, 1991.

– *The Trout and the Kingfisher*, selected articles on African Trout Fishing 1875-1975, The Entrepot, South Africa, 1993.

– *An Okavango Season*, The Entrepot, South Africa, 1995.

Mitchell, P, *et al.*, *Trout Fishing in Kenya*, Central Angling Advisory Board of Kenya Colony, 1950.

Norman, Charles, *Bass Fishing in South Africa*, Van Rensburg, Johannesburg, 1984.

– *Fresh and Saltwater Fly Fishing in South Africa*, Van Rensburg, Johannesburg, 1987.

– *African Angler*, Southern Books, Bergvlei, 1988.

Nuttall, Neville, *Life in the Country*, Argus, South Africa, 1973.

– *Trout Streams of Natal*, The Natal Witness, South Africa, 1947.

Nixon, Tom, *Fly Tying and Fly Fishing for Bass and Panfish*, Barnes, USA, 1968.

Pienaar, J, *The Freshwater Fishes of the Kruger National Park*, National Parks Board, South Africa, 1968.

Price, Taff, *Fly Patterns –-An International Guide*, Ward Lock, UK, 1968.

– *Stillwater Flies*, Vols 1,2,3, Benn, UK, 1979.

Reid, Arthur, *Trout and Angling in South Africa*, Speciality Press, South Africa, 1921.

Robinson, R & Dunn, J S, *Saltwater Angling in South Africa*, Robinson, Durban, 1923.

Salomon, M, *Freshwater Fishing in South Africa*, Van Rensburg, Johannesburg, 1978.

Salomon, M & Hendley, P, *Techniques of Freshwater Fishing in South Africa*, Sporting Pubs., South Africa, 1971.

Sawyer, Frank, *Nymphs and Trout*, Crown, UK, 1958.

Schoeman, S, *Strike! Fishing in South African Coastal Waters*, Balkema, South Africa, 1957.

Scholes, D, *Fly-fisher in Tasmania*, Melbourne University Press, Australia, 1961.

Scholtz, C H & Holm, E, *Insects of Southern Africa*, Butterworth, South Africa, 1985.

Schwiebert, E, *Matching the Hatch*, Macmillan, USA, 1985.

– *Nymphs*, Winchester Press, USA, 1973.

Skaife, S H, *African Insect Life*, Struik, Cape Town, 1987.

Skelton, Paul, *A Complete Guide to the Freshwater Fishes of Southern Africa*, Southern Books, Halfway House, 1993.

Skues, G E M, *The Way of a Trout With a Fly*, A & C Black, UK, 1921.

– *Itchen Memories*, Herbert Jenkins, UK, 1951 (published posthumously).

– *Nymph Fishing for Chalk Stream Trout*, A & C Black, UK, 1939.

– *The Way of a Man With a Trout*, Ed T Donald Overfield, Benn, UK, 1977.

Smith, Margaret & Dr J L B, *Fishes of the Tsitsikamma National Park*, National Parks Board of Trustees, South Africa, 1966.

Smith, J L B, *The Sea Fishes of Southern Africa*, CNA, South Africa, 1949, 1953, 1965, 1977.

Smith, Margaret & Heemstra, P C, *Smiths' Sea Fishes*, Southern Book Publishers, Halfway House, 1986.

Smithers, C, *Handbook of Insect Collecting*, Delta, Australia, 1982.

Sosin, Mark, *Practical Black Bass Fishing*, Crown, USA, nd.

Steves, H R & Koch E, *Terrestrials*, Stackpole Books, USA, 1994.

Stewart, Tom, *Fifty Popular Flies*, Vols 1,2,3,4, Benn, UK, 1962.

Sutcliffe, Tom, *My Way With a Trout*, Shuter and Shooter, Pietermaritzburg, 1985.

– *Reflections on Flyfishing*, Mark and Ronald Basel, South Africa, 1990.

Tabory, Lou, *Inshore Fly Fishing*, Lyons and Burford, USA, 1992.

Trethowan, S C, *Handbook and Guide to Rhodesian Waters*, Sarum Imprint, Rhodesia, 1973.

US Dept of the Interior, *Sport Fishing*, USA, 1971.

Van der Elst, R, *Guide to the Common Sea Fishes of Southern Africa*, Struik, Cape Town, 1981.

Venables, B, *Mr Crabtree Goes Fishing*, Daily Mirror, UK, 1960.

Veniard, J, *Fly Dressers Guide*, A & C Black, London, 1952.

– *Further Guide to Fly Dressing,* A & C Black, London, 1964.

– *Reservoir and Lake Flies*, A & C Black, London, 1970.

– *Fly Tying Development and Progress*, A & C Black, London, 1972.

Veniard, J & Downs, D, *Modern Fly Tying Techniques*, A & C Black, London, 1973.

Walker, C F, *The Complete Fly Fisher*, Barrie & Jenkins, UK, nd.

– *Fly-Tying as an Art*, Jenkins, UK, 1957.

– *Lake Flies and their Imitation*, Jenkins, UK, 1969.

Walker, Richard, Catching Fish, David and Charles, UK, 1981.

– *Dick Walker's Trout Fishing*, David and Charles, UK, 1982.

– *Fly Dressing Innovations*, Benn, UK, 1974.

– *Walker's Pitch*, George Allen & Unwin, London, 1959.

– *Still-Water Angling*, McGibbon & Key, UK, 1953.

Wallis, H F, *Where to Fish*, published annually, Field, UK.

Walsh, K, *Off the Beaten Track*, Bass Africa Safari Service, Zimbabwe, 1995.

Walton, Isaac, & Cotton, Charles, *The Complete Angler*, many printings, Rich & Marriott, 1653.

Watson, Rupert, *The Trout, A Fisherman's Natural History*, Swann-Hill, UK, 1993.

Wentink, Frank, *Saltwater Fly Tying*, Lyons & Burford, USA, 1991.

Whibley, I & Garratt, P, *The South African Fisherman*, Struik Timmins, South Africa, 1989.

Whieldon, Tony, *Stillwater Trout Fishing*, Ward Lock, UK, 1988.

Williams, A Courtney, *A Dictionary of Trout Flies*, A & C Black, London, 1949.

Wilson, T K, *Trout by All Means*, Angling Times, UK, 1966.

Witfield, A K, *Estuarine Fishes of South Africa*, ICTHOS, South Africa, 1990.

Yates, J H, *Angling Adventures in South Africa*, CNA, South Africa, 1950.

– *African Angler's Argosy*, CNA, South Africa, 1956.

Yates, Alan, '*Trout Flies of South Africa*', *Piscator*, vols 41-50, South Africa, 1958-60.

Yellow Spider, *Fly Fishing for All*, Maskew Miller, South Africa, 1965.

Index